D1140197

A Throne in Brussels

Britain, the Saxe-Coburgs and the
Belgianisation of Europe

Paul Belien

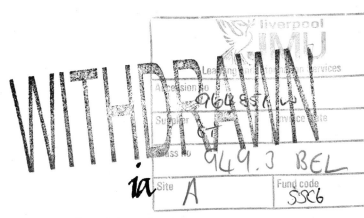

imprint-academic.com

Published in the UK by Imprint Academic
PO Box 200, Exeter EX5 5YX, UK

Published in the USA by Imprint Academic
Philosophy Documentation Center
PO Box 7147, Charlottesville, VA 22906–7147, USA

ISBN 1 84540 065 8 (pbk.), 2006
9781845400651

ISBN 1 84540 033 X (cloth), 2005
9781845400330

A CIP catalogue record for this book is available from the
British Library and US Library of Congress

Table of Contents

Preface to the Second Edition

When this book was first published, in 2005, it predicted that Belgium 'could fall apart in the next ten years.' Two years later the last episode of Belgium's history seems to have begun. 'A praline divorce is in order,' the *Economist* headlined on 6 September 2007. 'Even in a Europe riven by secessionist movements, Belgium takes the prize for the most fissiparous country of them all,' wrote the *New York Sun* on 11 September 2007.

The world awoke to Belgium's instability after the general elections of 10 June 2007. In Flanders, Belgium's Dutch-speaking northern half, these were won by two parties: CD&V (*Christen-Democratisch & Vlaams*) — an alliance of Christian Democrats and Flemish Nationalists which aims to transform Belgium into a confederacy of Flanders and Wallonia (the country's French-speaking southern half); and the Flemish secessionists — who aim for downright Flemish independence. Together they polled 56.1% of the Flemish electorate.

The huge gains of Flemish confederalists and secessionists resulted from deep frustration. Free-market-oriented Flanders, where 60% of the population lives, generates 70% of the country's gross domestic product (GDP) and is squeezed to subsidize socialist Wallonia. Belgium's constitution stipulates that no major decisions can be taken without a majority in both parts of the country and that the government should consist of 50% Flemings and 50% Walloons. In practice this means that 20% of the population (i.e. half of the Walloons) can veto every decision. This has made the *Parti Socialiste* (PS), the largest party in Wallonia, the power broker in the country.

After the 2007 elections, the inability of Belgium's politicians to form a government has led to the country's deepest political crisis ever. King Albert II, the descendant of a German prince from Saxe-Coburg who was installed by London in Brussels in 1831 because he was neither Fleming nor Walloon, sees the foundations under his throne crumble. Albert's popularity in Flanders has dropped to the lowest level ever.

What next? A breakup into two independent states might be achievable, or Flanders might join the Netherlands and Wallonia fall apart, with one piece going to France and another to Luxemburg. Brussels could join Flanders, be shared between two countries or become an independent city state, perhaps the last remnant of the Saxe-Coburg kingdom. In the latter case it would also become the first state in Western Europe with a Muslim majority.

No matter what happens, however, a Belgian divorce will leave the European Union with a headache. The thrones of the Brussels Eurocrats are trembling as well because Belgium, the EU's host country, is also the prototype for the EU project. If the Flemings and the Walloons are unable to live together in their federal kingdom, how can anyone expect the European Union, with its twenty-seven member states, to develop into one federal European state? As *The Independent* wrote on 11 September 2007:

> It is a great irony — beloved of Europhobes — that Belgium, one of the greatest advocates of a federal Europe, cannot make sense of its own federal system.

What an irony indeed. It indicates that the Europhile dream of Europe as a single state is doomed from the start.

This book, the only popular English-language history of Belgium and its royal family, helps the reader to understand Belgium and the roots of its crisis. It also offers extremely important insights into the nature of the EU. Yes Belgium *does* matter. It matters more than you think, and this book shows you why.

Paul Belien
15 September 2007

Prologue

A Nation Under Construction

On 6 November 1817, the 21-year-old British Crown Princess Charlotte died in childbirth. If she had lived, the course of history would have been different. Charlotte and her husband Leopold of Saxe-Coburg, a shrewd and ambitious German prince, would have succeeded to the British throne in 1830 and would have left their mark on a significant part of 19th-century British history. What happened instead was that in 1831 the International Powers installed Leopold on a throne in Brussels. He was appointed King of Belgium, a newly created state one-and-a-half times the size of Wales or New Jersey.

Belgium — its name referred to *Belgica*, the Latin word for the Netherlands — was an artificial state. It was inhabited by two different peoples: Catholic Dutchmen, referred to as Flemings (after Flanders, one of their historical regions) in the North, and French-speaking Walloons in the South (Wallonia). The country was the result of an international compromise. The Powers, however, were sceptical about the viability of their artefact.

The French diplomat Talleyrand described the new country as 'an artificial construction, consisting of different peoples.'[1] According to his Austrian colleague Dietrichstein, the Belgian nationality was 'a political attempt rather than an observable political reality.'[2] Nevertheless, Britain decided to give Belgium a chance. Lord Palmerston, the Foreign Secretary, liked the prospect of a weak and internally divided bogus state on his doorstep. But the grand old men of 19th-century European continental diplomacy, from Metternich to

1   Quoted in Stengers 1, pp. 90–2
2   Quoted in De Ridder, Alfred 3, p. 114.

Napoleon III to Bismarck, all thought that Belgium could not last longer than one or two generations. Leopold surprised them all by cleverly holding together his new state. He even vindicated his own Saxe-Coburg family by helping Albert, officially the son of his brother Ernst, but more likely Leopold's own, onto the throne of Great Britain. Thus Britain became an even stauncher defender of Belgium's independence and territorial integrity.

Leopold I and the five descendants of his House that have succeeded him since 1831 acknowledged the artificial nature of Belgium and the fact that it was unloved by the large majority of its citizens. They have been constantly in search of unifying elements to compensate for the lack of nationhood and the absence of genuine and generous patriotic feelings in their country. Belgium's history is a dramatic search for the civic glue that bonds 'normal,' i.e. non-artificial, countries.

Unlike normal states, artificial states have been *constructed* (in Friedrich Hayek's sense of constructivism: according to more or less specific plans or rationalist schemes) in places where no similar state had ever existed and where the people had no common identity that would enable them to acquire a national consciousness and, hence, become a genuine nation. Artificial states are either established through violence or drawn up at conference tables. They unite peoples of different cultural, linguistic, religious or ethnic backgrounds and are by definition multinational. Until the late 1980s, Europe had four of these artificial states: Belgium, Czechoslovakia, Yugoslavia and the Soviet Union. Today, only Belgium remains.

Belgium is sometimes compared to multilingual Switzerland. While Belgium is an artificial and multinational state, Switzerland is not. Switzerland was not constructed but grew organically, thereby gradually creating a Swiss national consciousness. In this respect Switzerland is more akin to the United Kingdom where historic accident brought together two of Europe's oldest nations, the English and the Scots, but where their subsequent common history fostered a British national consciousness, thereby creating a British nation encompassing both the English and the Scottish nations in a common home. Belgium is a state in which two peoples were forced to live together and where no common Belgian national consciousness developed.

Nevertheless, if there is no national consciousness binding Belgium, what has managed to keep it together for 175 years? The answer to this question has an importance beyond Belgium, because European politicians are at the moment trying to create, through constructivist planning at conference tables, a pan-European superstate. The European State currently in the making will resemble a 'Greater-Belgium' in that 'Europe' is also going to be an artificial, multinational construct, but it will hardly be a 'Greater-Switzerland.' Those who want to learn what the future of the European Union as a single state might be should study Belgium. Based in Brussels, and sharing its capital with Belgium, the European Union is greatly influenced — even infected — by Belgian political attitudes and habits. But, more importantly, Belgium acts as a model for the EU in the latter's efforts to 'construct a nation' out of different peoples with separate languages, cultures and traditions. Contemporary Belgium foreshadows Europe as a federal state.

Interestingly, the Belgian establishment realised one hundred years ago that Belgium could only survive if it were to become the nucleus of a European state. In this sense, *Belgicism* and *Europeanism* are the same thing. 'Have we not been called the laboratory of Europe,' the Belgicist ideologue Léon Hennebicq wrote in 1904. 'Indeed, we are a nation under construction. The problem of economic expansion is duplicated perfectly here by the problem of constructing a nationality. Two different languages, different classes without cohesion, a parochial mentality, an adherence to local communities that borders on the most harmful egotism, these are all elements of disunion. Luckily they can be reconciled. The solution is economic expansion, which can make us stronger by uniting us.'[3]

People like Hennebicq inspired the third King of the Belgians, Albert I, in the first half of the 20th century, to turn a peculiar mix of socialism and corporatism into the foundation of the Belgian state, thereby assuring the loyalty to Belgium of all those at the receiving end of an ever-expanding welfare mechanism. Belgium was built on a principle that was later, in the 1960s, described by Public Choice theorists as *rent-seeking*: 'the resource-wasting activities of individuals in seeking transfers of wealth through the aegis of the state.'[4] Belgium became basically a system of financial redistribution.

According to Mancur Olson 'distributional coalitions slow down a society's capacity to adapt to changing conditions, and thereby reduce the rate of economic growth.'[5] Belgium's history during the past decades confirms this. Economic stagflation and social rigidities have turned the 'national' conflict between Flemings and Walloons, which was until the 1960s mainly a linguistic conflict, into the ever-deepening socio-economic conflict that it is today. In other

3   Hennebicq, p. 278.
4   Buchanan, Tollison and Tullock, p. IX.
5   Olson 2, pp. 61–5.

words: an artificial state, based on rent-seeking, can survive as long as the economy performs reasonably well. Once the economy stagnates, tensions grow. The Belgian establishment is hoping that the transplantation of the Belgian model to a larger-scale European level will boost the economy, thereby averting the danger of the model imploding.

Meanwhile, however, the rent-seeking mentality of the Belgian establishment has led to corruption. In the case of 'normal' states, one can argue that these states have managed to become voluntary organisations resulting from generous motives of mutual concern and co-operation. They are based on a virtue called *patriotism*. In the artificially constructed state of Belgium, the absence of any patriotic feelings has forced the Belgian monarchs to make hard-headed calculated self-interest the foundation of the state. They have literally had to *buy* the adherence of the citizens (or a substantial group of them) to the state.

Belgium is sometimes considered to be a boring country – not the kind one would want to read a book about. How wrong can one be. *Boring Belgium* alliterates well, but *Baffling Belgium* does, too, and is nearer to the truth. Belgium is 'the land of a thousand scandals.'[6] It is striking to see how all the present characteristics were there from the very beginning. It is equally striking to notice how these characteristics were encapsulated in the Saxe-Coburg dynasty. Belgium's kings created their artificial country in their own image. Belgium's history is the Saxe-Coburg family tale. Belgium is their tragedy. The Belgian crown is their livelihood, but at the same time they all came to loathe Belgium with the 'decadence of its administration' and 'the ruinous abuses.'[7]

Corruption is, indeed, one of the basic characteristics of an artificial state. A second characteristic is the absence of the rule of law. If the latter were not absent and the state were able to survive while respecting democratic majority rights, it would no longer be an artificial state, but would have become a genuine nation-state. The third characteristic is its unreliability in international relations. The lack of sincere patriotic feelings has made the Belgians unwilling to make sacrifices for the common good. It has also made Belgium extremely unreliable to its allies.

Today there is a real danger that these three characteristics will infect the whole of Europe. In an Open Letter in 1998, a group of neo-Belgicist intellectuals wrote that they cherish the Belgian flag 'because

6   Rachel Johnson in *The Spectator*, 30 Oct. 1999.
7   Albert I in Willequet 4, p. 254.

the latter does not represent anything,' and that Belgium, precisely because it has no national consciousness, is 'an antidote against nationalism' much needed by the postmodern world.[8] According to the Belgian historian Louis Vos, 'a non-ideological postmodernism has become the predominant fashion in intellectual life, more eager to deconstruct the national identity than to make a contribution to it. Some go so far as to deny that the "invented" concept of national identity and community refers to anything real.'[9]

These 'postmodernists' claim that Belgium's lack of identity constitutes a supreme morality. This was also the opinion of Belgian King Baudouin who in 1993 stressed the importance of 'the European construction,' which, in following Belgium's lead, 'can best help us resist the temptation of egotism and narrow and disastrous nationalisms.'[10] The question must be asked, however, whether states that were established as artificial 'constructions,' according to rational constructivist schemes, can really be morally superior. This is a question that should be at the heart of the debate about the future European super-state.

The importance of this question goes even beyond Europe. Indeed, Belgium belongs to the category of the 'failed states' because it has never succeeded in generating a Belgian national consciousness that could become a genuine 'civic glue' binding the nation. Though failed states are exceptional in Europe and the Western world, where nation-states are the normal pattern of statehood, they are not exceptional on a global scale. Like Belgium, many of these states have fallen victim to mafia clans that colonise the state for their own purposes.

Hence, this book, while its primary purpose is to entertain the reader with a good story, is a work on several levels. It is a book about a royal family that is more closely related to the British monarchs than most people think, but also a political analysis of baffling Belgium. One cannot unravel these two stories, because they are connected as closely as Siamese twins. Finally, it serves as a warning concerning the European super-state currently in the making. Will Belgium's past be Europe's future?

8   *De Standaard*, 3 Mar. 1998.
9   Vos, p. 201.
10   Baudouin, vol. II, p. 1465.

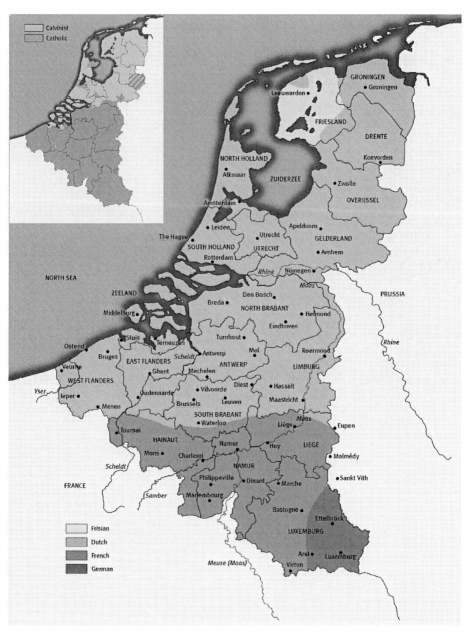

Map 1
The United Netherlands in 1815

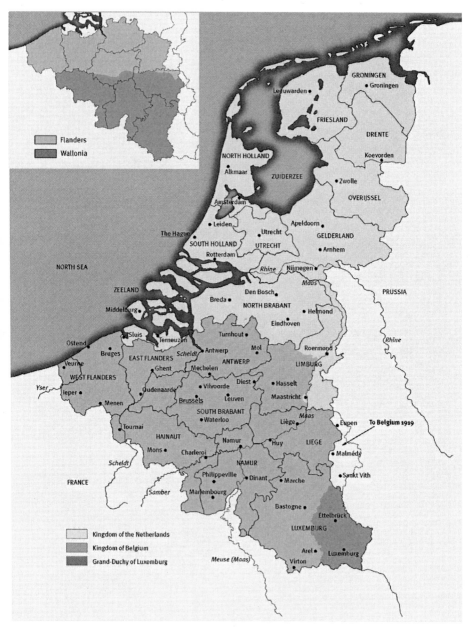

Map 2
The Low Countries after 1830

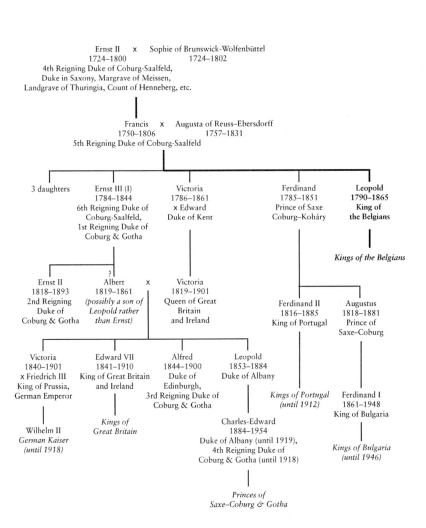

Ernst II   x   Sophie of Brunswick-Wolfenbüttel
1724–1800   1724–1802
4th Reigning Duke of Coburg-Saalfeld,
Duke in Saxony, Margrave of Meissen,
Landgrave of Thuringia, Count of Henneberg, etc.

Francis   x   Augusta of Reuss–Ebersdorff
1750–1806   1757–1831
5th Reigning Duke of Coburg-Saalfeld

| 3 daughters | Ernst III (I) 1784–1844 6th Reigning Duke of Coburg-Saalfeld, 1st Reigning Duke of Coburg & Gotha | Victoria 1786–1861 x Edward Duke of Kent | Ferdinand 1785–1851 Prince of Saxe Coburg–Koháry | Leopold 1790–1865 King of the Belgians |

Kings of the Belgians

| Ernst II 1818–1893 2nd Reigning Duke of Coburg & Gotha | ? Albert   x 1819–1861 *(possibly a son of Leopold rather than Ernst)* | Victoria 1819–1901 Queen of Great Britain and Ireland | Ferdinand II 1816–1885 King of Portugal | Augustus 1818–1881 Prince of Saxe–Coburg |

| Victoria 1840–1901 x Friedrich III King of Prussia, German Emperor | Edward VII 1841–1910 King of Great Britain and Ireland | Alfred 1844–1900 Duke of Edinburgh, 3rd Reigning Duke of Coburg & Gotha | Leopold 1853–1884 Duke of Albany | *Kings of Portugal (until 1912)* | Ferdinand I 1861–1948 King of Bulgaria |

Wilhelm II
*German Kaiser
(until 1918)*

*Kings of
Great Britain*

Charles-Edward
1884–1954
Duke of Albany (until 1919),
4th Reigning Duke of
Coburg & Gotha (until 1918)

*Kings of Bulgaria
(until 1946)*

*Princes of
Saxe–Coburg & Gotha*

The House of Saxe-Coburg
Reigning Dukes of Coburg & Gotha (1826–1918); Kings of the
Belgians (1831–present); Kings of Great-Britain (1837/1901–present);
Kings of Portugal (1837–1912); Kings of Bulgaria (1887–1946)

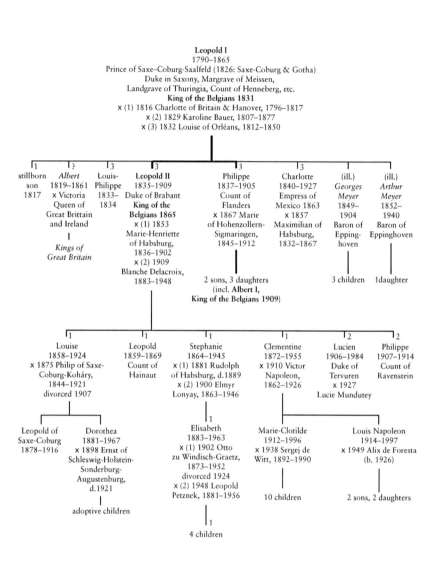

Leopold I
1790–1865
Prince of Saxe–Coburg-Saalfeld (1826: Saxe-Coburg & Gotha)
Duke in Saxony, Margrave of Meissen,
Landgrave of Thuringia, Count of Henneberg, etc.
King of the Belgians 1831
x (1) 1816 Charlotte of Britain & Hanover, 1796–1817
x (2) 1829 Karoline Bauer, 1807–1877
x (3) 1832 Louise of Orléans, 1812–1850

1 stillborn son 1817

? Albert 1819–1861 x Victoria Queen of Great Brittain and Ireland | Kings of Great Britain

3 Louis-Philippe 1833–1834

3 Leopold II 1835–1909 Duke of Brabant King of the Belgians 1865 x (1) 1853 Marie-Henriette of Habsburg, 1836–1902 x (2) 1909 Blanche Delacroix, 1883–1948

3 Philippe 1837–1905 Count of Flanders x 1867 Marie of Hohenzollern-Sigmaringen, 1845–1912 | 2 sons, 3 daughters (incl. Albert I, King of the Belgians 1909)

3 Charlotte 1840–1927 Empress of Mexico 1863 x 1857 Maximilian of Habsburg, 1832–1867

(ill.) Georges Meyer 1849–1904 Baron of Epping-hoven | 3 children

(ill.) Arthur Meyer 1852–1940 Baron of Eppinghoven | 1 daughter

1 Louise 1858–1924 x 1875 Philip of Saxe-Coburg-Koháry, 1844–1921 divorced 1907

1 Leopold 1859–1869 Count of Hainaut

1 Stephanie 1864–1945 x (1) 1881 Rudolph of Habsburg, d.1889 x (2) 1900 Elmyr Lonyay, 1863–1946

1 Clementine 1872–1955 x 1910 Victor Napoleon, 1862–1926

2 Lucien 1906–1984 Duke of Tervuren x 1927 Lucie Mundutey

2 Philippe 1907–1914 Count of Ravenstein

Leopold of Saxe-Coburg 1878–1916

Dorothea 1881–1967 x 1898 Ernst of Schleswig-Holstein-Sonderburg-Augustenburg, d.1921 | adoptive children

1 Elisabeth 1883–1963 x (1) 1902 Otto zu Windisch-Graetz, 1873–1952 divorced 1924 x (2) 1948 Leopold Petznek, 1881–1956 | 1 4 children

Marie-Clotilde 1912–1996 x 1938 Sergej de Witt, 1892–1990 | 10 children

Louis Napoleon 1914–1997 x 1949 Alix de Foresta (b. 1926) | 2 sons, 2 daughters

The House of Belgium 1831–1901
Legitimate, and illegitimate so far as known

Philippe
1837–1905
Prince of Belgium, Count of Flanders,
Prince of Saxe-Coburg & Gotha, Duke in Saxony,
Margrave of Meissen, Langrave of Thuringia, Count of Henneberg, etc.
x 1867 Marie of Hohenzollern-Sigmaringen,
1845–1912

| Baudouin 1869–1891 | Joséphine 1870–1871 | Henriette 1870–1948 x 1896 Emmanuel of Orléans Duke of Vendôme 1872–1931 \| 4 children | Joséphine 1872–1958 x 1894 Carlo of Hohenzollern- Sigmaringen 1868–1919 1935 benedictine nun \| 4 children | Albert I 1875–1934 King of the Belgians 1909–1934 x 1900 Elisabeth Wittelsbach Duchess in Bavaria, 1876–1965 |

| Leopold III 1901–1983 Duke of Brabant King of the Belgians 1934–1950 x (1) Astrid Bernadotte 1905–1935 x (2) Lilian Baels 1916–2002 | Charles 1903–1983 Count of Flanders Prince-Regent of Belgium 1944–1950 \| (ill.) Isabelle Wybo (b. 1938) | Marie-José 1906–2001 x 1930 Umberto II 1904–1983 King of Italy \| 4 children |

| Joséphine-Charlotte 1927–2005 x 1953 Jean (b. 1921) Grand-Duke of Luxemburg \| 5 children | (ill.) Michel Didisheim (b. 1930) x 1956 Countess Monika von Trauttmansdorff-Weinsberg (b. 1933) \| 5 children | Baudouin I 1930–1993 Duke of Brabant King of the Belgians 1950–1993 x 1960 Fabiola Mora y Aragon (b. 1928) | Albert II (b. 1934) Prince of Liège King of the Belgians 1993 x 1959 Paola Ruffo di Calabria (b. 1937) | Alexandre (b. 1942) x 1991 Léa Wolman | Marie-Christine (b. 1951) x (1) 1981 Paul Drucker (b. 1938) divorced 1981 x (2) 1989 Paul Gourgues (b. 1941) | Marie-Esmeralda (b. 1956) x 1998 Salvador Moncada (b. 1944) |

Alexandra (b. 1998)   Leopoldo (b. 2001)

| Philippe (b. 1960) Duke of Brabant x 1999 Mathilde d'Udekem d'Acoz (b. 1973) | Astrid (b. 1962) x 1984 Lorenz of Habsburg Archduke of Austria-Este (b. 1955) \| 5 children | Laurent (b. 1963) x 2003 Claire Coombs \| Louise (b. 2004) | (ill.) Delphine Boël (b. 1968) \| Joséphine O'Hare (b. 2003) (daughter of Delphine and Jim O'Hare) |

Elisabeth (b. 2001)   Gabriel (b. 2003)

The House of Belgium since 1901
Legitimate, and illegitimate so far as known.

The Belgian royal family has never acknowledged, officially or unofficially, that Count Michel Didisheim is an illegitimate son of King Leopold III. Consequently, this parentage cannot be proven. The author has it on the authority of sources in Brussels which he considers to be reliable.

Leopold of Saxe-Coburg and
Crown Princess Charlotte of Britain

Chapter 1

In Search of a Kingdom (1790–1831)

The Poorest Prince in Germany

The royal houses of contemporary Belgium and Britain were founded by Leopold (1790–1865), a prince from Coburg, a sleepy town in the middle of Germany. Leopold became the first King of the Belgians in 1831. Recent research indicates that he was probably also the biological father of Albert (1819–1861), the British Prince Consort, who in 1840 married Queen Victoria (1819–1901). Leopold, whom his family used to call *Poldi*, was as German as could be, without a trace of non-German blood in his veins. His father, Prince Francis of Saxe-Coburg, was the son and heir of Ernst Friedrich, the reigning duke of Coburg-Saalfeld, one of the smaller independent German states. It consisted of two unconnected pieces and some minor exclaves, in all barely 400 square miles (one-and-a-half times the Isle of Wight), with a population of barely 50,000, of which 6,000 in the town of Coburg itself.

Coburg is a little town in Upper-Franconia, the northern part of the present German state of Bavaria. It lies 548 feet below one of Germany's largest castles, the *Veste Coburg*, an impressive bulwark built by the counts of Henneberg in the 13th century on the southern edge of the dark Thuringian forests. In the late 16th century the lords of Coburg built a new residence within the city walls, on the site of a Franciscan monastery that had been dissolved in the Reformation. By the time of Leopold's birth in 1790, this residence, the *Ehrenburg Palace,* had become so dilapidated and the reigning ducal family so poor that they lived in a town house, directly behind the palace. In 1772 the duchy was declared bankrupt. With over 1 million thalers in debts, and an annual income of only 70,000 thalers, complete ruin with famine and foreclosures threatened the entire state. Fortunately, the Emperor came to the rescue by installing a Debt Commission that took over the administration of the duchy, assigning the reigning duke a meagre 12,000 thalers to run his household.

Poldi's father was a simple man, content with being an unambitious artist. Prince Francis loved to sing and play music and was good at drawing. He had two passions, one for copper etchings and engravings, of which he acquired the largest collection in Germany, another for birds, flowers and mineral stones, which he also collected. Francis died in 1806, at the early age of 56, six years after succeeding his father and inheriting a debt-ridden duchy, which was still under the charge of the Imperial Debt Commission. Little could he know that by the end of the century, the kings of Belgium, Great Britain, Portugal and Bulgaria would all be Saxe-Coburg descendants of his.

A tourist visiting Coburg today can only wonder how its ruling family escaped from this rustic backwater. This was, however, the achievement of two women. Unambitious Francis, content with collecting his etchings, plants and minerals, was a placid man. The ambition he lacked, his mother and his wife had in abundance. Francis' wife, Augusta von Reuss, the daughter of the Count of Reuss-Ebersdorff, has been described, by her granddaughter, Queen Victoria of Great Britain, as a woman 'with a most powerful, energetic, almost masculine mind.'[1] Her marriage with Francis was blessed with nine children. Two of them died young, but seven survived. The first three were girls: Sophie (born in 1778), Antoinette (1779) and Juliana (1781). The first son, Ernst, was born in 1784. He was followed by Ferdinand, born in 1785, Victoria (1786) and Marianne (1788–1794). Finally, there were Leopold, born on 16 December 1790, and Maximilian (1792–1793).

The children of Francis and Augusta came from a relatively modest family, but such was not the case for Francis' mother, Sophie of Brunswick-Wolfenbüttel. *Poldi's* paternal grandmother was the Duchess of tiny Coburg-Saalfeld through her marriage, but she was also a sister of queens, an aunt of kings, a cousin of one Russian Tsar and the aunt of another. Indeed, while Sophie had married the penniless princeling from Coburg, far better matches had been made for her sisters. Sophie's eldest sister Elisabeth had married Friedrich the Great, King of Prussia. Another elder sister, Louise, had married the Crown

1   Grey, p. 16.

Prince of Prussia, Friedrich's brother, and became the mother of the next Prussian king. And her youngest sister Julia was the wife of King Fredrik V of Denmark. Via his mother unambitious Francis was a first cousin of the kings of Prussia and Denmark.

For the future career of Francis' children, however, the Russian connections of grandmama's family proved far more important. In 1711 Sophie's aunt, Charlotte of Brunswick-Wolfenbüttel, had married Alexis Romanov, only son of Tsar Peter I. Aunt Charlotte's son, Tsar Peter II, ruled for only three years, dying of smallpox at the age of 15 in 1730. The boy was the last male descendant of the Romanovs. After Peter II's death, the tsarist crown was grabbed by Anna Romanov, daughter of Peter I's brother. Anna had no children, but in 1739 she arranged for her sister's daughter to be married to Anton Ulrich of Brunswick-Wolfenbüttel, the brother of Duchess Sophie of Coburg-Saalfeld. His son Ivan was born in August 1740 and was proclaimed Crown Prince of Russia. Two months later, when the Tsarina Anna died, the baby proceeded to the Russian throne as Tsar Ivan VI.

It is generally not a good thing for a baby to hold a throne. In November 1741, little Ivan was deposed by Elizabeth Romanov, daughter of Tsar Peter I. The child was locked up in a dungeon on the fortress island of Schlüsselburg, with no sunlight, nor people to talk to. Dressed in rags, he never matured and became a human vegetable. Many years passed. The House of Holstein-Gottorp succeeded to the Russian throne, Tsar Peter III was murdered by his wife, and in 1764 the new tsarina, Catherine the Great, visited Schlüsselburg. There she discovered poor Ivan VI, now 24 years old, still alive in his dungeon. She concluded that apart from his painful and almost unintelligible stammering, he was bereft of understanding and human intelligence, and had him murdered. One could consider it an act of pity.

What does all this Russian family business, where the women devour the men as some species of grasshoppers do after mating, have to do with the Saxe-Coburgs? In the early 1790s Catherine the Great was scouting Germany for brides for her grandsons, the sons of her only son, Paul. In 1793 the eldest, Alexander, had been married to Louise of Baden-Durlach. Now, in 1795, the time had come to find a suitable wife for the second son, the 16-year-old Constantine.

Grand-Duke Constantine was only three heartbeats away from the Russian imperial throne. This was a once in a lifetime chance for family fortune. In Coburg, two ambitious women, envious of their more fortunate family members and experts in the affairs of the Russian imperial family, were aware of the unique opportunity. They had three handsome eligible girls available. True, the girls were poor, but they were of noble birth and the Tsarina had to take what she could get, as many German princely families were not too keen on having their children marry Russians, after their barbarous treatment of two German princes, the tsars Ivan VI and Peter III.

On 7 September 1795, Francis' wife Augusta, with the blessing and encouragement of her mother-in-law, packed her three eldest daughters off in the carriage of the reigning duke, and departed for a six week voyage to St. Petersburg, determined to leave either the 17-year-old Sophie, the 16-year-old Antoinette or the little Juliana behind in Russia. For Leopold, not yet five years old, it was goodbye to a sister he hardly knew. For unambitious Francis, it looked as if it was going to be a life-long goodbye to one of his children — but he did not know which of the three, though he had a premonition. His wife and daughters arrived in the Russian capital on 18 October. 'It has happened, and as you expected, *Julchen* is the one whom Fortune has picked,' Augusta wrote to her husband from St. Petersburg on 24 October.[2] For it was Juliana, whom they called *Julchen* and who had turned fourteen during the voyage, who was chosen by the Tsarina. The next day, a huge party was held in St. Petersburg to announce the engagement. On 7 November, Augusta bade her child adieu and returned to Coburg. Before she set off, she was lavishly bestowed with jewels and gifts by the Russian Empress. She also received the sum of 60,000 rubles, while Sophie and Antoinette each got 50,000 rubles.

It was a triumph for Augusta when she arrived back in Coburg, covered in gold. It was a triumph for her mother-in-law, Duchess Sophie. With a bit of luck, they were going to be (great)grandmothers of a future Tsar of Russia. But for *Julchen*, it was the beginning of a nightmare. What her mother and grandmother did not know, or did not care to know, was that the Grand-Duke Constantine, like his father, the Crown Prince Paul, was a sadist and a pervert. On 25 February 1796, Juliana was baptised in the Russian-Orthodox faith, renamed *Anna Feodorovna* and married to the Grand-Duke. From then on, she was the Grand-Duchess Anna Feodorovna, and was forced to live through daily humiliations. She had to endure a husband who came to bed in riding boots and spurs, brought his friends into her bedroom, held orgies in his palace and gave her a venereal disease.

In November 1796, Catherine the Great died and was succeeded by her son. The Grand-Duke Constantine was now only two heartbeats away from the imperial throne of Russia, because the marriage of his

2   SAC A I 28 b 12 nr. 71, Augusta to Francis, 24 Oct. 1795.

elder brother Alexander was still childless. Every day the prospect of unambitious Francis becoming grandfather to a future Tsar of Russia looked more likely.

In Coburg, some of Anna Feodorovna's siblings benefited directly from their Russian family connection. In 1798, Antoinette married Duke Alexander of Württemberg, brother of the new Russian empress Maria Feodorovna (born Sophie of Württemberg), wife of Tsar Paul. It made Antoinette a sister-in-law of the Tsar, and an aunt of Grand-Duke Constantine, the husband of her sister. For Leopold, the Russian connection meant the certainty of a career in the Russian imperial army. Before the boy's sixth birthday the Russians made him a Captain in the imperial Izmajlovski regiment. One year later he was made a Colonel of the same regiment, and in 1803, when he turned 12, he became a General of the Russian cavalry. At first, however, apart from the right to parade around town in a beautiful uniform, this Russian military career did not mean much, for *Poldi* was still in Coburg, where his ambitious grandmother Sophie had taken his education in hand. Grandmama instilled in Leopold her own obsession with royal and imperial grandeur. From his grandmother he received the aloofness and conceitedness that became one of the main characteristics of his personality.

Then, in March 1801, dramatic events occurred. Tsar Paul was a madman. He had a paranoid suspicion towards everyone, including his sons, who lived in constant fear of their father's wrath. His behaviour had become so appalling that a group of noblemen entered his palace at night and strangled him in his bed. Paul was succeeded by his eldest son, Alexander. Constantine was now only one heartbeat away from the throne.

To an ambitious mother and grandmother in Coburg this should have been a cause for joy. Alas, they were put to shame by the very daughter they had brought so near to an imperial crown. Anna Feodorovna took advantage of the turmoil surrounding the murder of the Tsar to flee Russia. The 20-year-old Grand-Duchess could no longer bear the humiliations and torture inflicted on her by her husband. She had run away once before, to Karlsbad in Bohemia, but Tsar Paul had her brought back. This time she stood a better chance. With a large group of servants she arrived in Coburg, determined never to return to Russia. Her family greeted her with mixed feelings. Unambitous Francis, who had become reigning duke of Coburg-Saalfeld by now, was happy to see his daughter, but others were thinking about the possible repercussions. In a letter to the Coburg Finance Minister, her mother referred to the unfortunate events as 'the northern catastrophe.'[3] Her sister Antoinette, aunt to the new Tsar and his imperial brother, was equally angry. She reproached her: a wife should remain with her husband, even if he was an insane pervert, especially if he was the heir to an Empire.

But the new tsar, Alexander I, was more understanding than 'aunt Antoinette.' He knew his brother to be a wicked man and he liked Anna Feodorovna. There were even rumours that he had had an affair with her. He took pity on his sister-in-law and allowed her to settle in Switzerland, retaining her court, her subsidies and her status. Moreover, the Tsar had other preoccupations. In France, a Corsican upstart, Napoleon Bonaparte, had crowned himself Emperor, and this new 'emperor' was bringing war to every corner of Europe.

The Most Handsome Prince in France

In the summer of 1806, the Corsican invaded Germany. On 14 October 1806, Napoleon crushed the Prussian army at Jena, near Saalfeld. The fifteen-year-old *Poldi*, nominally a Russian artillery general, but one who had never seen a Russian canon, hid himself in an attic when the French arrived in town. His father, unambitious Francis, only 56 years old, died on 9 December, shortly after the French confiscated all his property and terminated his duchy's independence. On 15 December, his lands were integrated into the Confederation of the Rhine, a French vassal state. The Coburg heir, Leopold's eldest brother Ernst, suffered a nervous breakdown and spent several months in a Bohemian spa to recover. Fortunately, their mother Augusta knew what to do. She contacted her son-in-law, the Grand-Duke Constantine, and his brother, the Tsar.

After his victorious march through Germany, Napoleon was planning to invade England. To have his hands free in the East, he was eager for peace with Russia. Augusta convinced the Russians to make Coburg part of their deal with the Corsican. She pointed out that it would be a disgrace to imperial Russia for the in-laws of a future tsar to be a landless German family. As Tsar Alexander had only daughters, Constantine would some day be his successor, and after him — Augusta promised to make the Grand-Duchess return to her husband soon — his sons. Hence, it was imperative that the territories of Coburg and Saalfeld be returned to Constantine's brother-in-law.

On 25 June 1807, Napoleon and Tsar Alexander met at Tilsit. Napoleon got his peace with the Russians, and the Saxe-Coburgs got their duchy back. After personally taking an oath of allegiance to Napoleon

---

3	SAC A I 28 b 13 nr. 2, Augusta to Kretschmann, July 1800.

in Leipzig on 18 July, Ernst became the next reigning Duke of Coburg-Saalfeld. At Tilsit Napoleon had also promised to enlarge Ernst's duchy with parts of the adjacent principality of Bayreuth. Though he had not fulfilled his promise yet, Ernst and Leopold considered that the interests of the House of Saxe-Coburg were best served through collaboration with France. The Saxe-Coburg family motto was *Treue und Fest* (Loyal and Constant), and, as the most advantageous thing to be loyal to was the dominating force of the day, they decided to go to Paris, ask Napoleon to grant Leopold the privilege of serving at the Imperial Court and remind the French Emperor of his promise.

On 14 October, exactly one year after the Prussian defeat at Jena, the two brothers arrived in the French capital. It proved more difficult than expected to gain access to the Corsican. Nevertheless, the brothers had a good time. Ernst, who at 23 had already had plenty of experience with the fair sex, introduced his younger brother to the pleasures of life. Soon Ernst fell in love with Pauline Panam, an 18-year-old Greek girl who was a dancer in Paris, where she was known as *la belle Grecque*. Ernst decided that he had found in Paris all that there was to be found and returned home to govern his duchy, taking *la belle Grecque* along. *Poldi* regretted this, because, if one may believe Pauline's autobiography, he had got into the habit of enjoying her himself.

Leopold tried in vain to get his appointment with Napoleon. But the good-looking German prince, with his beautiful green eyes and delicate features, made many other appointments. The ladies at Court all fell for this handsome boy in his Russian general's uniform, and not yet seventeen. Leopold learned to use his charms. Napoleonic Paris was a decadent city where young noblemen could get all the ladies they wanted. 'Here, if you ask a lady to be seated, she goes to bed. That is the habit here,' he wrote from Paris to his eldest sister Sophie.[4]

Soon, the dashing prince caught the eye of Napoleon's promiscuous empress, Joséphine de Beauharnais. She was 44 but was considered to be the most beautiful woman in the world. Joséphine promised Leopold that she would arrange a meeting with the Emperor for him, if he returned to her often. According to Mademoiselle Ducrest, the Empress's lady-in-waiting, he saw her every day. He also attracted Joséphine's daughter, 24-year-old Hortense de Beauharnais, the wife of Napoleon's brother, Louis, whom the Corsican had made King of Holland. Hortense was as promiscuous as

---

4   SAP MP, Leopold to Sophie, 25 Apr. 1814, in Leopold I 2, p. 93.

her mother. 'I am a ship and you are the captain sailing it,' she told Leopold while she painted his portrait. He soon learned that he was not the only seaman to load this boat. In March 1808, Leopold finally had his appointment with Napoleon. He asked for permission to serve him as aide-de-camp. The French Emperor refused. Understandably, Napoleon, and his brother Louis, did not want Leopold around their women. Many years later, however, during his exile at Saint Helena, the Corsican would remember the young German: 'He was the most beautiful man that I ever saw at the Tuileries palace.'[5]

Poldi returned to Germany. A regiment of 400 Coburg soldiers served in Napoleon's *Grande Armée* in the wars in Tyrol and in Spain, but Leopold was not among them. He remained in Coburg where he assisted his brother. Ernst had decided to stop paying back the duchy's debts, which were still considerable, despite the efforts of the Debt Commission during the past 30 years. His decision brought him in conflict with the economist Theodor Conrad von Kretschmann, a former professor of the University of Jena and for many years the Coburg Finance and Justice minister. Kretschmann resigned and published a damning critique of the Coburg state finances. Leopold travelled to Munich and contrived to have the publication banned by the King of Bavaria. The latter did not want to upset the *protégés* of the French Emperor.

In the summer of 1809, Leopold visited his sister Victoria, who in 1803 had married Prince Emich Karl of Leiningen, 23 years her elder, to do her mother a favour. Leiningen was the widower of Augusta's youngest sister. Victoria gave him a son, Karl, and a daughter, Feodora. The Leiningens lived at Amorbach, a former Benedictine abbey which Napoleon had granted them. For Leopold, the place was aptly named. In Amorbach (which means 'Love Brook'), he fell in love with Polixena, the daughter of the Baron von Tubeuf, a courtier of Prince Leiningen. Polixena, whom he called Pauline, made him forget Hortense and the other Parisian women. He even asked her parents for permission to court and eventually marry their daughter. The Tubeufs refused. Her mother replied to Leopold that it was 'not done' for a girl of modest country nobility to marry the brother of a reigning duke.

Between 1809 and 1812, while his brother started extensive restoration of Coburg's Ehrenburg Palace, Leopold led an idle life. He resigned from the Russian army in 1810. He travelled around, visited Switzerland, Austria and Italy, and made several trips to Paris to safe-

---

5   Napoleon, 10 Nov. 1816, in Las Cases, vol. II, p. 298.

guard the Saxe-Coburg interests. Napoleon's efforts to subdue England had failed and his greedy eyes turned East. On 24 June 1812, the *Grande Armée* invaded Russia. Nearly 500 conscripts from Coburg were sent along. The Corsican, however, was not prepared for what awaited him. Thousands of young men perished in the Russian winter. Of the 600,000 men that Napoleon had forced to follow him into Russia, fewer than 50,000 survived. Of the 476 soldiers from Coburg, only 13 returned home. As soon as the news of the French defeat in Russia reached them, the Saxe-Coburgs changed sides and turned against the French. In March 1813 Leopold was the first German prince to present himself to Tsar Alexander at his headquarters in Poland. He was promptly reinstated to his former rank and became a General of the Russian Cuirassiers. This time he was not a 15-year-old boy with only a general's uniform, but a 22-year-old man with real Russian soldiers around him. On 29 August 1813, he participated in a victory over the French at Chlumec in Bohemia, one of the skirmishes preceding the decisive battle of Leipzig (16–19 October), where the French were crushingly defeated. Pursued by the Austrians, the Prussians and the Russians, the Corsican ran for France.

Leopold was absent at the battle of Leipzig, because the Tsar had needed General *Poldi* for something other than warfare. There remained an important family matter to be settled between the Saxe-Coburgs and the Romanovs. Alexander had ordered Leopold to persuade his sister to return to her husband. As wife of the heir to the Russian crown, she had to secure a next generation to the Romanov dynasty. After the skirmish at Chlumec, Leopold was sent to Switzerland, where the Grand-Duchess Anna Feodorovna had been living near Berne since 1801. During the past twelve years, she had had a number of liaisons, including one with her chamberlain, Jules de Seigneux, which resulted in the birth of an illegitimate son in 1808. This liaison had not been a happy one. Exit Monsieur de Seigneux. He was replaced as chamberlain by Dr. Rudolf Schiferli, a gynaecologist of the University of Berne. Anna Feodorovna seduced him too. In May 1812, he became the father of their illegitimate daughter. Schiferli was a married man and the father of two little sons. Nobody seemed to mind. To the nephews and nieces of the lustful Grand-Duchess, the adulterous Bernese gynaecologist was known as 'Uncle Schiferli'.

On 13 January 1814, 28,000 Russian troops marched through Basle, led by the Tsar and his brothers, the Grand-Dukes Constantine and Nicholas. The Tsar told Constantine to reconcile with his wife. He made it clear that without this reconciliation, Constantine would have to renounce his right to the throne in favour of his younger brother Nicholas. From Basle Alexander sent a message to Anna Feodorovna in Berne, saying that he was coming to visit her the next day. Instead of the Tsar, however, Anna Feodorovna saw her husband arrive at her château. During the next few days, Constantine and Leopold tried in vain to convince the Grand-Duchess to return to Russia. She refused. It made Constantine mad with rage, which in turn strengthened his wife's resolve not to give in.[6]

Leopold rejoined the Tsar at Vesoul on 19 January. The invasion of France had begun. On 31 March 1814, the Russian army marched into Paris, with Leopold in its ranks. 'I cannot remember a more beautiful moment than when, as a conqueror, I marched into the town where I had led such a miserable existence,' he wrote to his sister Victoria.[7]

* * *

In Paris, the first negotiations started between England, Austria, Prussia and Russia to redraw the map of Europe. Leopold approached his Russian master in an attempt to persuade the Tsar to speak for the interests of Coburg. But, as Leopold's sister would not reconcile with the Grand-Duke, and, hence, never be the mother to a future tsar, Alexander was not interested. Leopold concluded that the Russians would not mind Prussia annexing Coburg. It dawned on him that Austria was Coburg's only friend, because Austria was Prussia's rival in Germany. Although he personally disliked Prince Klemenz von Metternich, the chief negotiator for Austria, Leopold became a strong partisan of the Austrian position and his feelings were reinforced by his correspondence with the 'Austrian' members of his family, his brother Ferdinand, who had become an Austrian Field Marshal, and his sister Sophie, who in 1804 had married the Austrian diplomat Count Emmanuel von Mensdorff-Pouilly.

Metternich wanted the borders of Europe to remain largely as they had been before the French had set Europe ablaze in the 1790s. Austria would not let Prussia become too powerful. The only change to the pre-1790 borders Metternich insisted on was to surround France with strong buffer states. In order to achieve this, the Habsburgs were prepared to give up their claim to the Netherlands; the Catholic Southern Netherlands which the Habsburgs had, at great cost, suc-

---

6 For Constantine, the failure to convince his wife meant his hopes of becoming tsar were over. He officially divorced Anna Feodorovna in 1820 and renounced his rights to the Russian throne. The Grand-Duchess remained in Switzerland until her death in 1860, at the age of 79.

7 Leopold to Victoria, 11 Apr. 1814, in Buffin, p. 83.

ceeded in keeping after the Dutch revolution in the 1560s, were allowed to reunite with the northern provinces of the Netherlands. Of course, Austria could not let these united Netherlands become a confederation of sovereign republics, as the Northern Netherlands had been from 1579 until 1806. One good thing the Corsican upstart had accomplished, in Metternich's view, was to have done with republics. The United Netherlands would have to be a centralised, unified and autocratic kingdom, like all other civilised countries. Only the peasants in Switzerland and the colonists in America had confederal or federal republics, but these were regarded as uncivilised nations of marginal importance.

To reunite the Netherlands as a strong bulwark against France was a brilliant idea. Tsar Alexander and the Kings of Britain and Prussia all agreed on that. That the Netherlands should become a monarchy under the House of Nassau-Orange-Dietz — commonly referred to as Orange — was equally evident. It had provided the oligarchic Dutch Republic, a confederation of seven nominally independent provinces of which Holland was the most prominent, with six *stadholders*, one of whom had also been King of Great Britain. The Allies decided to make Willem Frederik, the son of the sixth and last *stadholder*, the first King of the Netherlands. The new king assumed the name of Willem I.

There was, however, one drawback. The eldest son and heir of the new king, the 22-year-old Prince Willem of Orange, was betrothed to the 18-year-old Princess Charlotte of Hanover, heiress to the British throne. The prospect of having a powerful state in the Low Countries united with Britain was not at all attractive to Austria, Prussia or Russia. As a consequence, they would have to thwart the engagement between Charlotte and young Willem. Tsar Alexander provided the Allies with a secret weapon for this mission: the most dashing prince in Europe, Prince Leopold of Saxe-Coburg.

In May 1814, Alexander summoned Leopold for a private and personal conversation. Leopold was worried. He thought this could only mean that the Tsar wanted to see him about Coburg — and that news would certainly not be good. To Leopold's surprise, the Tsar had a totally different message: 'We will soon leave for England,' he said. 'I intend for you to marry Princess Charlotte, the future Queen of England.' Leopold was stunned. 'She is betrothed to someone else,' he objected. 'But you are so beautiful, no woman can resist you,' the Tsar replied. Leopold also learned that the Emperor of Austria favoured the idea and that the Habsburgs would grant him the wealthy lordship of Holzkirchen near Würzburg in Lower-Franconia if he succeeded. And he learned that the Tsar had already sent ahead his own sister, Catherine, the widow of the Duke of Oldenburg, to befriend Charlotte and to speak to her of the attractive prince from Coburg.

In June, Alexander and Leopold arrived in London. Leopold liked the challenge. To his sister Sophie, he had written: 'I am going to London with the Tsar. I must honestly confess that I regard this journey as a kind of battle.'[8] He did really look forward to the contest between Orange and Coburg. The Tsar took his handsome 23-year-old protégé along whenever he visited the British royal family.

As King George III was plagued by severe bouts of madness, his son, the fat Prince of Wales, acted as Prince Regent. The future George IV was a pitiful figure. In 1785, as a young man of 23, he had married his one and true love, the 30-year-old widow Maria Fitzherbert. She was not only a commoner, but also a Catholic. Since 1701, however, English princes had been banned from ascending the throne if they married Catholics, so the marriage had been performed in secret. When he discovered what his son had done, an angry King George III — still sane at that time — forced his son to have the marriage annulled. He ordered the Prince to marry his cousin, Caroline of Brunswick-Wolfenbüttel. She was the daughter of Augusta, sister of George III. Her paternal grandfather was a brother of Leopold's grandmother Sophie.

The Prince of Wales married the 27-year-old Caroline on 8 April 1795, six days after her arrival in England. Caroline was no beauty and a bit on the plump side, though she possessed a certain blowsy blonde attraction. Prince George disliked her from the minute he saw her. His repulsion was such that he could not even force himself to come to his marriage bed and fulfil his 'dynastic duties'. He had to encourage himself by getting drunk. Their sad sexual encounter was blessed with a child exactly nine months later, on 7 January 1796. This was Charlotte, the girl the emperors of Russia and Austria wanted Leopold to seduce and marry.

After their wedding night, George and his wife did not sleep together again. The embittered Princess of Wales lived in a palace of her own, where she took many lovers, while he lived openly with his Catholic former wife. Little Charlotte was raised in George's palace, Carlton House, neglected by her father and away from her mother, whom she was allowed to see for only two hours a week. In 1814, she had become a plump and tall 18-year-old princess, 'a fine piece of flesh and blood,' very likely to have a weight problem soon, 'her bosom full, her shoulders large, and her whole person

---

8   SAP MP, Leopold to Sophie, 31 May 1814, in Leopold I 2, p. 101.

voluptuous,' according to Lady Charlotte Bury. She had, as one of her friends described it, 'blue eyes and that peculiar blonde hair which was characteristic rather of her German than her English descent.' However, 'when excited she stuttered painfully.' She was also very much her father's child, 'capricious, self-willed and obstinate.' Lady Glenbervie observed that she was 'full of exclamations very like swearing.'[9]

The fat Prince Regent had decided to marry his daughter off to Willem, the Prince of Orange. He was young, foreign and rich. He was also a courageous soldier who had fought with the Duke of Wellington against Napoleon in Spain. Wellington, however, did not have a high opinion of the Dutch Prince. 'He is very young, he is very shy and diffident. Too much is not to be expected from him,' he said.[10] But Charlotte did not dislike him. She found him amiable and kind, a bit shy and boyish, but 'by no means as disagreeable as I expected.'[11]

The trouble started when Charlotte discovered that because Orange's father was about to become the King of the United Netherlands, he, as the eldest son and Crown Prince, would have to live in the Netherlands — and so would his wife! Charlotte was afraid her father would use the opportunity of her absence to divorce her mother. She felt she had to protect her mother, who was, according to Charlotte, a 'very unfortunate woman, really oppressed and cruelly used.' As a consequence, the Princess almost overnight came to vehemently oppose marrying Orange. Instead of being an 'amiable boy,' he became 'that detested Dutchman.' Young Willem proposed a compromise whereby the couple could live alternately in the Netherlands and in England, but Charlotte did not accept that either. She was convinced that her father's only purpose in marrying her off to Orange was to get her out of the country.

At the end of May 1814, a new row started between the Prince Regent and his daughter, when Charlotte learned that her mother was not invited to the festivities in honour of the Russian guests who were arriving in London. The Regent intended to be present himself and he remained fixed in his resolution never to meet his estranged wife upon any occasion. Charlotte, who greatly resented this, must have been pleased when the absence of the Princess of Wales from a dinner held by her father in honour of the Tsar in Carlton House on 7 June led to an incident: a handsome Russian general, Leopold of Saxe-Coburg,

9   Quoted in Plowden, pp. 89 and 93, and Fraser, p. 223.
10   Wellington to Bathurst, 18 May 1813, in Colenbrander 3, p. 17.
11   Charlotte to Cornelia Knight, in Knight, p. 152.

caused the incident by requesting the Prince Regent's permission to visit his wife. The request was refused. Was this really a blunder by a naive Leopold, who did not know of the hatred between the Prince Regent and his wife and simply wanted to pay a family visit to his father's cousin? Or was it an ingenious plot to steal the heart of a girl who adored her mother, by showing consideration for this mother — a thing the Prince of Orange had never even thought of? The idea might have been conceived by the Tsar's sister, Catherine, who accompanied Charlotte daily and kept Leopold duly informed of Charlotte's state of mind. Catherine met Leopold at night, when, in his arms, she reported how much nearer she had brought him to the heart of Charlotte and to the throne of England.

But Charlotte was not impressed with Leopold. She fell in love with another German in the Tsar's delegation: Friedrich Augustus of Prussia, a 35-year-old notorious womaniser and the black sheep of the Prussian royal family. He led her on and did not tell her that he had a wife in Germany. Charlotte contrived to have several secret meetings with the Prussian, whom she referred to as 'F' in her letters. When 'F' left for Germany, she was devastated because of 'things having gone so far'.[12]

The Richest Prince in Britain

The whole situation surrounding Charlotte's engagement to Orange came to a crisis on 16 June. Exactly one week after the Russian delegation had arrived in town, Charlotte unilaterally broke off her engagement in a short letter to Prince Willem. Her father was furious. As a punishment, he kept her locked up for most of the time. But Charlotte remained determined. 'No threats shall ever bend me to marry this detested Dutchman,' she wrote.

Meanwhile, Leopold had become very active. He had written the Prince Regent a polite letter fully explaining his conduct. The Regent had graciously accepted Leopold's apologies and had even come to consider him a most honourable young man. Leopold had also been trying to catch Charlotte's attention. When she drove out in the Park he would ride up to her and endeavour to be noticed. He had called at her house, but she had not invited him in to drink tea with her. Charlotte was still in love with F and hoped that the latter, to whom she wrote ardent love letters, would return to England for her.

As it happened, Leopold spent barely a month in London. He cut short his stay because on 4 July 1814, the Prince of Leiningen, the husband of Leopold's sister Victoria, died. He returned home as soon as he heard the news. Although Leopold and Charlotte had hardly seen each other and had scarcely spoken, by early 1815 he had succeeded in becoming Charlotte's favourite. The reason why Charlotte picked 'the Leo' (as she called him) was a very prosaic one. She needed another man, as an alternative to Willem of Orange, to confront her father with. Since her first choice, F, had 'betrayed' her, the dashing Rusian general from Coburg simply was the first one that came to mind. Charlotte made a last desperate attempt to contact F on 11 November 1814, while at the same time she schemed to have Leopold suggested to the Regent as a possible husband. 'What odd mortals we are,' she remarked. 'That I should be as wholly occupied and devoted as I am to *one*, and yet think and talk and even provide for another would appear unnatural in the highest degree were it written in a novel, and yet it is *true*.' She wrote that she would still think of her Prussian Prince often, but with Leopold she would be less unhappy than if she were to remain alone.[13]

The affair with F was finally over on 18 January, when she got a letter from the Prussian. It left no further room for hope and broke her heart. Although she confided in her aunt, Princess Mary, that she was 'not the least in the world' in love with Leopold, she had a very good opinion of him, and for that reason would rather marry him than any other prince. She was encouraged by Princess Frederica, the Duchess of York, who praised Leopold abundantly. Frederica was in constant correspondence with Leopold and kept pressuring him to ask the Prince of Wales formally for the hand of his daughter. But Leopold kept putting this off. This procrastination even earned him the nicknames *'le Marquis peu-à-peu'* and *'Monsieur Doucement'* (Mister Softly-Softly) by the Regent, who seemed rather amused by the matter.

Leopold did not appeal to everyone, though. Lady Charlotte Bury, who had encountered him on her travels on the Continent in the autumn of 1814, disliked him. She had noticed that he never looked at the person he was speaking to. She thought him sly and was instinctively disinclined to trust him. Lord Frederick Fitzclarence, a bastard son of the Duke of Clarence, found him too smooth-spoken by half — 'a damned humbug.' According to Alison Plowden, the modern biographer of Princess Charlotte, there is no doubt that behind Leopold's 'suavely ingratiating façade lurked a shrewd, coldly calculating brain and a driving ambition.' He was, Plowden says, 'prepared to be agree-

---

13   Charlotte to Mercer Elphinstone, 11 Nov. 1814, in Charlotte, p. 165.

able while elbowing his way upwards.'[14] Leopold did not over hurry, he never said one word too many and took no initiatives unless he was certain of a successful outcome. Hence, Charlotte had to wait for over a year. Leopold was on the Continent and Charlotte remained virtually imprisoned by her father. Her letters to Leopold were smuggled out by the Duke of York, while Leopold corresponded with her via her friend Mercer Elphinstone. Meanwhile, Charlotte's relationship with her father gradually improved. She felt deceived by her mother, who had left England to live on the Continent, mainly in Italy. There the Princess of Wales caused much scandal by organising balls where, as Charlotte Bury wrote, she appeared 'dressed *en Vénus*, or rather not dressed further than the waist.'[15]

In the winter of 1814–1815, Leopold was in Austria as his family's official delegate to the international diplomatic Congress of Vienna, where the negotiations over the new borders of Europe continued, and where Duke Ernst of Coburg-Saalfeld, as a reward for his share in the victory over Napoleon, was assigned the territory of Sankt-Wendel in the Lower-Palatinate (today's Saarland) with its 22,000 inhabitants. When in the spring the news reached Vienna that Napoleon had escaped from Elba and had rallied the French in Paris, the delegates rushed home to raise their armies and prepare for battle. In Coburg, Duke Ernst and his family decided to lie low and await the outcome. None of the Saxe-Coburg princes participated in the battle at Waterloo, where the Allies crushed Napoleon on 18 June 1815 and Prince Willem of Orange was wounded by a musketball in the shoulder.

Meanwhile, in England, Charlotte was growing impatient. She urged 'the Leo' to ask the Regent for her hand, but he wrote to Mercer that it would be impossible for him to come to England that summer. Mr. Softly-Softly kept all options open, and as he was not certain whether the Regent would approve of his marrying Charlotte, he was reluctant to commit himself openly to her. Maybe he should marry someone else. While in Vienna, he had flirted with many girls. One of them was the beautiful and wealthy 31-year-old widow, Catherine Bagration, nicknamed 'the naked angel' because of her low necklines. Charlotte experienced moments of deep despondency. 'The more I really wish and think of this marriage for me, the more I begin to be in despair,' she told Mercer.

14   Plowden, p. 188.
15   Quoted in Plowden, p. 179.

Autumn came and Leopold was still dithering. He was in Paris with his brother Ernst, but he did not cross the Channel. 'Oh why should he not come over. It is but a run over of a few hours. I quite languish for his arrival,' Charlotte wrote desperately. At the end of October, when a couple of other German princes visited London with the thinly-veiled hope of winning themselves a British crown princess, Charlotte wryly told Mercer: 'I think the best thing I can do to make *all easy and equally* pleased is to *marry them all at once in the lump.'*

Again it was the Russian Emperor who paved the way for Leopold. When Tsar Alexander offered the Prince of Orange the hand of his youngest sister Anna, the Dutchman grasped this chance to become an in-law of the Russian imperial family. With his scheme of an Orange match definitely thwarted, the Prince Regent finally gave in to his daughter. She gained his permission to marry Leopold. Now, 'the Leo' hastened to London, where, on 26 February 1816, he saw Charlotte after a separation of 18 months.

For the Saxe-Coburg family 1816 was a year of glory. Imagine the triumph of Augusta, the Dowager-Duchess of Coburg-Saalfeld. In Vienna, on 2 January, Leopold's brother Ferdinand had married Antonia von Kohary, the only daughter of the immensely rich Hungarian Prince Kohary and the richest heiress of the Austrian Empire. Never before had Vienna seen such a wedding. The festivities, where an orchestra of 790 gypsies played Hungarian songs, lasted for nine whole days. And an even more glorious match was going to take place in London, between *Poldi* and the heiress of the Prince Regent. After the debacle in Russia, where *Julchen* had botched it, at last Augusta was sure that one of her grandchildren would some day wear a royal crown. This time nothing could go wrong, could it?

Leopold and Charlotte's engagement was announced in February. Leopold acquired British nationality and the rank of Field Marshal in the British army. He received a large sum of money from the Tsar and the Lordship of Holzkirchen from the Austrian Emperor. The poorest prince in Germany had become a wealthy man. While waiting for the wedding, Leopold remained at Brighton, recovering from neuralgia. Like his brother Ernst, the 25-year-old prince often complained of health problems. Hypochondria is a condition that apparently often occurs in highly-sexed men. His family sent him a doctor, Christian Stockmar, who arrived in Brighton on 3 April. The 28-year-old Stockmar was the official surgeon of the city of Coburg. Leopold and Stockmar became friends. Leopold asked him to stay and engaged him as his personal secretary.

Leopold's marriage took place on 2 May. Parliament settled upon him a stipend of £50,000 (the equivalent of £3.75 million or $6.25 million today), while his wife received an extra annual allocation of £10,000 pin money for her private expenses. It was agreed that if Charlotte died first, Leopold would enjoy the same income of £50,000 for the rest of his life. Furthermore, Parliament voted the couple a sum of £60,000 to be spent on furniture, jewellery and personal belongings necessary for setting up house for the first time. Charlotte also received a trousseau, consisting of thirty gowns, many embroidered in gold and trimmed with silver lace, dresses of satin decorated with Brussels point and flounces of Mechlin, and a wedding dress, also trimmed with Brussels point lace, which had cost more than £10,000.

The couple went to live at Marlborough House near St. James's Park in London and at Claremont House near Esher in Surrey. The latter was a huge Palladian mansion built in the late 1760s by the landscape gardener Lancelot 'Capability' Brown; a rare example of his work as an architect. The Prince Regent donated it as a personal gift to Leopold.

In the spring of 1817, the whole of England rejoiced in the news everyone had been waiting for: Princess Charlotte was pregnant. On 5 November, however, tragedy struck. Charlotte gave birth to a stillborn boy, after 52 hours of labour. The next day she died, only 21 years old. Leopold was shattered. 'It is true that I loved her for her physical beauty, but I can vow that what I loved *more* and came to appreciate more every day was her *noble heart*,' he wrote to his sister Sophie.[16]

* * *

After Charlotte's death, Leopold continued to live at Marlborough House and at Claremont. The provisions in the marriage contract had been extremely generous. No one had expected a tragedy like this — Charlotte dying without leaving the kingdom a successor to the throne, whom her surviving husband would then have had to raise in style. The inheritance Leopold received from his wife was large. There were some verbal protestations from his father-in-law and there was a painful squabble over a recently-painted portrait of Charlotte, but ultimately everything went to the German. Leopold lived frugally on his huge yearly allowance of £50,000, cleverly investing the fortune. He soon became the richest royal prince in England. Indeed, his stipend

16   SAP MP, Leopold to Sophie, 22 December 1817, in Leopold I 2, p. 169.

greatly exceeded the £25,000 which the Duke of York, the heir to the throne, annually received, or the £24,000 of the Duke of Kent.

Though officially Leopold remained in England until 1831, he spent most of his time on the continent. In 1819 he bought the castle of Niederfüllbach near Coburg. He often attended meetings of European freemasons and had a busy love life. He is said to have had children in Niederfüllbach and Coburg. His affairs with Countess Dorothée (Dolly) de Ficquelmont and with Jane Digby, Lady Ellenborough, did not go unnoticed; his relatives even thought that he was about to get married. Dolly he had to share with her husband, however, and Jane Digby, who was a nymphomaniac, with the whole of London. In Coburg, where Leopold had his own apartment in the Ehrenburg Palace, he frequently stood in for his brother Ernst, the reigning duke, when the latter went abroad for business or pleasure.

Duke Ernst had finally married in 1817. The bride was a relative, 16-year-old Louise of Saxe-Gotha. It was a marriage for dynastic purposes. She was the only child of Prince Augustus, the reigning Duke of Gotha-Altenburg. Her father's younger brother, Friedrich, was a childless homosexual, which made her the ultimate heir to Gotha-Altenburg. Louise, whose mother had died when she was but two weeks old, was a small, vivacious and intelligent girl. 'With long thick chestnut hair, and large blue eyes, though severely cross-eyed,' one of her nieces wrote, 'but when she smiles and talks, one assumes it to be a freshness in her expression, which suits her rather well.'[17] Because of her pleasant character, Louise was dearly loved by the people of Coburg. But the marriage was an unhappy one, owing to Ernst's continuing extramarital affairs. In the very year of his marriage, Ernst became the father of an illegitimate daughter by his 19-year-old Parisian mistress Sophie Fermepin. His reputation was further harmed by the publication, in 1823, of the saucy memoirs of *la belle Grecque*, his former mistress Pauline Panam, the mother of another of his many bastards. Out of revenge or out of loneliness, Louise soon started to take lovers of her own.

Ernst's first legitimate son, also called Ernst, was born in June 1818. A second son, Albert, was born on 26 August 1819. Theories abound over who Albert's real father might have been. According to Harald Sandner, the modern historian of the House of Saxe-Coburg, it probably was Leopold, who apparently stood in for his brother in the marital bed as well. Leopold was living in the Ehrenburg Palace from

17   Mary of Württemberg to Grand-Duchess Alexandra Feodorovna of Russia, 7 Oct. 1819, in Bachmann 2, p. 28.

September 1818 to May 1819.[18] He took a keen interest in the education of his nephews, especially of the youngest. The child grew very
fond of Uncle. 'Albert adores his uncle Leopold, never leaves his side,
ogles him, is constantly hugging him, and doesn't feel comfortable
unless he can be near him,' Louise wrote when the boy was two years
old.[19]

Duke Ernst, a promiscuous as well as a sanctimonious hypocrite
and highly suspicious of his wife, began to hate her. After Louise's
father died, he and his mother Augusta started scheming to rid themselves of her. On 29 August 1824, Ernst expelled Louise from Coburg,
while Augusta confiscated her jewellery. The people of Coburg
immediately went after their beloved Duchess, stopped her carriage,
stormed the Ehrenburg Palace and forced the Duke to take her back.
Ernst appealed to the Austrian Chancellor Metternich for help, but
Metternich refused to send Austrian troops to settle a marital dispute.
Nevertheless, on 2 September 'at the stroke of midnight,' so as to
avoid popular demonstrations, Louise left Coburg for Sankt-Wendel,
the distant Coburg exclave near the Franco-German border. 'There
nobody will see or hear anything from her, and she will soon be forgotten,' Augusta reckoned.[20]

Prior to her departure, Louise had signed all her possessions and
rights away, leaving Ernst everything and herself nothing. The fact
that she agreed to this may indicate that Ernst knew something he
could blackmail her with. At about the same time, the otherwise
miserly Leopold helped his brother out financially by giving him
£40,000. Louise wrote many sad letters to members of the family,
including Leopold and Stockmar, to be kept informed about her sons,
but she was never allowed to see the two little boys again.

As soon as Louise had been discarded, Augusta began to plan a
new marriage for Ernst, looking once more to the imperial family of
Russia, the major superpower of the day. For lack of a sister of the
Tsar, Augusta considered that a cousin of his would do. Her choice
fell on her own granddaughter Marie, the daughter of the late Antoinette of Saxe-Coburg and of Duke Alexander of Württemberg, the
Russian Minister of Roadworks and a maternal uncle of the Tsar. As
early as December 1824, Augusta was speculating that a marriage
with Marie would be financially rewarding, given that 'when she

18   Sandner, p. 56.
19   Quoted in Grey, p. 15. Also in Rhodes James, p. 24.
20   SAC Kohary Archives 32, Augusta to Ferdinand of Saxe-Coburg-Kohary, 6 Dec.
     1824.

marries, the Emperor of Russia will make a pecuniary effort for the sake of her late mother.'[21]

Before Ernst could officially repudiate his wife, however, he had to wait until Duke Friedrich IV of Gotha-Altenburg had died and Louise's inheritance had safely passed into his own hands. The gay duke passed away in 1825. The following year, Ernst became Duke of Gotha as well as Duke of Coburg. His territory doubled to 770 square miles (2,000 square kilometres) and the number of his subjects almost tripled. That same year, Ernst divorced Louise. Robbed of her inheritance, she married her *Rittmeister* but died shortly afterwards of a painful uterine cancer, only 30 years old. Ernst remarried his niece Marie of Württemberg. There were no children in that almost incestuous relationship. It was, once again, an unhappy marriage. 'Ernst is not made for marriage because he is extremely egotistical,' Leopold said.[22] In September 1838, Ernst became the father of twins by Margaret Braun, a servant girl.

* * *

In England, the tragic death of Princess Charlotte on 6 November 1817 had left the Crown without an heir, apart from George III's own children. Mad King George had fathered seven sons, but only the eldest, George, the Prince Regent, had been able to produce a legitimate heir. Now that this heir had died, it seemed that the ruling dynasty of Brunswick-Hanover was failing to guarantee the royal succession. In order to resolve this problem, the House of Commons encouraged the remaining four unmarried royal sons, the Dukes of Clarence, Kent, Sussex and Cambridge, to find suitable brides and get legitimate offspring as quickly as possible. To stimulate the princes in their duty to procreate, Parliament promised that the first to marry and get a legitimate child would be handsomely rewarded by the grateful nation. In less than seven months three of the brothers had rushed to the altar. The fourth one, 44-year-old Sussex, confessed to the Commons that he had already married secretly in 1793, but he had no children.

As the royal sons could only marry Protestants, their choice was restricted to German princesses, whose number was limited and whose child-bearing qualities, due to generations of inbreeding, were not always optimal. The youngest of the three brothers, the 43-year-old Duke of Cambridge, won the race to the altar. He married Augusta of Hesse and succeeded in having a son in 1819. Another brother, the 47-year-old Duke of Cumberland, also succeeded in get-

21   *Idem.*
22   SAP MP, Leopold to Sophie, 20 Apr. 1833, in Leopold I 2, p. 239.

ting a legitimate son in 1819 (the future King of Hanover). The 52-year-old Duke of Clarence discarded himself of his mistress, the actress Dorothea Jordan, the mother of ten of his bastards, and, as a sacrifice for Britain, married the ugly Adelaide of Saxe-Meiningen. She bore Clarence two daughters, the elder in 1819, the second in 1820. The children were poor in health, however, and both died young. The 50-year-old Edward, Duke of Kent, also rid himself of his mistress of 27 years, Julie de St. Laurent, the mother of two of his bastard sons. Intent on doing his patriotic duty to impregnate a German, he went to see Leopold for advice. 'Try my sister,' Leopold said and sent him to Amorbach, to Victoria, the 31-year-old widow of the Prince of Leiningen, and the mother of two lively children. For the House of Saxe-Coburg, this was a new opportunity to succeed to a royal throne. Leopold wrote his sister a letter, urging her to accept the marriage proposal of the Duke of Kent. At Amorbach, however, Kent fell under the spell of the beautiful Polixena von Tubeuf, Leopold's old sweetheart. He forgot that he had travelled to Germany to marry a princess and first proposed to Polixena, but she declined.[23] The Duke then turned to Victoria and married her in May 1818.

Their daughter was born on 24 May 1819. The baby was named Victoria after her mother. Seven months later, on 23 January 1820, Kent suddenly died from a cold which he had not treated. By a curious chance, young Dr. Stockmar was staying in Kent's house at the time. Two years after having watched Princess Charlotte die, he now stood by the deathbed of the husband of Leopold's sister. If Kent had survived, he would eventually have succeeded to the British throne and Victoria of Saxe-Coburg would have become queen, but this, too, was not to be. At Stockmar's advice Kent hastily prepared a will, ensuring the guardianship of his daughter to his wife.

Six days after Kent, his father, mad King George III, died. The Prince Regent became King George IV. He died in 1830 and was succeeded by his brother, King William IV, formerly the Duke of Clarence. When the latter died in 1837, Kent's 18-year-old daughter Victoria succeeded him and reigned for 64 years, the longest reign in British history. She married her cousin, Albert, officially the son of Leopold's brother but most likely Leopold's own. This marriage had been the last great ambition of her grandmother, the Dowager Duchess Augusta, who had destined the two children to marry each other

---

23   Vermeir, vol. I, p. 36. Vermeir quotes a letter of Victoria, Duchess of Kent, to Polixena, in which she says: *'Dir danken wir unser Glück'* (We owe our happiness to you).

from the moment that Albert was born, barely three months after Victoria. By marrying Albert, Victoria brought the House of Saxe-Coburg onto the British throne. In 1831, her uncle Leopold became the King of the Belgians. King Leopold and Queen Victoria collaborated in 1837 in bringing the eldest son of Ferdinand of Saxe-Coburg-Kohary to the throne of Portugal, while in 1887, the son of Ferdinand's second son became the King of Bulgaria.

There is some irony in the fact that of the seven children of unambitious Francis, the four youngest (Ernst, Ferdinand, Victoria and Leopold) became either monarchs or parents to one, while the three eldest (Sophie, Antoinette and Juliana) did not succeed in this respect. It had been these latter three whom their mother Augusta had taken to St. Petersburg in September 1795, to ensure that one of them became the mother of the future Tsar of Russia. When Augusta died in November 1831, however, her son Leopold was the King of the Belgians and her granddaughter Victoria the Crown Princess of Great Britain and Ireland. For a woman who was herself the daughter of an unimportant count, and who in 1777 had married a bankrupt prince, this was quite an achievement.

A Throne for an Equilibrist

When Kent died, he left his widow and eight-month-old baby hugely in debt. Though the Dowager-Duchess, who lived at Kensington Palace, received an annual pension of £6,000, this was hardly enough to raise the heir to the British throne. It fell far below the £50,000 that Leopold received annually. To help his sister out, Leopold offered her money from his own fortune, all in all £16,000 by 1831 — a period during which he received £700,000 (the equivalent of more than £52 million or $87 million today) out of the British Treasury. His sister and her child often came to stay for long periods with Leopold at Claremont. Here he could supervise little Victoria's education. Later, Victoria wrote that her childhood years at Claremont had been 'the brightest epoch of my otherwise rather melancholy childhood.' She grew very attached to her uncle. He was, she said, 'il mio secondo padre — or, rather, *solo* padre, for he is indeed like my real father, as I have none.'[24]

The brothers of the late Duke of Kent, including George IV and his successor, William IV, did not like this Saxe-Coburg influence on the royal heir at all. Leopold was given no official functions in Britain and led an idle life. When he was not on one of his frequent travels to the continent, he occasionally attended parties of the English aristocracy, where he was generally despised. 'The shabbiest ass,' Lady Cowper called him. 'His pomposity fatigues, and his avarice disgusts,' Lord Greville said. The Duke of Wellington, a member of the Tory cabinet, sometimes felt constrained to invite the shifty German prince. 'We are here with a crowd of bores,' Princess de Lieven, the wife of the Russian ambassador, reported to Metternich in January 1821 about one of Wellington's parties. 'Leopold,' she said, 'was wearying me with his slow speech and his bad reasoning.' 'He is a Jesuit and a bore.'[25] Even Wellington confessed that he was often 'bored to death.'

At home, in his mansion at Claremont, Leopold's company consisted of his servants, 'four dogs and two parrots, one of which can sing the overture to Weber's opera *Der Freischütz*,'[26] and his secretary, Christian Stockmar, whom Leopold had raised to the rank of a Baron in 1821. Stockmar not only promoted the interests of the Saxe-Coburgs, but also those of his own family. He knew that his master was leading a restless sexual life. Leopold had mistresses in London and abroad. In his capacity as personal surgeon, Stockmar, fearing that his master's promiscuous life would 'ruin body and soul,' advised the prince to marry. He told him that he had a cousin who strikingly resembled the late Princess Charlotte. In September 1828, Leopold departed for Prussia to meet this 20-year-old cousin of Stockmar's.

Karoline Bauer was the daughter of Christine Stockmar, an aunt of Leopold's secretary. She lived with her widowed mother in Berlin, where she was an actress at the Opera. There are indications that Karoline was a virtuous young woman. She had refused the advances of Count Bismarck and Prince Friedrich Augustus of Prussia (the late Princess Charlotte's infamous F).

Leopold was infatuated from the moment he saw Karoline in the theatre of the *Neues Palast* in Potsdam. He surprised the actress with a visit and proposed that she should come and live with him in England. At first Karoline was not enthusiastic, but Leopold courted her insistently. 'It is very hard for me to give up my career as an actress, but my heart asks me to make this sad, afflicted man happy again,' she wrote to Stockmar. 'Always, when I have decided not to give in, I see his dark melancholic eyes begging me. I will have to renounce my beloved job in Berlin for the only possible future that he can offer me: to join him in his loneliness in England.'[27] She finally gave in

25   Lieven to Metternich, 12 Jan. and 4 Feb. 1821, in Lieven, pp. 103 and 111.
26   Leopold to Marie-Amélie, Duchess of Orléans, 21 Apr. 1828, in Sabbe, p. 67.
27   Bauer to Stockmar, Jan. 1829, in Wangenheim, p. 76.

when during a visit to his castle in Niederfüllbach he promised to marry her.

In May 1829, Karoline and her mama moved to London. Leopold rented them a place near Regent's Park. Stockmar explained that the marriage had to be kept a secret, because Leopold might otherwise lose his British stipend. On 2 July, there was a small wedding party in Claremont House.[28] But Leopold's infatuation with Karoline was over as soon as he had conquered her. She became a burden to him. He was extremely angry when she spent too much money to his liking on a trip to Paris. Politically, too, she was a liability.

Since 1821, the people of Greece had been fighting a guerrilla war against their Turkish Ottoman overlords. In September 1829, the Turkish Sultan accepted the independence of Greece. The Greeks wanted a republic and had already chosen one of their leaders, Count Ioánnis Kapodístrias, as president. The Great Powers had decided, however, that Greece should become a kingdom. Hence, a kingdom it had to be. But who should be king? France supported Prince Johann of Saxony, while the candidate of King George IV of Britain was Prince Frederik of Orange, a younger brother of Prince Willem, who in 1814 had lost his fiancée to Leopold. Leopold decided to put himself forward as a better candidate. He knew he would easily get the backing of Russia. He visited France and persuaded Paris to accept him as second choice if Prince Johann was rejected. He went to Naples to meet Greek representatives. He sent the banker Karl Stockmar, the brother of his secretary, to Greece to meet Kapodístrias, who declared himself in favour of Leopold. He lobbied at the Foreign Office in London, where Lord Aberdeen was in charge, and he succeeded in obtaining the support of the Duke of Wellington, the British Prime Minister.

Their support for Leopold brought Aberdeen and Wellington into conflict with George IV. How could the Government be 'such fools as to think Prince Leopold could be any use?' the King exclaimed. George vetoed Leopold. This led to a government crisis. Wellington threatened to resign if Leopold was not accepted. The King 'grumpily' gave in. But having won his prize, Leopold was no longer interested and renounced the Greek crown. On thinking the matter over, he had begun to have doubts about the future stability of the Greek throne. 'It is a throne with only three legs,' Stockmar said, 'not fit for a King, but for an equilibrist.' His sister, too, wanted Leopold to remain in England. The Dowager-Duchess of Kent wished to have him

---

28   Sandner (p. 282) says that they were married in the chapel of Niederfüllbach Castle.

nearby, so that he could remain the protector of the interests of the House of Saxe-Coburg, as they were embodied in her daughter. Then, the 67-year-old King George IV became seriously ill. It was clear that he was soon to die (he died on 26 June). The Duke of Clarence was next in line for the throne, and immediately after him the 11-year-old Victoria. Was Leopold tempted by a possible glorious career in England, perhaps as the Regent for his little niece?

Leopold went to see the British Foreign Secretary. He told him that his acceptance of the Greek throne had only been conditional. The territory of Greece should be enlarged with the province of Candia (Crete). Aberdeen became angry. 'Notwithstanding all that has been arranged already, you are free to withdraw, but your decision cannot be explained by the case of Candia alone,' he said.[29] Nevertheless, on 21 May, Leopold officially declared that he would not accept the throne of Greece after all. Wellington and Aberdeen felt personally affronted. Lieven, the Russian Ambassador, called Leopold's behaviour 'downright scandalous,' because he renounced all the responsibilities he had previously accepted. Even the Prussian Baron von Stein, a friend of Leopold, wrote to the Archbishop of Cologne: 'It is all in the style of *Prince peu à peu*, as King George calls him. In cowardly fashion he lets go of the plough even before he has drawn the first furrow, and is already calculating his chances upon the death of the King. A man of such small stature is not worthy of a high position.'[30] Leopold denied that his real ambition was to become Regent of Great Britain, but many years later in a letter to Archduke Johann of Austria he would confess: 'If I had taken over power in England in 1830, things would have been different.'[31]

The Greek episode convinced Leopold of the urgency of discarding himself of his wife. If he had become King of Greece, his marriage to a commoner would have been a severe handicap. The children born within such a morganatic marriage would be unable to inherit their father's rank. If he had become king — or if he wanted to become a king in future and establish a respectable dynasty — he would either have to divorce Karoline Bauer or simply declare his marriage non-existent, as if she had only been his mistress. Leopold opted for the second solution. He told her that he no longer considered himself married. It is striking to see how he used the same argument towards his wife as he used towards the European Powers with regard to the

29   Aberdeen to Leopold, 31 Jan. 1830, in Bauer, Karoline 1, vol. III, p. 200.
30   Quoted in Vermeir, vol. I, p. 46.
31   Quoted in Bronne 1, p. 49.

Greek throne. He claimed that his marriage had only been conditional and that he could renounce it whenever this pleased him.

The deceived woman left England at the end of May 1830, only a few days after Leopold had officially rejected the throne of Greece. Karoline never met Leopold again. She committed suicide after writing her memoirs, in which she depicted the Coburg prince as a pedantic hypochondriac egotist. Ernst Stockmar, the son of Leopold's secretary, in a reaction to the publication of the memoirs, did not deny the fact that his relative had been wronged. However, he considered the marriage of the prince to his father's cousin no more than 'a small mistake, which was soon mended.' The whole episode, he said, 'does not even deserve to be mentioned.'[32] The official line is that the woman made everything up. Otherwise, one would have to concede that the founder of the royal dynasty of Belgium was a bigamist.

Indeed, within less than a year after Leopold renounced the crown of Greece, he accepted another: the crown of a country that did not exist at the moment of the Greek episode and that had never existed before — Belgium.

* * *

When in 1815 the provinces of the Southern Netherlands were reunited with those of the Northern Netherlands as a kingdom under Willem I of Orange, this meant the end of a separation of exactly 230 years between both parts of the Netherlands. Indeed, in 1585, the fall of Antwerp had marked the conquest of the South by the Habsburg King Philip II of Spain, but his Spanish troops did not succeed in subduing the flooded lands further to the North.

Understandably, France did not like the prospect of having the reunited Netherlands as a strong bulwark to the North of its border. As late as 1829 the French Prime Minister Jules de Polignac was proposing to redivide the Netherlands. He suggested giving the North to Prussia, the South to France, and the Dutch colonies to Britain. From the beginning, French agents fomented trouble in Willem's kingdom. To this end they exploited linguistic as well as religious divisions.

Willem's five million subjects were predominantly Catholic (3.8 million) and Dutch-speaking (3.8 million), but while religious divisions ran through the Northern provinces, linguistic divisions ran through the South. The people in the provinces of the Northern Netherlands (e.g. Holland, Zeeland, Gelderland) *shared one language, but different religions*: the 2 million inhabitants in the North were all

Dutch-speaking and predominantly Calvinist, although Catholics made up forty per cent of the population. In the South, the situation was the reverse. Here, there was *a unity of religion but a diversity of language*: the 3 million inhabitants in the Southern Netherlands shared one religion, Catholicism, but had three languages. The most populous northern provinces of the South (Flanders, Brabant, Limburg) spoke Flemish (a dialect of Dutch), the southernmost provinces (Hainaut, Liège, Namur) were predominantly Walloon (a dialect of French), while Luxemburg was Letzeburgian (a dialect of German).

The country had two capitals, Brussels in the South and Amsterdam in the North. King Willem had wanted to make Brussels the only capital of the realm, but the Great Powers had decided that there should be two. Parliament held its session alternately in Brussels and in The Hague, near Amsterdam. The government and the state administration travelled from one capital to the other, as did 600 families of functionaries and the diplomatic corps. Moving back and forth cost a lot of money, and much energy and time was lost transporting archives.

Willem I invested heavily in the South. Four-fifths of the industrial government subsidies went to the South. The King established an investment company, the *Algemeene Maatschappij* or *Société Générale*, which provided subsidies for the development of new industries in return for shares in the new factories. He gave his own private property as collateral security for the investment company. Ghent became the most modern centre of the textile industry on the European continent, with 30,000 well-paid jobs and 50 steam engines, processing 7.5 million kilos of cotton in 1829. Liège, a centre of the coal and metal industry, boasted 100 steam engines. The King diverted Dutch colonial trade mainly through Antwerp. The number of ships coming into its harbour rose from 585 in 1818 to 1,028 in 1829. By 1825, the harbour of Antwerp had become twice as busy as the Northern ports of Amsterdam and Rotterdam combined for trade in colonial goods.

Willem also cared greatly about education. Between 1815 and 1830 he had more than 1,500 new schools built in the South. As a result, the number of children attending classes doubled. The King also founded three universities in the South (none in the North). His efforts were directed towards the South to such an extent that it caused resentment in the North. When pro-French rioters rebelled in the South in 1830, many in the North grasped this opportunity to get rid of the South. This is the main reason why a French-inspired riot in Brussels led to the country falling apart, although the vast majority of the Southern population did not want the independence of the South — or 'Belgium' as it was to be called after the Latin word for the Netherlands.

The results of Southern independence were devastating for ordinary people. In 1832, Ghent processed a mere 2 million kilos of cotton, a drop of more than 73% compared to 1829. Most textile labourers had become unemployed and those who were fortunate enough to retain their jobs earned but 30% of their previous wages. By 1831, harbour activity in Antwerp had fallen from over 1,000 ships per year to only 398. For the common man, the Belgian Revolution was a catastrophe. King Willem I's reign ended in failure. In order to have been successful, he, too, would have needed to be more of an equilibrist.

A Most Violent Struggle

The riots in the South started on the evening of 25 August 1830. The month before, during the last days of July, there had been a revolution in France. The Bourbon King Charles X had been deposed. His distant cousin, Louis-Philippe of Orléans, succeeded him. Many French hoped that with the newly installed *July Monarchy* the glorious days of French expansion and conquest would return. This hope was shared by a group of French immigrants and exiles in Brussels.

The Southern Netherlands had been part of France from 1794 to 1814. During these twenty years the French authorities had pursued a policy of cultural imperialism. They had replaced all the civil servants in Dutch-speaking Flanders, Brabant and Limburg with Frenchmen. After the defeat of Napoleon at Waterloo, most of the French administrators and civil servants had remained in the Southern Netherlands. They were followed in 1815 by a second wave of immigrants from France. These were the most radical political opponents of the Bourbons, who, because of their political extremism during the previous decades, were persecuted in France. This group included the so-called 'regicides,' the surviving members of the first French revolutionary 'parliament,' the *Convention*, that in 1793 had voted in favour of executing King Louis XVI. King Willem granted them asylum. Most of them settled in Brussels, the nearest big city to Paris.

The most vociferous of the French immigrants was Prince Maurice de Broglie, the Bishop of Ghent. He was a French aristocrat, born in Paris in 1766. Broglie had been the almoner of the French Imperial Court. In 1807, Napoleon appointed him Bishop of Ghent. The so-called *Concordat* — the treaty between Napoleon and the Pope — of 15 July 1801 allowed the French Emperor to appoint the bishops in his Empire. As a result, all the bishops in the Southern Netherlands had become Frenchmen.

Although prominent ministers of the Dutch Cabinet, such as the Home Secretary, the Minister of *Waterstaat* (Public Works) and of the Colonies, and the Minister of Religious Affairs and Education were southern Catholics, King Willem opposed giving privileges to the Catholic Church. The bishops demanded, however, that Catholicism should be made the sole official state religion in the Southern provinces. When in 1815 the Dutch Constitution proclaimed religious freedom, Prince Broglie declared that it was 'a crime against God' to swear allegiance to it, thereby prohibiting Catholics from becoming civil servants. The Vatican representative in the Netherlands, Mgr. Capaccini, later regretted Broglie's decision. He wrote in 1829 that forbidding the faithful to swear allegiance to the Constitution had led to their underrepresentation in the government apparatus, 'with the consequence that the most influential posts in the Kingdom went to Protestants and to half-hearted Catholics.'[33] Bishop Broglie was so extreme that he did not even hesitate to use violence. Father Buydens, the dean of the parishes of Bruges, was physically assaulted by Broglie when he was called to account at the episcopal palace in Ghent after he had advised the Sisters Colettines in Bruges to obey the civil authorities.

* * *

At first, the revolution of 27 July 1830 in Paris did not affect Brussels. King Willem had been in town until 21 August and everything had remained quiet. There had been considerable nervousness and commotion, however, amongst the French immigrants and the Francophiles. They formed a small group, whose leaders were Charles Rogier, Count Félix de Merode and Alexandre Gendebien. Rogier, a journalist from Liège, was a French-born immigrant. Merode had been a senator under Napoleon. Gendebien was a lawyer whose father had been a *député* in the French Parliament. He was the contact person in Brussels of the revolutionaries who had taken over control in France. These groups wanted to take revenge for the defeat at Waterloo and restore France to what they considered its 'natural' border: the Rhine. They wished to occupy the whole west bank of that river, but especially the town of Antwerp, which Napoleon had called 'a pistol pointed at the heart of England,' because its port could dock a war fleet capable of reaching the Thames estuary in a single night.[34]

One of the new leaders in Paris was the 73-year-old Marquess of Lafayette, whose niece happened to be the wife of Merode. The

33   Quoted in Schmitz, pp. 274-5.
34   Terlinden 2, p. 155.

Marquess, who as a young man in his early twenties had participated in the American Revolution, was the commander of the French National Guard. He helped work out plans to set up a revolution in Brussels. On the evening of 25 August, rioters, led by the journalist Edouard Ducpétiaux, ransacked the offices of a Brussels newspaper and burned down the houses of the head of the Brussels police and the Minister of Justice. On the morning of 26 August, a French flag was hoisted over the Brussels town hall. The mob started a large-scale plundering of shops and factories. The Austrian Ambassador informed Metternich that the hooligans who started the riots had been paid by French secret agents.

On 27 August, the local authorities in Brussels were able to restore order. They established an armed guard of civilians, the Burgher Guard, to patrol the streets in order to avoid further plundering. Many of the guard's officers, however, were French immigrants, chosen for their military experience because they had been officers in Napoleon's army. One of them was Jean-Pierre Chazal, one of the members of the *Convention* that had condemned King Louis XVI to the guillotine in 1793. Chazal, whom Napoleon had made a Baron, had fled France after Napoleon's defeat to avoid punishment for his part in the regicide. Both Jean-Pierre and his son Pierre joined the Burgher Guard.

Meanwhile, the King had sent his eldest son, Crown Prince Willem, to Brussels with 6,000 soldiers. The choice of his son as the army's commander was very unfortunate. The Crown Prince had played a dubious role during the previous 15 years, often getting involved in conspiracies against his own father. In the winter of 1816–1817 the Prince had been involved in a plot of the exiled French intellectuals in Brussels to oust the Bourbon King of France and create, after seceding Belgium from the Netherlands, a new Franco-Belgian Kingdom with himself on its throne. When King Willem heard about this, he strongly advised his son to choose other friends, but the Prince took this as a personal affront. Three years later, the young man was involved in a similar plan. On 19 August 1820, the French government arrested some officers in Paris who were planning a military coup to put the Prince of Orange on the throne. King Willem once more warned his son against the company of the French exiles in Brussels. 'Without you they are nothing, but if you let them use you, you will become their toy,' he told his son.[35] By 1830 a reconciliation had taken place between father and son, but the King did not know that his

---

35   Willem I to Crown Prince Willem, 20 Feb. 1820, in Colenbrander 1, vol. VIII, II, p. 234.

37-year-old son was still harbouring the wild dreams of his youth. He still aimed for the crown of France. He had not understood that now that the Bourbon King of France had been toppled and replaced by an Orléans King, his former friends no longer needed their Orange toy.

Instead of bringing the army to Brussels, as his father had ordered, the Crown Prince left the royal troops at Vilvoorde, 20 kilometres to the north of the Southern capital and started negotiations with the French exiles. He entered Brussels with an escort of the Burgher Guard, including young Pierre Chazal. It must have been really easy for the Francophile party to persuade the gullible prince. They played their old tricks and enticed him with the prospect of becoming King of Belgium as a first step to becoming King of France. The Prince signed a petition to ask his father, in order to avoid similar riots in the future, to give the Southern provinces a separate administration with the Crown Prince as Viceroy.

Indeed, the Prince liked what he was told in Brussels. On 30 August, the poet Louis Jenneval, a French immigrant, had composed the first version of the *Brabançonne*, the future national anthem of Belgium. Its original text was not anti-Orange. The aim of the Brussels revolutionaries, it said, was *'greffer l'Orange sur l'arbre de la liberté'* (to put the Orange on the tree of liberty). Gendebien went to see the Prince to offer him the Crown of Belgium. The Prince was so blinded by the declarations of the revolutionaries' 'loyalty' to his person, that he did not notice that they were using him for their own purposes. Others, however, perceived exactly what was going on. 'I am very anxious about the course taken by the Prince of Orange,' the Duke of Wellington wrote to Lord Aberdeen. 'There is in that prince a foundation of vanity, levity, and thirst for vulgar popularity, which makes me tremble for the success of everything he undertakes. If he has consented to the establishment of the burgher guards he has lost the monarchy.'[36]

And, indeed, instead of bringing his army into Brussels, the Prince laid power in the hands of the Burgher Guard when he left the town on 3 September and went to the North to see the King with the proposal of an administrative separation between North and South. On 7 September, Charles Rogier arrived in Brussels with 300 armed men from Liège. Immediately they started building barricades in the Brussels streets. With the backing of the Liégeois, Gendebien installed himself at the head of 'The Commission of Public Security' which, he said, had taken over the city government in the name of the people.

36   Wellington to Aberdeen, 8 Sept. 1830, in Smits, vol. I, p. 206.

Apart from Leuven, however, which, situated on the road between Brussels and Liège, had been infiltrated by revolutionaries from both places, the whole Dutch speaking northern half of Belgium, remained calm. Major Flemish cities like Antwerp, Dendermonde, Ghent and Mechelen spoke out against every form of separation, administrative or otherwise, between North and South. The province of East Flanders stated that, in case of a division of the Netherlands, it wished to be attached to the North.

The rebellion remained limited to Brussels and the Walloon provinces, where French agents distributed alcohol to the mob. Sir Thomas Cartwright, the British envoy in Brussels, informed London on 10 September about the situation: 'The liberals or violent party hold the rabble in their pay and may put them in motion at pleasure accordingly as they will for their services, and the lower orders are willing at any moment to commence a general pillage.' According to Cartwright the radicals had devised 'a deep plan to throw the town into confusion.'[37] Meanwhile, Jenneval had written a new text for his *Brabançonne*. The aim of the Revolution had now become *'briser l'Orange sur l'arbre de la liberté'* (to smash the Orange on the tree of liberty).

On 16 September, the Brussels city hall was stormed and the French flag was raised once more. The mayor and the city councillors fled to Antwerp, where they asked Prince Frederik, the second son of the King, to march on Brussels. The same request was made by all Southern delegates in the Parliament in The Hague. They urged the King to put down the rebels by force. Even Baron Hoogvorst, the nominal head of the Brussels Burgher Guard, was hoping that the army would intervene. 'Everyone is suffering and wants to finish the Revolution,' Hoogvorst wrote to Gendebien.

In his reports to Aberdeen, Cartwright wrote that there were two factions in Brussels: the leftist radicals, supported by 'a mass of colliers of the lowest rabble' who had flocked into town from Liège Wallonia, and a group of moderates, led by Hoogvorst, and supported by the terrorised burghers of Brussels. 'A most violent struggle is at this moment going on between the two parties,' Cartwright wrote on 14 September. Exactly one week later, on 21 September, he reported that Hoogvorst was standing 'alone and unaided by anyone, and totally without a shadow of power.' In a summary report on 26 September, Cartwright concluded that 'had the Liégeois never entered Brussels, matters would not have come to such extremities. The moderates early in the business saw the grievous fault they had committed in admitting them to gain so firm a footing at Brussels, but all their endeavours to prevail on them to return to Liège were unavailing, and M. Ducpétiaux and the liberals knew too well their worth, to allow them to depart.'[38]

In the North tension was also rising. The Amsterdam newspaper *Algemeen Handelsblad* urged the North to discard the South: 'It would have been better if they had never been united with us. They have nothing in common with us,' it wrote on 8 September. The paper reminded its readership of the 'sacrifices' Amsterdam had been forced to bring for the benefit of Antwerp and Ghent. The head of the Amsterdam Police reported on 15 September that there was a general call in the city for a separation of the North from the South. An MP from Holland vented the general feeling in his province when he declared in Parliament that 'the North had gained nothing' from the union with the South, while Brussels had become 'a European city' and Antwerp had thrived. When the matter of the separation was put to the vote in Parliament, the majority of the delegates from Holland voted in favour of ridding themselves of the Belgians, including the Dutch-speaking Southerners in the Flemish provinces who were not rebelling. King Willem was now confronted with separatists in the North as well as in the South.

On the evening of 20 September, Prince Frederik received orders to march on Brussels with 52 canons and 14,000 soldiers — two-thirds of them Southerners. The next day, almost all the leaders of the rebellion fled the city. Cartwright remained an eyewitness to the events: 'The agitation and anxiety was intense during the 22nd., the barricades and breastworks were multiplied and strengthened, and every street was filled with groups of rabble who wandered two and three together through the town, armed with muskets taken from the burghers.' Although their leaders had run, the 'bandits' from Liège had stayed. 'They are in fact the principal actors in the defence.'[39]

On 23 September, Prince Frederik entered Brussels. Instead of marching to the centre of the town, however, he camped with his soldiers in the Park at the eastern end of the city, and remained there, inactive, for three days. During the first nights, the 'bandits' abandoned their barricades and went to the Brussels pubs. The Prince would have been able to take the barricades without bloodshed. But, like his brother four weeks earlier, Frederik was reluctant to use the army. He was an inexperienced soldier who had never before partici-

38   Smits, vol. I, pp. 315 and 380, and vol. II, p. 21.
39   Cartwright to Aberdeen, 26 Sept. 1830, in Smits, vol. I, p. 382, and vol. II, p. 21.

pated in battle. He offered an amnesty and hoped that the rebels would surrender. While he dallied, the leaders of the revolution returned. Gendebien arrived back in Brussels with a group of Frenchmen who had fought in the streets of Paris in July. When these French agents started shooting at the soldiers in the Park, Frederik decided to use force. But how! He bombarded the city and left the next night. To the amazement of the rebels, on the morning of 27 September, the Park was empty.

For the second time in a month, the Dutch army had unexpectedly retreated. Once more, this greatly encouraged the rebels. Volunteers came flocking to them from all over Wallonia and the North of France. Francophone generals of the Dutch army, like Duvivier (a brother-in-law of Gendebien) and Count du Val, declared themselves in favour of the revolution. In Namur, the military commander, General Joseph Van Geen, a Fleming, reported to the authorities in The Hague that his Walloon soldiers were deserting and that he could only trust those soldiers who came from the North, from Flanders or from Luxemburg.

On 4 October, a provisional government was established in Brussels. The revolutionaries who were in power now were a group of bright and radical young men. Gendebien, who was 41, Merode, 39, Lebeau, 37, and Rogier, 30, were the eldest of the leaders of the new regime. Chazal was only 22, Nothomb 25, Ducpétiaux 26, Van de Weyer 28. During the next half-century these men would dominate Belgian politics and use the new state as a vehicle to build themselves a fortune. They began by rewarding themselves handsomely and bestowed positions on themselves they could not have dreamed of two months previously — Chazal was made a general with an annual income of 7,000 guilders, while a high school teacher only earned 300 guilders a year. Others were similarly rewarded. They had much to lose now, which made them even more unscrupulous and ruthless.

The revolutionaries pretended to speak for both the Walloon and the Flemish provinces. Flanders reaffirmed, however, that it wanted to remain Dutch. Agents from Brussels, who had arrived in Antwerp and had offered money to the labourers if they would start a riot, were told off by them with the message that 'they rather worked to earn their living.' In Ghent the labourers held a demonstration in favour of the King. In Mechelen they wore orange ribbons in defiance of the revolution.

Reign of Terror

On 5 October, the Crown Prince arrived in Antwerp. Willem I, wishing to give his son a new chance, had sent him to the South to restore order. The foolish prince, however, still cherished his secret agenda. On the very day of his arrival in Antwerp, he received Ducpétiaux and started negotiations with the Brussels revolutionaries. He agreed to withdraw the Dutch army from the Belgian provinces and ordered the civil authorities in the whole South, including the provinces that were still loyal to his father, to participate in the elections of the Belgian 'National Congress' which the provisional government was organising in the areas under its control to give itself an appearance of legitimacy. The Prince hoped that this National Congress would, out of gratitude, elect him King of the new state — and the Brussels revolutionaries led him to believe that it might indeed do so. In reality, Gendebien and his friends wanted the National Congress to vote a request for annexation by France and disband itself as soon as annexation had been achieved. Hence, the National Congress was only elected for a six-month period. That was considered sufficient for France to absorb Belgium.

On 16 October, the Prince officially proclaimed Belgium's independence and put himself at the head of the new state. He ordered the soldiers from the North to return home and the soldiers from the South to form Belgian regiments and place themselves under his command. Knowing that the Prince was a fool, Wellington might well have realised that he was acting on his own, but the proclamation was a folly of such magnitude that even Wellington was baffled. The British government, so far opposed to dividing the Netherlands, concluded that the Dutch King himself wished an administrative separation of the South. Indeed, Wellington, on noting that King Willem had sent his son to Antwerp, 'whose propensities and partialities were well known, and who had already promised in September to the Belgians in revolt at Bruxelles that he would recommend to the King his father a compliance with their requisitions,' immediately concluded when he was informed that the Prince's 'first act was in fact a consent on his part to a separation of the Southern from the Northern part of the kingdom,' that this was also 'a consent on the part of the King.'[40] In fact, the King knew nothing of his son's initiative, let alone approving it. He wrote to the Prince that he was 'as surprised as afflicted' by his declaration. But it was too late.

---

40   Wellington to Aberdeen, in Smits, vol. II, p. 180.

The action of the Prince had a devastating impact. In Bruges, General Goethals defected to the Brussels government, as did General Daine in Roermond. The other generals disbanded their armies. By the end of October 1830, except for the garrisons in Antwerp, Maastricht and Luxemburg, King Willem had almost no troops left in the South. In Ghent, the city authorities begged the army to stay, but to their exasperation it left. A group of 400 Parisian revolutionaries arrived under the command of the French Viscount Pontécoulant. They occupied Ghent in the name of the Brussels government. They were, as one eyewitness recounted, 'a motley lot in rags, that is being called the *Légion de Paris* and that commits the greatest excesses everywhere.' They terrorised the population and plundered the Protestant church. One week later, they marched on Bruges, together with 600 hooligans from France, the *Corps de Roubaix*, led by a certain Grégoire.

Bruges had passed to the revolutionary regime after the defection of General Goethals, but on 21 October an anti-Belgian revolt took place which Pontécoulant and Grégoire were ordered to put down. Grégoire's *Corps de Roubaix* preferred to call itself *les Têtes de Mort* (the Skulls), but Grégoire considered his corps a civilised troop compared to the *Légion* of Pontécoulant which, he said, consisted of 'robbers.' After putting down the revolt in Bruges, the two 'armies' terrorised Menen, Ieper (Ypres) and Nieuwpoort. By way of reprisal they plundered the houses of the *Orangists*, the people loyal to King Willem. In Lichtervelde, the Catholic parish priest was molested when he refused to fly the Belgian flag from his church tower.

The Flemish provinces of Limburg and Antwerp were subdued by the revolutionary generals Daine, Niellon and Mellinet (the latter two were Frenchmen). As soon as the Dutch army had withdrawn, the revolutionary troops which consisted mainly of Liégeois, marched in. At Mechelen, they were able to catch Louis Gaillard, a Walloon from Liège, who was a colonel of the Dutch army and had remained loyal to King Willem. Gaillard was brought to Leuven, lynched and hanged from the so-called 'tree of liberty' in the market square.

Fortunately for the King, there were a number of Dutch generals in the South who refused to follow the Prince's orders. General Dibbets, the military commander of Maastricht, threw the representatives of the Brussels government who had arrived to organise the elections for the National Congress out of town. When they retorted that the Crown Prince had ordered the elections to be organised, Dibbets answered: 'I know but the King.' In Antwerp, the Dutch garrison did not leave either. On 23 October the city council asked to be treated like the rest of the North. Nevertheless, the army commander allowed the

civilian governor of the province to organise the elections for the
National Congress as the Prince had ordered. The town was plunged
into chaos. The Crown Prince left Antwerp on 26 October, and went
into exile in Britain, having become the most despised man both in the
North and the South. One day later, Dutch troops bombarded Antwerp after Belgian revolutionaries had infiltrated the city. A
significant part of the city went up in flames.

In Brussels, the Provisional Government of Belgium, with
Gendebien as Minister of Justice, started making preparations for the
annexation by France. On 5 October 1830, it was decided that the
whole administration should be run in French. 'The efforts of our government have to be directed towards the annihilation of the Flemish
language in order to prepare the fusion of Belgium with our great
fatherland France,' Charles Rogier wrote candidly to the British
Foreign Secretary.[41]

The judicial courts, which in 1815 had been ordered by King Willem
to use Dutch in the provinces where the people spoke Dutch, all had
to use French again, as in the days of French occupation. The schools,
too, were all forced to become Francophone. Most schools in Flanders,
however, were simply abolished. The number of primary schools in
the South was halved, from 4,000 to 2,000. The army, the backbone of
the new regime, was a Francophone institution as well. Of the 2,700
officers in the Belgian army in 1831, only 150 had been born in Belgium. Most officers were of French origin, and many had settled in
Belgium only since September 1830. The General Staff consisted of 28
generals: 24 Frenchmen and four Belgians.

'The first principle of good administration,' Rogier, the Belgian
Minister of the Interior, said in 1832, 'rests on the exclusive use of one
language, and it is obvious that in Belgium this language must be
French. To achieve this result, it is essential that all civil and military
posts be entrusted to Walloons, so that the Flemings, being temporarily deprived of the advantages deriving from such employment,
will be obliged to learn French.'[42]

* * *

In October 1830, 200 deputies were elected to the Belgian National
Congress. Of a total population of 3 million, only 46,000 men were
entitled to vote. Of these, more than one-third (16,000) boycotted the
elections because they were Orangists loyal to the King. The result
was that the National Congress was elected by only 0.075% of the

41   Rogier to Palmerston, in Verhaert, p. 52.
42   Quoted in Hermans, p. 72.

Belgian population. Of the 200 deputies, 28 were Orangists as well, while 156 wanted Belgium to be annexed to France.

During the first meeting of the National Congress, a naive delegate suggested that a proclamation should be issued to explain to the world why King Willem had been deposed by the Belgians. The suggestion was greeted with 'laughter and merriment.' According to Joseph Lebeau, an attorney from Liège and one of the intellectual leaders of the Belgian revolutionaries, such a declaration was unnecessary because it was not the law that ruled the world, but violence. 'The bayonets have spoken,' Lebeau said: 'Violence has undone what violence had imposed. Europe already knows this; a declaration is not needed.'[43] Charles Rogier, too, was of the opinion that a theoretical justification of Belgium's independence was 'unnecessary.' Moreover, the revolutionaries did not want Belgium to become independent; they wanted it to be annexed by France.

Paris, however, was threatened by London that if it annexed the Southern Netherlands there would be war. The new French king, Louis-Philippe of Orléans, did not want to run the risk of a war that could lead to the restoration of the Bourbons in Paris. Prince Talleyrand, the French representative at the Conference of London, which the European Powers had installed to deal with the problem of the Netherlands, proposed to divide the Belgian provinces between Prussia and France, while Antwerp would become a free state under British protection. This was rejected by Lord Palmerston, the Whig politician who had taken over as British Foreign Secretary from Lord Aberdeen, a Tory, on 17 November. When the Belgian revolutionaries realized that annexation by France was out of the question, they opted for independence and started procedures for the election of a Belgian king. But the Belgians were bent on deceit. They hoped that, by choosing a French prince as their monarch, they would eventually be united with France after all.

'I will vote for a prince accepted by France who will guarantee us a very close union with that country,' the Liégeois Gilles-François Davignon, one of the Francophile members of the National Congress said: 'Indeed, there are but a handful amongst us who would not admit that they have always been convinced that we shall soon return to France.'[44] The Belgians sent an envoy to Paris, threatening that if the French King did not allow his second son, Louis, the 16-year-old Duke of Nemours, to become King of Belgium, they would choose a

Napoleonist prince instead. On 28 January 1831, Louis-Philippe agreed to the Belgian plan. Six days later, on 3 February, the National Congress elected the Duke of Nemours as first King of the Belgians. He gained 97 votes, against 74 for the Napoleonist candidate, Auguste de Beauharnais, the 20-year-old Duke of Leuchtenberg.

On 1 February, however, Palmerston had outmanoeuvred the Belgians by forcing the Powers, including France, to sign a secret protocol banning both Nemours and Leuchtenberg from the Belgian throne. The Belgian delegation that travelled to Paris to present the throne to Nemours was kept waiting for ten days, before it was told that Louis-Philippe could not accept the offer to his son. 'Our national sovereignty has been transferred from Brussels to the British Foreign Office,' an angry Jean-Baptiste Nothomb exclaimed.[45] On 24 February, the frustrated National Congress decided to continue looking for a king. But the situation began to get out of hand. The revolutionaries were losing control over the Flemish provinces.

Ghent had elected itself a city council with an Orangist majority on 28 October 1830, which had been promptly disbanded by the Provisional Government. New elections on 15 December had led to an even more resounding Orangist victory. In retaliation, the Brussels Government had annulled the election result and deposed the mayor. This had led to anti-Belgian street demonstrations and the town had remained in turmoil ever since. In Antwerp, two consecutive municipal elections, the first on 7 December (which was annulled) and the second on 10 February 1831, had led to resounding Orangist victories as well. As in Ghent, the city council in Antwerp was deposed by the Belgian authorities. Even in Brussels, 62% of the voters had boycotted the municipal elections — a figure that was 30% above the national average — while 20% of those who did go to the polls voted for Orangist candidates.

The National Congress feared that the Orangists might win the coming elections for the new legislative body, a bicameral parliament, consisting of a Chamber of Representatives and a Senate, in May. To avoid this, the Congress committed a coup d'état on 12 April. It decided to postpone the elections and remain in power in its old composition of October 1830 which, according to the British envoy in Brussels, John Brabazon Ponsonby (later Viscount Ponsonby), was hostile to the majority of the people.[46] Gendebien declared a state of

45   Quoted in Huyttens, vol. II, p. 321.
46   Ponsonby to Granville, the British Ambassador in Paris, 19 Feb. 1831, in
      Kirschen, p. 191.

emergency. In many Flemish cities, he installed a regime of enhanced anti-Orangist terror. One of the victims was Willem Andries de Caters, the deposed Mayor of Antwerp. His house was plundered on 31 March. Caters, fearing for his life, fled to Germany. These excesses went on for many years. According to Prime Minister Joseph Lebeau 'plundering the houses of Orangists is, although regrettable, a terrible necessity to subdue the enemies of the public order.'[47]

In London, Prince Leopold had closely followed events in Belgium from the beginning. He had soon realised that Belgium might provide his second chance for a throne of his own. The ambitious prince knew it might very well be his last chance, too. Leopold was forty. It was now or never. Moreover, Belgium was an ideal place to be king. It was as close to England as one could get. It was the ideal position to see to the interests of Victoria and the Saxe-Coburg family.

By April 1831, it had become clear to the majority of the Belgian leaders that their revolution would get nowhere if they constantly offended England. When the Belgian envoy, Count Philippe d'Arschot, arrived in London with a letter for the British government, Palmerston sent him home with the message that 'he could keep his letters in his own pocket as long as the Belgians kept treating the Conference of London with disrespect.'[48] Those, like Lebeau, who wished to save the Revolution, knew they would have to mend relations with the British as soon as possible. On 20 April, a delegation of the Belgian revolutionaries arrived in London and met Prince Leopold and Stockmar. Leopold told them that he would not refuse the Belgian throne if the sovereignty of the new state was guaranteed by the Great Powers. On 4 June, the National Congress elected Leopold king with a majority of 152 members of the 197 that were present. Some of those who supported Leopold were very cynical about it. 'As I was unable to give Belgium to France, I gave it to the devil,' Count de Celles said.

In spite of the protestations of King Willem, the Powers accepted the creation of a new kingdom under Leopold of Saxe-Coburg. Hence, a totally new state came into existence. The revolutionaries who had created it had wanted it to be absorbed as quickly as possible into France. The majority of the people living on its territory had wanted it to remain part of the Netherlands. Being an artificial construction and not a nation, Belgium never became a fatherland that was loved by its people. Some loved France, some loved the Netherlands, others loved

47   Quoted in Fris, p. 123.
48   Palmerston to Granville, 25 Mar. 1831, in Buffin, p. 222.

their local Flemish or Walloon communities, but no one loved Belgium. Those who defended Belgium did so because it was their gravy train. One of these was Leopold.

He arranged with the Belgians that he would receive a yearly endowment of 1,300,000 guilders, or some £108,000 (£8.1 million or $13.5 million at today's value). This was a more than adequate compensation for the loss of the stipend of £50,000 the British wished him to renounce. London was unwilling to continue paying someone who had become the king of another country. Leopold, however, refused to relinquish his right to the annual £50,000. According to his marriage contract with the late Princess Charlotte, the British were obliged to continue paying him this sum for the rest of his life. Finally, on 15 July, a compromise was reached. The British would continue paying the £50,000. To Leopold this was of the utmost importance. It meant that he ran no risk in the Belgian venture. If things went wrong, he could always return to the British fleshpots. For so long as he remained King of Belgium, however, Leopold agreed to reimburse the British Treasury with whatever was left of his annuity after he had deducted (a) the money needed for the upkeep of his estate at Claremont plus (b) the sums needed to pay off the debts he had made while living in England.

The sum which Leopold said he needed annually for Claremont and its personnel was a staggering £20,000. The debts he had made in his 14 English years, were, he claimed, an even more staggering £83,000. The English were flabbergasted. How could a man who was generally perceived to be a miser, amass £83,000 in debts? Leopold refused to produce a detailed list of his debts. Nevertheless, the British government accepted the compromise. Leopold, however, did not return a single pound to the British Treasury until April 1834, after the British Parliament had threatened him with an official investigation into what he had done with the £150,000 that he had received since becoming King of the Belgians. Altogether Leopold of Saxe- Coburg cost the British taxpayers £1,440,000 (£50,000 annually from 1818 to 1833, and £20,000 annually from 1834 until his death in December 1865), the equivalent of £108 million or $180 million today. His marriage to Charlotte was by far the most expensive royal marriage the British have had to finance in their entire history.

Before departing for Belgium, Leopold contacted the King of France with the news that he would like to marry one of his daughters. By marrying a daughter to Leopold, Louis-Philippe, whose son had been forced to renounce the Belgian throne, could at least get a son-in-law on that throne. Leopold also promised that he would do his best to dismantle the so-called 'Wellington line,' a series of 21 fortresses that had been built along Belgium's southern border after Napoleon's defeat.

On 16 July, Leopold left England with Stockmar. Five days later, during a ceremony in Brussels, he officially became King of the Belgians by taking a solemn oath to uphold the Belgian Constitution. On 2 August, however, King Willem of the Netherlands sent an army of 50,000 soldiers to reconquer his Southern provinces. The army was under the command of Crown Prince Willem, who after a short exile in Britain had been reconciled to his father. The Belgians hardly put up a fight. 'Half my army betrayed me, the other half fled,' Leopold recalled later.[49] He fell ill and lamented to his Saxe-Coburg relatives: 'If I had been able to go to the army myself and had not suffered so much, I am certain that I could have changed the situation for the better.'[50] Stockmar relates in his memoirs how he went looking for his master and found him in a hut, lying in the straw, humming to himself in order to keep up his spirits.

Leopold called the French army to the rescue. This was a violation of the Belgian Constitution that he had vowed to uphold two weeks earlier. Article 121 of the Constitution stated that only an act of parliament can allow the intervention of foreign troops. Nevertheless, because the existence of the country was in danger, the King usurped parliament's powers. At Leopold's request, the French army crossed the border with 50,000 troops. Dutch soldiers encountered them on 12 August at Tervuren, a village fifteen kilometres to the east of Brussels. For a moment it looked as if an international war was about to start, but King Willem decided to call a cease-fire in order to defuse the situation.

The British demanded that the French troops leave Belgium at once. Leopold, fearing that their departure would lead to the collapse of his regime, asked the French to stay and in a letter on 8 September offered Louis-Philippe the immediate demolition of five Wellington fortresses of his own choosing. Palmerston assured the British Parliament that he was not going to let this happen. Leopold changed his mind three times about the fortresses, and finally gave in to the British who threatened to send an army to Belgium.

49   Leopold I to his daughter Charlotte, 1863, in Bronne 1, p. 75.
50   SAP MP, Leopold I to his brother-in-law Emmanuel Mensdorff-Pouilly, 3 Sept. 1831, in Leopold I 2, p. 201.

Talleyrand considered Leopold a 'pitiful sire' and the Belgians 'a useless riff-raff, unworthy of freedom.'[51] He proposed a new partition of the country. After lengthy deliberations in London, the European Powers reached a compromise. It was decided that Belgium could retain its independence, but had to yield territory of strategic importance to the (Northern) Netherlands, while the eastern (German-speaking) half of the province of Luxemburg became an independent Grand-Duchy within the German Confederation and was handed over to King Willem as a personal estate. The Powers also stipulated that Belgium would become a perpetually neutral state that was not allowed to ally itself with France (or any other nation) at any point in the future.

The Dutch King felt betrayed by perfidious Albion. He refused to give up his rights to Belgium and kept his garrison at Antwerp, even though the Treaty of London stipulated that he had to hand the town over to the authorities in Brussels. Willem had not been part of the Treaty and did not feel bound by it. The people of Antwerp agreed. In the local elections, held on 29 August 1831, the pro-Belgian candidate was defeated. 'What is to be done with these damned Dutch and Belgians?' Lord Charles Grey, the British Prime Minister, sighed. 'I believe that the best way would be to draw a cordon round Holland and Belgium, by sea and land, and leave them to fight it out.'[52]

During the next 12 months Willem received numerous ultimatums from the Powers to give Antwerp up to Leopold. Finally, on 5 November 1832, in a concerted Anglo-French action, the British Navy sealed the Dutch coast and blocked the Scheldt estuary so that Antwerp could not be reinforced, while a French army of 65,000 men with 105 canons marched to Antwerp to bomb the Dutch out of town. On 30 November, the French started shelling the Dutch. At first, the citizens of Antwerp had fled the city, but later, when they noticed that the French were only aiming at the soldiers in the Citadel, the bombardment became an attraction. A platform was installed on the roof of the local theatre, and for a fee one could climb up and watch the spectacle. On 23 December, the garrison surrendered.

In 1839, an exhausted Kingdom of the Netherlands, bankrupted by a Franco-British trade embargo, accepted the independence of Belgium. Meanwhile, Leopold's niece Victoria had become Queen of Britain in 1837. King Willem realised, that with the favourite uncle of the British Queen on the throne of his stolen provinces, his chances of

51   Quoted in Fris, p. 131.
52   Quoted in Thomas, p. 31.

recovering them were over. The Antwerpians, however, remained Orangists. When the German professor J.W. Löbell visited the town, he noted: 'Many common citizens here belong to the class and party that makes no secret of its Orangist tendency.' As late as 1845, another German visitor, C. Ludovic, observed: 'The mood among the citizens is everything but Belgian.'[53]

53   Quoted in Goris, p. 124.

H.M. Leopold, King of the Belgians
From the portrait by F. Winterhalter at Buckingham Palace

Leopold I
First King of the Belgians

Chapter 2

The Fox Hunter (1832–1865)

A Silent Sufferer

On 9 August 1832, Leopold married the 20-year-old Louise of Orléans, the eldest daughter of Louis-Philippe. The bride was a slight woman with blue eyes, blonde hair, a small mouth and a big nose. The nose was typical of her mother's Bourbon-Sicily family. Her maternal grandfather was King Ferdinand IV of Naples and Sicily, nicknamed *'Nasone'* (The Nose). Her paternal grandfather, Duke Philippe of Orléans, had had a nickname, too, but for political reasons. He was *Philippe Egalité*, because he had chosen the side of the Revolution in 1789. Grandpapa had cast the decisive vote which, on 21 January 1793, had brought his cousin, King Louis XVI, to the guillotine.

Louise cried when she left for Belgium on 13 August. 'I will have to give up all that is dear to me, for a man whom I care about as much as about any man who passes me by in the street,' she wrote to a friend. Leopold was not interested in the girl either. When Louis-Philippe had asked him over to France to meet his daughter before the marriage, he had replied that this was not necessary because he had already met Louise sixteen years previously, when she was four years old.

Louise had been a merry child, fond of sports, mischief and laughter, but, once in Brussels, Leopold did not allow this to continue. *'Pas de plaisanteries, madame,'* he said whenever she attempted a joke. He was a cheerless man, old for his age, and Louise soon forgot how to smile, too. Throughout the rest of her life, she wrote at least one letter a day — sometimes even two — containing five to six pages in her small handwriting to her mother, Queen Marie-Amélie of France.

While writing she always wept. It was her 'hour of tears.' Stockmar told his master that he did not think this 'scribomania' was healthy, but Leopold, whom she called 'le Léopich' in her letters, could not persuade her to give up the habit.

Louise had been a virgin when she married. She did not like having sex with Leopold, a man old enough to be her father. 'I do not have the same feelings for him as he has for me,' she wrote to her mother after one month of marriage. 'I am as indifferent to his caresses as I am to his familiarity. I put up with him, I let him have his way, but I feel more repugnance than pleasure. I cannot get accustomed to what one may call the animal aspect of my new position. Sometimes he notices and asks: 'Does my little wife no longer love me then?' Then I reassure him and do everything he wants.'

What made Louise feel even more lonely in Belgium was the fact that she sensed how unloved the new regime was. The Belgian nobility despised her husband, whom they loathed as a money-grubbing parvenu. 'The King, his dog and I live on our own,' Louise wrote. The old nobility of the Southern Netherlands refused to serve in the royal household and never visited the royal palace. The only social life Louise had were the occasional visits from her brothers, from Leopold's family and from members of the English community in Brussels. A frequent guest was also the American ambassador, Hugh Swinton Legaré. He was a 35-year-old aristocrat from the American South, who later became U.S. Attorney General. Harriet Beecher Stowe refers to him in her famous novel *Uncle Tom's Cabin*. Legaré was her source of inspiration for the slavedriver Simon Legree. He came to the palace to discuss prosaic matters with 'the Leopich,' such as the cotton trade and the future of the port of Antwerp.

Queen Louise often wrote to her mother how hurt she was by the attitude of the people. 'In a sad mood I return from High Mass at the church of Koudenberg. A small group of Orangists have inspected me from top to toe,' she complained on 27 March 1834. Sometimes Orangists would shout insults when the royal couple drove around Brussels in its carriage. On one occasion Countess Trazegnies stuck out her tongue at them. At the Opera in Ghent the boxes which had been crowded the previous evening were completely empty on the evening the King and Queen attended a performance.

The situation came to a climax in the spring of 1834, when the Belgian regime decided to sell the horses from the confiscated stud of King Willem at Tervuren. Orangist circles in Ghent, Antwerp, Brussels and some smaller towns decided to collect money, buy the noblest horses and give them back to the Dutch King. The collection was a success, in the cities as well as in small towns like Zinnik ('home to bigots and papists'). The list of those who had donated money was defiantly published in the newspapers. On 20 March the horses were sold. Four of the most beautiful animals were bought by the Orangists and transported to the Dutch border, where they were handed over to the Dutch authorities. 'Who knows, maybe these horses will return home one day, together with our freedom,' the *Messager de Gand* wrote. *Le Lynx*, a Brussels paper, was even more explicit: 'Soon, when the noble animals return, Belgium will have rid itself of its unwelcome guests.' The hope that Leopold would disappear and return to England was expressed in a satirical text which had Leopold say: 'After having fled with my gold, I will return home to Claremont and its lovely garden, to live there in luxury for many years.'

On the morning of 6 April, however, soldiers of the Belgian army attacked the homes of people who had donated money to the Orangist cause. 'You will never believe this, dear Mama,' Louise wrote. 'There is a mutiny going on here, but it is a mutiny in favour of the government. Yes, you will laugh: in favour of the government.' Houses were destroyed and Orangists molested in Brussels, Antwerp and Ghent. In Antwerp, the army returned several times to the Orangist club *La Loyauté*. In Ghent, the English industrialist Dixon, who was a friend of King Willem, was dragged from his home, while his attackers jeered 'Long live King Leopold. Long live Belgium' and sang the *Brabançonne*. In Brussels, the houses of the Orangist families Ursel, Ligne, Trazegnies, Marnix, Vonck and others were broken into. The countesses Trazegnies and Lalaing fled to the British Embassy. The Mayor of Brussels, Nicholas Rouppe, tried to persuade the vandals to stop, 'but not in a way to make much impression,' the British Ambassador, Sir Robert Adair, wrote to Palmerston.[1] Adair went to see the authorities, together with his Austrian colleague, Count Dietrichstein, to demand that order be restored. Leopold became angry and shouted: 'They are getting what they asked for.'[2] Finally, General Evain, the Belgian Minister of War, formerly a French general who had become a Belgian citizen only one week prior to his appointment as minister in May 1832, asked General Hurel, a French immigrant who was the military commander in Brussels, to restore order. By 5 o'clock in the afternoon Brussels was quiet again. The authorities had arrested 115 rioters. At their subsequent trial, however, all were

1   Quoted in Vermeir, vol. I, p. 142.
2   Bronne 1, p. 108.

acquitted. Louise defended them in a letter to her mother: 'They were decent people. Cheerfully, calm and unruffled, they marched to carry out the destruction as if they were fulfilling a duty. Everywhere they destroyed and wrecked, but nowhere, save for some exceptions, did they plunder.'

The Orangist cause was badly damaged. Following the events, a special secret police force was created to investigate Orangist activities. Parliament declared it a crime to make Orangist propaganda. To prevent the election of Orangist mayors and aldermen in Flemish towns and villages, the law was changed in March 1836: henceforth, mayors and aldermen would be appointed by the king instead of by the municipal council. In 1853, Leopold commented to the Russian ambassador: 'It is very fortunate that the King has been given the power to appoint the municipal authorities. No appointment is possible without my signature. This has secured my power.'[3]

Frightened by the possible repercussions of an open demonstration of Orangist convictions, many preferred to keep a low profile. The membership of *La Loyauté* in Antwerp dropped from over 170 in 1833 to a mere twenty in 1837. The press was silenced. The aristocracy switched allegiance from Orange to Saxe-Coburg. In Brussels, all Orangist members of the city council resigned and no Orangist candidate dared to stand for the 1836 municipal elections. In Antwerp, only one Orangist councillor remained after the elections; he had been the only Orangist candidate. Ghent, however, lived up to its age-old tradition of ardent stubbornness. It defiantly re-elected its Orangist city council with an overwhelming majority, but Leopold refused to appoint the local Orangist leader, Joseph Van Crombrugghe, as mayor. Belgium had come to resemble a totalitarian army barracks. The army, led by its French-born generals, was omnipresent and ever threatening. A population of 3 million had fallen under the control of a 100,000 man standing army, the largest of Western Europe, absorbing an annual budget of 47 million francs.

When in 1839 the Dutch King accepted the independence of Belgium, Orangism became an anachronism. Nevertheless, Leopold and his new kingdom remained extremely unpopular with the ordinary citizens. He was so utterly despised that in June 1841 the new King of the Netherlands, Willem II — who as Crown Prince had made such a fool of himself — became convinced that Belgium would soon be part of the Dutch Kingdom again. 'This Belgium will be ours sooner than one expects,' he said at a dinner party in Maastricht.[4] The stupid Orange was wrong again, for the Belgian army would not allow the people in the South to reunite with the Netherlands. And neither would France, nor the young Queen who in 1837 had ascended the British throne. This became very clear when in October 1841 a plot was discovered to reunite Belgium to the Netherlands. The leaders of the plot, Count Augustus Van der Meere and Baron Jacob Van der Smissen, were two Flemish generals who had been stripped of their rank for their Orangist sympathies. Their conspiracy was discovered, but even if it had not been, it is doubtful whether they would have had a chance of success. At Leopold's request, France immediately sent an army to the Belgian border, ready to intervene, while Britain made it equally clear that it would not let 'Uncle Leopold' down. It was obvious to the Flemish people that they were doomed if they rose in favour of Van der Meere and Van der Smissen. The sensible Flemings did not stir.

In February 1842 the conspirators were tried. General Buzen, the Belgian Minister of War, who had personally helped the plotters to prepare bullets and cannon-balls at Van der Smissen's house, was also accused of high treason. Buzen committed suicide while awaiting trial. Four of the conspirators were condemned to death, but Leopold did not want to create any martyrs. Van der Meere was pardoned on condition that he emigrate to Brazil, while Van der Smissen managed to escape from prison — suspiciously easily it seems — and fled to Germany.

When the Prussian diplomat, Count Königsmarck, travelled through Belgium in July 1844, he noticed that King Leopold was 'as generally unloved in his country as the Dutch King was loved.'[5] Only Leopold's British niece Victoria dissented. She greatly admired her *solo padre*. 'Uncle is so enlightened,' she wrote in her diary, 'so universally admitted to be one of the first politicians now extant, so beloved and revered by his Belgian subjects, that it must be a great compensation for all his extreme trouble.'[6]

* * *

The Orangist allegation that Leopold was interested in his Kingdom only for the money which he could extract from it was not unfounded. Leopold used his royal position mainly to enhance his personal fortune. Could this have been a subconscious form of

---

4   Quoted in Colenbrander 3, pp. 132–3.
5   Königsmarck, 14 July 1844, in Colenbrander 3, p. 167.
6   RAW QVJ, 21 Sept. 1836, in Victoria 2, vol. I, p. 168.

revenge for his modest, precarious youth? In his will, he later wrote: 'My first priority, one to which I have devoted a lot of energy, has been to amass a fortune for my children in order to protect them as much as possible against the adversities that many families have fallen victim to.'[7]

The Belgian state had provided Leopold with a stipend of 2.7 million francs.[8] The maintenance of his court and household cost him 1.5 million francs annually, which meant that he had 1.2 million for personal needs and private investments. He used his money to buy stocks and large estates, which he did judiciously. The bulk of his wealth, however, came from his ownership of shares of the *Société Générale*, the holding company that King Willem had originally founded to promote investment in his Southern provinces. After the Belgian Revolution, Leopold was able to buy shares of the SG with money the company itself had lent him. He owed this to the chief executive officer of the SG, its 'Governor.' This man, Ferdinand Meeus, had switched his allegiance from Orange to Saxe-Coburg in 1831 and became a close collaborator of the new regime. Leopold subsequently rewarded him with the hereditary title of Count de Meeûs d'Argenteuil. The SG controlled a substantial part of Belgium's economy, making Leopold one of the rare monarchs in Western Europe of whom it could be said, though with some exaggeration, that he virtually *owned* his country.

Count de Meeûs remained Leopold's loyal henchman. The King appreciated his loyalty and defended Meeûs' position at the helm of the SG, even when in 1848 a parliamentary investigation revealed that the Governor had enriched himself unethically. When Leopold refused to dismiss the corrupt Governor, all the directors of the SG resigned in protest. Meeûs remained in post until his death in 1861. The King's message was clear: those loyal to Belgium were entitled to enrich themselves, even if it involved a certain degree of corruption. 'Political and moral considerations are wasted on the Belgians. Their main attention is devoted exclusively to material interests,' the perceptive Marquess de Rumigny, the French Ambassador in Brussels, wrote about the ruling elite in the young state.[9]

Leopold also became one of the owners of the Belgian National Bank, a private institution that was granted a monopoly to issue

7   RAB Acquisitions nr. 229, Will of King Leopold I, 18 Apr. 1857.
8   This sum was voted in 1831 as 1.3 million guilders. However, Belgium soon changed from (Dutch) guilders to (French) francs. The Belgian and the French pre-1914 franc had the same value. One pre-1914 franc is worth about £3 or $5 today.
9   Rumigny to Guizot, 1842, in De Ridder, Alfred 4, p. 200.

money in Belgium. His real estate consisted of castles and domains in Belgium, totalling 5,300 hectares (12,720 acres). Outside Belgium, Leopold was known to own the castle of Niederfüllbach near Coburg, a castle in Bohemia, forests and farms in Moravia and Hungary, a house in Vienna, and the Villa Giulia (Villa d'Este) on Lake Como in Italy. The latter had once been the Italian home of his first mother-in-law, British Queen Caroline (George IV's estranged wife). When Leopold died, he left his children 13.2 million francs in real estate, 25.2 million in stocks, and 20 million on a deposit of the Rothschild Bank — a total of 58.4 million francs (£175.2 million or $292 million at today's value). Leopold's only confidants in his financial affairs were Stockmar, who acted as a middleman when Leopold bought land, and later, when Stockmar had left for England to assist Victoria in reigning over the British Empire, the equally discreet Viscount Edward Conway, a nobleman of Irish ancestry.

Apart from his personally-owned residences, Leopold could use the palaces that the state placed at his disposal in Brussels, Antwerp and Laken. The mansion at Laken, built in the second half of the 18th century, stands in a vast park 10 kilometres to the north of Brussels. It was the place Leopold's family came to live in for most of the year. The summers, however, Louise spent with her children at the coastal resort of Ostend, where Leopold rented a house — a modest one in an ordinary street, since he had to pay the rent from his own pocket.

Leopold and Louise had four children. The eldest, Louis-Philippe, was born in July 1833, but died as a baby. Their second son, Leopold (or Leo for short), was born on 9 April 1835, a third son, Philippe, on 24 March 1837, and their daughter Charlotte on 7 June 1840. Having a family did not make the King less of a penny pincher. Louise had to scrimp on everything Leopold paid for out of his own pocket. At one point a servant reported on the contents of little Leo's wardrobe: 'One pair of trousers in white cashmere, much too short to be worn in the drawing-rooms, one pair in grey cashmere which has been lengthened. Three jackets, one of which is too small but still good enough to be worn in Laken.' 'Very good,' Louise noted in the margin, 'it will not be necessary to have new suits made.' Leopold also ordered strict supervision of his palace's kitchens. As he had to pay for his personnel's food out of his own pocket, he considered '*le service de la bouche*' (the servicing of the mouth) 'one of the most costly services that exists.'[10] The King's own lifestyle was equally frugal. He hardly ever drank wine. William IV, the last Hanoverian King of Britain, disliked

10   Terlinden 1, p. 324.

this in him. 'God damn it, sir!' he told the Belgian King when the latter visited Windsor. 'Why don't you drink wine? I never allow anybody to drink water at my table.'[11]

Leopold had always been a withdrawn hypochondriac. Some days Louise did not see him at all. 'He has some lonely habits, and I know that he prefers to go off in search of adventure until late at night, though I think that is careless of him,' she wrote to Mama.[12] He was often away for several days, sometimes weeks, visiting his estates, where he went hunting, his favourite pastime. He never shot deer, but hunted boar, wild cats, wolves and especially foxes, a species he seemed to hate. Actually it was not hunting at all, but rather an exercise in target shooting. Servants drove the game towards a spot where the King had installed himself with his gun on a look-out. He once slaughtered 51 foxes in one single day. It has been calculated that he killed 2,800 foxes in a 20-year period.

Queen Louise was seldom taken along to the estates. In May 1840, her husband was gone for 25 days while she did not know where he was. It was a terrible time. She was expecting a baby any day and had had to lie flat since March. She was worried about the boys, because an epidemic of smallpox was raging in Brussels and 'the Leopich' sent no word at all. After their daughter Charlotte had been born one month later, the King stayed in Brussels for exactly nine days. Then he departed for the Ardennes to go hunting, leaving Louise, who had not yet recovered from giving birth, alone again. When he was gone, the poor woman confessed in letters to her mother how lonely she was, especially in the evenings. Afterwards she always regretted having complained to dear Mama. 'Also when he is at home,' she said, 'I seldom see the Leopich.'

Leopold's nights, unlike his wife's, were not spent alone. Like his brother Ernst, he was a man with a voracious sexual appetite. As Louise was unable to satisfy his hunger, he had to find satisfaction elsewhere. But the women sharing the Leopich's bed did not make him a happier person. Being a cold and calculating person who used people but trusted no one, he did not allow himself to become emotionally attached to anyone. In his later years, when he had grown old, this attitude changed. He took a permanent mistress, possibly because he felt the need for someone who could take care of him in his old age.

By 1843, the King's ministers had become worried about Leopold's dark moods. Jean-Baptiste Nothomb, the Minister of the Interior,

11   Quoted in Greville, vol. III, p. 377.
12   RAB FLI 642, Louise to Marie-Amélie, 12 Dec. 1833.

wrote to his wife: 'If the King is not drawn from his loneliness by some significant event, then in a few years' time he will have withdrawn completely; he will not want to see anyone any more, not even his own children.'[13] In May 1844, Louise, in a letter to her mother, considered her husband's dark moods a disease. She called them *'un état morbide.'*[14]

What was Leopold's problem? Maybe he was too ambitious to reign over an unimportant, unadventurous country, far too small in comparison to Great Britain, the prize that should have been his. Maybe he pined for something to do. He longed for activity. By 1839, when he had succeeded in consolidating the independence of Belgium, what more was there for him to do?

This Mystification Surrounding Our Position

Leopold had transformed the unstable country which the Belgian revolutionaries had given him into a stable kingdom. He had silenced the Orangists and purchased the adherence of the Francophile rebels of 1830. To this end he had even contributed some of his own money. Leading Belgian politicians, such as Rogier, Chazal and Lebeau, received regular sums of money from the King.

Leopold bought the press as well. In 1831, he had secretly founded his own newspaper *L'Indépendant*. Its editor, the Catholic politician Nothomb, could not publish a single line about the royal family (including its relatives in Coburg, Britain and France) without the King's approval. Having lived in Britain for many years, Leopold understood the importance of the press. He was prepared to manipulate it to serve his interests. He appreciated that the long term benefits of buying the media outweighed the short term costs. As *L'Indépendant* made a loss, the King subsidized the paper between 1831 and 1843 with an annual 40,000 francs. In 1858, he provided 200,000 francs to launch *L'Echo du Parlement*. He needed two papers because there were two political parties in Belgium: the Catholic Party and the Liberal Party. *L'Indépendant* spoke for the former, *L'Echo du Parlement* for the latter.

Leopold knew that as long as he could count on the army and on foreign military intervention on his behalf, there would never be a Dutch-inspired or Flemish rebellion against his monarchy. Flanders was a densely-populated, flat, open country, with no place for rebels to hide. There were no vast forests, no swamps, no mountains, no

13   Nothomb to his wife, 26 July 1843, in Bronne 1, p. 184.
14   RAB FLI 649, Louise to Marie-Amélie, 18 May 1844.

places to lie in ambush. Every uprising against the authorities could be subdued in no time, as Napoleon had proved in 1798 when an uprising of the Flemish countryside had been suppressed in a matter of weeks. The only way the Flemings could rebel was by ignoring the authorities where they could and by organizing their economic life as much as possible out of the government's reach. Tax evasion can be a form of rebellion. This, however, did not concern Leopold. It was not a direct threat to his throne, and as long as he could get more money out of Belgium than he had to contribute to it, he benefited from Belgium's existence.

Though a Lutheran and a freemason, Leopold had the sense not to repeat King Willem's mistake of antagonising the Catholic bishops. He knew the Church dominated the lives of the Belgians. This meant that if he made the Church hierarchy his ally, the people would remain loyal to his dynasty. Leopold valued the Catholic Church, because, as he told the papal Internuncio, Mgr. Raphael Fornari, in 1842: 'Catholicism teaches that respect for the God-given authorities is a duty.' Moreover, the Flemings and Walloons had *only* their religion in common. Leopold feared that the anticlerical Liberals by undermining the power of the Church, would also undermine Belgium's cohesion. 'Belgium has only one choice,' he wrote to Fornari: 'the choice between Catholicism and anarchy.'[15] To his father-in-law, King Louis-Philippe of France, he wrote: 'the only real and true Belgians are our good Catholics, the others are but a motley cosmopolitan group *fit for nothing.*'[16]

Leopold supported the Catholic Church, but he never considered becoming a Catholic himself. He was not a religious man. In his private letters to Louise, he vented his disdain for the Catholic religion, and also his contempt for his own position, always having to be friendly towards the bishops while 'sometimes things here overpower me with disgust, and then with regret to have put myself into such a despicable concern, and to have devoted to it what remained of the better part of my life.' But he knew he had to do so for the sake of his Belgian future. 'I have based this awful shop on a solid foundation, Catholicism,' he wrote — and mused: 'On the other hand, I have to admit that we are not too badly fed, not too badly accommodated and our beds are well made by the government, which is a lot and justifies a reasonable degree of cheerfulness.'[17]

15   Quoted in Vermeir, vol. I, p. 231.
16   Leopold to Louis-Philippe, 8 Nov. 1847, in Stengers 8, p. 171.
17   RAB FG AQL, Leopold I to Louise, 14 and 27 Nov. 1842.

Although liberal politicians all over the globe considered the Belgian King to be one of themselves, in reality he was a staunch authoritarian. One of the reasons why he regretted having opted for the throne of Belgium over that of Greece was that the Powers had allowed the Greek King to rule as an authoritarian monarch, while Belgium was a constitutional monarchy. Leopold considered the latter idea to be almost an impossibility and wrote: 'In ancient times, they kept slaves. Nowadays they have improved the matter and we keep creatures called constitutional kings. If one considers the fact that I am trapped in this fiction because of my own choice, one sees the mystification surrounding our position in the world as a good farce.'[18]

Leopold particularly disliked the freedom of expression and freedom of the press. But the reason he disliked it was sophisticated. He considered the press a danger to the people's adherence to the Catholic faith. 'The freedom of the press, without any restriction, as in Belgium, is a dissolving force of Catholicism and of society,' he said to the Ambassador of Piedmont-Sardinia in 1841. At that time Leopold was pressing his government to write a new education bill for primary schools. 'If I succeed in placing this education in the hands of the bishops and taking it out of the hands of the municipal councils, which are to a greater or lesser extent dominated by Liberal intrigues, the future of Belgium will be ensured, and I will have rendered religion a great service,' he told the Ambassador.[19]

The bishops returned the favour and supported Leopold in his policies. Monarchy and Church frequently conspired against Government and Parliament. In 1838, Leopold had Baron Goswin de Stassart removed as Speaker of the Belgian Senate because, as he wrote in a confidential letter to Mgr. Fornari, Stassart could 'not be trusted as a Catholic.'[20] Together with the Internuncio, Leopold also interfered directly in Belgian Church politics. The two men collaborated in forcing the Bishop of Ghent, Mgr. Van de Velde, to resign. This Flemish bishop, the successor to the reactionary Broglie, supported democratic ideas, such as those of the French priest Lamennais. Leopold considered 'democratic stupidities in the style of Lamennays' to be a threat.[21] The Bishop was bribed into resigning with 9,000 francs

18   RAB FG AQL, Leopold I to Louise, 16 Mar. 1842.
19   Quoted in Buraggi and others, p. 52.
20   Vermeir, vol. I, pp. 231–2.
21   RAB FG AQL, Leopold I to Louise, 20 July 1841. Félicité-Robert de Lamennais (1782–1854) tried to reconcile Catholicism with liberal political ideas like freedom of the press, freedom of conscience, republicanism, etc.

(£27,000 or $45,000 at today's value), plus a monthly allowance of 250 francs (£750 or $1,250 at today's value). Fornari had him replaced by Mgr. Delebecque, another Francophone reactionary. When Fornari was succeeded in 1843 by Joachim Pecci, Leopold found the new nuncio less obliging than his predecessor. For three years, the King relentlessly pressured the Vatican to recall Mgr. Pecci, which it finally did in 1846. Pecci was appointed Bishop of Perugia and moved on to become Pope in 1878. He reigned as Leo XIII until 1903 and was one of the 19th century's greatest popes, adopting a conciliatory position to democratic and social movements.

In 1857, Leopold strongly disagreed with the Liberal Belgian government, which he believed was intent on undermining the power of the Church. But, instead of quarrelling openly with his ministers, he contacted the French Ambassador to ask the Powers to interfere in Belgium and restore order if the Belgian government 'goes too far.'[22] Five years earlier, in 1852, Leopold had already asked London to intervene in Belgium in order to restrict the freedom of the press. The British were genuinely shocked by the request: 'It is a strange state of things when the Head of State encourages and seeks foreign intervention and influences to bear formally upon His Government in regard to Constitutional Law!' the British Ambassador in Brussels wrote to the Foreign Secretary, Lord Malmesbury.[23]

Indeed, Leopold was a 'Catholic' reactionary, often involved in conspiracies against his own government. But it was a secret well kept. Outwardly he behaved as if he was the most liberal monarch in the whole of Europe. He never criticised his country's constitution in public. It was not his habit to sail headlong into the storm. Once out of the public eye, however, Leopold bothered little about constitutional and legal obligations he did not like. He attempted to subvert and undermine that to which he paid lip-service. 'I am really disgusted with this idiot Constitution,' he wrote to his brother-in-law, Count Mensdorff-Pouilly. 'The Constitution,' he complained to Louise, 'is monstrous. It alone should have kept me from entering this *boutique* which is to blame for my horrid existence these past years.' In letters to Queen Victoria, he called it an 'absurd' and 'sad *Machwerk*' (concoction), 'fabricated' by 'a herd of mad democrats.'[24]

In his confidential letters, the King also boasted about his remarkable achievement of keeping the purely artificial Belgian nation

22   AQO, Barrot to Count Walewski, 13 Nov. 1857, in Stengers 8, p. 210.
23   Quoted in Stengers 8, p. 208.
24   RAW, Leopold I to Queen Victoria, 23 Dec. 1842, 14 June 1845 and 17 June 1859.

together. 'Belgium is a state only by virtue of its King; it is only by virtue of its dynasty that it defies immediate dissolution or perhaps even civil war,' he wrote to his Minister of Justice, Baron d'Anethan.[25] 'Its dynasty is the rock on which the political existence of the country is exclusively based,' he told Prime Minister Nothomb.[26] He also made this clear in various letters to Victoria: 'Belgium is *purement et simplement ma creation;*' 'Belgium owes me its sole existence;' 'With all modesty be it said, the directing hand in this corner of Europe is mine own;' 'The people owe me *all* they are.'[27] But did the Belgians deserve him? Probably not: 'Having great disunity,' he complained, 'they are without contradiction the most *insufferable* creatures that exist.'

* * *

Leopold wanted the young Belgian revolutionaries, whom he had made into ministers, governors, judges and generals in high positions, to do something for him in return. He longed for a colonial empire. 'Belgium,' he wrote, 'is but prose. Greece would have satisfied the poetic aspirations of my soul. I am the opposite of the sun. I have risen in the West, and I wish to set in the East.'[28] Lebeau, Nothomb, Rogier and the other ministers, however, thwarted all Leopold's colonial plans.

In 1840, the King sent an expedition to Abyssinia. It came back in 1842 with a message from King Gocho of Abyssinia to 'the Belgian Emperor,' telling him how pleased he was that Leopold was willing to 'alleviate the suffering of my people, Christians like yourself.' The *Société Générale* was willing to finance the Abyssinian colony, but the Belgian government vetoed the plans, because in 1842 Belgium had already sent 900 Flemish peasants to the swampy east coast of Guatemala at the King's request. Within five years half the colonists had died from exhaustion and disease and the Belgian authorities repatriated the rest.

Leopold's imperial dreams did not appeal to the Belgians. Those who did not care for the sight of the Belgian flag on their own town hall cared even less about raising that flag at the other end of the world. As the King knew very well: 'No patriotic feelings exist in Bel-

25   MFA Anethan Papers, Leopold I to Anethan, 27 Oct. 1845.
26   GSA Nothomb Papers nr. 1, Leopold I to Nothomb, 6 Jan. 1846.
27   RAW, Leopold I to Queen Victoria, 18 Dec. 1846, 23 July 1847, 19 Apr. 1850 and 13 June 1856.
28   Quoted in Bronne 1, p. 188.

gium.'[29] Leopold also had great recurrent difficulties in convincing Parliament to approve the annual military expenditure. Pacifist members of the Chamber of Representatives constantly tried to reduce the army's establishment, which they wished to bring down to 75,000 men, but which Leopold wanted to raise to 120,000.

Many Belgians saw the army as an occupying force and were not prepared to make sacrifices for the defence of a country that they did not love. This became all too clear in 1862, when Prime Minister Charles Rogier and General Pierre Chazal, the Belgian Minister of War, planned to build a ring of military fortifications around Antwerp. Rogier and Chazal, two former leaders of the Belgian Revolution and both of French birth, had, together with the King, worked out a plan to transform Antwerp into a fortress where in case of war the Belgian army could withdraw and await reinforcements from overseas. Thanks to the River Scheldt and its access to the sea, Antwerp could be easily provisioned from Britain, which the King reckoned was Belgium's natural ally. He believed that Britain would stand at her side in every war: 'We are of greater strategic importance to Britain than some parts of its own territory,' Leopold said.[30] He planned 'to render Antwerp very strong, and to collect there a thousand guns.'[31]

The people in Antwerp opposed the plans at once, unwilling to 'sacrifice the interest of our town to the interests of two Frenchmen.' Protest meetings were held and the leader of the protest, the journalist Jan Van Rijswijck, a member of a longstanding Orangist family declared: 'The Government wants to incarcerate us alive.' The Antwerp by-elections for the Senate were boycotted and only 151 of the 4,590 voters turned up. In an effort to defuse the situation, the city council was received by the King, but when they handed him a petition against the fortification plans, Leopold literally threw the petition back at the councillors and told them categorically that he would have the fortifications built at any price. The King was raging mad with 'the stupid Antwerpians' and 'Ryswick,' whom he despisingly called 'une espèce de poète flamand' (some sort of Flemish poet).[32]

After being snubbed by the King, 21 of the 26 Antwerp city councillors resigned in protest, while anti-royalist sentiment rose in the town. The Government, fearing a rising, declared a state of emergency. On 28 November Antwerp was taken over by the army. Heavily armed regiments, commanded by Walloon and French-born generals, descended

29   Leopold I to Nothomb, 17 Aug. 1858, in Thielemans, p. XXXIII.
30   Leopold I to Nothomb, 14 Apr. 1852, in Thielemans, p. XXXVIII.
31   RAB FLI, Leopold I to Sir Robert Gardiner, 16 Jan. 1853.
32   Leopold I to Nothomb, 6 July 1862, in Sabbe, pp. 228–9.

on the town. The people were sensible enough to know that they could not win a confrontation with the army. The street protests died down, but the protestors founded their own political party, the *Meeting Partij*. It became the first Flemish-nationalist party in Belgium. In 1863, it won the parliamentary elections in Antwerp. Its representative, Jan De Laet, refused to swear the oath of allegiance to the Belgian Constitution in French. He was the first to take the oath in Dutch.

Antwerp, however, could not stop the fortifications from being built. The Belgian authorities decided to bribe De Laet. The Flemish MP, who cared nothing for the artificial Belgian state, discovered that even a Fleming could *learn* to love and defend Belgium if it rewarded him handsomely. De Laet was bought by the authorities with 100,000 francs (£300,000 or $500,000 in today's value), to the dismay of his former companions. When Van Rijswijck attacked De Laet for his corruption, the former was brought to court, convicted for libel and imprisoned. He died shortly after. His allegation against De Laet later proved to be correct, though.

Another famous court case also related to the fortification programme. In April 1863, the authorities prosecuted Jacob Karsman, an Antwerp diamond trader, for publishing a poem criticising the government's plans. Referring to Article 23 of the Constitution, Karsman demanded that the court hear him in Dutch. The court, however, ruled that the constitutional right to use one's mother tongue in a penal court was a right of the judge, not of the accused. Karsman left the court room in protest and was sentenced in his absence to three months' imprisonment. The *Meeting Partij* was greatly boosted by the affair and went on to win the municipal elections of 1866. The newly-elected city council decided that French was no longer the official language in Antwerp and that the entire municipal administration would once again be conducted in Dutch, as it had in the days of Good King Willem.

Realising that he was unloved by a significant part of his people, while the others refused to approve his colonial plans, Leopold had already become a grumpy old man by 1840, when he was barely 50 years old. He came to loathe the Belgians so much that at Court he surrounded himself with Germans. Sarcastically the King wrote in 1845: 'I have the misfortune that for almost fourteen years now I have been obliged to spend my life in such a terribly prosaic place as Brabant. Awful!'[33] Queen Louise agreed. She confessed that she dreamed every night of being in France.

---

33   Leopold I to Louise, 14 Feb. 1845, in Kerckvoorde 1, p. 235.

For Men Must Work and Women Must Weep

The enhancement of the Saxe-Coburg family became Leopold's substitute for the colonial and imperial expansion that the petty and parochial Belgians would not grant him. He devoted as much energy to enlarging the fortune and the glory of his extended family as to his personal finances. In 1837, his beloved 18-year-old niece Victoria had been crowned Queen of Great Britain and Ireland. To assist the young and inexperienced in her new role — and also to keep an eye on her — Leopold sent her his own personal secretary as an advisor. From 1837 to 1856, when he retired to Coburg, Stockmar lived in England, where he became a trusted and discrete helper of the Queen and her husband, often to the displeasure of the British government, which tried to limit 'the Coburg influence' at Court. The discerning Princess Dorothea de Lieven, wife of the former Russian ambassador in London and one of the best informed women in Britain, remarked in 1837: 'England is at present living under Belgium's tyranny.'[34] When Lord Melbourne, the British Prime Minister, vented his dissatisfaction with Leopold's interference, Leopold wrote to Victoria: 'All I want from your kind Majesty is, that you will *occasionally* express to your Ministers, and particularly to Lord Melbourne, that you do *not* wish that your Government should take the *lead* in such measures as might bring on the *destruction* of your uncle and his family.'[35]

Together with Victoria and Stockmar, Leopold arranged for Ferdinand of Saxe-Coburg-Kohary, the 19-year-old eldest son of his brother Ferdinand, to marry the Portuguese Queen Maria II, a fat girl of seventeen. As a result Ferdinand became Titular King of Portugal in 1837 and laid the foundation for the House of Saxe-Coburg-Braganza that was to reign over Portugal until 1912. In his matchmaking efforts Leopold included his Orléans in-laws. He married three of Louise's siblings off to members of his own family. First, her sister Marie to Duke Alexander of Württemberg, eldest son of Leopold's sister Antoinette and a first cousin of the Tsar. Then, Louise's brother Louis, the Duke of Nemours, to Victoria of Saxe-Coburg-Kohary, the pretty daughter of Leopold's brother Ferdinand. They became the founders of the House of Orléans-Braganza, the Emperors of Brazil. Finally, Louise's sister Clémentine to August of Saxe-Coburg-Kohary, another son of Leopold's brother Ferdinand. They were the parents of the first Saxe-Coburg King of Bulgaria.

---

34   GSA Van de Weyer Papers nr. 110, Sylvain Van de Weyer, the Belgian Ambassador in London, to Leopold I, 19 July 1837.
35   RAW, Leopold I to Queen Victoria, 2 June 1838, in Victoria 1, vol. I, p. 148.

But Leopold's most prestigious matrimonial achievement was the marriage on 10 February 1840 of British Queen Victoria to Albert, officially the second son of his brother Ernst, the Duke of Coburg & Gotha. Leopold and Stockmar were instrumental in bringing about the marriage, although it took them many years and much pain to arrange it. Duke Ernst would have preferred Victoria to marry his eldest son, Ernst Junior, but Leopold insisted on Albert.[36] The two boys had been raised under Leopold's care in Brussels since 1836. In many ways Albert, as became apparent later on, resembled Leopold. He constantly suffered minor ailments and he grew old very quickly. But Albert won Victoria's heart, and, ultimately, that was the only thing that counted.

In the early 1830s, when Leopold and Stockmar began preparations to arrange Albert's marriage, the British King William IV and his government had done what they could to prevent Victoria from marrying her cousin. King and Government preferred Prince Alexander of Orange, second son of the Dutch Crown Prince Willem and the Russian Grand-Duchess Anna. 'I am really *astonished* at the conduct of your old Uncle the King,' an indignant Leopold had written in those days to Victoria. 'This invitation of the Prince of Orange and his sons, this forcing him on others, is very extraordinary. Really and truly I never heard or saw anything like it, and I hope it will a *little rouse your spirit*; now that slavery is even abolished in the British Colonies. I do not comprehend *why your lot alone should be to be kept a white little slavey in England*, for the pleasure of the Court, who never bought you, as I am not aware of their ever having gone to any expense on that head, or the King's ever having *spent a sixpence for your existence*.'[37] Leopold, as we have seen, had spent *a sixpence* for Victoria's existence when she was still a baby. He claimed a return on his investment.

Coburg defeated Orange again. Three years after Victoria ascended to the British throne, she married Albert. It was the vindication of Leopold's own British prospects that had been shattered when Charlotte died in 1817. Westminster, however, was less than enthusiastic about providing a purse for yet another Saxe-Coburg prince. The British Parliament offered Albert a stipend of 'only' £30,000. This was £20,000 less than what Leopold had been offered in 1816 when he had married Charlotte. The amount offered to Albert was, not by coincidence, equal to the £30,000 that Leopold, after much wrangling, had

36   Stockmar, p. 309.
37   RAW, Leopold I to Princess [*later* Queen] Victoria, 13 May 1836, in Victoria 1, vol. I, pp. 60–1.

reluctantly agreed to renounce when he left for Belgium. Reducing Albert's stipend from the usual £50,000 was an undisguised slap at Leopold and the Saxe-Coburg clan. 'Albert is very much irritated,' Leopold wrote to Victoria prior to the wedding. 'He does not care about the money, but he is much shocked and exasperated by the disrespect of the thing, as he well may.'[38] Of course, Uncle could have taken the opportunity to renounce his remaining annual British income of £20,000 in favour of his nephew, but did not do so.

Albert became Leopold's best ally in London. He consistently and constantly defended the interests of the Belgian monarchy and his family in Coburg. Some British newspapers claimed that Britain was now ruled by an 'Austrian-Belgian-Coburg-Orléans clique, the avowed enemies of England and the subservient tools of Russian ambition'[39] — a wild exaggeration that, however, contained a grain of truth. Albert had become, as his brother Ernst wrote to Uncle Leopold, 'the great channel through whom the Queen's will' was expressed.[40] In his letters to Uncle Leopold — he wrote to him at least once a week — he consulted the Belgian King on many things, including whom to invite for dinner at the palace. The Coburg influence forced Lord Palmerston to resign as Foreign Minister in 1851. This prompted the *Westminster Review* to condemn Victoria's inability to look with 'passive indifference' on foreign affairs because the 'high interests' of the Saxe-Coburgs prevented objectivity.

* * *

Belgium's foreign policy during Leopold's reign had two aims: maintaining Belgium's independence and serving the interests of the King's family. Leopold acted as his own Minister of Foreign Affairs with, as it was said, the nominal head of the department as his 'errand boy' and his wife as his 'chef de cabinet.' This was something poor Louise had longed for. At last 'the Leopich' placed some trust in her. Louise knew that he had other women to indulge his huge sexual appetite, and she accepted this. She blamed herself because she was a wife 'whose health did not allow her to fulfil her wifely duties.'[41] She accepted all humiliations, and never complained nor asked anything in return. She was, as she wrote to him, content to be 'your friend, your only friend. All my happiness, I owe to you: all that is lacking

38   RAW, Leopold I to Queen Victoria, 1 Feb. 1840, in Victoria 1, vol. I, p. 271.
39   Quoted in Rhodes James, p. 222.
40   SAC 567/WE22–76, Ernst to Leopold I, 17 Feb. 1840.
41   Louise, Queen, p. 290.

from my happiness is my fault alone, and I blame only myself for all that troubles me.'[42]

In 1843, Leopold and Louise succeeded in forging an alliance between Great Britain and France. They arranged a meeting between Victoria and Louis-Philippe at Eu, in Normandy. It was the first time since the 16th century that the royal heads of the two states along the Channel met. Victoria's trip to France was followed by her visit to Belgium. In order not to offend the French, Leopold persuaded Victoria not to go to Waterloo, where the flower of her nation had died 28 years earlier, defending the freedom of Europe against French aggression. Lord Aberdeen, the British Foreign Secretary, insisted on visiting the battlefield. He had to do so on his own, in private.

In February 1848, a revolution in Paris toppled Leopold's father-in-law. France again became a Republic. The French royal family fled to England. Leopold offered them his palace at Claremont to live in. Soon the whole household became ill. Two ladies-in-waiting and Louis-Philippe's private secretary died. They had been poisoned by drinking water from the lead pipes in the water system of a building that had not been tended for years, even though Leopold received £20,000 annually from the British government for Claremont's maintenance.

The new political situation in France forced Leopold to alter his foreign policy radically. As long as his father-in-law had been on the French throne, France had been the protector of the Belgian dynasty. But now that France resumed its position as Belgium's deadliest enemy, Leopold worked for a union between Austria and Prussia. He wanted Vienna and Berlin to form a solid block against France. 'To keep the two great continental powers united is our only hope and safety,' he wrote to his English friend, Lady Westmorland.[43] He especially favoured Austria. Like Belgium, the Habsburg Empire was not based on a nationality, but on the adherence of various peoples to a common Catholic religion and on their loyalty to the reigning family. Leopold regarded Austria as the linchpin of the existing order in Europe and opposed everything that might weaken it, such as the Italian and German unification processes. He gained the admiration of Prince Metternich, the grand old man of European diplomacy. According to the former Austrian Chancellor, Belgium was 'a miscarriage,' but with a king like Leopold, 'any country can survive.' He

---

42   Louise to Leopold I, 20 Feb. 1849, quoted in Corti and Buffin, p. 273.
43   GSA Acquisitions of the 4th section nr. 202, Leopold I to Lady Westmorland, 31 Dec. 1852.

considered Leopold one of the best diplomats he had ever met, 'very reticent, very prudent and cunning to the extreme.'[44]

After his retirement, Metternich settled in Brussels, where he came to admire Leopold's domestic policies, as well. In a letter to Prince Schwarzenberg in 1852, Metternich wrote that Leopold aimed constantly at expanding royal power in Belgium but was too intelligent to ever say so, because 'in accordance with his character, *he liked to remain behind the curtain.*'[45] If fate had granted Leopold the chance to become the King of Great Britain, he would undoubtedly have been one of its greatest monarchs. He most certainly was the best king England never had.

* * *

The events of 1848 left their mark on Queen Louise. When her father was driven from his realm, she understood that she had lost all political value for 'the Leopich.' As a wife Louise had already been feeling useless for years. She knew he did not find her attractive. 'I feel ashamed before him because I am already so old,' she wrote to her mother in April 1846, when she was 34 and he was 55. After 1848, she let her health deteriorate. Her mother sensed that she was losing her will to live on. 'On my knees I beg you to take care of yourself. My only comfort is that your health should improve. I beseech you, keep calm and take good care of yourself!' she told her daughter.[46] But Louise knew that she was not getting enough of the medicine she needed. In a letter of 30 July 1850 to Queen Victoria, she wrote: 'The reunion with your uncle has done me a world of good. The best of all medicines is to be able to be near your uncle.' The only thing she longed for was her husband's attention. But he deprived her of it.

While Louise suffered, Leopold left her for ever longer periods — either to go hunting in the Ardennes mountains or the Kempen moors, or to visit the German spa of Wiesbaden — and he took a permanent mistress. Leopold met Arcadie Claret in the early 1840s. In 1845, he had the 19-year-old girl marry one of the officers of his personal staff, his *Rittmeister* Friedrich Meyer, a widower from Coburg. Meyer had been ordered to marry Arcadie so she would have a position, but it was the King who bedded the bride.

Leopold installed young Madame Meyer, whom he called '*Meyerchen*' (Little Meyer), in a big house in the Rue Royale in Brussels, not far from the royal palace. Arcadie was given her own

44   Quoted in Bronne 1, p. 222.
45   Metternich to Schwarzenberg, 20 Mar. 1852, in De Ridder, Alfred 1, p. 280.
46   RAB FLI II 407, Marie-Amélie to Louise, 26 Aug. 1850.

servants, a carriage adorned with armorial insignia and liveried foot-men. Every afternoon Leopold walked from the palace to Arcadie's place and stayed for dinner. His ministers knew where to find him. Occasionally Leopold's friends, the ministers Van Praet and Chazal, stayed for dinner, too, together with the King and the woman whom he openly came to treat as his wife. He provided *Meyerchen* with a house in Liège, the little chateau of Stelenbosch near the royal resi-dence of Laken, and a house at Langenfeld in Germany. She also accompanied him on foreign travels

In 1847 the press published articles about the King and his mistress. To avoid similar embarrassment in future, Leopold began to bribe journalists not to write about his amorous adventures. The British Ambassador in Brussels reported to London that the King each year paid up to 125,000 francs in 'hush money' to 'scurrilous papers.' The Austrian Ambassador informed Vienna that 'His Majesty fears to irri-tate the press and buys its silence with regard to his person by paying his weight in gold.'

Louise was deeply hurt by the public nature of the affair. 'She is extremely nervous in her jealous affection,' the Marquess de Rumigny observed. Though in her daily letters to her mother she wrote down everything that was happening around her, even the most intimate details of her married life, this she never told her. It was too painful. The people in Brussels sympathised with Louise. In November 1849, Arcadie became the mother of a baby boy by Leopold. When she took her son out for a stroll in the summer of 1850, she was jeered at and eggs and excrement were thrown at her. When Leopold heard about this, he went mad with rage. He shouted insults at his ministers, com-plained about the ingratitude of the Belgians and threatened to resign, knowing full well that his ministers would never allow this to happen as it might jeopardise the existence of Belgium and, hence, their own livelihood. Then, one night in August, all the windows of Arcadie's house were smashed. The people were angry because they knew that at the royal palace Louise was lying seriously ill. The authorities feared an uprising if the Queen were to die. A senator said that he knew some citizens were preparing to burn Arcadie's house down and storm the royal palace.

Many politicians feared that the death of Louise could mean the end of the monarchy and of the state. Leopold's secretary, Viscount Conway, informed his master of his fears. 'I am concerned about the King and the Country,' he wrote. 'The mood amongst the public at this moment is of such harshness that it frightens me.' Conway's letter enraged Leopold as never before. 'I have never seen him so angry,' wrote Van Praet. 'His face had changed colour completely. He says he shall never be forced. He is considering abdication.'[47] Leopold ordered the removal of Louise from the tumult of Brussels to the calm of Ostend. He warned Van Praet: 'You are advised to ensure that things do not get out of hand there as well.'[48]

Louise's last trip was agony. She begged Leopold to be allowed to remain at Laken, but he refused. The Queen suffered terrible pains during the voyage. When she arrived at Ostend, being too sick to mount the winding stairs to the bedroom on the second floor of the modest terraced house that Leopold rented, she was hoisted up in a wicker basket. She died on 11 October 1850, only 38 years old. During her last seven weeks, Leopold had only occasionally been in Ostend, even though Van Praet had urged him to remain there. 'I am in a dreadful state when I am with her,' the King wrote to Victoria, as an excuse not to stay at Ostend.[49] He was present, however, at the moment Louise died. Also present were their children: 15-year-old Leo, the Duke of Brabant, 13-year-old Philippe, the Count of Flanders, and 10-year-old Charlotte.

Leopold outlived Louise by 15 years. In 1852, he and Arcadie had a second son, but his moods became darker than ever before. He hardly talked to anyone, not even to his children. One day a servant who had been working at the royal palace for sixteen years but had never ever heard the King's voice, accidentally stepped on the paw of Leopold's dog. 'You stupid fool,' scolded the King. Bewildered, the attendant ran to the servants' quarters, shouting: 'The King has spoken to me! The King has spoken to me!'[50]

Even his ministers often did not gain access to the King. There were no cabinet sessions for seven months in 1860, because Leopold, who chaired the sessions, had a disagreement with the Government. At other moments, he could rant and rave at the ministers. He constantly reminded them that 'the King has established this state and has saved it from certain doom.'[51] Therefore, the Cabinet had to do as he pleased. 'I try to control my outbursts of rage,' he confessed to his friend, General Pierre Chazal, the Minister of War, in 1864, 'but I find it very difficult.'[52]

47   RAB FLI III Conway 545/40: Van Praet to Conway, 24 Aug. 1850.
48   RAB FLI III Conway 496/2: Leopold I to Van Praet, 24 Aug. 1850.
49   RAW, Leopold I to Queen Victoria, 7 Oct. 1850, in Victoria 1, vol. II, p. 318.
50   Bronne 1, pp. 317–8.
51   Conway, 13 Nov. 1859, in Bronne 1, p. 318.
52   Leopold I to Chazal, 1 Dec. 1864, in Juste 2, vol. II, p. 625.

Leopold often refused to sign bills, even those approved by Parliament, if affairs had not been handled the way he wanted. 'Usually, he did not say a word,' minister Vandenpeereboom wrote in his diary, 'but he refused to sign them. If I insisted, he had someone — usually Van Praet — say to me that he was very displeased with me; that I treated him like a stableboy, while all the sovereigns had the greatest respect for him.'[53] Jules Van Praet held the rank of 'Minister of the House of the King;' he was Leopold's *chef de cabinet*. Once when a royal signature was urgently needed, the King departed on a foreign trip to Geneva. Prime Minister Rogier went after him to obtain the signature. Leopold scolded him, threw him out of his hotel room and told him he did not want to see him again. Because the government needed the signature, Jules Devaux, Van Praet's nephew and assistant, was sent to persuade the King. 'You are a good boy. I love you,' the King said to Devaux, but he did not sign.

In 1831, Leopold introduced the first Belgian ambassador to Vienna to Metternich with the words: 'I recommend you Baron de Loë; he has nothing in common with the [Belgian] revolution or the revolutionaries and will never be anything but the representative of his Sovereign.'[54] In 1864, the Austrian Minister of Foreign Affairs contacted his Belgian colleague to discuss a matter of common interest between the two countries. The reply was blunt: 'You know very well that our ministry does not conduct any foreign policy. That is the private territory of His Majesty.'[55] And at the centre of Belgium's foreign policy was the royal family's fortune.

When the French President Louis-Napoleon Bonaparte declared himself Emperor in 1852, the Second Republic came to an end. Four years earlier, it had confiscated all the property of the Orléans family in France, including possessions of Louise, Leopold's wife, valued at 30 million francs (£90 million or $150 million today). Consequently, her children had received an inheritance from their mother of only 8.4 million francs in non-French assets. Once Napoleon III had become Emperor, it became Belgian diplomacy's most important aim to have Louise's possessions restored. In 1856, Paris agreed to pay Louise's children an annual sum of 200,000 francs for fifteen years. In 1872 they also received a capital of 5.6 million francs. This enabled the Belgian Saxe-Coburgs to recover 8.6 million francs.

53   Quoted in Kerckvoorde 1, pp. 232–3.
54   Quoted in Corti and Buffin, p. 83.
55   Lambermont to Hügel, in Corti, p. 372; Hügel to Mensdorff-Pouilly, 3 Nov. 1864, in Bronne 1, p. 338.

Soon Leopold had new marriages to arrange. Always an admirer of the Habsburg family, the oldest and most prestigious dynasty in the world, he did his best to marry his own children to Austrian Archdukes. He succeeded twice. In 1853, his eldest son Leopold married Marie-Henriette, daughter of Archduke Joseph, a great-uncle of Emperor Franz Joseph. In 1857, his daughter Charlotte married the Emperor's brother, Archduke Maximilian.

Negotiating a dowry with a miser like King Leopold was a difficult undertaking. It took months before an agreement was reached for Charlotte's dowry. At first Leopold did not want to give his daughter anything because the Belgian Parliament was donating Charlotte 100,000 (Austrian) guilders. The Austrians insisted, however, that Leopold should also personally contribute to the dowry. He finally agreed to pay Charlotte an annuity of 20,000 guilders, while the Austrian Emperor gave her 130,000 guilders. Leopold also had to donate a huge trousseau, consisting of 44 dresses (many adorned with silk, Brussels lace, gold brocade), 23 necklaces (the largest consisting of 34 diamonds), 34 bracelets, 52 brooches, 11 rings and numerous smaller items such as lockets and watches. 'I am quite proud,' Maximilian wrote to his brother, Emperor Franz Joseph, 'that I have forced the old miser to part with a small part of that which he holds dearest in this world.' Also included in the trousseau were 360 shirts, 77 gowns, 216 handkerchiefs, 288 pairs of socks and 100 pairs of shoes. Even in aristocratic circles, it was customary to wash clothes only two or three times a year, which explains why the fine ladies needed a large wardrobe. Why Charlotte needed so many shoes is unclear. It is doubtful that these were polished even once a season.

Charlotte was Leopold's favourite child. She adored her father and shared his glorious dreams and grand ambitions for the Saxe-Coburg family. In 1863, the Belgian King supported Napoleon III's project to install an imperial regime in Mexico, with Maximilian as Emperor and Charlotte as Empress. The project appealed to Leopold's own dreams of imperial glory. Although Maximilian had serious doubts about the Mexican adventure, Charlotte pressured her dithering husband into acceptance. 'We, Coburgs, are a blessing to the families we align ourselves with,' she wrote to her brother Leo.[56]

King Leopold's last years were ones of physical suffering. His health deteriorated and he had to undergo surgery to remove kidney stones that caused him much pain. To the very end, he continued to quarrel with his ministers and kept demanding ever more money for

56   RAB FG PSDB, Charlotte to Duke of Brabant, 27 Jan. 1862.

his family. At Ostend a pavilion had been built for the royal family. Leopold wanted it to be more luxurious, but the Government had to foot the bill and was reluctant to come up with more money. The King wrote to Prime Minister Rogier: 'My grandchildren, for whom that vacation is a health necessity, are on the street and lodged in a way which is really disgraceful. The dynasty is not without its importance because I do not think that you will be given another one.'[57] As can be seen, after depicting the 'appalling condition' his grandchildren were in, he sternly lectured his ministers on the importance of the Saxe-Coburg family that guaranteed Belgium's independence. By threatening to sabotage the future of the country if he did not get his way, he blackmailed them into spending on his family.

Meanwhile, the international Powers were thinking of Belgium's future after the demise of the King. They doubted whether the artificial country could survive its monarch. Even Albert, the British Prince Consort, predicted in 1860 that France would seize Belgium once its ageing king was gone.[58] Napoleon III proposed to Austria and Prussia that Belgium be divided after Leopold's death. The North would go to the Netherlands, the South to France. In return, France would accept Austria's annexation of Southern Germany, while Prussia would be allowed to occupy Hanover. The Prussian Chancellor, Otto von Bismarck, did not like the idea, especially the suggestion that Austria could have the whole of Southern Germany. But Bismarck had his doubts about Belgium, too. 'My view is that Belgium is not viable in the long term,' he said, echoing the Prussian King Friedrich Wilhelm IV who in 1842 had told Stockmar: 'Belgium cannot last two generations.'[59] Even Leopold feared that his country might not survive him for long. 'Belgium has no nationality and, given the character of its inhabitants, it can never have one. Basically, Belgium has no political reason to exist,' he told Van Praet.[60] 'H. M. keeps repeating that nothing holds the country together and that it cannot continue to exist,' the Count of Flanders wrote to his brother Leo.[61]

In November 1865, the King went fox hunting for the last time. When he returned, he felt sick and tired. On 7 December, Van Praet received Leopold's last letter. He wrote in German and said he longed to die. He wished to see no one, except *Meyerchen*. Van Praet sent for

57   GSA Ch. Rogier Papers nr. 101, Leopold I to Rogier, 13 Mar. 1865.
58   Diary of Count Karl Friedrich Vitzthum von Eckstädt, Ambassador of Saxony in London, 14 Feb. 1860, in Weintraub, p. 381.
59   Wangenheim, p. 146.
60   Leopold I to Van Praet, 19 Nov. 1859, in Stengers 5, p. 478.
61   RAB FG PSDB, Philippe to Duke of Brabant, 29 Jan. 1865.

the King's Lutheran chaplain, the German Becker, but no one dared enter the royal bedroom for fear that the King would go into one of his rages.

Finally, on the morning of 10 December, Marie-Henriette, his Habsburg daughter-in-law, had the courage to enter the royal bedroom. The doctors had told the family that it was only a matter of hours now. Leopold did not mind her entering. She asked him whether he wished to see his son, the Duke of Brabant. 'No,' he whispered, but she had already been followed by the Duke, the Count of Flanders, Becker and Van Praet. Marie-Henriette went down on her knees and asked the dying king in German whether he regretted the sins he had committed in his life, and, more specifically, the scandal that he had caused. She was referring to his liaison with Arcadie Meyer. He answered: '*Ja*.' She then asked whether he was prepared to convert to Catholicism. He did not react. She repeated her question. '*Nein*,' he said, '*nicht Katholisch*.'[62] In a letter to the Dean of Windsor on 3 March 1862 he had expressed the wish to be buried in St. George's Chapel at Windsor, next to his first wife, Charlotte, who was a Protestant.

Leopold died as the morning drew to an end, at a quarter to twelve, with his hand in Marie-Henriette's. The same morning, Madame Meyer and her two sons left Belgium under police protection and travelled to Germany. The dead King was laid in state at the royal palace, dressed in his English mantle of a Knight of the Garter. He was buried on 12 December 1865, the day of his 75th birthday. Contrary to his wish, he was interred at Laken, next to Louise.

Queen Victoria was very upset about the refusal of her uncle's last wish to be buried in England. She had a statue erected for him in Windsor, and a grand monument in Esher near Claremont, with the inscription: 'In memory of the uncle who held a father's place in her affection — Vict. R.' Today, Leopold still lies in the royal vault at Laken. His place in Windsor, near to the British royals whom he used to call 'my English children,'[63] remains open. If some day the artificial state of Belgium should cease to exist, perhaps Leopold will be granted his last wish: to lie next to Charlotte, in the country that (but for her tragic death) should have been his.

---

62   Beyens, vol. I, p. 286. Beyens was given the account of Leopold's death by Van Praet, an eye-witness.
63   SAP MP, Leopold I to his brother-in-law, Count Emmanuel von Mensdorff-Pouilly, 29 Oct. 1851, in Leopold I 2, p. 403.

Leopold II
Second King of the Belgians

Chapter 3

The Cruel Pharaoh of the Congo (1865–1909)

Young Nasone

Two days after the death of his father, the 30-year-old Duke of Brabant took the constitutional oath and succeeded to the throne as Leopold II. From his father, Leo had inherited an obsession with money, burning ambition, and strong sexual urges. Like his father, he also was a hypochondriac. From his mother, he had inherited her most striking physical feature. Like Louise's maternal grandfather, the legendary 'Nasone,' the younger Leopold had a truly gigantic nose. When Leo was a child, his own mother wrote that he was 'disfigured by his enormous nose which gives him a bird-like appearance.' As soon as he was able to, the young Duke of Brabant grew a beard in an attempt to bring the rest of his face into proportion with his nose, but it remained, as Madame Baroche, pointed out, a remarkable *'nez romain un peu plus grand que nature.'*

Young Leopold had another conspicuous physical trait. He limped, owing to sciatic pains in his leg. This, however, did not prevent him walking long distances, always at a fast pace. He also complained that his lungs were weak and that he was very sensitive to colds. The Duke of Brabant grew up as a withdrawn boy, bullying his younger brother Philippe, the Count of Flanders. 'Leo has the Spanish moroseness,' the Belgian King complained to his Saxe-Coburg-Kohary niece, Victoria of Nemours. Like all little boys, Leo adored his Papa, but he did not get to see him often, which, according to his mother, 'saddened and confused' the child. Sometimes when Papa was around, the boy was confused as well. In a letter to Queen Victoria, King Leopold described how he attempted a joke at the expense of his three-year-old son. 'I said to him "*Bonjour Mademoiselle,*" which shocked him a great deal and he said gravely, "Prince is a boy and not a girl."'[1]

The education of the royal sons was consigned to their governor, Colonel de Lannoy, who received strict orders from the King. 'I wish to inculcate in them the sentiment of duty — everything must be made relevant to this sentiment: to allow them liberty to express an opinion would be disruptive.' Especially the Duke of Brabant had to be treated most severely, insisted the King. 'I recommend, especially for Leopold, that one apply greater strictness, even in the smallest matters of daily life.' The boys received harsh treatment and were submitted to many hours of study and training. They were raised in French, but they also had to learn to speak fluent German and English. Dutch, the language of the majority of the Belgians, was not deemed important, apart from an odd phrase such as '*Goede morgen*' and '*Lang leve België.*'

Every month the children — Leo, Philippe and their sister Charlotte — had to take exams in front of their mother and Viscount Conway, who, as he said himself, was called in because of his 'grumpy appearance which is likely to impress them.' Charlotte and Philippe usually did well, but the Crown Prince was a constant problem. 'My good friend, I was very disappointed to hear from the Colonel that you have again been lazy and that your dictations have been bad and careless,' Louise reprimanded her fourteen-year-old son in 1849. 'This is not what you promised me.'

As time went by, it was not so much Leo's lack of interest in his studies that worried his teachers, but the heartless and cynical way in which he treated his servants and his brother. Philippe suffered especially. Leopold tried literally to dominate him, ordering him around and demanding total submission. Things got worse after the premature death of their mother in 1850, when the royal children lost the only person in Brussels who really cared about them. Their self-centred father devoted what affectionate feelings he had solely to his mistress. Consequently, young Leopold became an ever more solitary, cold-hearted and sullen person. He grew into a scrawny, tall adolescent, outwardly resembling, as some contemporaries said, 'a stick of asparagus,' inwardly insensitive and callous. In November 1852, his educators approached Count Camille de Briey. The latter, a Frenchman who had been the Belgian Minister of Foreign Affairs in the early 1840s, had family connections to the Saxe-Coburgs, his aunt

1   RAW Y64/34, Leopold I to Queen Victoria, 27 Mar. 1838.

being the Countess of Mensdorff-Pouilly, the King's eldest sister Sophie. Briey wrote a letter to the King and drew his attention to young Leopold's *'sécheresse de coeur'* (dryness of heart).[2] The Crown Prince, however, had by now reached the age of seventeen, and his heart was to remain dry for the rest of his life.

In the spring of 1853, preparations were made for the marriage of Leo with 16-year-old Marie-Henriette, the fun-loving daughter of Archduke Joseph, the Palatine of Hungary. She was a rather plump girl, brown-eyed and fair. Leo wrote to his siblings from Vienna that she was 'a bit fat and not very pretty, though without being ugly.'[3] Marie-Henriette had also dreamt of a *prince charming* other than the one her parents picked for her, this sinister coughing six-feet-tall gimp with the biggest nose ever. She told her half-brother Stephan before leaving for Brussels that she felt 'like a nurse going to tend a patient with consumption.'[4]

It was, said Madame Metternich, a match between 'a stable boy and a nun, the nun being the Duke of Brabant.'[5] Lady Westmorland opined that, though the groom's 'body might even be too young for marriage, his mind is definitely not; he does not talk like a man, but like an old man.' Queen Victoria had her misgivings, too. She was particularly worried about 'the too young body' not being sexually appealing to the tomboy of Habsburg. When the newlyweds visited Windsor in early December, almost four months after the wedding ceremony, Victoria reported back to King Leopold that she doubted whether the marriage had been consummated. Young Leopold was to be blamed in this respect, because Victoria was certain that 'dear good Marie is much more alive to these duties than you think.' However, 'to ask her to obey a boy of 18, who tho' very sensible & clever, is *physically* 4 or 5 years her junior & decidedly her inferior in learning — wd be impossible.' Indeed, 'there is nothing a woman likes less than a man who is *not manly* in his person.' Alas, 'Leo does not demonstrate the slightest feeling of *love* or admiration for Marie, or *any woman* — and is so very underdeveloped, delicate and boyish looking as to be *totally incapable* (I am bound to tell you this *frankly* — as I as a *woman* can judge) of inspiring love — still less respect.'[6]

2   RAB FLI Conway 554, Briey to Leopold I, 24 Nov. 1852.
3   RAB F Count of Flanders letter 6, Duke of Brabant to Philippe and Charlotte, 15 May 1853.
4   Archduke Stephan to Archduke Johann, 21 Aug. 1853, in Corti 1, p. 205.
5   Dino, vol. IV, p. 112.
6   RAW Y79/11 and Y79/18, Queen Victoria to Leopold I, 6 and 26 Dec. 1853.

The British Queen knew exactly what to do. She had the Prince Consort instruct Leo in his marital duties. She informed her uncle that the ideal situation would be to have 'Albert at poor Leo's elbow constantly. Nothing short of that will do.' As late as April 1857, Albert was writing letters to Brussels to admonish the young couple 'to love each other with greater passion than displayed so far.'[7]

Unfortunately, especially for 'dear good Marie' who deserved better, young Leopold and Marie-Henriette were two incompatible personalities. She was a warm and ribald girl, who had been raised in Hungary, indeed as 'a stable boy.' He was aloof, cold and sarcastic. Her passion was horses, which she rode — Magyar style — at great speed through the puszta. Leo hated horses and detested riding. She was very fond of music, especially wild gypsy tunes, but also Viennese waltzes and anything lively. Leo abhorred music, which he called 'expensive noise.'[8] His passion was politics. She found it boring.

Like Louise of Orléans before her, Marie-Henriette soon lost her spontaneity and gaiety in Brussels. 'If God hears my prayers, I shall not go on living much longer,' she wrote one month after her marriage, to a friend in Vienna. The once so merry Marie-Henriette soon withdrew into herself and tried to find consolation in her hobbies. She established a *menagerie* with ponies, horses, dogs, parrots, even camels and llamas. Like Louise, she remained an unhappy woman for the rest of her life, in a foreign country where the people hated their kings and pitied their queens.

Her husband lacked all interest in her, except as a breeding machine for royal offspring. When the Austrian Archduke Maximilian visited Brussels, he found Leo boasting 'that he very frequently fulfilled his marital rights.' Soon, these efforts were crowned with success and Marie-Henriette became pregnant. 'The wise and practical advice you gave me has now borne fruit,' Leopold wrote to Cousin Albert in England.[9] Having discovered the pleasure of sex, young Leopold indulged in it — though not only with his wife. Historians do not know whether Marie-Henriette loathed sex with her unloving husband as much as Louise had done. Unlike Louise, she did not write her private feelings down during a daily 'hour of tears.' She probably wept on horseback, riding through the countryside, Magyar style.

7   RAB FG PSDB, Prince Consort to Duke of Brabant, 19 April 1857.
8   Marie-José, p. 135.
9   RAW M54/70, Duke of Brabant to Prince Consort, 19 Nov. 1857.

Leopold, however, confided to his diary that his wife's sexual performance did not at all satisfy him. He needed more women. 'My nature requires manifold encounters with the fair sex. I do not understand how clerics can live.'[10] It was the Saxe-Coburg nature.

* * *

Because of Leopold's chronic cough and the sciatic pains in his leg, his doctors in 1854 prescribed him a long stay in a warm climate. The Duke of Brabant wanted to visit Egypt, a country that fascinated him for the business opportunities it might provide. He presumed that the *Khedive*, the viceroy who ruled Egypt for the Turkish Ottoman Empire, would be greatly impressed by a visit from European royalty. 'I may be able to extort from the Khedive commercial advantages,' he wrote to Conway, 'I am the first foreign prince to be received by him and I think he will go out of his way to please me.'

Leopold went as far as Aswan to look for business opportunities. He obtained a permit from the Khedive to develop a regular steamship connection between Alexandria and Antwerp, and triumphantly wrote to Conway: 'I hope to get out of this venture 500,000 to one million francs. If I play my cards carefully, I may even be able to exceed this figure.' He also met Ferdinand de Lesseps, a Frenchman who was trying to raise money to build a canal from the Mediterranean to Suez. An excellent idea, according to Leopold, who hoped that Lesseps would fail, so 'that we can take up where he leaves off.'[11]

There were at least two important advantages in colonies, Leopold realised. Firstly, they brought in money, either through exploitation or trade. Hence, a Belgian colony would benefit Belgium's industrial and trading companies, and as many of these were controlled by the *Société Générale*, Belgium's largest bank and holding company, it would directly benefit the King who was the largest shareholder of the SG. Secondly, a Belgian colonisation project, as an undertaking of the Belgian nation as a whole, would provide a unifying element in a country that so far lacked any Belgian-nationalist feelings. In *normal* countries nationalism often led to colonialism. In an artificial country like Belgium colonialism might induce nationalism. The Belgians were not interested in colonies, as King Leopold I had discovered, because they lacked the necessary nationalist sentiments to be interested in planting their flag on foreign shores. The Duke of Brabant decided to work the other way round. He intended to bestow a colo-

---

10   Leopold II 3, p. 43.
11   Duke of Brabant to Conway, in Emerson, p. 19.

nial empire on Belgium — whether the Belgians liked it or not — and in doing so, foster Belgian nationalism.

'I regret the internal situation in my country,' the Crown Prince wrote in his diary. 'Thanks to King Leopold and Lord Palmerston, the Belgian State has nothing to fear from external enemies. Into this furnace we must bring a great and novel idea. That is what I am looking for in the Orient. We have to consider the question of national expansion.'[12] He wanted Belgium to become the centre of 'a Belgian Empire, that with God's help will consist of Pacific islands, Borneo, some places in Africa and America, as well as parts of China and Japan. *Voilà,* that is my goal. By arousing nationalistic fervour, I will acquire for myself apostles and supporters.'[13]

The Duke of Brabant returned home in August 1855 after an absence of nine months. It was the time of the Crimean War. Waging a war was also a good method for instilling nationalist fervour, Leopold reckoned. He tried to persuade the Belgian government to send troops to the Crimea to fight the Russians. The ministers were horrified at the idea. They feared it might constitute a violation of Belgium's neutrality. In 1857, he proposed sending Belgian troops to India to help put down the anti-British mutiny. In 1859, he tried to get Belgium to participate in an Anglo-French expedition against China. Apart from General Chazal, the Belgian Minister of War, Brussels did not want to hear of the bellicose plan. The Minister of Foreign Affairs informed Britain that the war scheme was a personal idea of the Duke of Brabant's.

The Crown Prince's most ambitious plan was to wage a war with the Netherlands. He dreamed of extending the Belgian border to the mouth of the Rhine by annexing the Dutch provinces of North Brabant, East Limburg and Zeeland. But above all, he wanted to force the Dutch to transfer their overseas colonies to Belgium. In February 1854 he sent his aide-de-camp, Adrien Goffinet, on a secret mission to the Netherlands to ascertain the strength of the Dutch army. He also invited Jerome Bonaparte, brother to the first Napoleon and uncle to the French Emperor Napoleon III, to Brussels to discuss his plans. Leopold proposed to the French that as the British would never allow them to extend their territory to the Rhine, Belgium would do so instead.

---

12   RAB FG Diary of the Duke of Brabant during his travel to the Far East, 28 Jan. 1865.

13   RAB FG Diary of the Duke of Brabant during his travel to Bavaria and Bad Gastein, 26 May 1861.

'The Kingdom of the Netherlands is a remnant of a scheme that was deeply hostile to France,' Leopold wrote. 'The Belgian Revolution of 1830 has undermined the Dutch Kingdom sufficiently to render it harmless to France, but insufficiently to derive for France as much profit as possible from the provinces that were detached from the Netherlands and at present constitute Belgium.' Hence, he offered Belgium as a proxy to France. Britain would never allow Napoleon III to wage a war of conquest in Europe, the Duke of Brabant wrote. Therefore, Napoleon should use Belgium to do this on his behalf: 'France does not need to extend its boundaries. That would lead to a contrary result. It has to surround itself by allies and friends, whom by its support, it can help to become more powerful, thereby becoming more powerful itself. This way one disturbs no one. Without costs and without noise, France will be able to surround itself with trustworthy defenders. It is evident that 6 or 7 million Piedmontese, 3 million Swiss, 8 million Belgians and 37 million French can provide [the French Emperor] with an armed force that is more considerable, more complete, better organised and better provisioned than an Empire of 50 million can provide. Everyone has the same goal, all the efforts are made together but the costs are spread. All the Emperor has to do is to give us his diplomatic support when we invade the Netherlands. The prestige of his support will allow us to gain a quick and easy victory. Then, in a few months from now, France will be able to draw on 200,000 Belgian auxiliaries along its Northern boundary. If the Dutch colonies pass to us, France will be able to withstand the whole of Europe. Our navy will be its ally, and combined we will be as strong as the British navy. And all this will not have cost France one single man or one single franc.'[14]

Leopold was convinced that Britain would not interfere if Belgium invaded the Netherlands. Queen Victoria considered Belgium, under the government of her Saxe-Coburg relatives, as an ally and friend. 'I do not care what Europe will say or think if we invade. The important thing is that it does not act against us,' Leopold wrote. 'If France does not react to our invasion, Prussia will not react, England will not want to do us a disfavour and we will remain the masters on the battle field. Then, as soon as we have grabbed the Dutch colonies in the East, our navy will become so powerful, that England will be kept in check.'[15]

Fortunately, the Duke of Brabant had not yet succeeded his father. The old King deemed his son's schemes unwise. He had heard

14 RAB FG, Duke of Brabant to Prince Chimay, 22 Apr. 1854.
15 RAB FG, Duke of Brabant to a collaborator of Prince Chimay, undated 1854.

rumours that Napoleon III was aiming at the outright annexation of Belgium and in compensation wanted to offer the Belgian royals a tiny crown somewhere beyond the Rhine or in Poland.[16]

* * *

The late 1850s were the time of the betrothal and the marriage of the Duke of Brabant's sister Charlotte to Archduke Maximilian, a marriage which her brother looked upon unfavourably. He did not want his sister to marry at all. According to Belgian civil law, a father's inheritance has to be divided among *all* his children in more or less equal shares. The civil law also applied to the royal family. Consequently, a Belgian royal daughter married to a foreign prince would eventually take part of the royal fortune abroad. The Duke of Brabant wrote a memorandum arguing that an exception to the civil law should be made for the royal family: a king's inheritance should pass only to his sons and exclude any daughters in order to keep the royal fortune in Belgian hands. The government rejected the proposal. When Leopold's first child, Princess Louise, was born in 1858, he greatly resented having fathered a girl. He could already see his own legacy going to a foreigner.

Luckily, on 12 June 1859 Marie-Henriette gave birth to a boy, who was christened Leopold and was made Count of Hainaut by his grandfather, the King. But in 1864 another girl was born, Stephanie. According to the Duke of Brabant, every daughter harmed Belgium's cause. In Windsor, Queen Victoria noted in her diary that Archduke Maximilian had warned her that the Duke of Brabant 'held such absolutist principles that he dreaded what might be if Uncle were no longer alive.'[17] The Archduke instinctively sensed what a dangerous cocktail lurked in this emotionally deprived but over-energetic young man, who was totally uncaring about others and whose only passion was the kindling of nationalist fervour through which he could exert power over others.

Uncle, however, was not dead yet. The Duke of Brabant would have to wait until he was 30 before succeeding to his father's throne. Meanwhile he had plenty of time to devote to his commercial and colonial projects. Leopold discovered that royal blood not only opened doors in foreign countries, but also allowed him to influence public opinion and get things done at home. Belgian diplomats abroad provided Leopold with a network of agents all over the globe,

16   Beyens, vol. I, p. 338.
17   RAW Z261/4, QVJ 31 July 1857.

which cost him nothing. He decided to use these advantages. In addition to being a Crown Prince, he became a businessman. His personal fortune steadily increased. Having made 1.5 million francs in profits since 1858, he was worth 5 million francs (£15 million or $25 million today) by 1864, and he constantly reinvested his money. Leopold also had unique assets of his own. He had boundless energy. He could switch his attention from one project to another and his mind produced a constant flow of new ideas. 'It is necessary to lay eggs all over the place. Some at least are sure to hatch,' he used to say.[18] He also had a knack for choosing his collaborators. He singled out the brightest, the most ambitious and the least scrupulous young men in the Belgian civil service, diplomatic corps and army, and had them work for him. Captain Adrien Goffinet became his aide-de-camp in 1853. He soon was Leopold's most trusted henchman in private and financial matters. Goffinet set up secret companies and partnerships to shield Leopold's fortune from scrutiny. The Captain remained in Leopold's service until his death in 1886, when he had become a Lt.-General and had been given the hereditary title of Baron. He was succeeded by his sons, the Barons Auguste and Constant Goffinet. They were twin brothers, two chubby fellows, Tweedledum and Tweedledee, who could hardly be kept apart. Both were plump, cross-eyed and bearded. Auguste became Leopold's factotum; Constant managed Leopold's finances. They knew everything about Leopold's private and financial dealings and were very discreet.

The Goffinets were perfect in carrying out orders, but hardly any good at solving problems. The ideal man for that job was Auguste Lambermont, a civil servant of humble background who worked at the Ministry of Foreign Affairs. He was a brilliant intellectual and workaholic, whom Leopold also rewarded with a hereditary baronetage. Another member of the inner circle was Captain Henri-Alexis Brialmont, a military engineer. Brialmont, of French descent like so many officers in the Belgian army, had just finished designing the Antwerp fortifications when he was taken into the Crown Prince's employment in the late 1850s. He provided Leopold with answers to technical details and data. 'The Duke of Brabant takes me for a statistical office,' he once complained. With Brialmont, the Prince authored a book that was published anonymously early in 1860: *The Sequel to the Achievements of 1830.* It advocated colonisation and economic expansion with emphatic nationalist arguments. It caused a political uproar. Leopold, however, was not deterred by '*la triste mentalité de son pays.*[19] He told Brialmont: 'Belgium does not exploit the world. We must teach her to develop a taste for it.' He soon surprised his henchmen with a novel and outrageous idea: he would acquire a colony of his own, as a private enterprise, which at a later stage, he said, he would bestow on Belgium.

One such privately-owned colony already existed: the sultanate of Sarawak, the personal property of Sir James Brooke. Brooke was an English adventurer who had become the adoptive son of the late Rajah of Sarawak. After the Rajah's death in 1842, Brooke inherited his country, rich in tropical woods, pearl fisheries and even some gold and copper mines. Leopold entered into secret negotiations with Brooke to establish a company for the economic exploitation of Sarawak.

The negotiations ultimately came to nothing. Brooke told his collaborators that the Belgian was only interested in 'how to squeeze money out of the people; he laughed at the idea of respecting the rights of the natives, and talked of having a garrison to coerce them into paying revenue.'[20] In Leopold's view, colonisation had to be ruthless. 'Submitting the lazy and corrupted peoples of the Far-East to forced labour is the only possible way to civilise and moralise them,' he told Brialmont.[21] He was greatly inspired by Sarawak. It proved that it was possible to own a colony as a private person, to exploit it with the help of private business companies, and to rule it as if one were a 19th century pharaoh.

In 1860, Leopold visited Constantinople. The Ottoman Sultan received him with lavish receptions, copious dinners and costly fireworks. But things took a nasty turn when, in his arrogance, Leopold stole a set of jewelled pipes from the Sultan. The theft was discovered and caused considerable embarrassment for the Belgian royal family. 'The Coburgs have no scruples,' *The Levant Herald* wrote in a biting commentary. 'They are always looking for gain, be it a vacant throne or a kitchen garden in Claremont.' In a stern letter, Leopold I warned his son that such 'childish conduct' was especially dangerous for a future Belgian king, because the Belgian nationhood was so frail. 'You have made yourself an object of ridicule. What we have to fear most are the forces working to destroy the Belgian nationality. You understand how dangerous it will be for you if one has no confidence in you and doubts your judgement.'[22]

19 Stinglhamber and Dresse, p. 67.
20 Quoted in Stengers 7, pp. 19–20.
21 Duke of Brabant to Brialmont, 26 July 1863, in Le Febve de Vivy, p. 20.
22 RAB FG PSDB, Leopold I to Duke of Brabant, 15 June 1860.

Young Leopold was not impressed. He did not think the moral qualities of the king mattered much in a country that had itself originated in immorality. What mattered were nationalistic feelings. To create these, he even considered robbing the Sultan of more than just a set of pipes. He wrote in his diary that a military assault on the Ottoman capital should be considered, to dethrone the Sultan and annex his empire to Belgium. 'It would not be impossible with five or six thousand determined men and a couple of steamboats to take Constantinople by surprise and proclaim oneself Emperor of the East. In Brussels we must organise a regiment of freebooters to grab a part or even the whole of the Turkish Empire.'[23]

In 1862, the Duke of Brabant spent a whole month in Seville, researching in the *Archivo General de Indias*, the Spanish Colonial Archives, to collect evidence on the profitability of the Spanish colonies. Later that year, he crossed to Algeria and moved on to Egypt. He wanted to see the work being carried out on the Suez Canal. In the autumn of 1864, he dropped by Suez again, and travelled on to Aden, Ceylon, India, Burma, Singapore, Sumatra and China. Along the way, he studied colonisation and trading methods and he penned trunks full of notes on what he had seen. In China, he visited Canton and Hong Kong, and he would have moved on to Peking, when he was ordered to return home because of his father's deteriorating health. Before 1865 had ended, the old King had died and the Duke of Brabant had become the second King of the Belgians. It was now up to him, as he pointed out to Queen Victoria, 'to uphold the Coburg reputation.'[24]

A Little Kingdom...

A King of the Belgians does not succeed upon his father's death, but only after taking a solemn oath to uphold the Constitution. Leopold II swore the oath in a ceremony before Parliament on 17 December 1865. The very first problem a Belgian King has to deal with is the problem of money. At the start of each new reign, the government sets the *civil list*, the sum of money the new monarch will receive annually from the taxpayer to cover the expenses necessary to maintain his status. Leopold I had received 2.7 million francs. The government proposed to pay the new King a stipend of 3 million francs (£9 million or $15 million today). Leopold II, however, demanded 3.5 million. After some haggling, a compromise was reached. He got 3.3 million francs,

---

23 RAB FG Diary of the Duke of Brabant during his travel to Constantinople, 15 and 16 May 1860.
24 RAW Q1/148, Leopold II to Queen Victoria on 19 December 1865.

plus an additional 700,000 francs during the first year of his reign to buy new furniture. Like his brother and sister, Leopold had also inherited a private fortune from his father. He received 15 million francs and immediately invested 7 million francs in the Suez Canal Company.

The ministers soon discovered that Leopold was difficult to deal with. 'He listens attentively and seems very anxious to do his best,' Alphonse Vandenpeereboom, the Minister of the Interior, had noted approvingly after the first cabinet meeting. But within a couple of months that opinion changed radically: 'He is sly and devious, if not two-faced at times. He hides his thoughts and argues obliquely in order to expose the inner thoughts of anyone opposing his views.'[25] If anyone should have known what was awaiting him, however, then surely it was Vandenpeereboom, who had been a confidant of the old King. Leopold I had warned Vandenpeereboom about his son – a warning the minister had even recorded in his diary. 'Leopold is subtle and sly,' the old King had said. 'He never takes chances. The other day, when I was at Ardenne, I watched a fox which wanted to cross a stream unobserved: first of all he dipped a paw in carefully to see how deep it was, and then with a thousand precautions, very slowly made his way across. That is Leopold's way.'[26] It was an apt description, and if one considers how much Leopold I hated the fox, it also says much about the relationship between father and son.

Leopold II inherited a Kingdom dominated by a Francophone bourgeois establishment. The right to vote and to be elected was restricted to wealthy citizens who paid a certain level of taxes. Parliament consisted of two parties, the Liberals and the Catholics, but they represented only a small minority of the population; barely five per cent of the people were allowed to vote. Outside Parliament, there was growing pressure from two other political forces: Socialism and Flamingantism.

A *Flamingant* was a Dutch-speaking intellectual from Flanders. The word had been coined as a term of abuse by the Francophone establishment, but the 'Flamingants' had adopted it as a badge of honour. They were schoolteachers, civil servants of inferior rank or parish priests, and they were demanding recognition of the linguistic rights of the Dutch-speaking majority in Belgium. Since the anti-Orangist terror of the 1830s, no one openly dared to call himself an *Orangist* and advocate a reunification of Flanders with the Netherlands. The

25   Quoted in Garsou 2, vol. I, pp. 24 and 29–30.
26   Quoted in Garsou 2, vol. I, pp. 30–1.

Flamingants stressed that they would be loyal Belgians, if only Belgium would recognise their rights.

In Flanders, Flamingantism and socialism overlapped to some extent, but Flamingantism had a broader appeal than socialism. It was a movement for the emancipation of the Flemish middle classes as well as the lower classes. Antwerp was the largest city where the Flamingants controlled the town council. It is customary for a new Belgian king at the beginning of his reign to visit the capitals of the various provinces to make his so-called *Joyeuse Entrée*. Antwerp was denied a 'joyful entry,' because, as Prime Minister Rogier put it, 'the city threw mud at the monarchy.'

Leopold I, understanding that his artificial country needed an element of unification, had opted for Catholicism as the binding element. Leopold II realised that this would no longer do in a modern late 19th century state. Something else was needed, a concept that, though modern, was as irrational as religion in its appeal to the lower and the middle classes. The shrewd Leopold knew exactly what it was. If he wanted to keep Belgium together, he had to forge Belgian nationalism.

Some things, however, would always remain the same. The leading political élite, intelligent enough to realise that Belgium was an artificial construct, would have to be bought. The young King was prepared to buy the new political generation, just as his father had bought the revolutionaries of 1830. Leopold immediately put Walter Frère-Orban on his secret payroll. His father had suspected that the young Liberal politician was an Orangist; Leopold bought him with 20,000 francs (£60,000 or $100,000 in today's value). He knew well enough that the brilliant and ambitious men — those who like the Saxe-Coburgs never stopped asking the question 'What is there in it for me?' — only defended Belgium because it constituted their livelihood, their source of money, titles and honours. Riding the gravy train, they were Belgium's *superpatriots*. The eldest of them, the veterans of 1830, were still in their prime when Leopold II ascended to the throne in 1865. They were people like Charles Rogier, Pierre Chazal and Jules Van Praet, men who were twenty or thirty years old when they made the Belgian Revolution in 1830–31, and only in their early sixties after 35 years of continuous 'service' to the state. Leopold intended to keep them aboard for as long as possible, though circumstances forced him to dump Rogier when he needed a scapegoat at quite an early stage.

Van Praet remained in post as *chef de cabinet* to the King until shortly before his death in 1887. He was a most secretive man, who intentionally dated all his letters and memos incompletely. After his death, his papers, assembled during 55 years as head of the royal secretariat, were all missing. According to Colonel Stinglhamber, one of Leopold II's personal assistants, Van Praet burnt everything before his death. He had shaped the royal cabinet into one of the most powerful institutions in Belgium, as it has remained to this very day. Some ministers called it the 'Camarilla' or the 'Seventh Ministry' (Belgium had only six ministers at the time). Often the ministers were directly instructed by the Camarilla about the positions the King wanted them to take. If they did not comply, they were scolded by Van Praet like disobedient schoolboys. It was one of the prerogatives of the King to demand the resignation of the government and both Leopold I and his son threatened to do so on more than one occasion if the ministers did not follow the Camarilla's orders.

The last years of Leopold I's reign had been characterised by growing political tensions between the Liberals and the Catholics in Parliament. As a result, the governing Liberals had become more and more stridently anti-religious, keen on undermining the position of the Catholic Church in society. It was an age of extreme polarisation that continued during the first decades of Leopold II's reign. In 1879, the Liberal government closed down Catholic schools and banned religious education from the schools. Because of their overreaction, the Liberals lost the elections in 1884, whereupon the new Catholic government reversed policies and imposed Catholic teaching on all schools. The episode of the 'School War' is generally seen as the biggest political crisis of 19th century Belgian history. Leopold II did not like the polarisation between the two parliamentary parties, but he did not take this threat to the stability of Belgium as seriously as his father would have done.

Commenting on the crisis, Jules Devaux, Van Praet's nephew and deputy, pointed out the difference between politics in Belgium and politics in Britain. 'In England the political spirit dominates the party spirit,' he wrote. 'Here it is the party spirit that dominates the political spirit. There, a *Whig* or a *Tory* will make sacrifices in order to allow the governmental machinery to continue. Here, our men sacrifice that machinery to their party interests.'[27] It seemed to bother Devaux, but Leopold did not really mind. It is only natural that the common interest should be sacrificed to private interests in an artificial country, where nobody cares about the common interest because nobody cares about the state. The only way to buy people's loyalty to an artificial

27   Devaux to Beyens, 16 June 1879, in Garsou 4, p. 368.

construction is to allow them to sacrifice the common interest to their own interests. In an artificial country the state can count on the loyalty only of those who can use the state as a means to achieve their private interests. The Coburgs knew it well enough, and so did the veterans of 1830 and Belgium's smart classes.

* * *

Leopold II's main interest in politics, however, was not domestic affairs but foreign politics. Shortly after ascending the throne, he started to make plans for the 'reunification' of the Grand-Duchy of Luxemburg with Belgium. Willem III of Orange, King of the Netherlands as well as Grand-Duke of Luxemburg, was short of cash and had indicated that he might be prepared to sell Luxemburg. The Grand-Duchy, however, was a member of the German Confederation, and the military fortress at Luxemburg was manned by a Prussian garrison. Owing to his diplomatic inexperience Leopold became trapped in Franco-Prussian power politics. France objected to Belgium acquiring the Grand-Duchy because Napoleon III wanted to buy it himself. Leopold was confident that he was going to get Luxemburg, until Count Beust, the Austrian Chancellor, proposed to allow Belgium to have Luxemburg in return for Brussels' ceding the area to the south of Mons, Charleroi and Namur, to France. Frère-Orban, the Minister of Finance, immediately rejected this trade-off. Leopold did not dare to oppose Frère-Orban and abandoned the Luxemburg project. Prime Minister Rogier had to take the blame for the debacle, which ended his political career. Frère-Orban succeeded him.

1867 was also the year of a second political debacle: the collapse of the 'Mexican Empire' of Leopold's sister Charlotte and her husband, the Austrian Archduke Maximilian. In 1864 the French Emperor Napoleon III had installed Maximilian as the 'Emperor' of a French protectorate which one of Napoleon's generals had conquered in Mexico when he had driven the Mexican president Benito Juárez from the area surrounding Mexico City and the coastal town of Vera Cruz. Maximilian was pressured into the Mexican adventure from three sides. He was deceived by Napoleon with solemn promises that he would never be let down. He was gulled by opportunist Mexican opponents of Juárez into believing that the Mexican people genuinely adored him. And he was goaded by his ambitious wife who wanted to be 'a Coburg blessing' to her husband by raising him to imperial status. Hence, the Archduke accepted the Mexican crown and set out on a fatal course which caused him to go down in history as the *archdupe*.

Charlotte and Maximilian arrived at Vera Cruz on 28 May 1864. They were an odd couple. Shortly after her marriage in 1857, Charlotte found out that Max, who had so far led a life of wild parties in the Viennese brothels, had no intention of changing his habits. There may have been something wrong with Charlotte, though. According to Archduke Karl Ludwig, Max's younger brother, Charlotte was 'too narrow for intercourse. The marriage was never consumated.' After Max infected Charlotte with a venereal disease two years after their marriage, she refused to let him into her bed. At the Mexican imperial palace in Chapultepec, the Emperor and the Empress continued to sleep apart. Max took numerous mistresses, one of whom was the under-aged daughter of one of the imperial gardeners and gave she birth to a boy in 1866. The boy was called Juliano Sedano y Leguizano, but the French would later call him *'le bâtard impérial'* — the imperial bastard. They had reason to do so, for Sedano was executed in France in October 1917 as a German spy.

To the outside world, Charlotte and Max remained a doting couple, but the Mexicans did not adore them. Juárez began a successful guerrilla war against the French. Napoleon III soon found himself stuck in a political and military quagmire. As French losses increased, public opinion in Paris clamoured for the withdrawal of the French troops. Others were drawn into the quagmire, as well. The Belgian army had sent a force of 600 volunteers to Mexico in 1864. For many years, Leopold and Baron Chazal, the Belgian Minister of War, had harboured the dream of involving their country in a foreign war. The Belgian Parliament had always rejected these wild dreams, but this time, as the Mexican Empress was a Belgian, Parliament could not object. The Belgians, under the command of Colonel Alfred Van der Smissen, the son of the Flemish general who in 1841 had attempted to depose Charlotte's father, did little to improve Max's popularity with the Mexicans. Some Belgians fought bravely, but others — unfortunately those remembered most vividly by the Mexicans — perpetrated excessive cruelties against the civilians, murdering entire villages. Many of the Belgians never returned home from the Mexican adventure. They fell in battle, they deserted or they were taken prisoner. Those captured could not expect much clemency. Chazal, who had encouraged his son Ernest to volunteer for Mexico, never saw his son again.

For Leopold, however, there was a bright side to the Mexican disaster. As a result of the collapse of her 'empire' and the execution of her husband by Juárez, Charlotte suffered a mental breakdown and went insane. This brought her fortune back into the hands where according to Leopold it belonged: his own. He entrusted Goffinet with the administration of his sister's possessions and, although this was illegal, he used them for his own business dealings and highly speculative investments.

In 1870, a full-scale war erupted between France and Prussia. For some years, Berlin and Paris had been secretly discussing Belgium's future. Bismarck, the Prussian Chancellor, frequently hinted at the fact that he would not object to dividing Belgium between Prussia and France, and explicitly told the French that he was prepared to see France extending its boundaries 'wherever in the world the French language is spoken.'[28] France, however, considered the whole of Belgium (including Dutch-speaking Flanders) to be a lost province, which sooner or later it would have to absorb if it was to reassert its international prestige. Leopold I had understood this well enough. The first Belgian King steered a cautious course, intent on not offending the French. In June 1865, he even had Vandenpeereboom prohibit the Flemish celebrations of the 50th anniversary of the battle of Waterloo. His son did not share the distrust of France. Leopold II reckoned that by subordinating Belgium entirely to France, he could neutralise the French appetite for the annexation of Belgium, because Paris would consider Belgium to be far more useful on the international scene as a proxy than as a province.

He was wrong, however, in his judgment of Napoleon III. In July 1866, seven months after young Leopold had succeeded his father, Prussia defeated Austria at the battle of Sadowa and absorbed the whole of northern Germany. Napoleon urgently wanted to redress the balance of power vis-à-vis Prussia by annexing Belgium. The week after the battle, Bismarck and Count Vincent Benedetti, the French Ambassador in Berlin, discussed a French invasion of Belgium. Benedetti presented Bismarck with a draft treaty, stating that 'His Majesty the King of Prussia, in case H.M. the Emperor of the French should be led by circumstances to cause his troops to enter Belgium or to conquer it, shall grant armed aid to France and shall support her with all his forces military and naval in the face of, and against, every Power which should in this eventuality declare war.'[29] It was the first Franco-German proposal in history to form a continental European coalition against Britain. Bismarck replied that the only difficulty he foresaw was to convince his King (whose son had

28   Lefebvre de Behaine to Drouyn de Lhuys, the French Minister of Foreign Affairs, 27 Sept. 1865, in Les origines diplomatiques, vol. VII.
29   Article IV of the so-called Benedetti Treaty, in Lademacher, pp. 212–3.

recently married Queen Victoria's daughter) to act against England, and carefully hid the draft treaty in his desk.

In the spring of 1870, Bismarck and Napoleon quarrelled over the succession to the Spanish throne. Tensions deepened. France mobilised its troops on 15 July and declared war four days later. Bismarck reacted by sending Benedetti's 1866 draft treaty to *The Times*, which published the document on 25 July. London was outraged. If Belgium were to disappear, Gladstone, the British Prime Minister, said it would be 'the most odious crime that had ever sullied the pages of history.'[30] He made it clear that Britain would go to war if either France or Prussia dared to violate Belgian territory.

Leopold suddenly saw his livelihood endangered and panicked. The Belgians, however, did not care about the threat to their country. In Brussels, the politicians were busy quarrelling over domestic issues. Some MPs of Frère-Orban's Liberal majority defected to the Catholic opposition. The cabinet resigned and elections were called. With war threatening its borders and the future of the country itself in jeopardy, the Belgian elections, taking place in the middle of the worst international crisis in decades, produced a resounding victory for the anti-militarist wing of the Catholic Party and for the Flamingants of Antwerp's *Meeting Partij*.

To Leopold's disgust, in early August, Baron Jules d'Anethan formed an anti-militarist government, which included Victor Jacobs, a Flemish politician close to *Meeting*. The message to the international community was clear. The Belgians did not care one bit whether their country disappeared or not. If Gladstone did not want Belgium to disappear, fine, *let the English defend it*. The Belgians were not going to lift a finger themselves. On 17 July Leopold had promised Victoria that within a week he would mobilise 60,000 soldiers to guard his frontiers and 30,000 to defend Antwerp. But Leopold and Chazal — 'a German and a Frenchman' according to the Antwerpians — had enormous difficulty in mustering these troops. It emerged that many of those who had done their military service in the 1860s could not be traced. The army had not kept track of their addresses and the local authorities were either unable or unwilling to cooperate.

Luckily for Leopold and Chazal, Belgium did not become involved in the Franco-Prussian conflict. The Prussians defeated the French in a matter of weeks. Napoleon III surrendered, France installed its Third Republic, and the Prussian King Wilhelm I became the *Kaiser* of Germany. France also lost its German-speaking provinces of Alsace and

30   Quoted in Emerson, pp. 51–2.

Lorraine to Germany. Indeed, as Bismarck had said, he was all in favour of 'extending a nation's frontiers to wherever in the world its language is spoken.'

The Franco-German war made a deep impression on Leopold. He decided to put his army to rights. In theory the Belgian army numbered 105,000 men. But the men were chosen by ballot, and if an appointee did not want to fulfil his two-year service with the colours, he was allowed to find a substitute. This *remplacement* system was flawed. It meant that rich men always paid poor men to serve in their place. As a result, the Belgian army consisted mostly of Flemish proletarians of dubious quality — more often than not illiterates who did not understand the orders that were given to them in French.

Leopold wanted to introduce a system of general conscription, where no *remplacements* were allowed. He informed Anethan of his plan. The Prime Minister immediately rejected it. The wealthy classes preferred a system that allowed them to buy their way out of the army, and the anti-militarists believed that Belgium needed no army, because Britain guaranteed Belgium's independence. Angrily, Leopold used his royal prerogative to force the government to resign. This he could do without calling new elections if he appointed another Prime Minister from within the Catholic parliamentary majority. He told Anethan and his anti-militarist cabinet to step down and had him replaced by the Catholic Jules Malou, a Governor of Leopold's *Société Générale* holding. Malou tried his utmost to introduce general conscription, but failed to convince Parliament of the need for conscription reform and additional military spending. A frustrated Leopold even asked the Pope to pressure the Belgian Catholics into accepting personal conscription. All to no avail.

When in 1875 French politicians offered Germany the renunciation of all French claims to the Alsace province in exchange for the annexation of Belgium, the Belgian public opinion reacted with complete indifference. 'The patriotism of 1830 has vanished,' the King observed in despair.[31] He drew a radical conclusion: such a complacent country did not deserve him. He shifted all his attention to a private business enterprise: acquiring an empire of his own. Not a colony of Belgium, but an exclusively personal one. From then on, he would devote his life exclusively to this goal.

31   Garsou and Stinglhamber, p. 202.

... And A Big Empire

In the fourth year of Leopold's reign, a personal tragedy befell the King. His son and heir, little Leopold, the Count of Hainaut, fell into a pond at Laken. The boy caught pneumonia and died, barely nine years old, on 22 January 1869. A few months later, after years of devoting his sexual attention to various other women, the King returned to the Queen's bed. Marie-Henriette gave birth to a fourth child in July 1872. Unfortunately, it was a third daughter, Clementine. Leopold was furious, but resigned to the fact that his successor would be the eldest son of his brother Philippe, the Count of Flanders. That boy had been born on 3 June 1869 and was called Baudouin, the French equivalent of *Boudewijn* (Baldwin), the name of nine medieval Counts of Flanders.

For the rest of his life, the King harboured a grudge against his wife and daughters. In a letter to Adrien Goffinet, which she asked him to burn, Marie-Henriette lamented Leopold's attitude. 'What can we do against the will of God!! One has to turn against Him, but not against children who cannot be blamed for the tragedy that happened, or against a wife, who would give her life (even if she cared about it, because in the current situation it would not be much of a sacrifice) to bring back that beloved son!'[32]

Marie-Henriette withdrew, even more than before, into a world of her own. Her plump figure had gone. The former Habsburg tomboy became a thin, sad woman. She no longer participated in official ceremonies and spent most of her time away from Brussels, at a house she had bought in Spa, a health resort in the Ardennes. She devoted her time to the breeding of horses and dogs. According to Prince Baudouin, the Queen smelled of her animals. She was constantly surrounded by a number of dogs, which she even allowed into her bed. The animals were a threat to visitors. Once Baroness Anethan was bitten by one of the Queen's dogs. 'Mummy, your dog is biting the Baroness!' Princess Clementine yelled, but Marie-Henriette behaved as if she did not notice the blood that showed on Lady Anethan's gown.

When she was in Brussels, Marie-Henriette spent many evenings at the opera. Leopold never accompanied her, but she often invited Pierre Chazal, the Minister of War. She adored the old General. He was as fond of horses, dogs and exotic animals as she was. Chazal owned a park with zebras, and in his living room he kept a monkey, which bit him once. It made him very ill and he nearly died. The General also used to take the Queen along to military manoeuvres, where

32   RAB FG Adrien Goffinet Papers, Marie-Henriette to Goffinet, 29 Aug. 1876.

— an excellent rider — she joined cavalry charges. In the old man's company, Marie-Henriette relaxed and behaved in an almost flirtatious manner. After Chazal retired to his native South of France in 1871, the Queen struck up an intimate friendship with the young royal veterinarian Henri Hardy. When she was ill, she preferred to be treated by the veterinarian rather than by a doctor. 'Treat me as if I were a horse,' she would ask.[33]

* * *

Leopold was greatly affected by the death of his son. Many Belgian biographies of the King suggest that Leopold's tenacity in building himself a colonial empire may be explained in terms of the King immersing himself in work after losing his heir. This view was put forward by Edmond Carton de Wiart, who succeeded Van Praet as chef of the royal cabinet. It is, however, false. Leopold had always been a workaholic and his colonial obsession dated from long before the death of the little prince in 1869. Barbara Emerson, Leopold's British biographer, accepts the argument that the King's colonial 'obsession' was caused by the death of his only son. It offers a nice psycho-analytical explanation. 'He had failed to provide his country with a son; instead he would bequeath Belgium a colony,' she says.[34] In reality, Leopold's aim had become to establish his *personal* colony, his own 'Sarawak.'

It would have to be an independent state, run as a business venture by privately-owned companies he controlled. Leopold was a thoroughly modern 19th century capitalist. He was also a precursor of a time yet to come: the age of the 20th century totalitarians. In his state, he wanted to be the supreme authority: no laws would be higher than his commands. Baron Lambermont, who had been given a top position at the Ministry of Foreign Affairs, had reliable Belgian diplomats scour the globe for *a Sarawak*. These diplomats had to be discreet, because the Belgian government was not allowed to know. Fortunately, the King could use his prerogatives to ensure that the key diplomatic positions were assigned to those diplomats whom he considered more loyal to his person than to the government. They were all rewarded by Leopold in the usual way, with a hereditary title of Baron: Beyens in Paris, Solvyns in London, Greindl in Madrid, ...

Unable to acquire colonies already owned by others, Leopold decided to go where no one else had been before. He became

33   Duchesne, Albert. 'Henri Hardy, vétérinaire en chef de l'armée et des écuries royales.' *Revue Belge d'Histoire Militaire*, 1988.
34   Emerson, p. 57.

intrigued by the vast blank on the map of Africa, the as yet unexplored central part of the continent, the basins of the rivers Congo and Lualaba. At that time no one knew exactly whether the latter connected to the upper reaches of the Congo or the Nile. This will be 'our share of the magnificent African cake,' Leopold said.[35] His competitors were European nations with vast resources, such as France, Britain and Portugal. Leopold was virtually a freelance, self-employed business maverick, albeit one who could draw on his royal status. He had three advantages. One, he could act more swiftly than nations. Two, the colonial nations did not regard him as a threat to their own interests. Three, he knew how to manipulate international public opinion.

Leopold attached great importance to propaganda. His father had already grasped the importance of the press as a political tool when he had secretly founded and funded his own newspapers. Leopold II set up an entire propaganda staff to influence papers both in Belgium and abroad. He also bribed various journalists to such an extent that Goffinet warned his master to hide all the accounts of the Civil List carefully so that they would never 'fall into the hands of the enemy or of revolutionaries, thereby revealing that you subsidized newspapers and paid pensions to journalists.'[36]

His target was not only Belgian but worldwide public opinion. He succeeded in the remarkable achievement of building himself a personal empire through the first disinformation campaign ever conducted on a supranational scale. He disguised his private colonial enterprise as an international Non-Governmental Organisation with a philanthropic, humanitarian goal — almost like a 19th-century Greenpeace or Médecins sans Frontières. Once he had phrased his objectives this way, he had public opinion on his side and for two decades could commit massive fraud, even atrocities, without anyone daring to question him.

In 1875, the Scottish explorer Verney Lovett Cameron crossed the southern end of the Lualaba basin and the Katanga region, which he annexed in Queen Victoria's name. To his frustration the British government did not want the territories. Cameron pointed out that the land was rich in crops and minerals, but London decided it already had enough problems to deal with in Egypt and in South Africa. In an article in *The Times* of January 1876 in which Cameron described the richness of Lualaba land and Katanga, he also mentioned the horrors

35   RAB FC 100/1, Leopold II to Solvyns, 17 Nov. 1877.
36   RAB FG, Adrien Goffinet to Leopold II, 22 Oct. 1870.

of the slave trade. The Lualaba basin supplied Arabia with most of its black slaves. Leopold read the article and had a flash of inspiration. He would tell the world that he was going to Central Africa *to abolish the slave trade!*

He organised a prestigious international geographic conference on Africa in Brussels in September 1876, inviting renowned explorers and scientists. All the participants' costs were paid and the King insisted that they be lodged in the glamorous surroundings of the royal palace. In the opening speech, he stressed that he was 'in no way motivated by selfish designs. No, Gentlemen,' he said, referring to Belgium and its well-known lack of interest in colonial expansion, 'Belgium may be a small country, but she is happy and contented with her lot.'[37] Since no one suspected that he was harbouring the crazy idea of establishing a personal colony, the delegates abundantly praised his philanthropy. The conference decided to establish an international organisation, the *Association Internationale Africaine* (AIA). It would build medical and scientific stations in the Congo and Lualaba basin, from which to explore the region and fight the slave-raiders. The conference was a huge public relations success. Leopold was recognized as the international leader of the crusade to fight slavery and bring civilisation to Africa. If the Nobel Peace Prize had existed in 1877, he would probably have won it.

The King soon found the man needed to establish his stations. The British-American explorer Henry Morton Stanley suddenly showed up at Boma, at the mouth of the Congo River on Africa's Atlantic Coast, on 17 September 1877, exactly 999 days after he had left from the Indian Ocean. Like Cameron, he had crossed the African continent from East to West, but Stanley had followed the whole course of the Lualaba, from its upper reaches to its very end, thereby proving that the Lualaba was the same river as the mighty Congo, *creeping through the black; cutting through the jungle with a golden track.*[38]

On his way home from Africa to London, in January 1878, Stanley arrived at Marseille and found two emissaries of Leopold awaiting him: Baron Jules Greindl and General Henry S. Sanford, a former American ambassador to Belgium who had become one of Leopold's business associates. They asked the explorer to come and work for the AIA. Stanley declined the offer. He wanted Britain to annex the Congo basin. His experience, however, was the same as Cameron's three years earlier: Britain was not interested. Leopold approached

37   Quoted in Banning 1, pp. 123–4.
38   N. Vachel Lindsay, *The Congo*, 1.

Stanley again in May, when the latter, frustrated with the British government, travelled to Brussels to meet the King. Leopold offered the explorer a five-year contract for the establishment along the Congo of permanent stations for philanthropic, scientific, but also commercial ends. The AIA, the King explained, had to make some profit to finance its activities. Because his employer was a non-governmental organisation, Stanley did not consider working for the AIA to be an impediment to the British annexation of the Congo basin at a later stage, and accepted.

To finance Stanley's expedition, Leopold formed the *Comité d'Etudes du Haut Congo*, a commercial enterprise with a capital of 1,000,000 francs. Leopold was the biggest subscriber with 265,000 francs, but there were also Dutch, American, British and other businessmen involved. In December, Stanley signed his contract with the *Comité* and departed to Africa. Having arrived at the Congo, he started building one station after another. When he finished one, he flew the blue flag with the golden star of the AIA over it, and moved further upstream to establish the next station. In November 1879, when it was clear that everything was working out as planned, Leopold dissolved the *Comité d'Etudes*. He paid the other shareholders back their investments plus a huge profit and became the sole owner of the stations. He wanted to have the Congo exclusively to himself. This meant, however, that he had to provide the capital needed for further stations out of his own (and his sister Charlotte's) private pocket. It was a great strain on his budget. The King was forced to sell many of his possessions and even had to take desperate measures such as mortgaging the livery of his servants and cutting the number of courses served at mealtimes in the royal palace.

Leopold was prepared to invest his entire fortune, which at the end of the 1870s amounted to about 50 million francs (£150 million or $250 million today), in Stanley's work. The explorer was deliberately kept ignorant of the fact that he was now working solely for the King. He was not informed of the demise of his formal employer, the international *Comité d'Etudes*. As late as 1882, Stanley received a letter from Leopold in which the King lied blatantly: 'It is indispensable that you should purchase for the Comité d'Etudes as much land as you can obtain, and that you should successively place under the sovereignty of that Comité, as soon as possible and without losing a minute, all the chiefs from the mouth of the Congo to Stanley Falls.'[39]

39   Leopold II to Stanley, 31 Dec. 1881, in Hird, p.183.

Meanwhile, Leopold had set up a new organisation, the *Association Internationale du Congo* (AIC), completely financed and controlled by the King alone. The name of the new institution closely resembled that of the *Association Internationale Africaine* (AIA), the anti-slavery organisation established at the Brussels conference six years earlier. This was done deliberately to confuse public opinion. 'Care must be taken not to let it be obvious that the Association du Congo and the Association Africaine are two different things,' the King told his collaborators.[40] The AIC also flew the same flag as the AIA, blue with one golden star. Instead of combating slavery, however, the AIC's purpose was to establish sovereign territorial rights in the Congo.

Leopold wanted his stations to form an autonomous state, but he needed international recognition. The philanthropist argument, however, sold extremely well in America. Sanford, Leopold's American lobbyist, approached various politicians, including Secretary of State Frederick Frelinghuysen and President Chester A. Arthur, and put forward the King's plans to transform his stations into 'independent States' (the plural was used on purpose vis-à-vis the U.S.), where the natives would be protected from slave hunters. The confusion between the AIA and the AIC proved very helpful in tricking Washington into recognising the King's personal AIC scheme as if it were the defunct philanthropist AIA. In a message to the US Congress on 4 December 1883, President Arthur referred to the AIC as the 'AIA' and gave it credit for establishing 'embryo states' around the stations, especially in view of the fact that 'it does not aim at permanent political control.' On 25 February, Congress recommended recognition of the 'AIC' flag (a correct reference this time) as that of the 'Congo Free States' (mark the plural). On 10 April 1884 the United States became the first nation to recognise 'the flag of the AIA' (wrong reference) as 'the flag of a friendly government.' The AIA, however, had long ceased to exist. It was the AIC flag that the Americans recognised, but, clearly, Washington did not know what it had recognised.

France, surprisingly, was the second nation to recognise Leopold's Congo State. Leopold knew that Paris wanted to have the Congo basin for itself. He also knew that London objected to this. On 23 April 1884, he made an astonishing offer to Jules Ferry, the French Prime Minister. If France recognised the AIC's claim to the Congo, Leopold in turn would offer France the right of pre-emption, meaning that if in the future Leopold should ever decide to get rid of the Congo, France would have the first option of buying it from him. The French imme-

40   Leopold II to Maximilien Strauch, 8 Jan. 1884, in Stanley, p. 21.

diately accepted the offer. They were convinced that Leopold would never be able to finance the huge operations involved in running a State out of his own pocket and that he would soon be obliged to sell all or at least substantial parts of the AIC shares. Leopold let them nurture this fallacy. The shrewd King now had France in his pocket, and Britain too. He could threaten that, if London refused to help him raise money to finance his Congo project, he would be obliged to sell his colony to France.

Convincing Germany to recognise the new state was more difficult. Leopold approached Bismarck with his usual philanthropic arguments, but that did not work with the perceptive German. *'Schwindel,'* Bismarck noted alongside the paragraph in Leopold's letter dealing with the repression of the slave trade. Leopold sensed that he would have to pay Bismarck a price and offered Germany free trading rights within the territories under AIC control. For Leopold this had the additional benefit that it now was in Germany's interest that the AIC territories extend as far as possible so as to reduce the French and British spheres of influence in Africa. In a letter to Bismarck, he revealed his wish to extend his state to the Nile basin. This was language to Bismarck's liking. 'It is not for us,' Bismarck told the French Ambassador to Berlin, 'to bridle these ambitions, seeing that the Company guarantees our trading freedom and that the benefit to us from application of this principle increases with the size of the Company's operations.'[41] On 8 November 1884, the German Empire formally recognised the AIC. Bismarck went even further. He convened an international conference in Berlin to settle the independent status of Leopold's state. The conference, attended by representatives of ten European nations plus Turkey, Russia and the United States, started on 15 November. It led to the international recognition of Leopold's State, now officially referred to as the Congo Free State (CFS).

When the Berlin conference ended in February 1885, Leopold was the internationally recognised ruler of the largest colony in Central-Africa: a state of 1 million square miles, 76 times larger than Belgium, five times as big as France, one-third the size of the continental USA, and up to 20 million inhabitants. In addition, he was an absolute ruler who could do what he liked in his country. He was literally its proprietor. One of the first decrees of the new state stipulated that all the land not under cultivation by the natives belonged by right to the state. The state being Leopold in person, it made him the largest private landowner in the world; possibly even in modern history. The

41   AQO Correspondance politique Allemagne 58, 30 Aug. 1884.

Belgian government kept a deliberate distance from Leopold's African project. The only positive remark Prime Minister Jules Malou made about the whole business was that he assumed it to be 'not a bad thing that a king like ours should have a favourite hobby to drain off his surplus energy.'[42]

The Coburg Reputation

Leopold was an extremely energetic man. 'Time is money,' he used to say in English, as he switched from one activity to another. Apart from politics, money and sex, he was passionate about one thing only: like his father and grandfather, he was a fervent botanist. At Laken, he had immense hothouses built, the largest one 25 metres high, to contain precious exotic plants, flowers and trees.

Leopold was a callous and vengeful man. He demanded unconditional assent from everyone. 'He accepts no criticism and demands absolute obedience to his orders. He even goes so far as to impose his own conscience on others,' Albert Thys, one of Leopold's closest Congo aides, wrote to a friend.[43] To make his point perfectly clear, Leopold always took revenge. Baron Chazal, the long-time Minister of War, had dared to oppose the King over a minor defence issue. When Chazal retired and returned to live in France, he discovered that he was not receiving his Belgian pension (an annuity of 12,000 francs). The King himself had stopped it.

Leopold's daughters also had much reason for complaint. In 1875, the 16-year-old Louise was married off to 31-year-old Philip of Saxe-Coburg-Kohary, a prince who was renowned in Vienna for the sexual orgies he organised at his palace. The fat and ugly Philip was a paternal as well as a maternal cousin. His grandfather, Ferdinand, was an elder brother of Leopold I, and his mother, Clementine of Orléans, a younger sister of Leopold II's mother. Louise was a virgin when Philip married her. During their wedding night at Laken, she became scared, ran away from the connubial bed and fled into the royal hothouses. Marie-Henriette had to bring her back to her husband.

After returning to Vienna, Philip enticed Louise with alcohol, showed her erotic pictures from the Far East, 'which no girl can watch without blushing,' and gave her 'Dionysian lessons.'[44] She must have taken a liking to it, because she turned nymphomaniac, hopping from

42 Quoted in Daye, p. 203.
43 RMCA Thys Papers, Thys to Cito, 26 June 1904.
44 Louise, Princess, p. 80.

one man's bed into another and causing great scandal. Philip did not mind as long as she returned to him after her adventures. She had two children, Leopold and Dorothea, which, one supposes, were his as well. She even flirted with her husband's little brother Ferdinand, two years younger than her, whose hobby was to perform Satanist rituals and who in 1887 became the first Saxe-Coburg King of Bulgaria, and with Archduke Rudolf, the son and heir of Emperor Franz Joseph of Austria. In her autobiography Louise claims it was her idea to marry her sister Stephanie to the Austrian Crown Prince.

Archduke Rudolf, perhaps hoping for a bride as wild as Louise, travelled to Brussels in 1880, accompanied by the actress Fanny Winkler, one of his mistresses, and proposed to the 16-year-old Stephanie. 'You get exactly one day to answer the Archduke's proposal,' Leopold II told his daughter, making it clear that he expected a *yes*. Stephanie gave the answer that was expected of her and was married to Rudolf in May 1881. Stephanie's life at Vienna was made into a living hell, especially by her mother-in-law, the Austrian Empress Elisabeth. The Empress was an astonishingly beautiful woman, but she behaved towards her son's bride almost as the envious stepmother towards Snow White. This envy was all the more peculiar because poor Stephanie was rather plain. 'Stupid cow, insignificant goose, tiresome lout' were some of the insults the Empress shouted at her daughter-in-law. Stephanie did not resemble her sister and led a quiet life at the *Hofburg*, the imperial palace. She gave birth to a daughter Elisabeth ('*Erszi*') in 1883. Unfortunately, *Erszi*, as all women, was barred from succeeding to the Austrian throne. Hence, when Rudolf in 1884 infected his wife with a venereal disease that made her infertile, Stephanie lost all significance for the hypocritical Habsburgs. She would never be mother to a future Emperor. By the time she turned 21, in 1885, her bright future seemed to be over.

In 1885, the year in which Leopold became King-Sovereign of the CFS, he was discredited for the first time in the international press. It had nothing to do with politics, but with a topic that was to gain Belgium worldwide notoriety one century later: paedophilia.

Leopold was as energetic in his sex life as in politics, and his sexual exploits were almost as remarkable as his colonial achievements. He was a frequent visitor of Parisian nightclubs, where expensive prostitutes with pseudo-aristocratic names rendered their carnal services. Three of these ladies, La Belle Otéro, Liane de Pougy and Emilienne d'Alençon, were known as the 'Grand Three' or the '*Grandes Horizontales*' and were considered to be the top of the bill. Leopold was particularly fond of Alençon. The King also had mistresses in

Nice and the other fashionable resorts of his time, and, of course, in Brussels, where one of his girlfriends, Marguerite d'Estève, who kept a 'salon' at the Avenue Louise, was known as 'Margot, the Queen of the Congo.'

The allegation that Leopold was a paedophile was made in a London courtroom. A former servant of a 'disorderly house' owned by one Mrs. Mary Jeffries testified that the Belgian King paid £800 a month for a steady supply of young virgins, ten to fifteen years old, to be shipped to Brussels.[45] Further allegations were made by William Stead, the editor of *The Pall Mall Gazette*, in a series about child abuse.[46] It was said that a hundred girls were sold each year to the King. Stead possessed a letter that had erroneously been delivered to a Miss Mary Jeffries of Chelsea, but was in fact addressed to her namesake, Mrs. Mary Jeffries, the brothel-keeper. In the letter, an Italian asked for the delivery of 'a lively young girl of sixteen years, nice complexion, with pretty throat.' As his reference the author named King Leopold. The allegations were never conclusively proven, apart from the confession by Mrs. Jeffries of the delivery of a young girl to the Belgian royal yacht *Alberta* when it was moored in the Thames during one of Leopold's visits to London. Leopold remained undisturbed by the affair. The Belgian press devoted hardly any attention to it.

* * *

Money had now become Leopold's most urgent problem. Between 1879 and 1885, he had already spent 10.5 million francs on his colony. He knew that if he wanted his CFS to bring in revenue, he would have to invest many millions more. The country urgently needed a railroad. The banks considered the King's one-man colony a huge financial risk and refused to lend him money. Once again, Leopold was lucky in his collaborators. The King's equerry, Captain Albert Thys, proved to be a clever young man with a salesman's talent. Against all odds, he collected 8 million francs from Belgian, British, German and American investors. Leopold was also aided by the new Belgian Prime Minister. In 1884, he dismissed Frère-Orban's cabinet and replaced the latter as Prime Minister with August Beernaert, a 55-year-old lawyer. The aim of Leopold's 'coup d'état of 1884,' as some historians have called it, was to install a government in Brussels that was more supportive of his Congo plans. Beernaert had been a Belgian member of the philanthropist AIA in 1876–77. He was a Cath-

45   *The Pall Mall Gazette*, 10 Apr. and 11 Apr. 1885.
46   *The Pall Mall Gazette*, 6–10 July 1885.

olic idealist who genuinely believed in bringing civilisation to the world (he received the Nobel Peace Price in 1909) and he wanted to help the King in his endeavour to 'ban slavery from the Congo basin.'

Moreover, Leopold put political pressure on the gullible man. In March 1886, he threatened to abdicate if the government did not help him in his financial predicament. Beernaert feared that the King's abdication would lead to the collapse of the unstable Belgian state. Leopold's threat came at a time when Wallonia was hit by severe strikes and violent protest demonstrations of workers singing the *Marseillaise*. The government called in the army to restore order. Meanwhile, the King kept repeating his threat. 'I have told Beernaert that if I get no help, I will resign,' he told Goffinet. 'I will abandon the party. The country is lost. Let them find someone else!'[47] Aware that the very existence of the artificial Belgian state depended on a King who happened to be a close relative of the Queen of Britain, the government granted Leopold a loan of 10 million francs from the Belgian Treasury.

Thanks to Thys and Beernaert, the King could establish a company to build the Matadi-Leopoldville railroad. It was registered as a Congolese company. This implied that any legal dispute had to be settled according to CFS law. Congolese law was written and promulgated by Leopold, who was accountable to no one, and he could change the law at will. In his colony, Leopold's power was absolute; he was the supreme legislative, executive and judicial authority. An embryonic CFS government, which took its orders directly from the King-Sovereign, consisted of three Secretary-Generals — one for Foreign Affairs and Justice, one for Finance, and one for the Interior. They resided in a building at the Brussels *Brederode Straat*, immediately behind the royal palace. Their representative in the Congo itself was the Governor-General, who was based in Boma at the mouth of the Congo River.

By 1889, there were 430 Europeans in the Congo. Most of them were adventurers working as mercenaries for the state. There was also a large group of Protestant missionaries, belonging to organisations such as the *Congo Balolo Mission* and the *American Baptist Mission Union*. These young idealists had been lured by Leopold's alleged philanthropy. They believed that the CFS under his totalitarian rule was about to become a modern-day Utopia. They went to the Congo to help establish this paradise: a heaven for the natives as well as for all American Blacks who wanted to return to the continent of their ancestors.

---

47   RAB FG Adrien Goffinet Papers, handwritten report by Adrien Goffinet, 2 Dec. 1886.

In 1889 Leopold's Congolese expenses amounted to 3 million francs, ten times as much as his receipts. Congolese exports, mainly ivory, amounted to 2 million francs a year, but Leopold received only 300,000 francs of these. The Berlin Conference had stipulated that the CFS was a free trade zone. Companies, beyond Leopold's control, traded heavily in the Congo. The biggest traders were the Dutch. Leopold regarded them as parasites living off *his* Congo. Other parasites were the Arab dealers in the Eastern provinces, who made a fortune, not only on slaves but on ivory as well. Leopold decided to snatch this income away, from the Dutch as well as the Arabs. He played his philanthropy trick again and announced that it was his intention to eradicate the Arab slave traders. He added that, unfortunately, he did not have the money to launch a military campaign against the slavers. Hence, he proposed an exemption to the Berlin Treaty and asked to be granted the right to collect import taxes and to establish toll barriers in the Congo basin. Leopold had Beernaert organise an international Anti-Slavery Conference in Brussels to revise the Treaty. The King managed to enlist Britain's support. 'The bastion of the slave-trade is, alas, in the Congo State and import duties are needed by the State to combat it,' he wrote to Victoria.[48] He had Stanley initiate a press campaign advocating his humanitarian case and he launched an attack, both in the media and in diplomatic circles, on the 'caprices' of the Dutch, who wanted to thwart his philanthropist initiative out of capitalist greed. An international agreement was reached in February 1891; the shrewd Belgian fox obtained everything he wanted.

Once the international community had abandoned its fundamental principle that the CFS was a free trade zone, Leopold grabbed everything. In September 1891 he issued a CFS decree that gave the state — hence, Leopold himself — a monopoly in the trade of both ivory and rubber. The decree forbade everyone, including the natives, to hunt elephants or harvest wild rubber unless the entire harvest was handed over to the state. Anyone buying these products would be considered guilty of receiving stolen goods. All trade in these products was forbidden except when carried out by state agents. In one stroke, Leopold unilaterally confiscated all the ivory and rubber in the Congo. He had now become not only the biggest real estate owner in the world, but also the biggest ivory and rubber baron.

Though Leopold's methods later became common practice in totalitarian communist states, for a state to confiscate a country's entire capital in resources was unheard of in 1891. The honest men amongst the King's collaborators protested against the decree. The Governor-General at Boma, Camille Janssen, resigned. He was replaced by Edmond Van Eetvelde (later a Baron). Another critic was Emile Banning, one of Leopold's closest collaborators for almost thirty years. 'The doctrine of state ownership,' Banning wrote, 'should not be allowed to prevail, either against the natural rights of the indigenous population, which it would in effect dispossess, nor against the rights of the Powers as laid down in the Berlin Act.'[49] Furious, Leopold fired Banning from royal service. As Leopold owed Banning very much, his dismissal made a big impression. 'The King treats men as we use lemons,' Beernaert remarked. 'When he has squeezed them dry he throws away the peel.'[50]

Beernaert, too, disapproved of the CFS decree. He threatened to resign as Belgian Prime Minister if the King did not modify it. By way of compromise, Leopold divided the CFS into three parts, of which only one, the *Domaine de la Couronne*, was to be exclusively exploited by the state. The two other regions would in principle remain open to commercial companies. Leopold could not dismiss Beernaert, because in 1891 the latter was doing his best to obtain a new loan for the King from the Belgian Treasury. The year before, Leopold had asked the Belgian Parliament for an interest-free loan of 25 million francs. In return, he had promised to publish a Will stipulating that his colony would become Belgian after his death. Legally, he was in no position to make such a promise, since in 1884 he had signed an agreement with France that gave Paris the first option of acquiring the Congo if he (or his natural heirs) ever renounced it. But Leopold had never cared much about honouring contracts and promises.

Beernaert persuaded Parliament to grant Leopold his loan. The conditions were that the King either pay back a total sum of 25 million francs after ten years, or, in the event that he could not do so, allow Belgium to annex the CFS. Meanwhile, he was not allowed to contract any new debt with third parties without the consent of the Belgian Parliament and was obliged to keep the Belgian government fully informed of the state of the Congo finances. Leopold promised to respect these conditions and pocketed the money on 3 July 1891. Only then did he sign the Will, which he back-dated to 'August 2, 1889,' to give the impression that he had bequeathed Belgium his colony long before it had granted him the loan. One year earlier, he had confided to Thys that he would only 'sign the Will when the loan is signed: the Will will be ante-dated.' The King did not inform Belgium about the state of the Congo finances. Strangely enough, the Belgian government never asked about it.

Leopold, however, did not forget that the Prime Minister had obstructed him in his attempt to claim a trading monopoly in the whole of the CFS. He took his revenge three years later, when the politician had lost his value. Leopold was far too shrewd for Beernaert. The latter's obstruction over the trading monopoly for the whole of the CFS did not really make a difference, because within weeks of establishing so-called 'free trade zones' within the CFS, Leopold granted exclusive exploitation concessions for entire provinces to a number of private companies. These were companies under Congolese law, and they were controlled by Leopold, who as a rule owned 50% of the shares. The most important one was the Anglo-Belgian India Rubber Company (ABIR), nominally run by an Englishman, Colonel John Thomas North.

The companies were given long-term concessions for the economic exploitation of specific areas. They received permission to administer the area in which they operated on their own terms. They could make their own laws, were allowed to levy their own taxes and had their own police force. They transformed their zones into gigantic concentration camps, where human rights violations were rampant and a man's life counted for naught. The only thing that counted was the revenue of the Pharaoh.

Red Rubber, Green Gulag

With his Belgian loan, Leopold financed an expedition by the CFS army, the *Force Publique*. It was composed of natives forcibly enlisted by white agents. Since many of the officers were Belgians, Leopold's modern-day crusade was also an ideal opportunity for fostering Belgian nationalism. The ruthless Belgian mercenaries were depicted as valiant national heroes for generations to come. Belgium even acquired two national martyrs, when Lieutenant Joseph Lippens and Sergeant Henri De Bruyne were captured by the Arabs and murdered. The commander of the army, the hard-headed Captain Francis Dhanis, had refused to negotiate for the release of the two officers. 'If any of you has the misfortune to be taken prisoner by the enemy,' he had warned his men, 'I shall regard him as dead.'[51] Aided by superior weaponry and auxiliary troops consisting of cannibals, Dhanis

51   Quoted in Slade, p. 110.

crushed the Arabs in 1892–93. Dhanis' victories were somewhat discredited by his troops, who 'after each combat rushed to eat the slain.'[52] Such lurid details, however, were omitted from the glorifying reports in the Belgian press. Dhanis went on to become a Baron.

The King then cast his eye on the Sudan. After the Mahdist rising in the 1880s the Anglo-Egyptian troops had evacuated the upper reaches of the Nile. Leopold decided to take advantage of the vacuum and have the CFS annex the Sudan as a first step towards driving the British from Egypt altogether. To the Belgian Prime Minister, Leopold confided that he found nothing more exciting than 'the glory of being a real pharaoh.'[53] 'Egypt,' he told CFS Governor-General Van Eetvelde, 'is my glory: its occupation has been my objective for years. Rather than renounce I will resort to violence.'[54]

Leopold financed many *Force Publique* expeditions to the Nile. The first one, in 1887–1888, was led by Stanley. Its purpose was to convince a German doctor-turned-warlord, Eduard Carl Schnitzer, known in the Nile valley as Emin Pasha, to work for Leopold and become CFS Governor of the Southern Sudan. Stanley reached the Pasha after a gruelling march through the Ituri rain forest which took months and during which most of Stanley's men died. The Pasha was not interested in Leopold's offer. Leopold was not discouraged. When Stanley returned to Brussels, Leopold proposed to him 'the taking of Khartoum.'[55] The explorer politely declined and ran for London. Subsequently Leopold sent a Belgian, Captain Guillaume Van Kerckhoven. He was an aggressive commander, who rewarded his men per human head they brought him. On his way from the Congo River to the Sudan, Van Kerckhoven terrorised the natives to such a degree that they all fled, depopulating the whole area for two years. Then his army plunged itself into the experience of the Ituri rain forest, where Van Kerckhoven was killed by one of his own soldiers. In 1891, another Belgian, Lieutenant Charles de la Kethulle, succeeded in building a number of CFS stations on the upper reaches of the Nile. During the next years Leopold sent new expeditions deep into the Sudan.

He soon extorted another loan from the Belgian government. In 1894, Beernaert had been succeeded by the stupid Jules de Burlet. The King confessed to Burlet that, although Belgium had lent him 25 mil-

52   Slade, p. 110.
53   Quoted in Daye, p. 413.
54   Quoted in Collins, p. 157.
55   RMCA Stanley Papers, Autographical Journal of Henry Morton Stanley, vol. 3, in Hird, p. 276.

lion francs in 1891 on the condition that the King should not contract any new debts without the consent of the Belgian Parliament, circumstances had forced him to borrow an additional 5 million francs in November 1892. This sum, he said, he had borrowed at 6% over a three-year period from the Antwerp banker Alexandre Browne de Tiège on the security of 40 million acres of land in the Congo. The land would be forfeited if the loan was not repaid by the end of June 1895. Leopold asked Burlet for 6.5 million francs to be able to repay the banker and keep 'Belgium's future colony' intact. Meanwhile, France had heard (perhaps through the sly Leopold himself) of the plan to bequeath the Congo to Belgium. In May 1895, the French Secretary for African Affairs, Gabriel Hanotaux, protested in Brussels, invoking the French pre-emption right to the colony. Burlet firmly replied that Belgium had a better claim to the Congo, because of the huge financial liabilities of the latter to the former; and, to prove his point, paid back Leopold's Browne de Tiège loan. In reality, however, the loan was a hoax. The Antwerp banker was a middleman acting on Leopold's behalf. The 5 million francs he had lent to Leopold were Leopold's own. The King had simply transferred the money from his Belgian private accounts to his Congo Treasury; and he had cleverly used the transfer as a device to extract new funds from the Belgian taxpayers — funds he cashed and never repaid to the Belgian State. As usual, he rewarded those who collaborated in his schemes by receiving them into the Belgian nobility: Alexandre Browne de Tiège became a Baron.

Leopold used the money to raise another army, which in October 1896 left Stanleyville under Baron Dhanis. It was 3,000 men strong — the largest of all 19th century African expeditions — and under secret orders to march on Khartoum. Dhanis, however, got stuck in the tropical inferno of the Ituri. In February, his auxiliary troops, cannibals from the Southern Congo, mutinied. They devoured some of their white officers, thereby literally eating into Leopold's resources, and fled.

By 1901 British intelligence reported that Leopold was building the Lado Enclave, his station on the left bank of the Upper-Nile, into a military stronghold. In 1902 the *Force Publique* had 2,400 native troops and 60 European officers based in the tiny enclave. This was the largest concentration of soldiers anywhere in Africa, apart from South Africa where the British were fighting the Boers. In 1903, additional arms and ammunition entered Lado and new contingents of troops arrived, while an expedition was sent deep into the Sudan. By the turn of the century, however, the British had grown tired of the King's attempts to take the Sudan from them. Queen Victoria had died and

London suggested withdrawing its commitment to uphold Belgium's independence and neutrality. This greatly alarmed the Belgian politicians. Even Leopold's supporter Baron Greindl declared that 'the King cannot have two policies, one in Europe as King of the Belgians, the other in Africa as Sovereign of the Congo; being the friend in Europe of Powers whose enemy he is in Africa.'[56] Hence Leopold reluctantly relinquished his Nilotic dreams. Everything he and his father had obtained — their fortune, the artificial state of Belgium, the vast empire along the Congo — had been obtained thanks to the British. But London did not want to grant him the Nile. He would never be a real Egyptian pharaoh.

Meanwhile, the financial return on Leopold's investments in the Congo boomed. In 1890 the state had received 150,000 francs from its domains, mainly from ivory; in 1893 Leopold got 3.5 million francs from ivory and 1 million from wild rubber. By 1901 he was making 18 million francs a year, mostly from rubber. After John Dunlop invented the pneumatic tyre in 1888, the demand for wild rubber skyrocketed. The CFS exported 100 metric tons of rubber in 1890; 250 metric tons in 1893; 1,300 metric tons in 1896; 2,000 metric tons in 1898; and 6,000 metric tons in 1901. Leopold's wealth increased enormously. He could easily afford to pay Belgium back the interest-free loan of 25 million he had obtained in 1891, but he had no intention of doing so. The 1891 contract, however, stipulated that if the King did not pay back in 1901, Belgium had the right to annex his colony. Leopold conceded that the contract gave Belgium this right, but he pointed out that it did not stipulate *when*. 'Let us leave the door open; that will suffice. The country must have confidence in me,' he wrote in an arrogant letter to his new Prime Minister, Count de Smet de Naeyer.

Smet proposed a bill adjourning annexation *sine die*. Beernaert, angry as he realised that Leopold had cheated him in 1891, strongly objected, but most of his colleagues in Parliament accepted Smet's bill. The richer Leopold became, and by now he grew richer every day, the deeper the Belgian establishment grovelled at his feet. They were hoping for a share of Leopold's Congo booty. As a young man Leopold had already held that *money is power*. But it was the power, not the money, that really interested him. He needed money to buy loyalty and adherence. Even his apologists concede this. The newspaper *La Nation Belge* wrote in 1926: 'Leopold II wanted the King to be rich, so that he would be in a position to compensate, personally and

56   Greindl to Lambermont, 28 May 1894, in Willequet 2, p. 15.

generously, those who served the common good but were not recognised or were forgotten by the politicians in power.'[57] In Belgium the servants of 'the common good' had to be bribed by the head of state.

Many of the King's employees, however, were not rewarded. Those whom the regime did not need to uphold the 'common good' got nothing. The King's domestic staff, whom he had to pay out of his own pocket with money from the Civil List, did not benefit from the Congo fortune. In the early 1880s when Leopold had been short of cash to sustain his colony, he had abolished his employees' traditional New Year's bonus. In the 1890s, the servants asked to have the bonus again. The King refused. 'They are already paid too much for the work they have to do,' he said. 'What is more: if they do not like it here, they are free to leave.'[58] Like his father, Leopold was very stingy on personnel costs, even though he paid only a small portion of the total cost. The large majority of his secretariat consisted of civil servants who were detached from Belgian ministerial departments and whose salaries were paid directly by the ministries. Similarly, the Belgian government had allowed the King to deploy Belgian army officers in the CFS. The officers who volunteered for service in the *Force Publique* were paid by the *Institut Cartographique*, as if they were scientific explorers serving the Belgian State. In this way, Belgium directly subsidised Leopold's tropical gulag.

Leopold's Congo was not at all representative of European colonialism. The CFS was not a cash economy and the country had no currency. Its entire economy was based on barter. The millions of natives were legally obliged to trade exclusively with the state. The CFS, however, levied a tax, which, for lack of cash, had to be paid in kind. Every adult male had to work 40 hours a month for the state. If one compares this to a normal European working week of 40 hours a week, the blacks were expected to labour one week a month for Leopold. Their situation, however, was worse than that. The 'tax payers' were forced to collect wild rubber. They had to tap the rubber vines high into the trees. The rubber was collected by white mercenaries who were awarded bonuses according to the amount of rubber which they extracted from the natives. It was the mercenaries who decided how much rubber was to be collected in 40 hours of labour. Predictably, they demanded excessive amounts.

In 1985 the Flemish anthropologist and Congo researcher, Daniel Vangroenweghe, calculated that in the rubber area the natives had to

57   *La Nation Belge*, 16 Nov. 1926.
58   Quoted in Stinglhamber and Dresse, p. 34.

toil for up to 24 days a month in order to fulfil their tax obligation. Once the rubber trees nearest to the villages had been harvested, the men were forced to penetrate ever more deeply into the green hell of the rain forest, up to several days' journey on foot. They had to work almost continuously for the state. The CFS was a genuine slave camp.

In the 23 years of Leopold II's rule half the population of its approximately 20 million inhabitants perished.[59] No other 19th-century colony had a death toll as high as the CFS. In the so-called *Domaine de la Couronne*, some tribes were reduced to 20% of their number. The Domain's governor, Charles Massard, killed at least one of the Black porters with every load of rubber that was brought to him, just to frighten the others. The Crown Domain earned Leopold 50 million francs (£150 million or $250 million in today's value) between 1895 and 1905. He literally plundered the whole area of its rubber. By the time all the rubber was gone, the country was depopulated. Another notorious sadist was Léon Fiévez, who governed the Equator Province. The natives called him *'Ntange'* (the Devil). In 1894 the Scottish missionary Joseph Clark wrote that the death squads of Fiévez reduced the population of one rubber-gathering village, Ngero, from 2,000 to 10 in one year.[60]

Leopold had the Congo rubber shipped to Antwerp, where he sold it for 6.5 francs a kilo, while each kilo cost him only 0.25 francs to extract it from the Congo. Ivory, the other Congo commodity Leopold was most interested in, was 'purchased' from the natives for the equivalent of 0.82 francs a pound and sold in Europe for 12.5 francs a pound.

For lack of a money economy, physical chastisement was the only punishment available to deal with natives who failed to pay Leopold's 'taxes.' This punishment was inflicted using the *chicotte*, a whip made of hippopotamus hide that sliced like a knife. Frequent punishments were rape and cutting off the hands and feet of women and children. Contrary to what the CFS propaganda was saying in Europe, the cutting-off of hands was not an indigenous tradition in the Congo. It was first introduced by CFS commissary Fiévez in the early 1890s. Fiévez wanted to control the amount of ammunition used by the *Force Publique* soldiers during punitive raids. To account for the bullets they fired, he ordered them to bring their white officers the right hands of the victims they killed. Soon the soldiers were chop-

---

59   The estimate that the population had 'been reduced by half' during Leopold's
      rule was first given by a Belgian government commission in 1919 and has been
      confirmed by recent research. See Hochschild, pp. 232-3.
60   Vangroenweghe 1, pp. 67 and 73.

ping-off the hands of living people. In this way they could keep spare bullets to go hunting in the forest. In some CFS stations, where the officers required the soldiers to prove that they had killed men and not women, the soldiers had to bring in penises.

Outside Leopold's Crown Domain, the most horrendous abuses occurred within the provinces assigned to the concession-holding companies. Natives who fled the killing fields of the ABIR were hunted down by cannibals who had permission to eat everyone they could capture. Before consumption they had to present their victims to the ABIR representatives. 'They carried the corpses on their back, like the blacks carry the wild boars they have killed. They presented them in this fashion to the white officers, saying that they were going to eat them, which, indeed, they did,' Raymond De Grez, an ABIR official wrote.[61]

The companies were interested only in making the highest profit at the lowest price. The value of each of the 2,000 ABIR shares (Leopold owned half of them) rose from 500 francs in 1892 to 14,600 francs in 1898 and to 25,250 francs in 1900. To make labourers deliver their rubber quotas as fast as possible, their wives and children were imprisoned without food or water. In 1904 Baron Dhanis wrote to the ABIR-headquarters in Antwerp that he was 'absolutely appalled' by what he had witnessed during a visit to the ABIR-concession: 'Women and children are starved to death in gaol.'[62] Fernand Waleffe, a CFS official who visited the *Anversoise* concession in 1900, also had doubts about the effectiveness of the measure. It was simply not possible for the labourers to fulfil their quotas in time. Try as they could, by the time they managed to pay their rubber taxes, their wives and children were dead.[63]

Did Leopold know what horrors were going on in his Congo? The question might be as irrelevant as the question whether Stalin knew what was going on in his Gulag and Hitler knew what was happening at Auschwitz. Leopold had deliberately created a system that permitted the greatest cruelties. He was the first totalitarian ruler of the Modern Age, the supreme authority in a slave state, accountable to no one and, hence, ultimately responsible for the death of the millions of men, women and children who perished or were mutilated as a result of the system he had installed. 'We should not give in,' Baron Van

61   De Grez to Morel, 17 February 1905, in Vangroenweghe 1, p. 105.
62   RMCA Dhanis Papers, Dhanis to ABIR, 7 and 9 July 1904.
63   Waleffe, Fernand. 'La Vérité sur les accusations portées contre le grand roi Léopold II et ses collaborateurs belges.' *Journal des Tribunaux d'Outre-Mer*, 15 Oct. 1952, pp. 129–34.

Eetvelde wrote to the King from the Congo in 1904. 'Those who criticise the taking of hostages do not know what they talk about: one should simply call it an imprisonment of people who do not pay their taxes, and the whole matter no longer sounds extraordinary. I have never ceased to recommend the necessity of the measure.'[64]

Only in Monuments Glory Survives

From 1890 onwards, reports of the Congo atrocities began to reach Europe and America through letters from Protestant missionaries. At first, Western public opinion was not really disturbed. The King of the Belgians was reputed to be a philanthropist. It is a reputation which, once acquired in the media, seems to stick well and long. In 1895, however, Leopold's mercenaries committed a serious public relations mistake. They murdered a white man. Charlie Stokes, an English ivory trader working for the Germans in East Africa, was hanged without trial when caught violating Leopold's trade monopoly. His execution led to an outcry in the British and German press and drew attention to other Congo atrocities. Van Eetvelde complained that people in Europe gradually came to believe that the Belgians were 'essentially a cruel race.'[65]

Leopold used the growing anti-Belgian feelings to his own advantage. They helped to foster Belgian jingoistic sentiments in his own country. Belgian newspapers were bribed by the King with money from the Civil List to run articles claiming that the stories were lies by vindictive British agents who were angry that the Catholic Belgian King, rather than the Protestant British had been able to get hold of the Congo. Numerous newspapers, from the Liberal *Le Soir* to the Catholic *Le XXᵉ Siècle*, willingly accepted the King's money. Leopold's propaganda line worked remarkably well. The Belgian public became genuinely convinced that the British were only criticising their King and his colonisation methods out of spite. By the turn of the century, directly and indirectly, Leopold's colony provided employment for thousands of Belgians. All the ivory and rubber that Leopold extracted from his colony was transported to Antwerp, which, as a consequence, became the world's biggest ivory and rubber market. Its port handled 7,000 ships a year with a total cargo of over 18 million tons. The CFS provided the livelihood of many families in Antwerp. Because to criticise the Congo State was to criticise Leopold II, every foreign criticism of Leopold and his Congo colony was seen as a direct

64   GSA Van Eetvelde Papers 35, Van Eetvelde to Leopold II, 23 Feb. 1904.
65   FO 123/429, Phipps to Lansdowne, 31 May 1903.

threat to their very livelihood. These people did not see Leopold as a cruel, heartless tyrant, but as their benefactor. Moreover, he used the fortune he extracted from the Congo to embellish Belgium.

Brussels was the focus of the King's attention. He wanted it to become the worthy centre of an empire; not just a European capital, but *the* European capital. Leopold started by eradicating the Dutch character of Brussels. For centuries, the city had been part of the Netherlands, a pre-capitalist and proto-democratic society, dominated by its *burghers*, the hard-working, productive and prosperous middle classes. The Dutch cities were remarkably alike, in the sense that their pride was their belfry or city tower, symbolising municipal autonomy, their guildhalls along the main market square, and their *burghers'* houses along the canals and the smaller market squares. In the middle of the 19th-century Brussels had many winding streets and market squares along the Zenne River and its branches and canals. In 1871 Leopold had the Zenne vaulted and the canals filled up. Brussels became the only European capital without river banks. With the exception of the immediate neighbourhood of the *Grote Markt* (the Great or Main Market, renamed in French as *Grand Place*) and the *Zavel* and *Marollen* district along *Hoog Straat* (High Street), all quarters of the old town were demolished and replaced by straight boulevards. 'In Paris we find the examples we have to copy to embellish Bruxelles,' Leopold wrote to his brother Philippe.[66] The demolished medieval quarters of Brussels were, according to Leopold's collaborator, Gustave Stinglhamber, 'but a jungle of narrow little streets of no historic importance. The gem of the *Grand Place* only shines more brilliantly next to the modern style arteries.'[67]

With the new look came a new language. The new Francophone elite came to live along the new boulevards. The Dutch language disappeared together with the former inhabitants into the *Marollen*. Towering high above the latter, Leopold built the *Palais de Justice*, described by Neal Ascherson as 'a black ziggurat approaching the size of Gibraltar which throws the whole city into its cruel shadow.'[68] Actually, the building is white, but even Leopold's man, Stinglhamber, referred to it as 'Babylonian.' It is a truly colossal building complex, bigger than the Vatican's St. Peter's basilica, with a huge dome-covered tower. This Tower of Babel is the seat of the *Cour de Cassation*, the highest judicial authority in Belgium. It served as a warning to the Flemings

66 RAB Count & Countess of Flanders Papers nr. 3, Duke of Brabant to Philippe, 22 July 1863.
67 Stinglhamber and Dresse, p. 225.
68 Ascherson, p. 219.

living in the district below, signalling to them that their native tongue was no longer officially tolerated in Brussels. One of the locals dared to protest. He was Joseph Schoep, a Brussels labourer, who did not understand French. Schoep was brought to court because he refused to have the birth of his son registered in French. A stubborn man, Schoep demanded a trial in Dutch. In May 1873, as an immediate result of this case, *Cassation* ruled that the use of Dutch at courts in Brussels was forbidden. Schoep was fined 50 francs for 'civil disobedience' and ordered to pay the full costs of the trial.

One of the many destroyed neighbourhoods was the Saint Rochus borough, a buzzing district along the *Hofberg*, the steep slope covering the 40 metres between the Zenne valley and Koudenberg Hill. Leopold renamed the area the *Mont des Arts* and planned to redevelop it with museums and a national library among terraced gardens. The Mayor of Brussels, Karel Buls, a Fleming who gained international renown as the author of the book *Esthétique des villes* (1894) in which he defended the idea that cities should grow organically instead of through constructivist planning, was an outspoken opponent of Leopold's urban schemes. After his election as mayor in 1881, Buls tried to stop the demolition of the old neighbourhoods. He quarrelled with the King for many years and was vehemently attacked by the Francophone newspapers. The fiercest was *L'Indépendance Belge*, whose editorials about the Hofberg were occasionally written by the King himself.

Buls resigned in 1899. He was, he wrote in his diary, sick and tired 'of the constant interference of the King to have us adopt in our public works plans of which I disapprove.'[69] Nothing, however, could stop the King. During the demolition of the Hofberg, he had a special box suspended from an adjacent building, from which he could get an overall view of the Saint Rochus neighbourhood. He wanted to witness its destruction, just as the Romanian dictator Ceausescu was to witness the destruction of the old town of Bucharest in the 1970s.

Though he had no respect whatsoever for the historical record of Brussels, Leopold was all the more concerned about his own record in history. He believed that, to be remembered by posterity, a statesman had either to wage war or to construct monuments. But monuments were more important than war. 'The glory of Rome has survived to this very day in its monuments,' Leopold said, 'while its power and its conquests are but history.'[70] In 1905, he had a gigantic Triumphal

69   Buls 2, p. 143.
70   Quoted in Stinglhamber and Dresse, p. 240.

Arch erected in the Jubilee Park in Brussels' fashionable East End. From the Arch, a magnificent avenue, 57 metres wide and twenty kilometres long, led to Tervuren where, on the site of the former residence of the Prince of Orange, Leopold built a palace in French Classical style to house the Royal Museum of Central Africa.

The historic town of Antwerp suffered a fate similar to that of Brussels. Around 1870 Antwerp was a city with many medieval burghers' houses lining a criss-cross pattern of canals. In the early 1880s the canals were either vaulted or filled up. In 1884 the oldest part of the town was pulled down completely. The harbour town of Antwerp had originated on a land spit in the River Scheldt. This piece of land, called the *Werf* (Wharf), had given its name to the city: *aan 't werf* — 'at the wharf.' Leopold, however, wanted Antwerp to have a straight waterfront, which could serve as a quay for his Congo liners: the bend in the river had to go. The *Werf* quarter, with the 13th-century Saint Walburgis Church, the oldest church in town, was demolished and the land on which it stood was dug out and hauled away. The result was the most blatant case of 19th-century urban destruction. The oldest part of the town and the site on which it stood disappeared forever.

* * *

While their father concentrated his attention on his colony and building projects, Leopold's three daughters grew ever more miserable. The first disaster occurred in 1889 when Archduke Rudolf, the heir to the Austrian throne, murdered a 17-year-old mistress and committed suicide. Rudolf was the husband to Leopold's daughter Stephanie. The only thing Rudolf left her, apart from her daughter *Erszi*, was her sterility, the result of the venereal disease he had infected her with. Rudolf's parents, the Emperor and his dreadful wife, blamed Stephanie for the affair. Their reasoning was that if a man needs a whore, his wife is to blame.

Eleven years later, in 1900, the 36-year-old Stephanie married a Hungarian land owner, Count Elmyr Lonyay. Furious, Leopold wrote to his daughter that 'the Belgian monarchy does not need a shepherd in the family.' He told her that he never wanted to see her again and denied her the right to continue her correspondence with her sister Clementine, still living at Laken. Queen Victoria tried to soften Leopold's attitude: 'You treat Stephanie as if she had committed a murder. Her marriage to the Archduke was arranged by you. Surely, after all the suffering that has brought her, she now has the right at her age to choose a husband for herself whom she can love and respect. I cannot comprehend how you can treat your child the way you are doing now. As far as I am concerned, I shall always remain her loyal friend.'[71] Leopold replied that the matter was none of Victoria's concern.

Another family matter concerned Leopold's eldest daughter, Louise. For twenty years she had been unhappily married to Philip of Saxe-Coburg-Kohary. In 1895 Louise met Count Geza Mattacic-Keglevic, a 26-year-old cavalry lieutenant and the son of impoverished Croatian nobility. Louise, although ten years older than Mattacic, fell in love and eloped with the young lieutenant. In retaliation, her influential husband had Mattacic arrested and sentenced to six years imprisonment on false charges of theft, while Louise, with the approval of her father, was confined to a lunatic asylum. When Mattacic was released in 1902, he rented a room near the asylum where Louise was imprisoned, kept a close watch for almost two years and managed to arrange her escape in August 1904. 'There is a God after all,' she cried as she was liberated after having been incarcerated as a lunatic for many years. She, too, never saw her father again. Mattacic died in 1923 in Paris, weakened by sickness and deprivation. Six months later Louise, totally bankrupt and forsaken by everyone, passed away in Wiesbaden.

Clementine, Leopold's third and youngest daughter, also had a miserable youth. Like her father, Clementine was extremely tall. She had also inherited his large nose. 'She grows and grows, and it does not make her more beautiful. I am afraid we will never get her married,' Marie-Henriette remarked about the teenager.[72] Getting a princess married, however, is not a matter of love, but of politics. Leopold wanted Clementine to marry her cousin Baudouin, the eldest son of his brother Philippe and the heir to the Belgian throne. In this way, the King would become the grandfather to his Belgian successors. Young Clementine, who was infatuated with her handsome cousin, did not mind, but Uncle Philippe objected to a marriage between first cousins. Other candidates were rejected because Leopold did not want Clementine to marry. As ever preoccupied with keeping the royal inheritance in Belgium, he believed that she should remain at Laken and die an old spinster there. In addition, since the queen had retired to Spa with her stinking menagerie of dogs, horses, camels and llamas, Clementine was the acting 'first lady' in Brussels. Leopold expected her to accompany him at various official ceremonies.

71   RAB, Victoria to Leopold II, 2 Apr. 1900.
72   Quoted in Kerckvoorde 3, p. 239.

The princess was over thirty when, in 1904, she fell in love with Prince Victor Napoleon. He was the Bonapartist pretender to the throne of France. Ten years older than Clementine and still a bachelor, he lived as an exile in Brussels. Clementine asked her father for permission to marry the prince, but the King refused. He said that he did not want to offend the French republican government by having his daughter marry a Bonaparte. When she kept pressuring Leopold for his approval, the King unleashed a full-scale propaganda campaign against her.

He had the Prime Minister, Count de Smet de Naeyer, as well as the Catholic Party leader Charles Woeste, write hostile letters condemning the marriage. Woeste, especially, was a man much feared. The son of a Protestant Prussian diplomat who had settled in Brussels after the Belgian Revolution, he had converted to Catholicism in order to join the governing Catholic Party. His power was such that when a Catholic priest, Father Adolf Daens, founded a movement for Flemish emancipation and was elected a Member of Parliament, Woeste succeeded in having the priest suspended by the Belgian bishops and formally condemned by the Vatican, as Leopold had requested. Woeste's message to the devout, conscientious Clementine was clear: it was her God-given duty not to marry. The leading editorial in the influential newspaper *L'Indépendance Belge* said: 'Princess Clementine, we are utterly convinced, cannot repay the affection of the Belgian people by forgetting her duty towards them, towards her father, and towards the Dynasty which is for ever inseparable from the great Belgian family.' This text had been anonymously written by Leopold himself. Clementine surrendered. In 1910, however, immediately after her father's death, the 38-year-old princess did marry Victor Napoleon. She was lucky that Leopold had died in time for her still to have children. Her daughter Marie-Clotilde was born in 1912 and her son Louis Napoleon in 1914. Through Clementine, the blood (and the nose) of the Bourbons was brought into the Bonaparte family. Victor Napoleon died in 1926, Clementine in 1955.

* * *

Leopold II had many illegitimate children. Like Leopold I before him, he literally was father to quite a few Belgians. Like a cuckoo, he laid an egg in many a nobleman's nest. Famous royal bastards are Jean-Félix de Hemptinne, the later Catholic Bishop of the Katanga, and Etienne de Vrière, a large landowner in Beernem near Bruges. Vrière is said to have ordered the kidnapping and murder of Baron Henri d'Udekem d'Acoz, whose wife he coveted, as well as the murders of five others who knew about the affair. The murders were committed by Vrière's own bastard, Hector Hoste, who was sentenced to twenty years for one of the deaths, but was prematurely released after six years. He was, after all, a royal grandson.

The King also had numerous children abroad. For the largest part of the year, Leopold lived outside his country. The German, Austrian and French spa resorts, Paris and the French Riviera were his favourite holiday places. He had established his second home at Cap Ferrat, near Villefranche, between Nice and Monaco. In a 1999 interview Herman Liebaers, *Grand Maréchal* (head of the ceremonial department) at the Belgian royal palace in the 1970s, recalled that every year an old man, an illegitimate son of Leopold II, travelled from the South of France to the royal palace at Brussels, where Liebaers had to hand him a sealed envelope filled with money. 'Usually, however, such *delicate* matters were dealt with by the *Société Générale*, that handled these affairs discreetly.'[73]

In Paris, Leopold owned an apartment at the Avenue d'Eylau. It was connected by a secret door to an adjacent apartment. Leopold's servants had to make sure that the King had a permanent supply of girls. One stay in Paris in 1895 consisted of an orgy that lasted ten days and ten nights. 'Dancers, singers, demi-virgins and professional call-girls were all fetched round to satisfy his astonishing sexual appetites,' writes his biographer Neal Ascherson, who also stresses that 'his elaborate and incessant affairs with women never for a moment interfered with the routine of his work,' and that very often 'the assumption that he went to Paris to make a tour of the brothels conveniently obscured the political business he had to transact there.'[74] Leopold was a friend of the French President, Félix Faure, who assisted him in his Congo dealings. They shared at least one other interest. Faure died of a heart attack in his presidential office on 16 February 1899 while the model Marguerite Steinheil was performing oral sex on him. Faure, only 58 years old, must have had a very weak heart indeed. One century later, an American President engaged in similar acts in the Oval Room and survived; his heart was stronger. As for Leopold's heart, his sister-in-law, the Countess of Flanders, maintained that he lacked the organ.[75]

73 Liebaers in *Humo*, 23 Nov. 1999.
74 Ascherson, p. 218.
75 RAM WC XVII–XVIII, Countess of Flanders to Augustine Cerrini di Monte Varche, 22 Aug. 1898.

In the summer of 1900, the 65-year-old Leopold met Blanche Caroline Delacroix, a 17-year-old prostitute, whom he engaged to stay with him. Like his father before him, Leopold decided that, as he was unloved by his own family, he needed a permanent mistress, a woman to nurse him in his old age. When Queen Marie-Henriette died, in 1902, Leopold took Blanche along to the funeral, while forbidding his 'sheep-herding' daughter Stephanie to attend.

The King showered Blanche with gifts. He bought her the Villa Vanderborght, a luxurious mansion within walking distance from the royal residence at Laken. At Ostend, too, he bought Blanche a private residence, the Villa Caroline, which was connected to the *Chalet Royal* by an underground tunnel. He gave her expensive jewels, including a diamond necklace of 75,000 francs. He bought her the Château of Balincourt in Arronville near Paris. It boasted silver bath tubs with golden taps and a bed adorned with gold under an immense canopy of handmade Brussels lace. The opulence was so excessive that one might wonder whether he kept Blanche Delacroix, with her vulgar manners, as his mistress just to insult his daughters.

Blanche came to dominate the ageing King. From time to time the servants could hear her shout at him. When he was cross with her, she lit a cigar and concentrated on puffing it. She also resumed her contacts with her former pimp, Antoine Durrieux, who visited her in secret. One afternoon Leopold walked in unexpectedly at Villa Vanderborght to find Blanche and Durrieux together. She introduced Durrieux to the King as her brother. Leopold would have been a fool if he had believed it, but he tolerated Durrieux's presence near his girlfriend. The French crook soon became a common figure in the royal entourage at Brussels. Socialist pamphlets alluded to 'an indecent triangular relationship.' The Catholics were more respectful but, as the King's behaviour caused offence, a local priest in Ostend felt obliged to call Leopold to account. 'Sire, I have heard rumours that you have a concubine,' he told the King. 'Good heavens, Father! I have heard the same rumours about you,' Leopold retorted: 'But you know, Father, *I* do not believe them.'

Indignation in Belgium about his love life was not Leopold's main concern; certainly not in Ostend, where he was very popular. He had given Ostend a race course, a casino, luxury hotels and galleries, beautiful parks and elegant boulevards. After Brussels, he had selected Ostend to become a showpiece of Belgium's national *grandeur*. The King transformed the town from a sleepy fishing village into a renowned port of call for the late 19th-century equivalent of the modern jet set. The royals of Europe and even the Shah of Persia were frequent guests. Leopold, however, never forgot to look for business opportunities. While embellishing Ostend, he acted as a real estate developer. Together with Constant Goffinet he worked out ways to buy land at the cheapest possible price. On reselling he made huge profits. Through his British middleman, Colonel North, he bought a large stretch of dunes from the Belgian state. He made it into a new city quarter with villas which he sold at high prices to the very wealthy. He also intended building a gigantic royal residence in Italian style along the beach. This project, however, never got started. It was delayed because Leopold was too busily engaged in scores of business projects in Belgium and abroad. Together with the late 19th-century Belgian captains of industry, men like Solvay, Empain and Boël, he invested in coal mines, steel factories, real estate, tramways and railroads, in Southern and Eastern Europe, Egypt, Russia and China. And everything this modern Midas touched turned to gold.

The Fox Empties the Shell

Leopold's main concern during his last years was to keep *his Congo* out of the hands of Belgium and his inheritance out of the grasp of his daughters. In Britain public discomfort about the atrocities in the Congo had been rising to the point where the British Government could no longer afford to ignore it. In 1904, the British Foreign Office published a White Paper on the Congo atrocities, written by Roger Casement, the British Consul in Boma. London officially put forward the *Belgian solution*: Belgium should annex the CFS as a colony.

Leopold was furious. He reacted to the White Paper by setting up a special branch within his propaganda department directed against Britain. He also had a propaganda magazine published, for international use. It was called *The Truth about the Congo* and was widely distributed in various languages, and could be found, for example, on the bedside tables of all European *wagons-lits* train coaches. The Belgian King was a major shareholder of the Wagons-Lits Company. He also bribed (sometimes offering up to 100,000 francs) journalists, newspaper owners, and politicians, in Britain, France, Germany, Austria, Italy and America.

International public pressure, however, continued to rise. In March 1904, the English journalist Edmund Dene Morel officially established the Congo Reform Association. Morel, the editor of the *West African Mail*, had become intrigued by the Congo whilst working in Antwerp for the Liverpool shipping line of Elder Dempster in the late 1890s. Leopold had granted Elder Dempster a monopoly on all traffic between Antwerp and the CFS. Morel noticed that enormous quantities of ivory and rubber were arriving in Antwerp, while hardly anything was ever shipped to the Congo, apart from machine guns, rifles and ammunition. This aroused his suspicion. When the young man inquired too much into the Congo matter, he lost his job. Following his usual tactics, Leopold tried to bribe Morel, but the Englishman refused the offer. Morel wrote numerous pamphlets and books about Leopold's rule and, being a born campaigner, he organised meetings and demonstrations throughout Britain. These attracted influential supporters, such as the novelist Arthur Conan Doyle, many Anglican bishops and MPs.

Pressured by the British government, the Belgian authorities decided to send an international commission to the Congo to investigate Casement's allegations. They let Leopold choose the members of the Commission. He appointed the Belgian Edmond Janssens, Attorney General at the *Cour de Cassation* in Brussels, the Italian Giacomo Nisco, President of the Court of Appeal of the CFS at Boma, and the Swiss Edmund Schumacher, brother of the Belgian honorary consul in Luzern. The Commissioners started their voyage along the Congo River in October 1904. By February they decided that they had seen enough. Deeply shocked, they returned home.

When the Belgian government read the Commission's official report, confirming the state's regime of deliberate terror in the Congo, they considered it so damaging for the King that they locked it away. The report was filed as a top-secret document in the archives of the Foreign Ministry, stamped with the message: 'Never to be communicated to researchers.' In the early 1970s a Belgian diplomat, Jules Marchal, who was serving as ambassador in West Africa, accidentally learnt of its existence. When he asked permission to read it, he was denied access to the document. He was told that there is 'a rule in the Foreign Ministry Archives' that no one is ever allowed access to 'material that is bad for the reputation of Belgium.'[76] Marchal pestered ministry officials for more than a decade. Finally, a senior official allowed him to see the file, 'but only if you promise not to write anything based on it.' He refused to make such a promise and continued his struggle until 1985, when he finally obtained permission to read the 80-year-old document. In 1988 Marchal published a book about the findings of the report. The book was written in his native Dutch and published under the pseudonym A. M. Delathuy. It was ignored in Belgium. After his retirement in 1996, Marchal privately published a translation of his book in French. This, too, was ignored in Belgium, but it was used by the American author Adam Hochschild as a basic source for his award-winning bestseller *King Leopold's Ghost*, published in 1998.

With the independent Commission of Inquiry confirming the atrocities, the Belgian government felt it had no option but to take over the colony. In February 1906, Parliament started the annexation process. It installed a working group, the so-called 'Committee of Seventeen,' to arrange the take-over. The Committee encountered severe difficulties. When it asked the King for the Congo State's accounts and budgets, it did not get them. 'The Congo Free State is not beholden to anyone except to its Founder. No one has a right even to ask for its accounts,' Leopold said.[77] He also refused to inform Belgium about the contents of the CFS Treasury. To this very day it remains a secret how many millions this Treasury contained and what the King did with the money. A 'conservative estimate' puts Leopold's Congo profits at a minimum of 220 million francs (equivalent to £660 million or $1.1 billion today).[78]

While the Committee worked on, Leopold outmanoeuvred the politicians. He informed the government that he was prepared to cede his colony on one condition only: the Belgians would have to respect all commitments that the CFS had entered into with third parties. During the whole of 1907, the King obstructed the negotiations with the Committee, in order to gain time. He was busy reducing his colony to an empty shell. He awarded several new Congo exploitation concessions to foreign companies, most of which he owned himself through middlemen, and to three newly created companies, owned by the *Société Générale* holding, such as the *Union Minière du Haut-Katanga*. In exchange for additional SG shares, Leopold assigned virtually all the mineral wealth of the Congo to these companies under SG control. This was a masterstroke. When the Belgian Government took over the Congo it did, indeed, respect the contracts with the new companies. The SG, which already controlled the Belgian economy, was a leviathan — a power within the Belgian state — whose might no government dared to defy.

Throughout the following decades, the *Union Minière* was beyond all political control. Worse, it was the UM which controlled Congolese politics. This was especially the case after 1945, during the Cold War,

---

77   Quoted in Emerson, p. 259
78   Calculation made by Ambassador Marchal in 1997, in Hochschild, pp. 277 and 334.

when Katangese uranium was of vital strategic interest for the Western world. Through the UM, the Belgian royal family, the largest shareholder of the SG, grew rich on the mineral wealth of the Katanga in the Southern part of the Belgian Congo. The UM income was considerably higher than the Congo's rubber income had ever been.

Leopold incorporated his private rubber concession, the so-called *Domaine de la Couronne*, into a new legal entity: the Crown Foundation. By tying the assets up in a foundation, he hoped to be able to disinherit his daughters. Belgian civil law obliged the King to leave each of his three daughters at least one-quarter of his immense fortune. In a will he had drafted in 1900, Leopold assigned only 11.25 million francs to his daughters — 3.75 for each of them — considering this more than sufficient. According to its charter, the Crown Foundation's purpose was to embellish Belgium with monuments and to provide an annual sum for the construction of large boulevards, 50 metres in width, which were to connect the Belgian cities and allow modern motor vehicles to travel rapidly along these 'national arteries.' It is often said that Adolf Hitler invented the motorway, but Stinglhamber stresses that King Leopold II was the first man ever to have a vision of an '*autostrade*.'[79]

The Crown Foundation resembled the so-called *Donation Royale*. In 1901, Leopold had brought most of his Belgian real estate together in the *Donation Royale*, which he gave to the state on condition that the successive Belgian Kings (but only those of the House of Saxe-Coburg) would be allowed to use these domains and enjoy the usufruct of the properties. The *Donation Royale* included the royal castles of Ciergnon, Villers-sur-Lesse, Fenffe, Ardenne, Stuivenberg, the *Chalet Royal* at Ostend, the coastal estate of Raversijde, the royal greenhouses and other properties at Laken, Tervuren, Brussels and elsewhere, as well as a portfolio of shares. This was a blatantly illegal act, as the *Donation Royale* was obviously a scheme to disinherit his daughters in favour of the future Belgian Saxe-Coburg monarchs. Rather than a gift to the Nation, the *Donation Royale*, valued between 15 and 20 million francs, was a perpetual annuity to the Crown. Although the illegality of the scheme was clearly pointed out by Beernaert, it was accepted by Parliament.

The Belgian government, however, was not prepared to accept the Crown Foundation, which owned one-sixth of the territory of the whole Congo colony. To Leopold's dismay and under his loud protests, the Foundation's Congolese territories were integrated in the

Belgian Congo colony. In compensation, the Belgian government created a *Leopold II Fund*, to be financed not from Congolese profits but by the Belgian taxpayers, for completing building works in Belgium already begun by the King. Leopold at once demanded 150 million francs for the fund. He obtained 'only' 80 million, but when the government decided that, in addition, the King would be given 50 million francs from the Belgian state as a mark of gratitude for all the great sacrifices he had made for the Congo, he gave in. Finally, in February 1908, an agreement was reached for the Congo transfer to take place by the end of the year.

Once he had cashed his reward, Leopold lost all interest in the whole Congo business. 'I will do nothing to help annexation, I will do nothing to stop it, I just don't care about it,' he told his secretary, Count Edmond Carton de Wiart.[80] 'I will give them my Congo, but they do not have the right to know what I have done there,' he confided to Stinglhamber.[81] In August 1908 he had all the archives and accounts of the CFS burned. It took eight full days to have every document at the Congo State headquarters in the Brussels *Brederode Straat* thrown into the flames. People such as Stinglhamber, the Goffinet twins, Carton de Wiart, who worked for Leopold but were paid by Belgium, either actively cooperated or stood by passively while the King destroyed all evidence relating to his Congo dealings. Valuable information, including the financial data which the Belgian authorities had tried to obtain from Leopold the previous year, was burned, while people who considered themselves Belgium's true 'patriots' and 'guardians of the common good' looked on.

A similar, deliberate destruction of incriminating evidence occurred when the complete archives of the ABIR were burned on Leopold's orders. 'Seldom has a totalitarian regime gone to such lengths to destroy so thoroughly the records of its work,' writes Hochschild. 'In their later quests for a higher order, Hitler and Stalin in some ways left a far larger paper trail behind them.'[82] The only document Leopold's henchmen forgot was the report of the Commission of Inquiry in the archives of the Foreign Ministry.

On 18 October 1908 Leopold signed the Treaty of Cession. The British government demanded that the Belgian government immediately abolish the labour tax in the colony. Julien Davignon, the Belgian Minister of Foreign Affairs, replied that, although Belgium intended such

80   Carton de Wiart, p. 190.
81   Stinglhamber and Dresse, p. 52.
82   Hochschild, pp. 294–5.

a reform, it could not do so at once, nor even openly declare its intention to do so, because this would amount to criticism of the King's Congo regime. Davignon, the grandson of one of the revolutionaries of 1830, knew that in an artificial country such as Belgium, where the King is the only institution symbolising the nation, every criticism of this symbol can undermine the state's cohesion and must be avoided. The Belgian government even backed the King in his grudges against the British. This became clear when Leopold discovered that the city of Antwerp had invited David Lloyd George, the President of the British Board of Trade, for a visit. The King had Carton de Wiart write a stern letter to the government to ensure that Antwerp did not give Lloyd George too warm a welcome. 'Such a welcome,' Carton pointed out, 'would be highly inappropriate, as Mr. Lloyd George has signed an appeal criticising His Majesty as Sovereign of the Congo State. It would not be fitting to honour someone who has insulted His Majesty.' The government at once replied: '*Care shall be taken to ensure* that the reception will not be more welcoming than politeness requires.'[83]

*   *   *

In 1905, Blanche Delacroix became pregnant by the 70-year-old King. She gave birth to a son, Lucien, at Cap Ferrat in February 1906. Leopold rewarded her with the title of Baroness de Vaughan. Her son received the title of Duke of Tervuren. One year later, in October 1907, a second son, Philippe, was born at Lormoy, Leopold's castle south of Paris. He was given the title of Count of Ravenstein, a title referring to a German lordship of the Saxe-Coburg family. As Leopold was 72 years old at the time of Philippe's birth, many doubted whether he was the boy's real father. Gossips had it that Antoine Durrieux — Blanche's former pimp, who now called himself the Baron de Vaughan — was a more likely candidate. Leopold had not been too sure either during Blanche's pregnancy, but his uncertainty vanished when he saw the newborn child. The baby had a deformed right hand. 'It has a stump, like the Negroes whose hands Leopold chopped off,' some remarked wryly. To the King, however, this proved his fatherhood. The German Kaiser Wilhelm II, a son of Vicky, the eldest daughter of the British Queen Victoria and Prince Albert of Saxe-Coburg, had also been born with a deformed hand. 'It is a hereditary trait of the Coburgs,' Leopold said proudly.[84]

---

83   RAB Leopold II nr. 391.
84   Quoted in Van Audenhaeghe, p. 80.

During his last years, the King devoted much energy to military matters. In 1909 he finally succeeded in having Parliament vote a bill introducing general military service. Leopold had proposed the bill as long ago as 1871, but, as the Belgians clearly were not interested, he had devoted his time to other things. After a visit to Berlin in January 1904, Leopold resumed his efforts. The visit to Berlin had convinced him that a new Franco-German clash was imminent. Wilhelm II had proposed that Germany and Belgium carry out a joint military strike against France. Leopold refused and at once returned to Brussels to strengthen his own army. The Kaiser felt insulted by the departure of his guest. His wife, however, was relieved and had the court chaplain exorcise the rooms where Leopold had been staying. The Kaiserin was convinced that he was the Devil in person, who chopped off children's hands and, like Bluebeard, devoured a virgin a night.

On 14 December 1909, Parliament approved the general conscription bill. It came just in time for Leopold to put his very last signature under it. The King had fallen ill at the beginning of December. He died in the early hours of 17 December. Three days before his death, he had a Catholic priest marry him to Blanche Delacroix. The groom was 74, the bride 26. Baron Raoul Snoy, the King's aide-de-camp, and Baron Auguste Goffinet acted as witnesses.

His widow left Belgium with eight suitcases full of bank notes, gold, jewels, and company stocks. Baron Snoy and Baron Baeyens, the Governor of the SG, helped her smuggle the valuables out of the country. Blanche settled in France and married her former pimp Antoine Durrieux in August 1910, when he adopted her two sons. They divorced in May 1913 after they had gambled away her entire fortune. Mother and sons afterwards lived in great poverty in Paris. Philippe, the Count of Ravenstein, died of diphtheria in 1914, at the age of seven. In 1946 the Belgian government decided to pay Blanche a small monthly allowance in remembrance of her husband. She died in 1948. Her son Lucien, the Duke of Tervuren, died childless in 1984 and is buried in Cambo-les-Bains near Biarritz in the South of France. He lies under a stone with the inscription: *Lucien, Duc de Tervueren, Prince de Saxe-Cobourg-Gotha.*

Albert I, Third King of the Belgians,
and Prince Leopold

Chapter 4

Reluctant Ally
(1909–1934)

The Making of a Belgicist

Albert I, the third King of the Belgians, was born on 8 April 1875. His father, Prince Philippe, the Count of Flanders, was Leopold II's younger brother. Philippe was a gloomy man. His moods were worst when his wife, Marie of Hohenzollern-Sigmaringen, was around. Fortunately, she liked to travel and spent much of the year abroad.

Philippe lived in his Brussels palace in the Rue de la Régence on Koudenberg Hill. He devoted his time to collecting antiques and rare books. His library eventually contained over 30,000 volumes. Part of the collection was of a pornographic nature. Of all the grandchildren of Duke Francis of Coburg-Saalfeld, Philippe most resembled his paternal grandfather in his lack of political ambition. He was not interested in founding dynasties and building empires. The fact that he had started to grow gradually deaf in his twenties, helps to explain his attitude. 'The Count of Flanders is very nimble, clever and prudent — but unfortunately stonedeaf,' Queen Victoria said about her cousin.

In 1866, the Romanians elected Philippe as their king without asking him. He responded by sending a simple telegram to Bucharest. In one sentence he refused the offer. The crown of Romania subsequently went to Prince Karl of Hohenzollern-Sigmaringen. The following year the Count of Flanders married a girl Queen Victoria had picked for him. It was the myopic Marie of Hohenzollern-Sigmaringen, a younger sister of the new King of Romania.

Between 1869 and 1875, the Count and Countess of Flanders had five children. A boy, Baudouin, was born in 1869. Two twin daughters, Henriette and Joséphine, were born in 1870. Baby Joséphine died barely two months old. Another daughter, also called Joséphine, was born in 1872. Finally, in 1875, a second son was born. He was called Albert, after his Saxe-Coburg cousin, Queen Victoria's late husband. Marie and her children only spent the winter months at Brussels. Each spring, they travelled for a holiday to her mother's residence at Umkirch near Freiburg in south-western Germany. The Count, whom his children mysteriously called 'die Päppin' (a plural in the feminine gender), seldom accompanied them. He made his own trips to Italy, where he went to purchase art, and to Paris for pleasure. In the summer, they spent their time in one of the South-German or Swiss castles of the Sigmaringens (later the Count of Flanders bought his own Swiss residence, the Villa Haslihorn on the shores of Lake Lucerne), or at the castle of Les Amerois, near Bouillon in Belgian Luxemburg. Each autumn, a second or third visit was made to Germany, before returning to hibernate in Brussels.

When in Brussels, the Flanders family was expected to have dinner with the royal family at Laken every Tuesday and Thursday. The children hated this. They invented strange nicknames for the sovereigns: the King was 'der bäcktelein' and the Queen 'die bäckin' (without capital letters). They noticed that the bäcktelein was not interested in children, not even his own, while the bäckin was often 'bissig' (short-tempered) towards them and was only kind to her dogs.

In 1876, Leopold II appointed Jules Bosmans, a 30-year-old Flemish polyglot who had studied at the universities of Leuven, Bonn and the prestigious Sorbonne in Paris, as tutor to Prince Baudouin, who was the heir to the Belgian throne. Bosmans also taught Latin, Economics, Law and Dutch to Albert. Every week, Albert had four hours of tuition in the Dutch language; Bosmans complained to Prince Philippe that he was bad at it. According to his teachers, Albert was undisciplined. The teachers also complained that the boy was insincere. Albert often felt insecure, which he tried to hide behind fits of rage.

The Countess Marie, a pious Catholic, did not like the influence of the non-religious Bosmans on her sons, but as Bosmans was the King's choice, she had to accept him. In 1888, the Count of Flanders appointed a governor for Albert, a young officer, Harry Jungbluth, the son of a German father and an English mother. The Countess disapproved of Jungbluth as well. He was a Protestant and an avowed bachelor who did not engage in stable relationships with women.

One of the King's collaborators, Baron Greindl, warned that Albert's tutors were giving him 'dangerous books' — works by socialist authors such as Marx and Bebel, and free-thinking philosophers, like Herbert Spencer. Leopold II, however, was not much interested in Albert. The boy was of no importance to him. Albert was impressed by the books, which convinced him of the inevitable rise of socialism as a political force. When the socialist deputies made republican speeches in Parliament, Albert was greatly disturbed. In March 1895, he wrote in his diary: 'The socialist movement is anti-dynasty. Something must urgently be done about this. Unfortunately, the bäcktelein and the Päppin are not very popular; they do not do enough and do not show themselves enough.' In a letter to her daughter Henriette, the Countess of Flanders regretted that Albert looked at the world 'through the obscure eyes of a socialist.'

During his formative years, Albert also reached another conclusion that he would adhere to throughout his life: the 20th-century was going to be the age of the Anglo-Saxons. He came to this *belief* — for it was, indeed, a religious conviction — during his years as a student at the Belgian Royal Military Academy at Terkameren, near Brussels. The most remarkable professors at the Academy in the early 1890s were two Protestant brothers, Charles and Eugène Lagrange. They were mathematicians who had developed a historical and political theory, based on what they called *Brück's Law*. Major Nicholas-Rémy Brück was a Belgian military engineer, who had 'discovered' that a literal reading of the Bible combined with mathematical calculations contained the key to predict future political developments. The Lagrange brothers 'improved' Brück's theory by adding the measurements of the pyramid of Cheops. Hence, they had 'calculated' that the world would come to an end exactly 5,160 years after the creation of Adam. The complete history of the world could be divided into ten periods of 516 years, each of which were dominated by a leading people. The tenth and last in this series of dominating peoples were the British and the Americans. They were the descendants of the lost tribes of Israel.

The Lagranges' teaching had an enormous influence on their pupils. One of them, Emile Galet, later became the head of the Belgian General Staff. Galet's successor as head of the General Staff, Prudent Nuyten, was also an adept of Brück's Law, as was General Raoul Van Overstraeten, military advisor to King Leopold III in the 1930s and 40s. In 1924, Albert asked the British King George V to help produce a movie about the origin of the Stone of Scone and the identification of the British people with the lost tribes of Israel.

Another newly constructed semi-scientific theory that made a lasting impression on the prince was *Belgicism*. This ideology was devised in the 1890s by two Walloon intellectuals, Edmond Picard and Henri Pirenne. Picard, a socialist member of the Belgian Senate, was an outspoken anti-Semite, who held that the superior Aryan race was locked in a class struggle with the 'capitalist' Jews. His anti-Jewish sentiments were shared by other prominent Walloon socialists, including Jules Destrée and Louis Bertrand, the editor of the newspaper *Le Peuple*. Picard was a prolific writer and polemicist. In 1893, he wrote the essay *La révision des origines du christianisme* about the allegedly non-Jewish roots of Christianity. In 1895, he published *Comment on devient socialiste* (How to Become a Socialist). In 1897, his most influential essay, *L'âme belge* (The Belgian Soul), was published. In this work, Picard argued that while the two peoples living in Belgium may differ in language, they still belong to the same Belgian 'race.' In fact, according to Picard, no Flemings or Walloons existed, but only Belgians.

To the governing Belgian elite, Picard's theory came as a godsend. Even the non-socialists embraced it wholeheartedly. It offered comfortable moral reassurance. Thus far, the ruling classes had never denied the artificiality of the Belgian state. Thanks to Picard, they no longer needed to feel like parasites living off a state they were bound to defend because it was their livelihood. Now they could pretend to be defenders of the unity of 'a real nation' and hence argue that their defence of this nation was inspired by the altruistic, generous virtue of patriotism. Thanks to Picard, the base, materialistic personal interests of those running the Belgian state could be wrapped in a moral principle.

Albert was one of those who eagerly accepted Picard's notion of the 'Belgian Soul.' To the *bäcktelein* and the *Päppin*, the Flamingants fighting for the rights of the Flemish people against the artificial state of Belgium were dangerous political opponents capable of destroying the Saxe-Coburg family business. To Albert, the Flamingants were utterly immoral as well. There existed no Flemish people, only a Belgian people to which the Flamingants were traitors.

One year after the publication of *L'âme belge*, Picard embarked on another anti-Semitic crusade, writing *L'Aryano-Sémitisme*. He left it to others to expand his theory of Belgicism. Picard may have invented the concept of the 'Belgian Soul,' but its foundations were laid by Henri Pirenne. The latter was a Walloon historian from Liège who had been given a job at the University of Ghent, where he became one of Europe's leading specialists in the economic and social history of the Middle Ages. In 1899, Pirenne, inspired by Picard's revelation of the 'Belgian Soul,' set out on an enormous project: to rewrite the entire history of the Southern Netherlands from a Belgicist perspective. Pirenne's *Histoire de Belgique* appeared in seven volumes, published between 1900 and 1932. According to Pirenne, Belgium was one of the oldest nations in the whole of Europe, instead of a 19th-century invention. To Pirenne, Charlemagne, 'the father of Europe,' had been a Belgian. Charlemagne's Frankish Empire, where people of Latin and Germanic origin lived together, had been a precursor of Belgium. The independence of Belgium in 1830 was an inevitability, said Pirenne, because the Belgian nation — the very core of the state of Charlemagne — still existed, and was bound to reappear like a phoenix.

Pirenne rejected the Flamingants' argument that the Flemings and the Walloons were different peoples because they had never spoken the same tongue. In his *Histoire de Belgique*, he asserts that Flanders had *always* been bilingual. He 'proved' this by referring to medieval documents of the Flemish nobility written in French. (Using the same argument, one can also 'prove' that the English are the same people as the French.) From this assertion, Pirenne drew political conclusions. He argued that, as Flanders had 'always been bilingual,' the Francophones were entitled to the same linguistic rights as the Dutch-speakers in Flanders. Pirenne — like Picard — did not deny the Flemings the right to use Dutch in their own country, which was more than the Belgian regime allowed them in the 19th century, but Dutch was clearly inferior to French.

When in the 1930s, the Flamingants succeeded in having Flanders (excluding Brussels) recognised as a Dutch-speaking region where French ceased to be an official language, Pirenne and other Belgicists were furious: Flanders had been 'stolen' from them, they said. The Flamingants were not only traitors, they were thieves as well, robbing Belgium of its soul by denying the Francophones the right to speak French in Flanders. The Belgicists had effectively turned the argument around. They portrayed the Flamingants, who were fighting against the linguistic discrimination of the Flemish people, as intolerant ideologues because they denied others the right to impose French as an official language in Flanders.

Because of Picard and Pirenne, the Flamingants lost the moral high ground to the Belgicists. The Flamingants had another major disadvantage as well: they lacked foreign allies. Their Belgicist adversaries, through their writings in French, had direct access to international public opinion. The Flamingant's books, written in Dutch, were not read abroad. Even in England, the traditional geopolitical ally of the

Flemings, Flanders disappeared from the picture. Flemish cities such as Mechelen, traditionally known in England as *Mechlin*, came to be referred to by the French name, *Malines*. The Dutch-speaking Flemings no longer existed as a people. They were Belgians now, who spoke French if they were educated, and otherwise some kind of Low-German dialect, called 'Flemish'.

* * *

With the exception of Albert's mother and Baron Greindl, few people were disturbed by the fact that the prince was acquainting himself with socialist theories and weird ideas such as Brück's Law. The focus of all public attention was Albert's elder brother, Baudouin. By January 1891, the 21-year-old Baudouin was a dashing Colonel and a reputed lady-killer. He was also the pawn in a power game between King Leopold and the Count of Flanders. The relationship between the *bäcktelein* and the *Päppin* had become strained, as the latter kept vetoing a marriage between Baudouin and the King's daughter Clementine. Officially Philippe objected to a marriage between first cousins, because he feared this would lead to genetic degeneration. He said he suspected his own deafness to have been caused by the (distant) relationship between his parents. He also referred to the haemophilia that had afflicted Queen Victoria's offspring.

In reality, Philippe used the genetic argument as an alibi to thwart his brother's marriage scheme. He did not want Leopold to become the grandfather to a future Belgian King. That was his way of taking revenge on his elder brother. This became perfectly clear when three years later, in 1894, he gave his daughter Joséphine, who had inherited her father's hearing impediment, permission to marry her first cousin, Prince Carlo of Hohenzollern-Sigmaringen.

While Leopold II and Philippe quarrelled about marrying Baudouin to Clementine, tragedy struck. Baudouin died unexpectedly on 23 January 1891 of pneumonia. The death of his brother dramatically changed Albert's hitherto quiet life. Suddenly 'the red prince' was the heir to the Belgian throne. At once, the *bäcktelein* started interfering with his nephew's education. The King's collaborators, people such as the Barons Lambermont and Dhanis, came to instruct the young man about Belgian politics and Congo matters.

It became part of Albert's duty as Crown Prince to represent the King at various official occasions. In 1896, Albert travelled to Russia to attend the coronation of Tsar Nicholas II. The journey took him through Warsaw, which, in a letter to Jules Bosmans, he described as 'extremely filthy and packed with miserly Jews.'[1] The Prince's duties also included opening festivities in Belgium. When Albert had to make speeches in Flanders, he did his best to deliver at least a couple of sentences in Dutch, which he carefully read from a piece of paper. They were written according to Albert's wishes by Jules Bosmans and invariably stressed the importance of Belgian unity and the need for all Belgians to cooperate — moral imperatives which, according to Albert, the Flamingants were undermining. 'When speaking to the Flemings, one must never forget to talk in this fashion,' Albert instructed Bosmans.[2]

Meanwhile, the Prince had met two men who would remain close collaborators for the rest of his life. Emile Sigogne was a Professor of Elocution at the University of Liège. Jungbluth had advised Albert to take some lessons from Sigogne in order to improve his French. Sigogne, a French-born immigrant, was a prominent member of the Masonic lodge and an influential advisor of the socialist Belgian Workers' Party (BWP). He encouraged Albert to study Marx more thoroughly and helped him in his efforts to reconcile the BWP to the Saxe-Coburg dynasty. To this end, in 1905, Sigogne authored a political essay, *Socialisme et monarchie — Essai de synthèse sociale*, which he dedicated to the Prince. It argued that a monarchic regime was not incompatible with social progress.

Jungbluth also introduced the Prince to Emile Waxweiler, a young engineer who had just returned from the United States. In 1898, inspired by Waxweiler's enthusiastic stories of America and his own belief in the ascendancy of Anglo-Saxon world domination, Albert asked permission from both the *bäcktelein* and the *Päppin* to travel to the United States. His father replied that he did 'not understand what could possibly attract him in America.' But the King granted his permission and used the opportunity to charge Harry Jungbluth to contact American business companies and recommend 'the good quality of Congo rubber.'

The Prince and his party arrived in New York in March 1898. They travelled to San Francisco and back, before returning home in July. Albert was greatly impressed, but at the same time came to loath the Americans — these 'parvenus' as he called them. In a letter to Bosmans, he wrote: 'This nation has until now limited its activities to commercial and industrial undertakings. It will, however, turn militarist and become a danger to the world. Within the next twenty years

1   RAM WC, Albert to Bosmans from Moscow, 28 May 1896.
2   RAM WC, Albert to Bosmans, 19 Aug. 1897.

it will have the biggest fleet in the world, which it will abuse to inter-fere in situations that are none of its business. That is going to be the biggest danger of the coming century.'[3] According to Brück's Law, the Anglo-Saxon ascendancy in world politics was an inevitability, but this did not mean that Albert liked the prospect.

While the Prince was in the U.S., a war erupted between America and Spain. Albert wrote to his father that he hoped the Americans would lose the war, 'in order to calm their jingoism.' If the Americans win, he warned, 'they will become incurable and their arrogance will grow unbearable.' A couple of years later, during the Anglo-Boer War, Albert was equally partisan in his anti-British feelings. 'The Eng-lish have been beaten,' he rejoiced, 'that will teach them a lesson.'

In 1898, Albert, by now 23 years old, asked his uncle's permission to marry Princess Isabelle of Orléans. King Leopold refused, arguing that he did not want to offend the French Republic. He made a counterproposal, offering Albert his granddaughter, the Austrian Archduchess Elisabeth (or *Erszi* as the family called her), in marriage. If Albert accepted, the King would give him the Congo Free State as a wedding present. Albert was not interested in marrying the Arch-duchess who, being eight years his junior, was but a child. By 1900, however, he considered life at his parent's home to have become utterly unbearable. He wanted to move out as soon as possible, and even marry Erszi if need be. 'Papa nowadays has periods of very bad depressions, black melancholy and vicious rage,' he wrote to his sister Joséphine. 'The Päppin have also introduced the rules of a convent here, but at the same time he remains hopelessly inactive, always repeating the same things. What I most lack here is life.'[4] When, how-ever, Count John d'Oultremont wrote to the King on Albert's behalf that the Prince was willing to marry the Archduchess, Leopold replied that such a marriage was out of the question. His daughter Stephanie had recently married the 'sheep-herding' Count Lonyay without his approval. As a consequence, he did not consider her to be his daughter anymore and, hence, did not want anything to do with Stephanie's daughter either.

Whilst turning down Albert's request, King Leopold proposed that his nephew marry a Russian Grand-Duchess, but Albert had Oultremont inform the King that 'the Grand-Duchess is ugly.' Two weeks after the King's veto of Erszi, Albert, afraid that the *bäcktelein* would propose yet another ugly princess, presented his uncle with a

3   RAM WC, Albert to Jules Bosmans from San Francisco, 25 Apr. 1898.
4   Quoted in Albert I 2, p. 30.

choice made by his sister Henriette: Elisabeth Wittelsbach, a 24-year-old cousin of Henriette's husband, the Duke of Vendôme. Albert travelled to the Vendôme residence at Neuilly near Paris, where he met Elisabeth for the first time during a family dinner arranged by Henriette. He preferred Elisabeth's younger, and prettier, sister, Marie-Gabrielle, and was disappointed to learn that the latter had already been promised to Crown Prince Rupert of Bavaria. Hence, he had to make do with Elisabeth. 'I think she is excellent,' he wrote to Henriette after his return to Brussels; 'I was more impressed with her than I have shown.'

Henriette replied that she would invite Elisabeth and her parents over to Paris again as soon as possible. Albert could then ask her father for her hand. The Count of Flanders objected that the Wittelsbach family was not rich enough to his opinion. 'They do not have a penny,' he remarked, but King Leopold made no objections. Consequently, the meeting of Albert and the Wittelsbachs at Neuilly was arranged for 29 May. *Liesel*, as Elisabeth was called at home, was one of three daughters of Prince Karl Theodor, the Duke in Bavaria. The Dukes belonged to a collateral branch of the royal House of Bavaria. Both Wittelsbach branches, the Kings *of* Bavaria, as well as the Dukes *in* Bavaria, were known for their eccentricity, due — it was said — to excessive inbreeding.

Things went very fast. The engagement was officially announced on 30 May. The next day Albert returned to Brussels. The betrothed promised to write each other every day. In his letters, the Belgian prince was very prosaic. Marriage 'is always a lottery,' he wrote, advising Elisabeth to enjoy her freedom while she could: 'Afterwards we will not be able to change our minds.' She, however, as befitted a Wittelsbach, was very passionate. 'If only I could be inside this letter and embrace you when you open it and cover you with kisses,' she wrote, 'I am so impatient to see you again, I shall cuddle you to bits.' And in another letter: 'I should so love to come to you and embrace you and tug at your hair, I love you so much that I would jump into water and fire for you.'[5]

The next summer, Albert travelled to Bavaria with his father. The *Päppin*, who preferred tall, big women, was not impressed with his future daughter-in-law, who in his opinion lacked a pair of firm breasts and a round bottom. 'The young Elisabeth is not very pretty, she is rather small and does not have much shape,' he wrote to his daughter Joséphine. 'We are used to beautiful tall princesses, like your mother was and still is, as well as you two, my good daughters. I think the public will be disappointed with the small Elisabeth.'[6]

Albert and Elisabeth were married in Munich on 2 October 1900, in the presence of Albert's two royal uncles, the Kings of Belgium and Romania, and Elisabeth's cousin, the Prince-Regent of Bavaria. According to Article 60 of the Belgian Constitution, the Belgian government had to approve the marriage of the Crown Prince. Failure to do so would *automatically* mean that the Prince would lose his rights of succession. The ministers, however, were never asked for their approval. It is possible that the vindictive Leopold II deliberately 'forgot' to do so. No one seemed to bother about it — at least not for the time being.

The groom was a tall, pessimistic, self-doubting man. He was myopic, like his mother, and had to wear glasses, but he was handsome like his maternal Sigmaringen relatives (no Bourbon nose here) and had a little beard. Later Albert would shave the beard, keeping only a moustache. The bride was a small, vivacious woman, with short hair and a sharp, long and bony face. She had a strong personality and was uninhibited. *Liesel* was one of the first German nudists, convinced of the benevolent influence of the sun on one's naked body. Her nudist practice tanned her skin, so she powdered it to look paler as fashion required. Like her father, she was a gifted musician and had very liberal ideas about morality and religion. Nominally Elisabeth was a Catholic, but she was very unorthodox; she believed in reincarnation and astrology.

Albert and Elisabeth were a good match. Though Elisabeth was a feminist, she allowed Albert to boss her around. She called him *'Männele'* (dear husband), he called her *'Liesel,' 'Sabeth,'* or *'Kind'l'* (dear child). When he talked about her in the third person, he referred to her as *'das Kind'* (the child). He sent her written instructions, like: *'Das Kind* has to take good care of itself. It has to have a good breakfast. It has to eat well around noontime. It has to cover itself well, certainly not wear thin socks, and it has to put on booties that keep its feet warm.' She said she felt like a *'Hund'* that had to listen to its *'Herrle,'* — a dog that had to listen to its master — but she did not mind. She pretended to listen to *'Männele,'* and continued to do things her own way.

After their marriage, the newlyweds went to live in a huge house, the *Hôtel d'Assche* in Brussels' quiet and elegant Leopold Quarter. Albert felt obliged to pay daily visits to his father, but he hated it.

6   Quoted in Albert I 2, p. 34.

'These visits demand much of me,' he confessed to Henriette. 'We feel like strangers. *Les bonnes Päppin* [the good Päppin: plural, feminine gender] have grown very old. There is only one thing dominating them: the hatred of the bäcktelein — and it has really become a genuine hatred.'

The first decade of the 20th-century saw the old generation of the Saxe-Coburgs pass away. Queen Victoria died in 1901; the *bäckin* in 1902; the *Päppin* on 17 November 1905; the *bäcktelein* in 1909. Only the Countess of Flanders survived the decade: she died in 1912. Meanwhile, a new generation was born. The birth of Albert's first child, Leopold, on 3 November 1901 was greeted with 101 cannonshots. A second son, Charles, followed in 1903; and in 1906 a daughter was born, christened Marie-José after her maternal grandmother.

Albert prepared himself thoroughly for the day that he would succeed his uncle. He met a young hardworking intellectual of Flemish origin with left-wing sympathies, Jules Ingenbleek, whom he engaged as his personal secretary. Ingenbleek and Albert discussed social problems, visited Britain to study social conditions in the English industrial areas, and closely watched the development of the socialist parties in Belgium and its neighbouring countries. After making the acquaintance of the French social-democrat Alfred Léon Gérault-Richard in February 1906, the Prince concluded that 'in the future the socialist movement will inevitably be linked to more reformist and less revolutionary attitudes.'[7] This was a comforting conclusion: it made an alliance of interests possible between the socialists and the monarchy.

The Pontiffs of Socialism

The *bäcktelein* had been one of the most controversial men in Belgium. At Leopold II's funeral, while the royal coffin was being driven on a carriage through the streets of Brussels, onlookers shouted insults at the corpse, turned their backs to the hearse and spat at it. This caused Albert to panic. That evening, on 22 December 1909, he tried to memorise the constitutional oath that he was to take the next morning in Parliament. He became extremely agitated. 'I cannot do it,' he cried, 'I will not take the oath.'[8] Elisabeth, unable to calm him down, summoned Ingenbleek to the palace. The latter argued with the Prince till the early hours and was able to talk him round.

7   Albert I 2, p. 42.
8   Albert I 2, p. 348.

The next day, Albert took the oath. Everything worked out well, apart from a minor incident when some socialist MPs yelled: 'Equal voting rights for all.' The leader of the Belgian Workers' Party, Emile Vandervelde, later apologised to Albert: 'We did not criticise you, but the bastards in the government.'[9] Since 1894, Belgium had had an electoral system with plural votes: every male citizen from the age of 25 had one vote, but supplementary votes were given — to fathers from the age of 35, to intellectuals holding a degree of higher education, and to men who owned their own house — with a maximum of three votes per individual. The Socialists demanded a *one man, one vote* system. After the inauguration ceremony, the new King rode to Laken. He stopped at the *Maison Populaire*, the headquarters of the BWP, to greet the red flag.

Albert was relieved that the inauguration had passed smoothly and that the Socialists accepted him. Only a Flamingant lawyer from Ghent, Alfons Jonckx, questioned his authority. Jonckx argued that Albert had lost his rights to the crown because the Government had not explicitly approved his marriage to Elisabeth in 1900, as Articles 60 and 64 of the Constitution required. In the Brussels Liberal newspaper *Le Soir* of 6 January, Beernaert, the eminent jurist and former Prime Minister, acknowledged that there had indeed been 'a theoretical violation of the letter of the Constitution.' However, as everyone seemed to be quite happy with the King, it was better to 'smile and forget the whole affair.'

There was also some criticism of Albert's alleged *red* sympathies. 'He is said to adhere to a certain socialism,' *Le Soir* wrote. The paper referred to a secret memorandum from the Papal Nuncio in Brussels to the Vatican, which had been leaked to the press. It stated that the King was 'deplorably half-hearted as a Catholic,' that he read 'dangerous books' and that he had surrounded himself with 'free-thinkers, freemasons, even socialists.'[10]

The Belgian bishops, however, supported Albert. The Archbishop of Mechelen and Primate of Belgium, Cardinal Désiré Mercier, was careful not to undermine the foundation which underpinned the Belgian state. None of the Catholic newspapers, all of them under direct control of the Church hierarchy, published even the slightest criticism of the King. On the contrary, they emphatically described him as 'a most Catholic king.' Mercier had become Archbishop in 1906 with the approval of Leopold II. The Cardinal was a Walloon and an outspo-

9   Vandervelde 2, p. 182.
10   *Le Soir*, 18 and 26 Dec. 1909.

ken Belgicist. 'Patriotism is a Christian virtue,' he said, referring to Saint Thomas Aquinas. By patriotism, Mercier meant Belgian nationalism, not Flemish patriotism, which to Mercier was not only treason but a sin. In the seminaries young trainee priests were taught that the Flemish Movement was an invention of the Devil: '*Motus iste flandricus, a diabolo inventus.*'[11]

Through its entire history, from the early Middle Ages right up to the Belgian Revolution of 1830, Flanders had been one of the most prosperous regions in the whole of Europe. The industrialisation process that Dutch King Willem had started in Ghent, Antwerp and other Flemish cities, was suddenly brought to a halt in September 1830. In the new state, the government's attention was focused almost exclusively on Wallonia, the southern Francophone part of the country. From the beginning, the Francophone revolutionary elite, the creators of the new state, made very clear to the King what part of the country he had to cater for. When in 1834 Leopold I decided to build the first Belgian railway line between Brussels and Antwerp, Alexandre Gendebien, one of the fathers of the Belgian Revolution, objected that the railroad had to be constructed between Brussels and his Walloon home province of Hainaut, whose economic interests, he said, were being 'sacrificed' to those of 'Orangist Antwerp.' In a speech in Parliament on 11 March, Gendebien warned the King. 'Bear this in mind,' he said, 'If you refuse to listen to the language of reason, we shall have you hear the language of violence.' Leopold realised his mistake. From then on he bore Gendebien's warning in mind, and so did his successors.

The result was that of the 2.93 billion francs spent on railroad infrastructure between 1832 and 1912, 68% went to the four Walloon provinces, where only 38% of the population lived. During the same period, the government devoted a total of 4.29 billion francs to transport infrastructure (by land, rail and canals) and harbour works, but only 35.6% went to Flanders and more than 55% to Wallonia. By 1914, the Walloon provinces of Luxemburg (230,000 inhabitants) and Namur (350,000 inhabitants), both boasted 1,200 kilometres of paved roads, while the Flemish province of Antwerp (as large as each of these Walloon provinces, but with 950,000 inhabitants) had only 600 kilometres of these roads. Flanders lagged behind in all areas. The Walloon district of Dinant had 15 post offices more than the equally large Flemish district of Aalst, even though the latter had 100,000 inhabitants more than Dinant.

11   Quoted in Boudens, p. 101, n. 169.

Wallonia was pampered for two reasons. First, its geography made it far less easy to control by an occupational army than the open Flemish flatlands. Wallonia consisted of a long industrial axis in the valley along the Maas and Samber rivers, surrounded by mountains and the vast Ardennes forests. Secondly, at least when compared with the placid Flemings, the Walloons are a hot-tempered and rebellious 'Latin' people. The Francophone Walloons had risen against King Willem in 1830 in order to join France. Their plans had been thwarted. To appease them, a price had to be paid. The authorities in Brussels bribed Wallonia into complacency: they bought Walloon loyalty to the artificial Belgian state with money they extracted from the Flemings.

Indeed, the bulk of Belgium's tax revenue was used for investments in Wallonia, though most of that revenue came from Flanders. Wallonia accounted for only 30% of the direct and indirect taxes collected between 1832 and 1912. This financial drain had a dramatic effect on the Flemish provinces. In less than three decades Flanders deteriorated from one of Europe's most developed regions to one of its poorest areas. One million emigrants left Flanders after 1850. This was a considerable demographic loss for a people of 5 million. Emigration caused the population of the Flemish provinces to drop from 60% of the Belgian total in 1830 to 53% by 1880. (It rose again to 60% only in the second half of the 20th century).

Even in the most terrible years of destitution and poverty, the Flemings still contributed a disproportionate percentage of Belgium's taxes. The Belgian fiscal system taxed an individual according to the number of inhabitants in the municipality where he lived. Because Flanders (13,708 square kilometres) is a smaller country than Wallonia (15,743 square kilometres) and because it had larger municipalities, its tax burden was substantially heavier.

Another tax advantage for Wallonia was that corporate taxation was virtually non-existent in Belgium. The Belgian industrialists, including the royal family with its stake in the SG, were taxed at only 2% of their gigantic profits. It was not until 1880, after an interruption of half a century, that the industrialisation process began to gain momentum again in Flanders. In 1890, 16.7% of all corporate taxes were paid in Flanders; in 1900, 18.6%; in 1910, 28.4%. When the Walloon tax advantage diminished, the Belgian authorities decided to raise corporate taxes.

Flemish intellectuals who protested against the unfair treatment of their people faced the immediate wrath of the authorities. In the aftermath of the 1830 Revolution, anyone suspected of harbouring

Orangist sympathies had been either dismissed from the civil service or the army, or degraded to inferior positions. This purge removed the entire administrative elite of young Dutch-speaking Flemish intellectuals appointed by King Willem. In 1848, Charles Spilthoorn, a 44-year-old lawyer from Ghent tried to incite an uprising. He was arrested and condemned to death. In 1855, after seven years of imprisonment, Spilthoorn was released on condition that he leave the country: he boarded a ship bound for New York. Another 'revolutionary' was the Catholic priest Benedict Beeckman from Bruges. He was an avowed Orangist and a democrat. In 1848 he founded *Het Brugsche Vrye* (The Bruges Freestate), a journal that campaigned for political rights for the Flemings. He soon ran into trouble with the authorities and with his bishop. As a result, *Het Brugsche Vrye* ceased publication in 1853. Father Beeckman was forced into submission by the Church and died twelve years later in obscurity in Brussels. In 1858, the Brussels poet Michiel Van der Voort refused to pay his taxes. The authorities claimed the taxes in a letter in French, a language Van der Voort did not understand. He was taken to court and condemned for insubordination.

Men of a more cautious nature became the founders of the so-called *Flemish Movement*. As involvement in activities in favour of Flemish political rights was too dangerous, the Flemish Movement initially focused on the cultural emancipation of the Flemish people. Only from the 1860s onwards, did it start to make political demands and its members became known as Flamingants. The Flamingants did not dare to advocate reunification with the Netherlands, but they campaigned for the official recognition of Dutch as the administrative language in the Flemish provinces.

The suppression of the Dutch language in Flanders was most dramatic in the fields of justice and education. The execution in 1860 of Jan Coucke and Peter Goethals, two Flemish labourers who were sentenced to death by a court that had refused to hear them in Dutch, greatly disturbed the Flamingants. In the field of education, all the efforts of King Willem between 1815 and 1830 to fight illiteracy in Flanders were undone. The result was devastating. By 1900, Belgium had a higher proportion of illiterates than any of the neighbouring countries: 10.1% of its army could neither read nor write, against only 2.3% in the Netherlands, 4.7% in France, and 0.5% in Germany (a country extending far into Eastern Europe). Although the 1910 census revealed that 98.4% of the Flemish population spoke Dutch, there was not a single Dutch-language secondary school in the entire country,

apart from one Antwerp school that had been privately established by
Marten Rudelsheim and S. Samson, two Jewish Flamingants.

The anti-Flemish policy was felt most severely in Brussels. After the
imposed Frenchification during the French occupation of the Southern
Netherlands in 1794–1814 and the subsequent influx of French Republican and Bonapartist immigrants, the number of Francophones in the
city had risen to five per cent. By 1900, after seventy years of Belgian
rule, the number of Francophones in Brussels totalled over half the
population. In 1911, two nurses at a Brussels hospital were disciplined
for speaking 'Flemish' (Dutch) to each other. The doctor who ran the
hospital commented: 'It is already bad enough that we have to tolerate
the patients speaking Flemish.'[12] Even primary school children in the
rural Flemish countryside were familiar with the violation of the freedom of opinion, education and language in Belgium. In his childhood
memoirs the popular Flemish novelist Ernest Claes (1885–1965)
describes how he was caned by the headmaster because he had said in
class: 'Flanders is my fatherland.'[13]

Denying the Flemings education in their own language was a
means of keeping the Belgian ethnic majority in a minority position.
The Church applied this policy as rigorously as the State. It is indicative of the position of the Catholic hierarchy that, while the vast
majority of schools in Flanders were run by the Church, the bishops
refused to provide any secondary and higher education other than in
French. When the Flamingants pleaded with the Church to allow
Flemish children to study in their mother tongue, the bishops replied
with a document in September 1906, stating that Dutch was 'unfit as a
cultural and scientific language.' Mgr. Waffelaert, the Bishop of
Bruges, added that it was 'unchristian and against the Catholic principles to aim for a Dutch-language university.'[14]

* * *

Albert lacked the shrewdness and the self-confidence of Leopold II,
but he had one idea that would be the leitmotiv of his entire reign: he
wanted the socialist movement to become the new supporting pillar
under the Belgian structure. He understood that if the Socialists were
unable to extend their power-base in Flanders, they needed a united
and centralised Belgium because this would allow them to use their
dominance over Wallonia as a lever to exert power over Flanders and
its growing economic potential. Hence, the Socialist Movement was

12   Quoted in *Het Laatste Nieuws*, 30 May 1911.
13   Claes, Ernest, p. 281.
14   Quoted in Boudens, p. 98.

by definition a Belgian-nationalist force. 'Three enemies lie around my throne,' Albert wrote, 'Conservatives who are against the State; Flemish-activists who are against the monarchy and the Belgian Nation; and demagogues who adhere to a certain Catholicism resembling French popular democracies. To hold out against them, I can only count on the support of Socialism, which is national, in favour of Belgian unity, and in favour of centralism — three elements that make it an ally of the dynasty.'[15]

In order to get the Socialists into power, the King had to get rid of the Government. Since 1884, the Catholic Party had held an absolute majority in Parliament. The Liberal Party, dominated by the Masonic lodges, was the main opposition party. The Socialists had entered the Chamber of Representatives with 28 seats in 1894, when all Belgian males of 25 and older had been given at least one vote. By 1910 the BWP had grown to 35 MPs. It was assumed that if a *one man, one vote* system were introduced and the plural votes for family fathers, home-owners and educated people abolished, the number of Socialist MPs would rise even further and the Catholic Party might lose its absolute majority in Parliament.

Moreover, Albert's advisors reckoned that democratisation combined with proportional representation would result in greater power for the King. Indeed, whenever a government depending on a parliamentary majority of only one party had a strong leader, as Beernaert had been in the 1880s, the King's political influence was limited. A government depending on a coalition of two or more parties would be inherently weak, and hence the King could pose as an independent arbiter. Thus, it was in the Crown's interest to promote the introduction of a *one man, one vote* principle in a system with as proportional a representation as possible. Such a change to the Constitution, however, required two-thirds of the votes in Parliament. As the Catholic Party was opposed to these reforms, the government of Prime Minister Frans Schollaert had to be toppled first and an alliance forged between Liberals and Socialists.

In 1911, Schollaert came up with a novel idea. He proposed the introduction of school vouchers. Parents would receive a voucher for each child under 15. The voucher was to be handed over to a teacher or a school of their choice. The teacher could then cash the voucher and receive a subsidy from the government. The voucher bill was attacked by the anti-clerical Liberals, who saw it as a sly ploy to give government subsidies to schools run by the clergy. It was also rejected

15   Albert I to Henriette, in Wilmet 1, p. 156.

by the Socialists, who wanted to abolish all private schooling. Their common opposition to the voucher bill provided the ideal opportunity to bring Liberals and Socialists together. When Schollaert presented his bill to Albert to obtain the required royal signature, the King refused to sign. After long and bitter bickering, Schollaert resigned as Prime Minister. The episode made the King very popular amongst the left. When the royal couple paid a visit to Charleroi in November 1911, Socialist activists took to the streets cheering 'Long live the King.' The local Socialist newspaper explained to its readers: 'The cry "Long live the King" actually signifies "Long live the delivered people" or "Down with the clergy." These are all synonyms.'[16]

Schollaert was replaced as Prime Minister by a relatively unknown Catholic politician, Baron Charles de Broqueville, the son of a French aristocrat and a daughter of Leopold I's former hunting companion, Count Camille de Briey. In June 1912, new elections were due. Waxweiler, Jungbluth and Ingenbleek persuaded the Liberal Party leader, Paul Hymans, to join forces with the Socialists and participate in the elections as one political formation. To the amazement of the King and his advisors, however, the Catholics won the elections. They gained 101 seats in the Chamber of Representatives, against 83 for the Liberal-Socialist alliance and two for the Flemish-nationalist Daensists, increasing their majority to 16 seats instead of the previous 6. In Flanders, where many Catholic candidates tended to be anti-militarists sympathising with the Flamingants, the Catholics obtained a clear-cut majority of 61 seats, against only 25 for their opponents. In Wallonia, however, the Liberals and Socialists gained an equally clear-cut majority of 44 seats, against only 28 seats for the Catholics. In Brussels, the Catholics got 12 seats, against 14 for their opponents — a figure roughly corresponding with the number of Flemings and Francophones in the capital.

The elections gave the Catholics a democratic mandate to introduce the voucher system. They received this mandate from a majority of all Belgians, but the Francophones were not prepared to accept this. In Liège, there was a popular outcry against the Flemings. 'There is much talk here of a separation from Flanders,' a correspondent from Liège warned Hymans in Brussels. The Walloon anti-Semite and Socialist MP, Jules Destrée, wrote an open letter to the King, stating that the Flemings were becoming ever more demanding in Belgium. 'Sire, allow me to tell you the truth, the large and horrifying truth: *il n'y a pas de Belges!*' Destrée exclaimed, and he argued in favour of introducing federalism as a means to neutralise the Flemish democratic majority within Belgium. Albert told Ingenbleek: 'What Destrée says is true enough, but it is no less true that an administrative separation will lead to far greater inconveniences and dangers than the present situation.'[17] For the sake of national unity, the King wanted the Catholics to renounce their democratic mandate.

Ingenbleek was sent to see Broqueville. Pale and in tears, he said: 'I beg you, save the King!'[18] Broqueville did as he was asked. The voucher bill was buried and never mentioned again. George Helleputte, the new Minister of Agriculture and Public Works, who was a moderate Flamingant, was very critical of the King: 'It is always the politics of the Court to weaken the Catholic Party and to ally itself with the so-called moderate Liberal Left,' he wrote in his diary. The collaboration of the royal entourage with the Socialists went so far that in 1913 the King's men secretly paid the BWP one million francs to organise a general strike in favour of the one man, one vote electoral system. Belgian Catholic politicians did not dare to criticise the King, but when Albert visited Switzerland shortly before the outbreak of the First World War, they had the Swiss Catholic newspaper *La Liberté* attack 'the pontiffs of Socialism' reigning at the Belgian royal palace.[19]

* * *

At Laken, Albert acquainted his three children — Leopold, the Duke of Brabant, Charles, the Count of Flanders, and their sister Marie-José — with their future duties. He took them along to all kinds of ceremonies. The children were often bored to death. Equally boring were the hours spent with their mother. The music-mad Elisabeth played the violin every morning from eleven to half past twelve. The little princes had to sit on the sofa and keep still. The Queen, who was very authoritarian and demanding, wanted them 'to learn how to listen.' From an early age, they were taught to play the piano and the violin. Other studies were deemed less important and even harmful, because, according to Elisabeth, studying 'distorts the instinct.' They received no religious instruction, either. 'My parents were extremely discrete about everything related to religion,' Marie-José wrote in her memoirs. '*Ask the chamber maids*, my father told me when I once questioned him about an image of the crucifixion.'[20] Albert, however, made sure that Leopold and Charles were introduced to his own

17 Albert I to Ingenbleek, 30 Aug. 1912, in Albert I 2, p. 435.
18 Albert I 2, p. 391.
19 Albert I 2, p. 499.
20 Quoted in Marie-José, pp. 59, 62–3.

philosophy and the things he valued. The boys were taught world history according to Brück's Law and learned to count using Lagrange's calculations based on the pyramid of Cheops.

Albert and Elisabeth were not only demanding with regard to their children. The Queen was also extremely authoritarian towards her staff. Once, the poet Emile Verhaeren, whom Elisabeth often invited to the palace because she liked him, gave the manuscript of one of his poems as a gift to the governess of Princess Marie-José. Apparently, Verhaeren fancied her at least as much as the Queen. Elisabeth, who had noticed this, confiscated the manuscript from the governess as soon as the poet had left.

Apart from music, the Queen devoted her time to painting and sculpting. Ornithology was another passion. Elisabeth was mad about birds, and especially about their 'music,' which to her was literally of a divine order. 'Bird songs = cosmic music,' she wrote, 'the bird = the Holy Spirit, the spiritual side of man.'[21] She wanted to discover the divine messages of her feathered friends, and she tried to 'talk' to the birds, taking these efforts very seriously. In 1938, the Queen hired an entire BBC-team to record birdsong in the royal park at Laken. The BBC people worked day and night for weeks, and recorded 35 species. This resulted in a collection of 250 gramophone discs, the equivalent of 50 CDs today. The Queen sent a compilation to politicians, foreign embassies and musicians. 'We still listen to the Birds of Laeken,' the British ambassador wrote many years later, 'the whole thing is very funny and always a source of joy.'[22]

To Be or Not To Be Neutral

Belgium was a neutral country. Unlike other neutral countries, its neutrality was involuntary. The Treaty of London of 1831 prohibited it from joining any military alliance. Britain had imposed this neutrality on Brussels because it feared that Belgium would ally itself with France. In return, the British agreed to guarantee Belgium's independence, which obliged them to go to war with any country violating Belgium's borders. The Flemish majority of the Belgians favoured this neutrality. The only advantage of being a Belgian, was that one never had to fight or die for Belgium. 'This nation,' Albert complained to Prime Minister Broqueville in June 1912, 'guards what it pretends to be a liberty: not to have to defend itself.'[23]

---

21 RAB SAE nr. 621.
22 RAB SAE, Knatchbull-Hugessen to Elisabeth, 3 Feb. 1957.
23 Albert I to Broqueville, 22 June 1912, in Albert I 2, p. 426.

The majority of Broqueville's Catholic Party, as well as the Flamingants, were fervently neutralist and anti-militarist. Most of the Belgian Francophones, however, were both militarist and anti-neutralist. They considered the prohibition preventing Belgium from joining a military alliance with France a limitation of Belgium's sovereignty. The Liberal leader Paul Hymans was their main spokesman, but Emile Vandervelde, the leader of the Socialist BWP, also belonged to this group. Both Hymans and Vandervelde had Flemish grandparents who had moved to Brussels where the Frenchification process had transformed their grandchildren into Francophones. Like many Frenchified Belgians of Flemish descent, they considered Dutch an inferior language of uneducated people, as their own grandfathers had been. This group of middle-class civil servants living in Brussels formed the hard-core Belgian nationalists. They were no Walloons and had ceased to be Flemings; their only identity was Belgian.

The King was the only Belgian militarist who did not belong to the pro-French group. He wanted a strong Belgian army but wished to remain neutral as well. To Albert, the only thing that mattered in case of a Franco-German war, was to stay out of it, or end it on the winning side, whichever side that might be. As Belgium was an entirely artificial country, the risk was that if the King backed the wrong side and ended up with the losers, the victors would simply abolish his kingdom after the war. When Albert left for a visit to Potsdam in November 1913, Baron Léon Van der Elst advised him to tell the Kaiser that Belgium intended to defend itself in case of military aggression. The King did not do this. He told Van der Elst: 'I am not that much in favour of Germany myself, but one has to take into consideration what is in the interest of our country.'[24] Hence, all options had to be kept open.

The Belgian general staff, however, was not much impressed by Germany's military power. A bunch of conceited Francophiles, they reckoned that the German troops would be vastly inferior to the Belgian and French armies. Some even hoped for a German attack on Belgium, which would allow them to counterattack towards Cologne and Trier and occupy the entire Rhineland. 'Such an offensive is within our means' stated a secret report of the Belgian general staff in the summer of 1913.[25]

The First World War began when Austria declared war on Serbia on 28 June 1914. Tensions rose between France and Germany. The *Kaiser*

24   Albert I 2, p. 449.
25   Quoted in Albert I 2, p. 88.

presented Brussels with an ultimatum on the evening of 2 August: Belgium had to allow a free passage to the German army on its way to France. At two minutes past eight on the morning of 4 August, German troops crossed the Belgian border. In London, later that morning, the British Cabinet, with fifteen votes against two and four abstentions, declared war on Germany.

Albert issued a proclamation to call his people to arms. He addressed himself explicitly to 'Flemings' and 'Walloons.' It was the first time ever that a Belgian King called directly upon the Flemish people. It was generally interpreted as a promise that if the Flemings fought loyally for Belgium, they would be granted their rights within the Belgian framework once the war was over. Consequently, even Flamingants volunteered to fight for the King.

According to Article 68 of the Belgian Constitution, the King is not only the theoretical Commander-in-Chief of the Armed Forces, but he actively commands them in the field when the country is at war. As a result, Albert was the only head of state in Western Europe personally to lead the military operations of his country's army. Not even the *Kaiser* did this. In Britain, the royal prerogatives are diminished in case of war,[26] in Belgium they are enlarged. Contrary to his peacetime political competence, a Belgian King does not need the approval of either Government or Parliament for his wartime decisions. When the very existence of the artificial Belgian state is at risk, it is the King, and he alone, who decides about the country's fate. Though this may seem an odd rule, there is some logic behind it: as the King is the person whose private fortune depends most directly on Belgium's existence, he is the man that can best be trusted to uphold the artificial Belgian construction.

Albert and his generals soon discovered that the Germans' military strength was vastly superior. Instead of marching victoriously on Cologne and Trier, the Belgian field army, 117,000 men strong, was forced to retreat. Two weeks into the war, the field army had dwindled to 90,000 men, not only through casualties, but also through defections. Albert wrote to Broqueville on 14 August that the army was undisciplined; that the privates did not salute their officers; that they were incapable of marching. 'After ten kilometres, the soldiers are exhausted. They all complain they have sore feet.'[27] It took General Scheere's men five hours to cover a distance of barely ten miles, without luggage! The Belgian defences collapsed. Brussels fell with-

26 Hardie, pp. 141–3.
27 Albert I to Broqueville, 14 Aug. 1914, in Albert I 2, p. 515.

out putting up a fight on 20 August. By the end of August, Albert withdrew with the field army to Antwerp. It had been reduced to 70,000 men. Antwerp, however, had a city garrison of another 70,000 men.

In early September, the Germans turned their attention to France and ignored the Belgians, apart from an occasional bombardment of Antwerp with zeppelins. Queen Elisabeth left the city for Britain with the royal children and 200 million francs in gold. The Queen was not the only fugitive: twenty per cent of the Belgians fled abroad in the autumn of 1914. Of the entire Belgian population of 7.6 million, one million went to the Netherlands and almost half a million to Britain and France. Ninety per cent of those who had fled to the Netherlands later returned; those in Britain and France were unable to do so. As a consequence, 8 per cent of the Belgians spent the First World War outside Belgium. Two-thirds of them were Flemings.

When, after the battle of the Marne, the Germans turned on Antwerp in early October, the King lost heart. He decided to give himself up as a prisoner to the *Kaiser*. A shocked Broqueville protested violently; Ingenbleek also tried to make the King change his mind; even Winston Churchill, the First Lord of the Admiralty, came to Antwerp on 3 October to encourage Albert. Luckily, Elisabeth had returned as well. On 6 October, she was able to talk him round. Victory might still come, as the Flemish provinces to the West of the River Scheldt had not been conquered yet.

The royal couple and the field army left Antwerp for Ostend in the early hours of 7 October. The Antwerp garrison remained in town. After the King had left, 30,000 soldiers from the garrison fled to the Netherlands. The remainder surrendered to the enemy on 10 October. Meanwhile, the King's forces, rapidly dwindling to 55,000 men through defections, were in a chaotic state. The officers were all Francophones, while the Flemings made up the lower ranks. As the latter were commanded in French, frequent misunderstandings occurred. Artillerists who received the French order '*Visez la meule*' (Shoot at the haystack) dutifully destroyed a nearby mill ('*meulen*' in their native tongue).[28]

The only Belgian success during the campaign was the achievement of the royal propaganda department. German atrocities were emphasised and exploited to the full. A decade earlier the royal propaganda staff had appreciated how effectively Leopold II's adversaries had exploited the pictures of children with their hands cut off. Now they

28   This and other examples can be found in Vanacker 2, pp. 30–43.

concocted stories of German soldiers chopping off the hands of little Belgians and used these to win international sympathy for Albert's cause.

After the Belgians had evacuated Ostend on 15 October, the King went to the little coastal village of De Panne, the last hamlet before the French border. He settled in the Villa Maskens, literally the last house on Belgian soil, situated in the dunes. Albert was determined to await the arrival of the Germans and to surrender. He forbade Belgian soldiers to cross the border and continue fighting the *Kaiser* from France. They had to give themselves up with him. According to Albert, Belgium had merely defended its own territory against aggression, but it had never joined the Allied side. He hoped that this argument would persuade Berlin to allow him to keep his kingdom.

Broqueville disagreed. He wished to continue the war together with the Allies. He argued that constitutionally the King could not surrender without the approval of the Government. Albert replied that according to the Constitution the King was the Commander-in-Chief of the army and could do as he pleased. Two simple Flemish civilians, however, saved the day. They suggested flooding the Yser estuary, to create a water barrier of one mile wide between the Belgians and the enemy. Water was the only natural defence the Dutch people (in Holland as well as in Flanders) had ever had. In the 16th century they had used a water barrier against the Spanish; now the Belgians used water to stop the German advance. The flood gates were opened on 27 October, submerging the Flemish meadows. Hence, the German offensive came to a halt less than ten miles to the east of Albert's residence on the Franco-Belgian border.

The danger now came from the south: 25 miles from De Panne lay the medieval town of Ieper (Ypres), unprotected by water. The Belgians had fled Ieper on 7 October, allowing a German cavalry unit to enter the town. The British were able to recapture Ieper on 13 October. They held on to it during the following four weeks at the heavy toll of 58,000 men. In the spring of 1915, the Germans launched a new offensive against Ieper. The second battle of Ieper cost the British and Canadians another 59,000 men. The Belgians took no part in the battles around Ieper. They defended the submerged front of 24 miles between the sea and Diksmuide, 7 miles to the north of Ieper.

During the following years, the Belgians remained passive onlookers of the war. They gradually built up their military strength by enlisting all men in the small area that was left of Belgium and with volunteers who arrived via Holland. They numbered 79,000 men in December 1915, and 167,000 men by the autumn of 1918 when male

Belgian fugitives in France and Britain had also been enlisted. But the Belgians hardly fought during the entire war. Albert pretended that, as he was 'neutral,' he had nothing to do with the conflict between Berlin on the one hand and Paris and London on the other. Compared to the military losses of other belligerents, Belgium suffered relatively little. Proportionally its death toll was about seven times less than that of the Allies. Only 41,000 Belgian soldiers died (0.6% of the population), against 700,000 for the British Isles (1.75%), 1.5 million for France (3.5%), and 1.95 million for Germany (3%). Of the Belgian casualties, one-third perished through disease. Less than 27,000 actually fell on the battle field. There were also 6,500 Belgian civilian war casualties.

* * *

Albert and Elisabeth remained in De Panne throughout the war. Their three children lived in Britain. The King had asked Lord Curzon, a member of the British war cabinet, to look after them. Curzon was the widower of Mary Leiter, the daughter of a Jewish Chicago real estate magnate. He had three daughters, the only heirs to the Leiter business empire. As soon as the Belgian princes 'invaded' Hackwood, Curzon's Hampshire mansion, the quiet life of the girls was over. On noticing Bobby, the dog of Curzon's youngest daughter Ba-Ba (Alexandra), Charles at once gave it a treacherous kick, while Marie- José pulled its tail. Cimmie (Cynthia) Curzon, the second daughter, threw a picture of the *Kaiser* on the floor and invited the Belgian guests to trample on 'this grandson of Queen Victoria.' Leopold immediately fell in love with the hot-blooded girl of sixteen. Irene Curzon, nineteen, and the meticulous lady of the house since her mother had died, had a hard time keeping everything in check, especially when Charles and Marie-José spilled oil paint all over their room. Lord Curzon's nerves were sorely tried. One night, he had a nightmare. In his dream, he saw the Belgian princes kick his precious antique Greek statues to pieces, while he tried to stop them but could not.[29]

Occasionally, the children were allowed to go to De Panne to meet their parents. Elisabeth was staying with Albert at the Villa Maskens. The only permanent resident at the Villa was the Belgian Chief of Staff, General Emile Galet. Four years older than the King, he was one of Albert's best friends. The royal couple received many visitors. Albert and Elisabeth became immensely popular in the Allied press.

The Belgian propaganda portrayed them as mythical figures. Albert complained that he had far too many visitors, and he did not like all of them. Baron Léon Lambert, a Belgian banker and an in-law of the Rothschilds, he found 'a real Jew and a snob.'[30]

Despite his popularity in the Allied countries, Albert blamed them for the position he was in. On 17 April 1915, he wrote in his diary: 'The Allies have not served us well. Though the Germans have violated their obligations towards us, the others have not been able to keep them.' Colonel Eugène Génie, the French military attaché at De Panne, sensed the King's resentment. The Frenchman, whom Elisabeth in her diary described as 'a false dog,'[31] reported to Paris: 'The King, supreme commander of the army, is not up to his present heavy responsibilities. Not only is he technically incapable of leading an army, but, what is worse, he completely lacks the character and the temperament which is indispensable for doing so.'[32]

Albert decided to enter into secret negotiations with the Germans. If the *Kaiser* would reinstate him in Brussels, Albert was prepared to withdraw from the war. In the autumn of 1915, he wrote in his diary that the Allies were destined for 'total defeat.' 'In the Central Empires, there is discipline and unity, while on the Allied side everything depends on the politicians, on irresponsible and incapable men. The sovereigns of England and Russia are nonentities,' who 'allow Parliaments — already totally incapable in times of peace — to take decisions at decisive moments when the vision and the energy of a superior man is needed.' Albert was particularly harsh on 'the incredible vanity of the English,' while 'France allows itself to be abused by England.' 'If only France would understand that it is not in her interest to spill her blood to serve the egotistical aims of the English with regard to the Continent.' Belgium had to detach itself from London and Paris. 'For us, it is more than time to focus our attention on the means by which to recover the territories that the Allies are unable to conquer.'[33]

Albert's unilateral peace negotiations started in September 1915. He used two maternal aunts of Elisabeth as his intermediaries. They came to De Panne for so-called family visits. The Duchess of Bourbon-Parma came in September. Her sister, the Countess of Bardi, arrived in late October. The Countess brought a message from Albert's brother-in-law, the German diplomat Count Hans Törring,

30   RAB KAD, 5 Mar. 1916.
31   Elisabeth's diary, 30 Sept. 1914, quoted in Marie-José, p. 161.
32   Génie, in Albert I 3, p. 81.
33   RAB KAD, 17 Oct., 12, 17 and 25 Nov. 1915.

the husband of Elisabeth's sister Sophie. Except for General Galet and Emile Waxweiler, the entire royal staff was sent away during the aunts' visits. While the Countess of Bardi waited, Albert and Waxweiler worked on a letter to the Germans. 'The contacts between London and Brussels have been cold and distrustful for twenty years,' the King wrote. Before the war, 'public opinion, while really hostile to England, was not unfavourable to Germany, despite a press campaign in favour of France, which I disapproved of and fought.'[34] On 24 and 25 November, Törring and Waxweiler secretly met at Zürich in Switzerland. After the first round of talks, Törring went to Berlin for instructions and met Waxweiler again for a second round on 29 November. The Belgian government knew nothing of this, nor did the Allies. In England, however, Lord Curzon was worried. Albert had sent Curzon a pessimistic letter on 8 November. 'The powerful countries on the Allied side lack unity of direction, practical sense in action and a clear sight of the real situation of the war. That leads to complete defeat,' it said.[35] Curzon showed the letter to Herbert Asquith, the British Prime Minister. Asquith concluded that the King was depressed because London was not doing enough to reconquer Belgium. He at once ordered the preparation of a plan for a large-scale military offensive in Flanders.

Meanwhile, Waxweiler had returned to De Panne with the news that Berlin wanted Belgium to abandon its neutrality and become a German ally. Berlin also demanded that, in post-war Belgium, Flanders should have its own civil administration separate from Wallonia. The King could agree to the first demand, but not to the second. In a letter to Törring on 10 December he told his brother-in-law that he refused to negotiate any further if the Germans did not accept the principle of non-interference in the internal affairs of Belgium. Berlin subsequently dropped its pro-Flemish demand, but insisted on Albert becoming their military ally. But if he joined the German side, he risked losing the Congo. Albert feared that the British would take his colony. To avoid this, he had to involve Britain in his peace negotiations with Germany.

The King wrote Curzon a letter on 8 December to invite him over to De Panne. 'I am always more and more convinced that the Western front will remain unmoved,' he said. Albert wanted to imply that the only way out of the quagmire was a negotiated Peace. Curzon did not grasp the implicit message, because the letter also stressed that the

---

34   Albert I to Törring, 30 Oct. 1915, in Albert I 2, p. 605.
35   Quoted in Albert I 2, p. 617.

King remained confident in Britain's power: 'The rumours on our less sympathetic feelings towards England are entirely deprived of foundation,' he wrote, 'I keep an entire faith in the future and the power of Great Britain.'[36]

A new round of negotiations between Waxweiler and Törring took place in Zürich on 5 and 6 January. Apart from Germany now accepting Belgium's internal autonomy, Waxweiler returned empty-handed. On 7 February Albert received Curzon and Field Marshal Sir Douglas Haig at De Panne. They talked for almost three hours, but, to the King's annoyance, mainly about military issues. Curzon and Haig proposed a huge British military offensive in Flanders: a massive land strike from Ieper in the direction of Passendale. They were amazed when the King rejected the plans. They asked him what offensive he had in mind then, and were even more amazed to discover that he rejected every offensive on Belgian soil. At the end of the meeting, the King confronted Curzon with the question that he had been longing to ask all along: was there any basis for an agreement between Germany and England? Curzon does not make any reference to this question in his own report of the meeting,[37] but in his war diary Albert writes extensively about the answer he received. It came as a cold shower. 'No,' the Englishman had said, 'there will be no agreement. What is at stake in this war is British supremacy. We will never lay down arms.'[38]

Waxweiler and Törring resumed their talks in Switzerland on 25 and 26 February, but with Britain occupying Germany's African colonies, and London eager to continue the war, the situation was deadlocked. It was their last meeting. Waxweiler's constant travelling between De Panne and Zürich had raised the suspicion of the French secret service. Four months later, the 51-year-old Belgian whom Albert wanted to have as his post-war Prime Minister was run over by a taxi in Le Havre. He died on the spot.

The Foe of the Flamingants

In Berlin, the Kaiser decided to put his Belgian cousin under pressure. On 5 April 1916, the German Chancellor, Count Theobald von Bethmann-Hollweg, announced in the *Reichstag* that Germany would grant the Flemings everything Belgium had always denied them. Until the beginning of 1916, the Germans had kept the Flamingants at a dis-

---

36   Quoted in Albert I 2, p. 626-7.
37   PRO Cab. 37/142, Curzon to British Cabinet, 8 Feb. 1916.
38   RAB KAD, 7 and 8 Feb. 1916.

tance. The Flemings had been wary of the invaders as well. A group of Flamingant fugitives in the Netherlands had founded the newspaper *De Vlaamsche Stem* (The Flemish Voice), expressing strong anti-German indignation. The paper was smuggled into occupied Belgium. On 11 July 1915, the editors organised a meeting in Bussum near Amsterdam. They sent a telegram to the King in De Panne. 'The thousands of Flemings assembled at Bussum pay homage to Your Majesty, trusting your high wisdom to safeguard an autonomous Flanders in an independent Belgium,' it said in Dutch. When Albert received the telegram, he refused to acknowledge it. The editors, Alberic Deswarte and René De Clercq, supposing that they had offended the King by addressing him in Dutch, sent a second telegram with the same message in French. Albert informed Broqueville that, 'as I was offended' by the first telegram, 'I did not answer it. Now I have received one in French. I think it useful to answer them by teaching them a lesson.'[39] A reply was sent, deliberately not signed by the King, but by Ingenbleek, to 'Deswaerte and Declercq' (misspelling both their names) stating: 'H. M. is of the opinion that once the Nation will have recovered its sovereignty, the constituted authorities will take all measures to safeguard the aspirations and interests of the Belgian people. Meanwhile, the King calls urgently on all the Belgians to have no aim but the liberation of the country's territory.'

The reply did not mention the Flemish people and only referred to 'Belgians.' The editors were greatly disappointed. Fewer than three months later, Albert had De Clercq, who was also a teacher at the Belgian School in Amsterdam, dismissed from the school for 'unpatriotic activities.' In private letters to Broqueville, the Minister of Education acknowledged, however, that De Clercq was 'a patriot and a royalist who could not be reproached for anything.'[40]

As a direct result of the King's hostile reaction, the Flamingant movement, which until then had been loyal to Belgium, split into two groups: the *Passivists* and the *Aktivists*. The Passivists, led by the Catholic MP Frans Van Cauwelaert, believed that nothing should be attempted until after the war ended. The Aktivists concluded that the King would never be prepared to give Flanders just treatment, that Belgium was Flanders' real enemy and that, since the enemy of one's enemy is one's friend, it should actively ally itself with Germany. Many Flamingants, including De Clercq, returned home, prepared to

39 GSA Broqueville Papers, Albert I to Broqueville, 13 July 1915.
40 GSA Broqueville Papers nr. 182, Poullet to Broqueville, 10 Sept. 1915.

collaborate with the Germans. A worried Van Cauwelaert asked the King for an urgent audience; he travelled from Holland to De Panne via England and France, but Albert refused to receive him.

By the end of 1915, at the same time that Albert was secretly negotiating with Berlin, the Aktivists approached the Germans. They were a heterogeneous group: one of their leaders was an anti-militarist Protestant vicar from Ghent, Jan Domela-Nieuwenhuis-Nyegaard; others were Catholic Conservatives, such as August Borms and René De Clercq; Communist revolutionaries, like Joseph Van Extergem; and Zionist Jews, such as Marten Rudelsheim, Maurice Friedman and Lode Oudkerk. Another Jew, the Antwerp diamond trader, Salomon Kok, financed Aktivist organisations and publications.

The Aktivists achieved a great deal. All Belgian laws were translated into Dutch. For the first time since 1830 Flemish municipalities were administered in Dutch. Children again received education in their mother tongue. The University of Ghent, until then a Francophone institution, became a Dutch-language university. In February 1917, the Aktivists opened their own Parliament, the Council of Flanders. However, when the Council of Flanders proclaimed the Flemish Declaration of Independence on 22 December 1917, Berlin censored it. New negotiations were being conducted with King Albert, who, once again, seemed prepared to change allegiance to the German side. Hence, the *Kaiser* wanted to give his cousin a second chance and had the Flamingants silenced.

Albert had been brooding over new solutions for his Congo problem, the colony which he was bound to lose if he became a German ally. Perhaps the United States, still neutral in 1916, could help. He invited Colonel Edward House, an envoy of President Woodrow Wilson, to De Panne on 8 February 1916 in order to kindle American interest in Africa. When House suggested that the King sell the Congo to the Germans, Albert realised that he would have to corrupt the Americans in the same way that the Belgians had been corrupted to defend the interests of their artificial nation: by making it financially rewarding to do so. He wrote to Broqueville: 'Let us draw the attention of the Americans to our colony by giving them huge concessions. They must have something to gain from our retention of all our possessions. Let us give that powerful Republic a very good reason to immerse itself in African politics.'[41] Broqueville, unaware of the King's secret dealings with the Germans, did not understand why the Congo was suddenly an issue on the King's mind and made no special

---

41   GSA Broqueville Papers, Albert I to Broqueville, 4 Mar. 1916.

efforts to welcome the Americans to the colony. Albert became utterly dissatisfied with the Prime Minister. He told him that he did not want to see him anymore. If Broqueville had something to say, he had to do so in writing, as 'one letter teaches me more than ten conversations.'[42]

In the autumn of 1916, the Franco-British military debacle at the River Somme, which cost them 600,000 men (and the Germans 'only' 470,000), strengthened Albert's conviction that Germany was about to win the war. He contacted Berlin again. This time, the secret negotiations went through the Marquess of Villalobar, the Spanish Ambassador to Belgium. Germany reaffirmed that it was prepared to respect Belgium's internal autonomy, though Chancellor Bethmann-Hollweg remained sceptical about Albert's ability to decide in favour of the German side. The Chancellor wrote to King Ferdinand of Bulgaria, a German ally and a Saxe-Coburg cousin of Albert, that the Belgian King 'is under close surveillance of English and French troops and is also in disaccord with his own government. Hence, he cannot impose his own initiatives.'[43]

Albert's position became even more complicated when the United States joined the war on the Allied side in April 1917. This made his Congo scheme impossible. But it also worried him for another reason. President Wilson had proclaimed that every nation, however small, was entitled to self-determination. The King feared that the Americans would see no difference between the Flemings' right to independence and that of the Poles. He believed that if the Flamingants put their case to Wilson, they might gain his support. The King's only hope to avoid this danger was an early peace treaty between Germany and the Allies, before the Americans became too influential. He asked Emile Vandervelde, the leader of the Belgian Socialists, to have his comrades in various countries pressure their governments into peace negotiations. Vandervelde and Albert were political allies. The King had every reason to be satisfied with the Socialist leader. Within the Cabinet, he was, together with the anti-Flemish hardliners Paul Hymans and Henri Carton de Wiart, demanding the death penalty for Flamingant soldiers who were assumed to be undermining army discipline.

Indeed, apart from the Passivists and the Aktivists in the Netherlands and German-occupied Belgium, there was a third group of Flamingants: the *Frontists*. These were men serving on the front in

---

42   GSA Broqueville Papers, Albert I to Broqueville, 7 July 1916.
43   Bethmann-Hollweg to King Ferdinand of Bulgaria, 16 Oct. 1916, in Willequet 4, p. 170.

King Albert's army. Some of them had signed up as volunteers after the King's explicit call to arms of 'the Flemings' in August 1914. Once in the army, however, they grew bitterly disappointed about the way they were treated. Others were young Flemings, previously uninterested in politics, who became Flamingants while serving because they felt humiliated by their Francophone officers. Although 80% of the privates were Flemings, there were hardly any Dutch-speaking officers. The staff of 5,000 officers consisted almost entirely of Walloons.

To make matters worse, many of the Francophone officers deliberately pestered their Flemish subordinates. Some of the highest ranking Belgian officers, such as General Jules Jacques, to whom Albert gave the title of Baron Jacques de Dixmude in 1915, had learned their trade by committing crimes against humanity as commissaries in King Leopold's CFS. General Jacques was a sadist who in the Congo had aimed, as he himself put it, for 'the absolute submission or the complete extermination of the natives.'[44] In Belgium, the army did not aim to exterminate the Flemings, but it did its best to achieve absolute submission. At the military training camp of Honfleur, Walloon privates were allowed to march with empty rucksacks, while the Flemings had to carry stones in theirs. Private Jules Billiaert, who did not understand a French order, was told that 'in Africa even the niggers understand their orders' and was sentenced to one week in gaol for insubordination. When Corporal Karel De Schaepdrijver, a lawyer, asked permission to speak Dutch while defending a Flemish soldier at a court-martial, the military judge told him: 'You can speak Hebrew if it pleases you; the result will be exactly the same.' Father Robert Mortier, a Jesuit army chaplain who had prayed the Lord's Prayer in Dutch during a funeral, was told that he fomented discord with his 'Flamingant and separatist propaganda.' He was removed from his post and sent to work in an ammunition factory in France.[45] Many officers regarded all Flemings as Germanophiles and began to speak of 'Flamingoths' or 'Flamboches' — Goth and Boche being French terms of abuse for a German. Military censors carefully scrutinised all Dutch-language publications. Even a poem by the late author Guido Gezelle was censored: the words 'dear Flanders' had to be omitted. As a rule, the army censored all references to Flanders which did not mention Belgium as well. The situation can be likened today to one

44   Jacques to Post Chief at Inongo, reprinted in *The West African Mail*, 16 Mar. 1906.
45   These and similar examples can be found in Vanacker 2, pp. 61, 212, 223–4, 239, 251, 283.

where all references to England or Britain that do not simultaneously mention Europe would be prohibited.

From 1915 onwards, groups of disillusioned Flemish soldiers began to organise themselves in what they called the *Front Movement*. In August 1917, the leaders of the Movement were rounded up and deported to Belgian prison camps and penal colonies in France. Life in the camps was worse than in the trenches. Ten per cent of the inmates died. Dr. Alfons Van de Perre, who led an official committee to investigate living conditions at Fresnes, a Belgian army prison not far from Paris, wrote: 'The prisoners do not know when they will be released. They live in filth, they do not get half the food ration needed to survive, many suffer from consumption, many go insane. Many die. It is awful. It is a disgrace. Our prisoners of war get better treatment in Germany.'[46]

While the Belgian authorities were rounding up the leaders of the Front Movement, the British were fighting the third battle of Ieper. From August to November 1917, they advanced six miles to the north into the hamlet of Passendale. It cost them 245,000 men. The fact that Albert kept his troops out of any offensives explains why many Flemish soldiers remained royalist, despite the discrimination and humiliations they had to suffer in the army. Even the most ardent Flamingants were grateful that the King had refused to participate in the British attack. In Flanders fields, having to undergo the humiliations of the Belgian authorities as the Flemings did, was preferable to having to die for Belgium like rats, as the poor British did. Even the Frontists never criticised Albert in person. They began to hate Belgium as it hated them, but they thanked God for its king.

* * *

With the declaration of Flanders' independence by the Aktivists on 22 December 1917, the genie was out of the bottle. The Germans tried in vain to keep the declaration secret. Finally, on 19 January 1918, they allowed the publication of a censored version, which spoke of Flemish 'autonomy' instead of 'independence.' Soon, the news reached De Panne. 'The Council of Flanders is about to declare (or might already have done so) the independence of Flanders and announce a referendum on the subject. This news has greatly shocked the government,' Albert wrote in his war diary.[47] He called the cabinet over to meet him. 'We have all been scandalised by the news of the formation of a

46   Quoted in Deleu, vol. I, p. 540.
47   RAB KAD, 25 Jan. 1918.

Flemish government that declares itself autonomous. We have also received the news that a popular consultation will be held about the question of Flemish independence. These are events of which the gravity cannot be denied,' he told the ministers.[48]

The declaration of Flemish independence made Albert look for moderate Flamingants who were prepared to accept Flemish autonomy within a Belgian framework. Van Cauwelaert, the leader of the Passivist Flamingants, was called over from Amsterdam. Albert asked him what concessions were needed to prevent the Flemings from breaking with Belgium altogether. Van Cauwelaert voiced three demands: the introduction after the war of Dutch-language education at all levels, including at university level; the establishment of a Dutch-language civil administration and of Dutch-language courts in Flanders; and the immediate division of the army into separate Flemish and Walloon regiments. Albert and his advisors discussed these demands at length. They concluded that though the first two demands could be accepted, the third demand was entirely out of the question. 'I have the feeling, if not the certainty, that the Walloons are not going to accept this passively,' Albert said. 'Especially the officers will be profoundly troubled.'[49]

Amongst the Flemish soldiers in the trenches, the news stirred up emotions. It led to dozens of spontaneous demonstrations. Officers trying to stop the demonstrations were beaten up by their men. One soldier who had attacked a Sergeant was court-martialled. Despite requests for mercy, he was executed. 'There have been demonstrations and the number of leaflets keeps growing,' a worried Albert wrote in his diary. The King was realistic enough to see that 'it would be wrong to believe that the enemy has fomented this wave of unrest; given the Belgian character, an influence from abroad can achieve nothing here or only very little.'[50] Albert was not prepared to take responsibility for the order to open fire on demonstrating soldiers. The Government had to do this. 'Discipline is fading,' he told the Cabinet. 'Concessions have to be made. If not, an inexorably harsh repression might be necessary to restore order. Are you unanimously prepared, in the present situation, to approve and support such a repression?'[51] Hymans and Vandervelde answered assertively, but the Catholic ministers hesitated.

---

48   Cabinet meeting, 1 Feb. 1918, in Albert I 3, p. 446.
49   Preparatory notes for the cabinet meeting of 1 Feb. 1918, in Albert I 3, p. 443.
50   RAB KAD, 6 Mar. 1918.
51   Cabinet meeting, 20 Mar. 1918, in Albert I 3, p. 452.

The King's troubles deepened when the Germans began two new offensives, one military, the other diplomatic. A large-scale German attack, that began on 21 March, dealt severe blows to the Allies, who were forced back 40 miles along the Somme. At the same time, Count Törring re-emerged on the scene. Albert's brother-in-law contacted Fernand Peltzer, the Belgian Ambassador in Bern. Peltzer and Törring met a first time on 27 March.

Given the strength of the German military offensive, London and Paris asked the King to join an Allied counterattack. Albert refused. The French President Raymond Poincaré, the French Prime Minister Georges Clemenceau and the British Prime Minister David Lloyd George all came to De Panne in efforts to talk Albert round. They failed. When Broqueville tried to do the same, the King decided to rid himself of the Prime Minister. Broqueville was forced to resign on 24 May. Albert's new Prime Minister was Gérard Cooreman, the Governor of the SG, a man totally subservient to the King.

Peltzer and Törring met again on 30 June. Albert had finally decided in favour of a separate Belgo-German peace. On 10 July, the new German Chancellor, Count Georg von Hertling, made the necessary overtures. He announced in the *Reichstag* that Germany would guarantee Belgium's independence and integrity. The Council of Flanders, the Aktivist Parliament in German-occupied Belgium, was prohibited from convening again. That same day, General Galet, still living with the King at the Villa Maskens, wrote: 'We are convinced that Germany will give us our country back and that it will be happy to pay that price in return for peace. France will continue the war in order to conquer the Alsace-Lorraine province, and England in order to assure its world prestige. These are the war goals of the big nations for which we are not prepared to spill one drop of Belgian blood.'[52]

A week later, however, there was a dramatic turn of events. On 18 July, the British and French succeeded in stopping the German advance. Albert decided to wait and see how things developed. On 2 August, the French won the second battle of the Marne; on 8 August, British troops dealt a severe blow to the exhausted Germans near Amiens. Soon German resistance collapsed on all fronts. On 26 September, Albert put the Belgian army under Allied command. He was no longer 'neutral.' The final Allied offensive started on 29 September. It was the first offensive of the war in which the Belgians participated. The Belgian army put the most militantly Flamingant

---

52   Galet manuscript, 10 July 1918, in Albert I 3, p. 157.

regiments in the first line. As General Honoré Drubbel said, they were
to erase 'the regimental dishonour' with their blood.

On 17 October, Admiral Roger Keyes of the British Royal Navy
escorted Albert and Elisabeth to Ostend, liberated by Keyes the day
before. 'We are witnessing the agony of the dragon,' Elisabeth
exclaimed, 'It is the wish of all the Belgians to fight to the last and
never to see a German in Belgium again.'[53] Suddenly, Albert and his
wife were the greatest enthusiasts for the war in Europe. General
Galet was told to leave the Villa Maskens. Fernand Neuray, one of
Broqueville's friends, wrote to the former Prime Minister after having
met Albert's secretary Ingenbleek: 'Galet has been cast aside and
dumped completely. It is as if he does not exist anymore.'[54] Galet was
a liability to the King, because he knew too much about Albert's 'unpatriotic' attitude during the war; but he was a soldier and kept silent.
Broqueville was a liability as well. Ingenbleek went to see the Baron to
sound him out. Broqueville told Ingenbleek that the King need not
worry: he was most loyal to the institution of the monarchy and
would never discredit it. Albert rewarded Broqueville by making him
a Count. When the Germans asked for an armistice early in November, the King was greatly disappointed. The French President
Poincaré, who met him on 9 November, wrote in his diary that Albert
was 'saddened by the news of the armistice, which, he says, robs him
of his victory.'[55]

After the German surrender on 11 November 1918 and the triumphal return of the King and the Government to Brussels, any willingness to appease moderate Flemings had vanished. The Dutch-
language university of Ghent was abolished at once. The royal argument was that 'Belgium cannot grant in a legal way what the occupying Germans had wanted to impose illegally.'[56] A purge began, as
ruthless as the anti-Orangist terror of the 1830s. Every professor who
had lectured in Dutch at Ghent was brought to court on the charge of
treason. They were all convicted at the so-called 'Trial of the Professors' in 1919 and given long prison sentences. One of them was sentenced to 25 years. Even Ludovic Dosfel, a professor of Law, who,
though lecturing in Dutch, had warned his students to keep out of
Aktivist politics, was sentenced to 10 years. The students were also
punished. One student was sentenced to 8 years in prison because he
had recruited other students. Every student who had obtained a

53   Quoted in Weber, p. 107.
54   GSA Broqueville Papers nr. 165, Neuray to Broqueville, 8 Nov. 1918.
55   Quoted in Willequet 4, p. 166.
56   Marie-José, p. 357.

Dutch-language degree at Ghent lost his diploma. They, as well as all others who had enrolled during the war, were prohibited from continuing their studies at any other Belgian university. 'Had to fob off lots of weeping mothers and desperate ex-students these past days,' the new Chancellor of Ghent University (now again a Francophone institution) maliciously wrote in his diary.[57] Hundreds of Aktivists were arrested by the police. The mob was allowed freely to plunder houses and shops of 'Flamingoths,' while the police looked on. In Ghent, an elderly Aktivist who tried to prevent his house from being plundered was shot; another man was beaten to death, as was his girlfriend. Many hundreds were imprisoned without trial and remained in gaol for weeks. The exact number of those unlawfully imprisoned was never revealed. Wives and daughters of Aktivists, or girls who had befriended German soldiers were publicly humiliated and their hair was shaved off. Some were branded on the forehead with a hot iron.[58] King Albert did not raise his voice to stop the atrocities. On the contrary, 'for the zealotry of those who in the painful hour that the country was in danger, aimed for its total ruin, no amnesty is imaginable. The culprits have to experience the harshness of severe punishment,' he said in his first public speech after his return to Brussels.[59]

This harshness affected only Flanders. Over 300 Flemish teachers of primary and secondary schools, who had graduated during the war, lost their degrees, while not a single Walloon was disturbed for the same reason. Some 3,240 Flemish civil servants were dismissed for alleged 'Aktivist and Orangist zealotry.'[60]

Thirty-nine people were sentenced to death, including the Protestant vicar Jan Domela-Nieuwenhuis-Nyegaard, and the former editor of *De Vlaamsche Stem*, René De Clercq. They both fled to the Netherlands. Domela-Nieuwenhuis-Nyegaard was the victim of a second political sentence 25 years later, when the Nazis murdered his son and sent the elderly vicar to a concentration camp. One Aktivist 'zealot,' Arthur Faingnaert, accumulated 268 sentences (all for political reasons). He, too, fled to the Netherlands, as did 500 others, including the Jewish Flamingants Lode Oudkerk, Maurice Friedman, Hendrik Van Praag, and S. Samson, whose valuable library was confiscated by the Belgian authorities. The Aktivist Saul De Groot later became the leader of the Communist Party in the Netherlands. The

57   Quoted in Vanacker 1, p. 360.
58   Van De Woestijne, p. 478.
59   Quoted in De Schaepdrijver, p. 293.
60   Deleu, vol. I, p. 90.

anti-Flamingant purge of 1919 led to a brain drain that robbed Flanders of a significant part of its political and intellectual elite.

The most prominent Aktivist arrested by the Belgian authorities was August Borms, the Minister of Defence of the Aktivist government. Borms, a Catholic, had refused to flee. He (somewhat naively) expected a fair hearing in court, but the trial was a sham. It took place in the Brussels *Palais de Justice*, the awe-inspiring Babylonian ziggurat of Leopold II, and was conducted entirely in French. Borms refused to speak French. 'I will teach him to understand French,' the police officer guarding the prisoner yelled at the judges, adding that he hoped they would sentence him to death. Borms did, indeed, receive the death penalty, but he escaped execution because Pope Benedict XV asked the Belgian government for clemency. Of the less prominent Aktivists, fifteen received life imprisonment; 51 were sentenced to fifteen years or more; 52 got between fifteen and ten years; and many hundreds were condemned to sentences of less than ten years. In prison they received harsh treatment. Marten Rudelsheim died in gaol of deprivation. Professor Dosfel became severely ill, was released and died shortly afterwards, barely 44 years old. Jan Hainaut committed suicide in his cell.

The authorities hoped to intimidate the Flemings into submission. Henri Pirenne, the father of Belgicism, rejoiced: 'The last miasmas of Flamingantism have dissolved in the bright sunlight of the French victory!'[61] The intimidation left its mark. When the census of 1920 was held, only 31.7% of the inhabitants of Brussels still dared to declare themselves Dutch-speaking, against 44.7% in 1910. It was dangerous to be a Fleming, as the death of Herman Van den Reeck illustrated. During a parade in Antwerp on 11 July 1920, the 19-year-old student carried the Flemish flag — a black lion on a field of gold. The police tried to confiscate the flag, the young man refused to hand it over and was shot in the stomach. He died the next morning.

The Great Equaliser

The aftermath of the war led to a polarisation between Flemings and Walloons. Already during the war, Father Jules Callewaert, a Flemish Dominican monk who was a parish priest in Stockport near Manchester, concluded: 'Belgium is an unnatural State, which *as such* is a danger for the survival of the Flemish people.'[62] In August 1917 Charles Magnette, a Liberal MP from Liège and the Grandmaster of the

61   Quoted in Florquin, vol. VIII, p. 286.
62   Quoted in De Schaepdrijver, p. 195.

Masonic *Grand Orient de Belgique*, warned the King: 'It is intolerable that after the war 4.5 million Flemings decide about the fate of 3 million Walloons. I have heard many people, even civilised and cultivated men, declare that rather than to live under the yoke of the Flemings, rather than allowing a culture and a language which is not theirs imposed on them, they prefer to go where the affinity of their race calls them: to France.'[63]

For a while, a number of revolutionary Flamingants, inspired by Ireland's Easter Rising of 1916, considered the possibility of a Flemish Rising. They concluded, however, that armed rebels would have little chance of success. 'The anti-Flemish terrorism will increase tenfold, hundreds of innocent people will be gaoled, public opinion, under the influence of the clergy, will turn against us.'[64] In February 1919 two bombs exploded. No one was injured. These were the only terrorist acts ever committed by Flemish-Nationalists. When a message was smuggled to the imprisoned Borms to ask if he agreed with an armed attempt to liberate him from gaol, Borms's reply was negative. When Irish Sinn Féin members offered their assistance to liberate Borms, the Flamingants turned the offer down because this would cost lives. 'Of course,' the Irish said, 'how many dead do you need?'[65]

The Belgian regime did not respect the Flamingants for their principled non-violence. It did, however, fear and respect the explicit threats of the Walloons to join France, and it pursued a Francophone and Francophile policy to appease them. The King also feared the Socialists. He had promised to bring them to power after the war if they would support the monarchy. He kept his word. Before re-entering Brussels with the victorious army in November 1918, Albert launched a coup d'état.

Albert and Elisabeth left De Panne on 24 October 1918 and settled at Loppem Castle, near Bruges. There, on 11 November, the very day of the armistice, the King received two leading politicians: the Francophone Liberal Paul-Emile Janson and the Flemish Socialist Edward Anseele. They had lived in occupied Belgium during the war, where, following the German collapse, they cleverly filled the political vacuum. The last weeks of the German occupation had been very chaotic: a Soviet of German soldiers took over control in Brussels and hung red flags on official buildings. They invited the Belgian Socialists and Communists to join them. Anseele, who had been a personal

63   RAB FH nr. 242, Magnette to Albert I, shortly before Aug. 1917.
64   Cyriel De Wael to (presumably) Jules Charpentier, in Vanacker 1, p. 353.
65   Vinks, p. 178.

friend of the German revolutionaries Karl Liebknecht and Rosa Luxemburg for more than a decade, was a sly opportunist. His friends in the German Soviet provided him and Janson with an army vehicle that brought them to the King at Loppem Castle. There, Albert together with his SG subordinate, Prime Minister Cooreman, and his two guests unilaterally changed Belgium's Constitution, in particular its franchise law.

According to the Belgian Constitution, no constitutional changes can be made without a special procedure that requires preliminary elections to appoint a new Parliament with a mandate for changing the Constitution by a two-thirds majority vote. The Loppem four disregarded this and decided there and then to have the next Parliament appointed according to a new electoral procedure, based on proportional representation and one single vote for every Belgian male of 21 and over. Women were deliberately excluded from the franchise because the King feared that they would be more inclined to vote Conservative, while the only aims of the Loppem four were to break the Catholic parliamentary majority and to force coalition governments to include the parties of the Left.

Since the Government and the Parliament would insist on following the constitutional procedure, Albert had to neutralise both institutions. The Government had quite different intentions than those of the four conspirators. In 1917, Broqueville had agreed with the Liberals and Socialists to introduce universal suffrage after the war for every Belgian, including women, aged 25 and over, plus a second vote for every Belgian of 40 and older, again including women. Because this proposal would receive the constitutionally required a two-thirds majority in Parliament, the Loppem four worked out a scheme to remove Parliament and Government for at least one week, leaving the King as the sole legislative and executive power in the country. Two days after the Loppem meeting, Cooreman presented the resignation of his cabinet, to the surprise of the Cabinet itself, where only a few hours earlier the ministers had agreed that they would remain in office until the first post-war plenary session of Parliament the following week. Albert was now the only political authority in the country for a whole week. He used this opportunity to usurp the powers of both Parliament and Government, disregard the Constitution and proclaim the new franchise law devised in Loppem.

On 22 November 1918, Parliament convened in Brussels for its first session since 4 August 1914. The King gave the opening speech, entirely in French, announcing the decisions that had been taken in Loppem. The inhabitants of Brussels looked upon Albert as the greatest of all war heroes, who had single-handedly driven the enemy from Belgium after doing battle with them in the trenches for four years. This was not the right moment for any politician to criticise the King. Hence, the blatant illegality of the Loppem decisions was left unmentioned. As Beernaert had said about the previous violation of the Constitution in 1909, it was better to 'smile and forget the whole affair.'

Albert appointed a new government that included as many members of the Liberal-Socialist alliance as of the Catholic parliamentary majority. Of the twelve ministers, only three lived in Flanders, and none had Flamingant sympathies. On the contrary, the King had removed three war-time ministers because he considered them too Flemish-minded. Vandervelde became Minister of Justice, Anseele got Public Works and a third Socialist, Joseph Wauters, the Department of Labour.

On 16 November 1919, the first post-war elections in Belgium were held according to the Loppem franchise system. As these elections were unconstitutional, they were strictly speaking invalid. But no one dared say so with the post-war purges still raging. After the elections, in which the Catholics lost their absolute majority, the King installed a new coalition of Catholics, Socialists and Liberals. It established the framework of Belgium as it still exists today and as it had been devised by Albert and his late friend, the engineer Emile Waxweiler, when they were brainstorming before the war about a social welfare construction that could unite the Belgians. It is a unique system, where the Government runs the State together with so-called 'Social Partners.' These 'Social Partners' are the *Fédération des entreprises de Belgique*, the official representative of the Belgian employers, and three trade unions (a Christian-Democrat, a Socialist and a Liberal one) recognised as the *only* official representatives of the employees. Economic and social policies are decided in consensus between the Social Partners, rather than in Parliament. The management of the entire welfare system has been delegated to the 'Partners.'

Indeed, in Belgium the three official unions, not the state, pay unemployment benefit. Each year the government gives them the necessary funds and also pays them a fee for every unemployed person they cater for. The perverse result is that it is in the unions' interest to have high unemployment: the more people without a job, the richer and more powerful the unions become.[66] All Belgian civil servants are *automatically* union members: the government pays their membership

---

66   In 2001, the unions received 4.78 billion francs (about £72.4 million or $119.5 million) from the government to pay unemployment benefit.

dues directly to the unions — even if an individual does not want to join. In that case his dues are divided proportionally amongst the three official unions.[67] The authorities deal only with the three officially recognised unions; all other unions are called 'independent unions.' The latter are small and powerless. Employers who negotiate with them run into serious trouble with the three big ones.[68]

The mandatory health insurance system is also run by the Social Partners. Each of the official unions is linked to a sickness fund. These funds are represented in the state organisations supervising the health care system. They own hospitals, pharmacies and health resorts. The three big conglomerates also have their own insurance companies, their own savings and investment banks, and their own Members of Parliament. The Social Partners finance the party of their political affiliation and appoint their representatives in the party structures, at national as well as local level. Because at least two of the three so-called 'traditional' parties are needed to form a government coalition, the Social Partners are always represented in the Cabinet. Consequently, it is impossible for any government even to try to diminish the influence of the Social Partners.

The post-war governments also created the legal framework to allow the state to interfere directly in the economy. In 1923, rail transport and telegraph services became government monopolies, and the national airline company Sabena was established. All this happened in close cooperation with the Social Partners, who came to share directly in the power of the state. They secured (well-paid) representatives on the boards of all government-run companies and institutions, such as the National Rail Company, the Belgian postal services, Sabena, the Belgian Central Bank, the broadcasting company, the University of Ghent, etc.

As the official unions, their sickness funds, banks and insurance companies operate in Flanders as well as Wallonia, and have huge financial and political interests in both parts of the country, they are — like the monarchy — by nature Belgicist institutions. The Social Partners do not tolerate any questioning of the Belgian State and its unity, because of the real risk that any successor to this state will be less generous to them. They are always prepared to mobilise their

---

67   In 2001, the government paid the unions 2,815 francs (about £42 or $70) per civil servant, or a total of over 1.82 billion francs (£27.6 million or $45.5 million).

68   In 2001, the three official unions had a combined membership of over 2.9 million — almost 30 per cent of the whole Belgian population. Over half the members (53.8%) belonged to the Christian-Democrat Union, 39% to the Socialist Union, and 7.2% to the Liberal Union.

members and their clients (the unemployed, the sick, everyone at the receiving end of the generous 'social' subsidies provided by the state, as well as those who earn their living providing the welfare state's 'care') against 'political adventures,' such as Flemish separatism. By gradually handing over the Belgian State to a limited number of unions whose vested interests spanned the linguistic divide, Albert mobilised the Social Partners against the Flamingants and their goal of an independent Flanders.

This 'unionisation' of the state — this process of handing over state authority to the three official trade unions and their subsidiaries, while at the same time strengthening the Belgian national union — was not yet fully completed when Albert died. In fact, it was only completed in the 1950s, the early years of the reign of his grandson Baudouin. But the Loppem Coup marked the start of the process that gradually transformed Belgium into a corporatist state, where the Flemings and the Walloons are bound together within one single welfare system spanning the linguistic divide. It had an immediate effect: in 1919 the membership of the Socialist Trade Union exploded from 120,000 to 720,000. This was ample proof of the efficiency of Albert's scheme, which made social-corporatism the main pillar upholding Belgium.

* * *

The Belgian electorate remained remarkably stable during the 1920s and '30s. In the 1919 elections the Catholic Party won 73 seats in the Chamber of Representatives, the Socialists 70 seats, the Liberals 34 seats, and the *Front Partij*, a new party, established by Flemish war veterans, five seats. The *Frontists* were the radicals amongst the Flamingants. Moderates, like Frans Van Cauwelaert, believed that it was better to work within the three traditional parties. Many Flamingants joined the Catholic Party. In Parliament Van Cauwelaert could count on some 40 MPs. In Flanders, 51.7% of the electorate had voted for the Catholic Party; 25.3% for the Socialists; 14.1% for the Liberals; 5.2% for the Frontists.

Apart from the Catholic losses to the Flemish-Nationalists, the preferences of the Flemish electorate hardly changed during the next two decades. In 1939, the Catholics gained 41% of the Flemish electorate; the Socialists 26%; the Liberals 12.6%; the *Vlaams-Nationaal Blok* (formerly *Frontists*) 15%. This gridlock of the electorate was visible among the Belgian Francophones as well: between 1919 and 1939, the Socialists received the support of about half the electorate in

Wallonia. While the Catholics in Flanders saw a number of their voters defect to the Flemish-Nationalists, the Communists and the Fascists were only able to break through amongst the Francophones. On the eve of the Second World War, this resulted in 17 seats in the Belgian Chamber of Representatives for the Flemish-Nationalists and 13 seats for the totalitarian parties of the extreme Left and the extreme Right. The latter 13 seats were exclusively Francophone. In Flanders, neither Communism nor Fascism made an electoral breakthrough.

In Albert's 'unionised' state, where the real powers were vested in the Social Partners instead of in Parliament, it did not matter which of the three 'traditional' parties a citizen voted for. They all defended the status quo of the corporatist system. The only votes that made a difference were votes against the system. In Flanders, this meant voting for Flemish secession; in Francophone Belgium, it meant voting for a revolution of either the extreme Left or the extreme Right.

The inter-war years witnessed a rapid succession of twenty government cabinets, one of which lasted only one day, another only six days. There were eleven so-called 'national' coalitions of Catholics, Socialists and Liberals; six coalitions of Catholics and Liberals; two of Catholics and Socialists; and one Catholic minority government (lasting nine days). The introduction of the corporatist system led to the *end of politics*: it is, indeed, hard to tell where the twenty inter-war cabinets differed. When they fell, it was usually over personal intrigues within the government, rather than basic disagreements about political options. There were ten government crises in the fourteen years between the 1919 elections and Albert's death. This gave the King frequent opportunities to interfere directly in politics. In Belgium, even today, the King plays the decisive role in forming governments. Without having to account to anyone, he unilaterally appoints the so-called *formateur* who brings the parties together for coalition talks. Belgium is the only monarchy where after the First World War the King's powers increased. Albert, however, longed for the period between 1914 and 1918 when his political power had been almost absolute. 'Let's admit it: it was far more interesting during the war. It takes a political crisis for me to have anything to do,' he told Vandervelde.[69] To his sister Henriette he complained: 'The profession of a constitutional monarch is a very bad farce. I would take any opportunity to leave this prisoner's role.'[70] It is no surprise that he greatly admired Benito Mussolini, a fellow authoritarian as well as a corporatist.

69   Quoted in Vandervelde 2, p. 218.
70   RAM WC, Albert I to Henriette, 28 Oct. 1924.

Another constructivist scheme was devised for the Congo. This scheme, too, had been masterminded by Albert's friend Waxweiler. He saw colonisation as a utilitarian enterprise. The natives were the valuable manpower needed by the mining industry in the Katanga and Kasai provinces. Leopold II had murdered half the colony's indigenous population, but, under Albert's rule, population management became a priority.

In 1906, Leopold II had brought the Congo economy under direct control of a number of SG companies, such as the *Union Minière* (UM), its mining subsidiary. As manpower was especially needed in scarcely populated mining areas of the Katanga and the Kasai, the UM imported labourers from other parts of the Congo to supply the workforce for the mines. The labourers were selected by physicians according to strict medical criteria, because 'recruiting weak elements is not only a cruelty, but a useless cruelty and economic nonsense.'[71] They had to live in labour camps of a quasi-military nature. They were well-fed, well-housed, well-cared-for, but closely controlled. Various types of camps were drawn by Waxweiler's *Institut de Sociologie* and different methods of disciplining the Congolese were studied, in order to give optimal long-term labour results. Waxweiler even conducted research into the ideal diet to guarantee the highest labour productivity at the lowest cost.

In the early 1920s, the Belgian social scientists concluded that all labourers had to marry. 'Married men have a better morale and a higher morality than single men. As a consequence, their ratios for sickness, mortality, desertion and absenteeism are lower and their productivity is much higher,' Waxweiler's pupil, Dr. Leopold Mottoulle, the head of the UM's social policy division and a leading member of the *Institut Royal Colonial Belge*, wrote. The UM went very far in its policy. It forced all its non-married Black employees to marry. The company selected the brides. The UM actually bought young women, paying the traditional African dowries to their families. The women were recruited according to medical criteria which envisaged the 'production' of future labourers of quality standard.

Whenever an already married Black man applied for a job at the UM, his wife had to pass medical tests as well. If she was considered physically 'insufficient,' her husband did not get a job. The marriages were duly registered in order to allow the company to control the breeding process. Keeping a concubine was forbidden for the Black employees, as was polygamy and adultery. The labour camps were

71   Mouchet and Pearson, p. 5.

transformed into so-called *'villages indigènes,'* where the labourers had to live with their families. This allowed the workforce to supply the company with children that could be moulded from the cradle into workers of optimum quality.

The so-called 'indigenous villages' soon developed into huge townships where the inhabitants were pampered, but where at the same time they were guinea pigs for the Belgian social engineers. It was a closely controlled totalitarian society. 'If one could say that the *Union Minière* was a state within the colonial state, then it was in any case a social and altruistic state,' a 1992 book about the system states.[72] In some aspects the UM villages did, indeed, resemble the ideals of the 'social and altruistic' welfare state. Every family had its own house with a garden. The houses were semi-detached and built along avenues and streets lined with trees. The Blacks were fed by the company with a protein-rich diet and much attention was paid to hygiene. Health care was free, as was the education of the children, who had to be sent to kindergarten and to primary school, where they learned basic skills, including French. Parents who did not send their children to school were punished by lowering the food ration of the mothers (not the fathers, because they had to labour in the mines). Education beyond primary school was not deemed necessary. The aim of the school was to discipline the boys into 'becoming good labourers' and to teach the girls how to be good mothers.[73]

Female behaviour especially was closely monitored in the 'indigenous villages'. Women were perceived to be potentially more subversive elements in society than men. The women were not allowed to leave the camp. If they wanted to visit their own families, they needed a permit. Breastfeeding the children was discouraged, because the UM wanted to boost feminine fertility in order to create as large a pool of future labourers as possible. To enforce this policy, mothers had to bring their children to kindergarten from the age of one to be fed by the company. If a woman insisted on breastfeeding her child, her food ration was lowered.

The culmination of the Belgian social engineering project in the Congo was the creation of a new people: the Tshanga-Tshanga. Dr. Mottoulle considered it a good idea to diminish the ethnic tensions between the various tribes and peoples of the Congo by substituting them with a new race, wiping out all previously existing differences. Inter-ethnic marriages were enforced in order to artificially construct

72   Lekime, p. 94.
73   Mottoulle, p. 33.

this Tshanga-Tshanga people. Its name was devised by the Congolese themselves, Tshanga-Tshanga meaning 'The Great Equaliser.' In 1937, the Belgian Prof. J. L. Frateur wrote a study about this racial project for the *Institut Royal Colonial Belge*, entitled: 'The Notion of Race in the Light of the Results of Experimental Heredity.' The Belgians tried to discover what ethnic mixture would make the Tshanga-Tshanga people economically most profitable for the mining industry. As Dr. Van Nitsen, one of the leading racial constructivists in the Congo, wrote in 1932: 'Our aim is not to make an elite, but simply to create a strong, healthy, disciplined workforce of devoted labourers.'

Nevertheless, the project was a failure, despite the fact that, as Bruno De Meulder of Leuven University concluded in 1996, it was 'undoubtedly one of the most consistently applied attempts at social engineering ever.'[74] Indeed, the 'devoted labourers' frequently rebelled and often went on strike. Charles de T'Serclaes, the SG representative in Leopoldville, opined that 'a certain moral and even physical coercion' was necessary, 'because laziness is the cause of the moral decline and the physical deterioration of the race.'[75] As in the old days of Leopoldian tyranny, the *chicotte* was frequently used to whip the Blacks into submission. In 1941, after incidents at Likasi, Mottoulle wrote that he was sick and tired of the attitude of the ungrateful Tshanga-Tshanga. He regretted that the army had not opened fire and 'killed two or three hundred' to set an example.[76]

* * *

Belgium did not feel properly rewarded after the First World War. At the Versailles Peace Conference in 1919, it demanded the annexation of the Grand-Duchy of Luxemburg and a dismemberment of the Netherlands. Though the Dutch had not committed any aggression on Belgium and had not even been involved in the war, Brussels claimed large parts of the Netherlands. 'The Belgians are on the make and they want to grab whatever they can,' Lord Hardinge warned the Dutch Ambassador in London.[77]

The Belgian demands became so vociferous that in the summer of 1919 the Dutch army planned a pre-emptive military strike on Antwerp and Brussels. U.S. President Wilson, however, assured The Hague that the United States would guarantee the Dutch borders.

74   De Meulder, p. 122.
75   T'Serclaes to Gaston Périer, 30 Oct. 1933, in Brion and Moreau, p. 305.
76   Quoted in Vellut, p. 157.
77   Ambassador E. Marees van Swinderen to Herman Van Karnebeek, the Dutch Minister of Foreign Affairs, 18 Dec. 1918, in Provoost, vol. I, p. 46.

Ultimately, Brussels only obtained Rwanda and Burundi (two tiny German colonies in central Africa), a monetary union with Luxemburg (despite the fact that the Luxemburgians voted against it by referendum), plus a number of German-speaking municipalities bordering on Belgium's eastern border. Germany was also forced to pay Belgium a large financial indemnity of 2.5 billion gold marks. The Treaty of Versailles also abolished the neutral status that the Treaty of London had imposed on Belgium in 1831. Brussels received the right to join international alliances, and at once signed a military pact with France. Because the impoverished Germans were incapable of paying the full war indemnities immediately, Belgium and France invaded the Rhineland and occupied Frankfurt and Darmstadt in April 1920. Paris hoped to trigger a secession of the German Rhine provinces and the establishment of an independent Rhine Republic. Britain condemned the Franco-Belgian aggression. In June, Brussels asked the Belgian ambassador in London, Ludovic Moncheur, to organise a media campaign to pressure the British government into joining the Rhineland occupation. Despite his expertise in such matters, Moncheur, who as ambassador to the U.S. in the early 1900s had been involved in bribing American politicians and journalists on behalf of Leopold II, was unable to influence the British cabinet.

King Albert concluded that a Belgian press agency had to be created to provide the Belgian papers with international news not filtered through Reuters in London. The King personally approached Belgian industrialists to sponsor such a venture. This resulted in the establishment of the *Agence Belga,* which, as Max-Léo Gérard, Albert's private secretary, wrote, 'is an indispensable instrument for our foreign policy.' The King was also in favour of a major reinforcement of the Belgian army. This, however, antagonised the Marxist wing of the socialist BWP. Hence, after the November 1921 elections, Albert installed a coalition of Catholics and Liberals, led by Georges Theunis, a Franchophone Catholic, who had previously been on the payroll of the SG.

Angered by the fact that the Rhinelanders did not secede and that Germany was still unable to deliver its war indemnities, an army of 32,000 French and 25,000 Belgians crossed the Rhine on 11 January 1923 and occupied the Ruhr region as well. One week earlier, during a summit meeting in Paris, the British had warned the French and the Belgians in vain not to squeeze the Germans dry. The Ruhr province was Germany's industrial powerhouse; its coal mines and steel works were a direct competitor to the coal and steel industry of the SG in Wallonia. Because the Germans could not pay up, the French and the Belgians intended to destroy the German economy to the benefit of their own industries. The Franco-Belgian army used brutal force to break up protest demonstrations of German civilians, killing 132 unarmed men and women. When the protests continued, Belgium persuaded France in April to introduce an even harsher occupational regime. All factories that were of no use to the Belgians and the French were shut down, coal mines were flooded, electric plants were closed, and the import of all commodities except basic food products was prohibited.

The occupation of the Ruhr brought on the economic collapse of Germany and led to hyperinflation. The value of the German mark plummeted, from 7,525 marks for one U.S. dollar on 3 January to over 4,210 *billion* marks by 21 November. This ruined the entire German middle class, as the British correctly perceived. Lord Robert Cecil later commented that 'the Ruhr occupation was probably one of the stupidest things that a government has ever done.' The French historian Maurice Baumont has called the Ruhr occupation 'the beginning of the birth of Nazism.' According to R.J. Schmidt, it was the 'seedbed of World War II.'[78]

As Flanders benefited from a strong German economy, because the Ruhr was the hinterland of the port of Antwerp, the Franco-Belgian military operations against Germany led to rising tensions between Flemings and Walloons. Because the issue was considered to be disruptive to the cohesion of the artificial Belgian State, the Belgian establishment did not want the Ruhr occupation to be mentioned in public debate. Belgium's three 'traditional' political parties even forbade their representatives to discuss the matter in Parliament. When the Catholic Flemish Senator Van Overbergh asked Prime Minister Theunis a question related to the Ruhr occupation, his colleague and party member Wittemans shouted him down: 'The agreement is to keep quiet about this. One should not talk about it.' Only the MPs of the *Front Partij* mentioned the topic, but the government refused to answer the questions of these '*Flamingoths.*'

Albert intervened frequently to prevent the Theunis cabinet from falling. The result was that it lasted a record three and a half years, making it the longest-serving government in Belgium between 1918 and 1954. With the Socialists in opposition, there was, however, one danger. 'There is one thing which we cannot fear enough,' the King told Theunis in June 1922: 'a coalition between the Socialists and the Flemings.'[79] Hence, as soon as the army had been reinforced, in the

78   Cecil, pp. 142–3; Baumont, vol I, p. 279; Schmidt, *passim.*
79   Quoted in Willequet 4, p. 188.

spring of 1925, Albert installed a cabinet of Catholics and Socialists. But the spectre of Flamingantism began to haunt Laken. The *Front Partij* launched a campaign to renew the neutral international status of Belgium. This drew much popular support in Flanders. In protest against the Franco-Belgian treaty, a number of Flemish conscripts refused to serve. They were condemned to long prison sentences. Some of the prisoners went on hunger strike. One of them died, three others became permanent invalids.

From the early 1920s onwards, Fascist Belgicist groups like the *Légion Nationale* and the *Action National* of Baron Pierre Nothomb, a grandson of one of the leading 1830 revolutionaries, waged vicious anti-Flemish and anti-Semite campaigns. They regarded both the Flamingants and the Jews as unpatriotic elements. They wanted Flemish activists to be disenfranchised and all Jews to be deported from Belgium. The vilest anti-Semites were two Antwerp Belgicists, Charles Somville and René Lambrichts. The Flemish-Nationalists on the other hand welcomed Jewish organisations in the Antwerp headquarters of the *Front Partij*. On 13 November 1922 *De Schelde*, the party's newspaper, was probably the first paper outside Germany to run an editorial warning against the anti-Semitism of an obscure German politician, one Adolf Hitler, whom two years later it called a 'persecutor of the Jews.'[80]

As the Flamingant Movement was growing stronger all the time, Albert asked the Catholic Church, the only authority the Flemings seemed to recognise, formally to condemn Flemish-Nationalism. As early as 1920, the King had asked the Papal Nuncio in Brussels, Mgr. Nicotra, for the direct intervention of Pope Benedict XV. Albert also sent Cardinal Mercier, the Belgicist Archbishop of Mechelen, to Rome to ask the Holy Father to prohibit the faithful from 'engaging in passionate conflicts that divide citizens from the same country.' Benedict adopted a cautious position. He wrote a letter about the '*Quaestio Flandrica*' in February 1921, exhorting only priests and seminarians, but no lay people, to abstain from political activities.

In 1926, the King asked for a new intervention from the Vatican. Albert personally wrote to the new Pope Pius XI. 'The Flamingant clergy has disobeyed the previous papal letter,' he complained. 'Its extremist propaganda, especially its separatist intentions, threaten the social order and the unity of the country.'[81] Baron Beyens, the Belgian Ambassador to the Vatican, was even more explicit in a let-

80   *De Schelde*, 13 Nov. 1922, 30 Jan. and 2 Mar. 1924.
81   Stengers 9, pp. 205–6.

ter to Cardinal Pietro Gasparri, the Vatican Secretary of State: 'The Flamingant leadership wants a total autonomy for the Flemish part of the country. They call it an administrative separation, but they actually aim for complete independence, a disruption of national unity. I regret that I have to add that the most fervent and blinded propagandists of an independent Republic of Flanders belong to the lower clergy and to the religious orders. These clerics remain deaf to the admonitions of the Holy Father and oppose the authority of the Bishop of Mechelen.'[82] Pius XI reacted favourably. Though he did not excommunicate the Flamingants, he complied with the Belgian request to change the traditional formula in Holy Mass that stated that Mass was said 'in communion with the Pope of Rome and the local Bishop.' In Belgium, it was replaced by the formula that Mass was said 'in communion with the Pope, with the local Bishop and with King Albert.'

On 9 December 1928, the *Front Partij* gained a victory that rocked the Belgian establishment. The party had put August Borms, the former Aktivist leader, forward as its candidate for the parliamentary by-elections in Antwerp. Borms was still in gaol serving his life sentence, but obtained 83,058 votes or 65.2% of the electorate. The authorities, arguing that a prisoner could not take up his seat in Parliament, proclaimed Borms's election invalid and appointed the losing candidate, the Liberal Belgicist Paul Baelde, MP for Antwerp. In order to appease the indignant people, Borms was released from prison on 17 January 1929.

The so-called 'Borms election' persuaded the Belgian Bishops to interfere directly in the electoral process. In 1929, Thomas Debacker, a war veteran and a popular schoolteacher from the rural Kempen area to the east of Antwerp, founded a new Flamingant party, the *Katholieke Vlaamse Volkspartij*. Cardinal Joseph-Ernest Van Roey, who had succeeded Mercier as Primate of Belgium after the latter's death in 1926, had a letter read from the pulpit in Debacker's constituency during Sunday Mass. He forbade all Catholics to vote for Debacker. This did not prevent Debacker from winning a seat in the Chamber of Representatives. In June 1930, Van Roey published a pastoral letter declaring that loyalty to the Belgian State was a Catholic duty. 'As shepherds of your souls we declare and teach that for all, Flemings and Walloons, Belgium is the fatherland,' the Cardinal's letter said. It was read from the pulpit in every church.

---

82   MFA Beyens Papers, Beyens to Cardinal Gasparri, 1 Feb. 1926.

In 1932, the Flamingants won the municipal elections. In Debacker's home town of Mol, they became the largest party. Mol was also the town of Count Broqueville, who had meanwhile returned as Prime Minister. Though Debacker had the support of 9 of the 15 members of the municipal council, the King refused to appoint him as Mayor and appointed a politician from Broqueville's official Catholic Party (4 seats) instead. Though this was undemocratic, it was not illegal, because according to Belgian law the King appoints the mayors. Unlike Albert, Debacker was a democrat. In the party journal, he warned against Hitler's 'totalitarian civilisation from which Flanders can expect no good,'[83] but he also made it clear that he would never volunteer to fight for Belgium again, as he had done in 1914.

In the late 1920s, the anti-militarist campaigns of the Flamingants attracted the attention of the German-Swiss physicist Albert Einstein, a self-declared pacifist, as well as a would-be social engineer. Unfortunately, the latter prevailed over the former in his priorities. Einstein believed in World Revolution and admired the Soviet Union, 'the first country that through its powerful action has proved the practical possibility of a planned economy.'[84] When Einstein visited Brussels in 1927, Albert, who cared greatly about his international reputation, invited him over to Laken. Einstein at once felt at home with the Belgian monarch and his schemes of social engineering. He also became a close friend of the Queen, whose Soviet-friendly opinions originated in talks with Einstein. Until the early 1920s, Elisabeth had been outspokenly anti-Soviet as well as anti-Semite. In November 1919, during a visit to the United States, the Belgian royal couple had amazed Assistant Secretary of State, Breckinridge Long, with remarks about 'the part played by the Jews in Bolshevism, their designs for control of the world.' Especially the Queen, the American noted in his diary, 'spoke several times of Jewish ambitions and connected the Zionist movement with it. She asked of Justice Louis D. Brandeis, of the propriety of his connection with Zionism.'[85] Albert, too, believed in dark Jewish conspiracies. 'The Jews love the freemasons and hope for their triumph,' he noted in his war diary in 1916.[86]

83   Debacker in *De Nieuwe Kempen*, 5 May 1934.
84   Quoted in Erauw, p. 176.
85   Third Assistant Secretary of State Breckinridge Long, Diary, 10 Nov. 1919, p. 314 (3), in Library of Congress, Washington D.C., Division of Manuscripts.
86   RAB KAD, 17 Mar. 1916.

In the 1930s, Einstein, although a Jew, became a political advisor of the King. Albert asked him how to deal with the Flamingant conscripts refusing to serve in the Belgian army. Einstein replied: 'It seems to me that the Belgian army is an instrument of defence and not at all an instrument of aggression. Hence, it is indispensable for the security of Belgium.' He advised, however, not to imprison those who refused to fulfil their service, but to 'have them work in the mines, or nurse contagious people.'[87] The two Alberts, Einstein and the King, also shared a mutual distrust of the U.S. They suspected America of harbouring dangerous imperialist dreams. Already in March 1917, in a conversation with Colonel Génie, King Albert had proposed a Franco-Belgian alliance as a device 'to resist America which is about to join the war, not to suffer with us, but to conquer us.' Einstein, as one learns from his letters to Laken, shared this distrust of the Americans, whom he called 'minuscule demi-Gods' with 'childish illusions,' who impose 'a new sort of colonialism through the money they invest in foreign countries. And those who defend themselves against this, are an enemy.'[88]

Blood on the Rocks

There are many indications that Albert and Elisabeth grew apart in the 1920s. The King became the father to at least one bastard son. The Queen also had a sex life of her own. During a vacation in Italy in 1922, the 16-year-old Marie-José witnessed her mother flirting with King Victor-Emmanuel III of Italy, who 'could not keep his eyes from my mother.' Victor-Emmanuel followed Elisabeth around whenever she went swimming and sunbathing. They locked themselves up for hours in a little cabin on the beach. Marie-José also noticed that he had stolen a kiss from her mother in an elevator. The Belgian Queen's habit of lavishly powdering her face betrayed him: 'When he left the elevator, he had some of her powder on his nose.'[89] Apparently, King Albert did not mind. After a period of marital tension in late 1918 and early 1919, Albert and Elisabeth had reached a *modus vivendi*, allowing each other their own erotic adventures.

The relationship between Albert and his two legitimate sons was strained. Crown Prince Leopold, the Duke of Brabant, was a tall and handsome Adonis, with blue eyes and blond curly hair. He had

---

87   Einstein to Albert I, 14 July 1933, in Marie-José, pp. 401–2.
88   Einstein to Elisabeth, 20 Nov. 1933, 12 Jan. 1953 and 22 Jan. 1955, in Marie-José,
       p. 396.
89   Quoted in Petacco, pp. 50–1.

inherited the Saxe-Coburg looks of his great-grandfather Leopold I, and none of the ugliness of his mother's Wittelbach family. This had apparently all gone to his brother Charles, the spitting image of his mother, with the same long, bony face. Leopold craved his father's approval. Once, when he was 23 years old, an angry Albert scolded his son. 'I left feeling very miserable,' Leopold recalled many years later. 'I went to a public park and, feeling so upset by the row with my father, I spent the night there... on a bench.' Charles, the Count of Flanders, was more phlegmatic than his timid older brother. When Albert reprimanded Charles for his bad school results, Charles replied: 'The second worst student of the class is such a genius that it is impossible for me to surpass him.'

Albert appointed Jacques Pirenne, the son of the Belgicist historian Henri Pirenne, teacher and advisor to the Crown Prince. Jacques Pirenne was one of the leaders of the anti-Semite *Jeunesses Nationales*. He exerted a great influence over Leopold by constantly flattering him. The Papal Nuncio in Brussels, Mgr. Clemente Micara, noted in 1933 that the Crown Prince was 'impressionable to the highest degree.'

In 1920, Albert and Elisabeth attended the wedding of 'Cimmie' (Cynthia) Curzon to a promising young British MP, Sir Oswald Mosley. With Cimmie's aid — and the fortune of her American Jewish grandfather — Mosley later founded the British Fascist Party. Her sister, 'Ba-Ba' (Alexandra) Curzon, became an ardent Fascist, too, as well as one of Mosley's mistresses (which earned her the nickname *Ba-Ba-Blackshirt*). King Albert probably regretted that all three Curzon daughters, heirs to Levi Leiter's immense fortune, married Englishmen. They would have been a good match for Charles. Albert preferred the aristocracy of money above that of blood. 'Personally I would prefer my son, or my sons, to become the sons-in-law of John Rockefeller,' he wrote. 'There lies the future: the only kings left are the kings of money, and only they establish new dynasties.'

Crown Prince Leopold, however, had to marry for the sake of politics, rather than money. On 10 November 1926, the Duke of Brabant married the Swedish princess Astrid. As with Albert's marriage 26 years before, the constitutionally-required approval by the Government was not asked. The 21-year-old Astrid was a daughter of Carl Bernadotte, a younger brother of King Gustav V of Sweden. She was tall and friendly, with green eyes and dark brown hair, and looked more like a blushing farmer's daughter from the South of France, than a Northern princess. The House of Bernadotte was founded by one of Napoleon's generals, a Gascon of humble origins, who in 1810 had been adopted by the King of Sweden. Astrid's mother was Princess Ingeborg of Denmark, whose grandmother was a Princess of Orange. Thus, King Willem I of the United Netherlands, who in 1831 had lost the Belgian provinces to Leopold of Saxe-Coburg, was one of Astrid's ancestors. Her elder sister Martha was the wife of Crown Prince Olav of Norway. The marriage of Leopold to Astrid linked Belgium to Sweden, Denmark, Norway and the Netherlands — four neutral Northern countries.

Indeed, the Belgo-Swedish marriage signified the beginning of a shift in Albert's foreign policies, away from the Franco-Belgian alliance, and towards a renewal of Belgium's neutralist position. By the mid-1920s, King Albert had begun to doubt the wisdom of the Franco-Belgian military alliance because it obliged Belgium to join France in every European war in which Paris got involved. In 1925, Belgium and France pulled their troops out of the Rhine and the Ruhr provinces after Germany formally recognised its new western borders. The German eastern border, however, remained under dispute. Paris had signed treaties with Poland, Czechoslovakia and Romania to guarantee them French military assistance in case of an armed conflict with Berlin. Unlike the French government, Albert was not prepared to jeopardise his army for countries he felt he had nothing to do with. As the 1920s drew to their close, the King began to fear a new European war, which made it even more urgent for him to detach Belgium from France. 'France has concluded alliances that will engage it in foreign wars. We have to ensure that Belgium is not drawn into any conflict foreign to our interests,' the King told Hymans, his Minister of Foreign Affairs.[90] 'Of this we may be certain,' Lord Tyrrell of the British Foreign Office wrote. 'Unless the knife is at her throat, Belgium will not fight except in her own defence: never say for Poland or Roumania.'[91]

In 1926, Albert reappointed Emile Galet, whom he had so abruptly discarded in September 1918, as Chief of Staff of the Belgian army. In December 1930, when Hitler was not yet in power in Germany, Albert told Galet's pupil, General Raoul Van Overstraeten: 'The fight for the hegemony within Europe is not at all finished. It will lead to new wars between England and Germany.'[92] Both the marriage of his son to Astrid of Sweden and that of his daughter Marie-José to Crown Prince Umberto of Italy in 1930 must be seen in the context of a gradual shift

90   Hymans, vol. II, p. 602.
91   FO 371/10.531 W11181/9992/4, annotation Tyrrell, 25 Dec. 1924.
92   Van Overstraeten 1, p. 78.

in Belgium's international policy from pro-French to once again neutralist. The day after Marie-José's marriage in Rome, King Albert
attended a party parade of the Fascist Militia, something he was not
obliged to do, but did out of sympathy for Mussolini.

Leopold's marriage also fulfilled its dynastic purposes. According
to Colonel Van den Heuvel, Leopold's aide-de-camp, the car of the
Duke and Duchess of Brabant often stopped during their trips
through the countryside. The driver had to go for a walk while the
Prince and his wife disappeared into the fields. On 11 October 1927,
Astrid gave birth to her first baby, Joséphine-Charlotte. On 7 Septem-
ber 1930, Astrid's first son was born: Baudouin, the Count of Hainaut.
On 6 June 1934, the Duchess of Brabant gave birth to a second son,
Albert. The baby received the title of Prince of Liège.

Meanwhile the King's financial worries increased. The finances of
the Belgian royal family, like those of many others, were severely hit
in the late 1920s. We do not know the details of the losses, but Albert
complained to his sister Henriette: 'Everyone has lost money, including me. I am in a situation that is far from brilliant.' Only occasionally
the public could catch a glimpse of the King's private financial situation. One such occasion occurred in February 1932 when the Communist politician Henri Glineur revealed that Albert owned a stake of 9.3
million francs in the Walloon coal mine of Marchienne-au-Pont.
Glineur was angry after a mining accident there which occurred
through negligence on the part of the management and which had
killed sixteen miners and seriously injured eleven. The King paid a
visit to the injured, prompting the Communist to write that Albert
was a 'sadist' coming to view 'the cooked flesh of the good miners that
had died for the glory of the personal profits and the good reputation
of the House of Albert and Co.' As a result of the article, Glineur was
brought to court. He was condemned to one year's imprisonment for
insulting the King. The verdict was hardly noticed. Apart from *Le
Peuple*, none of the major newspapers devoted any attention to it.

Albert also had a major stake in the biggest Belgian steelworks, the
Cockerill Company in Seraing near Liège, and the royal family was
the largest shareholder of the SG. This holding controlled over 40% of
the Belgian economy. In 1932, a Dutch economist calculated that it
owned 10% of the Belgian cotton industry, 25 to 30% of its coal mines,
48% of its iron and steel works, 60 to 75% of its zinc industry and 100%
of its copper industry. The SG also owned Belgium's largest bank, the
Banque Générale or G-Bank. In the late 1920s, Albert had Emile
Francqui, the Governor of the SG, appointed a cabinet member to
watch over the interests of the holding.

The fruits of socialism and corporatism were bitter: they had brought economic sclerosis to the huge coal and steel works of Wallonia, where economic growth had stagnated. The number of Walloon industrial jobs remained static at 400,000 between 1896 and 1937. In Flanders, with its many small and medium-sized private enterprises, the economy boomed and industrial jobs grew in the same period from 184,000 to 400,000. Proportionally, the Walloon share in Belgium's industrial production fell from 55.9% (1896) over 49.9% (1910) to 40.0% (1937), while in Flanders it rose from 27.4% over 33.3% to 40.1%. Most of Brussels' 200,000 industrial jobs were filled by Flemings as well: they worked harder than the Francophones, were less demanding, and tended to distrust the trade unions — those pillars of the Belgian regime. Flanders also remained the dominant agricultural area in Belgium, with over 370,000 farmers in 1939, against less than 300,000 in Wallonia.

The growing political, demographic and economic power of Flanders left the Belgian regime no other option but to grant the Flemings more linguistic rights. In 1930, exactly one hundred years after the Belgian revolutionaries had banned Dutch, the State University of Ghent became a Dutch-language institution. Half the cabinet ministers were Flemings by now, some of them were even moderate Flamingants who no longer accepted the argument that Dutch was unfit as a language for higher education. The establishment of a Dutch university came as a blow to Belgicists such as Henri Pirenne, who resigned as a professor at Ghent in protest. His son, Jacques, started a campaign to keep Ghent University at least partly French. The King, too, wanted Ghent to become a bilingual university, as did the Church. They were, however, unable to persuade the politicians. The Catholic Party, fearing that it would lose too many votes to the Flemish-Nationalists, insisted on an entirely Dutch university. Once Ghent had become a Dutch-language institution, the Catholic University of Leuven was forced to follow suit, lest it lose all its Flemish students to Ghent. At Leuven, however, the Church succeeded in slowing down the inevitable development. Leuven became a bilingual university and remained half Francophone until as late as 1968.

Soon, new concessions had to be made to the Flemings: In 1932, Dutch became the official language of Flemish public primary and secondary schools. In that same year, the vernacular also became the language of the civil administration in Flanders. Meanwhile King Albert was growing ever more dissatisfied with his subjects. He became embittered and was subject to morose moods, which he tried to remedy by climbing rocks in the Ardennes on his own. This physical exercise became an addiction. Had Albert's pessimism anything to do with the concessions that the politicians were making to the Flemings? Or does it put a strain on a man to be the king of an artificial country, of a people whose adherence to the state has to be bought? The fact that there was no generosity in the 'patriotism' of the Belgians seemed to bother him. Once, after he had spoken to a crowd, the King told an aide: 'It is themselves that they acclaim by acclaiming me.' When Count Louis de Lichtervelde told Albert that there were more monarchists now than ever before, he retorted: 'The bourgeoisie know that they are defending their own lives and possessions.' Belgium only appealed to feelings of greed, self-enrichment and immorality, never to sacrifice or charity. Belgium corrupted and perverted its inhabitants. The King complained, again to Lichtervelde, in 1931 about 'the decadence of the senior administration' and 'the ruinous abuses.'[93] He frequently announced his intention to abdicate and retire to Switzerland.

In 1929, Lichtervelde had an English-language hagiographic biography *Léopold of the Belgians* published in New York and London. Its preface states that 'the Belgians, now that they do him justice, have become passionately proud of the great and heroic figure of Léopold II.' The King knew this to be a lie. 'I am still to find the first Belgian who will defend Leopold II,' he told General Van Overstraeten in February 1931. Albert was angry that part of his uncle's fortune had been lost to him. 'The public could not bear the fact that the Head of State was rich. When King Leopold died, all the statesmen did their utmost to disperse his inheritance. They made the people sympathise with his daughters, who had become but strangers. Indeed, the monarchy was really robbed then.'[94] In public speeches he began to praise the late *bäcktelein* as 'one of those rare men whose deeds testify to their *grandeur* better than any words can.'[95]

In the autumn of 1933, Count Broqueville proposed an amnesty for Flemish civil servants who had lost their jobs after the anti-Flamingant purge in 1919. The Prime Minister wanted a reconciliation between the Belgians, arguing that after bitter conflicts all nations try to reconcile the previously warring factions. In an artificial country like Belgium, however, magnanimity is impossible. It endangers the very existence of the state. Broqueville's amnesty bill led to fierce

93　Willequet 4, p. 254
94　Quoted in Willequet 4, p. 252.
95　Albert I in Namur, 1928, in Stinglhamber and Dresse, p. 234.

protests from Belgicists who took to the streets and petitioned the King not to be forgiving.

To Albert, too, an amnesty for the 'unpatriotic' Flamingants was out of the question. In January 1934 he personally intervened to prevent the amnesty. He wrote a stern letter to the cabinet condemning the bill, and had the letter leaked in the Francophone papers. The government at once buried its proposal. The Francophone press unanimously praised the King. 'He has affirmed his right, both constitutional and sovereign, to revise the decision of his ministers, even of the entire cabinet,' *La Nation Belge* wrote.

The prevention of the amnesty was Albert's last political act. The King, not yet 59 years old, was found dead, his skull cracked, at the foot of the rocks at Marche-les-Dames in the Maas valley on the evening of 17 February 1934. He had set out to climb the rocks on his own in the afternoon. It was an easy climb, which he had often done alone. The fatal accident of a healthy and experienced mountain climber, on a spot he knew well, at once led to speculations. The British Military Intelligence suspected that the King had been murdered, either by French secret agents or by Francophile Belgians, because he was about to formally renounce the Franco-Belgian military treaty. When Colonel Sir Graham Seton Hutchinson defended this thesis, it led to official protests from the Belgian Embassy in London and to indignation in the Belgicist press.[96]

By the beginning of 1934, the King was, indeed, on the point of formally renouncing Belgium's military alliance to France. Not only was he unwilling to join France in a war with Germany over Eastern Europe, but he was also no longer prepared to assist France in case the latter was attacked by Nazi Germany. If France were to lose the war, he did not want his dynasty and Belgium to go down with it. Unlike *real* countries, artificial countries are perishable goods. Albert wished to return to the tried and tested policy which his House had always pursued: *stay out of any war unless you are sure to end up on the winning side.* 'So far,' the King told General Van Overstraeten in December 1933, 'we have been loyal to our Allies, but, if need be, we will reconsider this.'[97] He was saying the same thing that he had been saying until September 1918. He had come full circle. Belgium was, once again, an unreliable ally.

96   *La Nation Belge*, 7 May 1934.
97   Quoted in Van Overstraeten 1, p. 100.

Leopold III, Fourth King of the Belgians,
and Lilian Baels

Chapter 5

A King Crowned With Thorns (1934–1950)

Like Father, Like Son

King Albert was buried on 22 February 1934. The next morning, the 33-year-old Leopold took the constitutional oath and ascended the throne. His mother Elisabeth went to live in the Palm Pavilion in the royal park of Laken, about one kilometre from the Palace. There the Queen Mother often invited friends over. One of them was her physician, Dr. Karl Gebhardt, a German orthopaedist and a Colonel in the SS. Gebhardt greatly influenced Elisabeth. As Nazism was a constructivist ideology of social as well as human engineering, Elisabeth was naturally attracted to it. In June 1939 she told Gebhardt that she admired Hitler's 'constructive work.'[1]

During the first year following Albert's fatal accident, it appeared that the late king's death had tipped the balance in favour of the defenders of the Franco-Belgian military treaty, to the disadvantage of the neutralists. On the day of King Albert's funeral, the Belgian Minister of Defence, Albert Devèze, a Francophone Liberal, began to negotiate an extension of the treaty with the French.

Devèze forced Leopold to dismiss General Prudent Nuyten, an adherent of General Galet, who had succeeded Galet as Chief of Staff of the Belgian army in January 1933. In his memoirs, written half a century later, Leopold wryly recalled: 'Devèze came to see me shortly after my accession to the throne. Bluntly he declared: "I am sorry to disturb the King whilst he is still grieving for his father, but he shall

---

1   Quoted in Lambrechts, p. 93.

have to choose between his defence minister and the chief of the general staff.''' Devèze threatened to bring the government down if Leopold did not dismiss Nuyten at once. The inexperienced King did not dare to risk the resignation of the cabinet. 'I was trapped. The highest military authority in the country was fired without being given a chance to defend himself.'[2]

But Leopold sought revenge. When in 1936 he felt at ease in his new role as king, he dismissed Devèze. In a speech on 14 October he publicly revoked the Franco-Belgian military treaty and announced Belgium's return to international neutrality. Unlike the neutral status that had been imposed on Belgium by the international powers until the First World War, this was a voluntary neutrality. For the first time in its history, Belgium had willingly and publicly disengaged itself from France; this was seen by many Francophones as treason. To these Belgicists, the King had become a... Flamingant! 'This will have serious negative consequences for the institution of the monarchy,' the Walloon Socialist newspaper *Le Peuple* warned prophetically.

In Flanders, too, the King's policy was interpreted as an overture from the monarchy towards the Flemings. This impression was reinforced in 1938 when the Belgian army was divided into separate Dutch- and French-language regiments. For the first time since 1830, soldiers in Flanders received their orders in their own tongue. George Van Severen, a former MP of the *Frontists*, literally embraced the Belgian flag. He renounced his erstwhile separatist and democratic convictions and began a campaign for a new 'Burgundian Empire' — a greater Belgium, a bilingual state encompassing both the Netherlands and Northern France, with a Mussolini-style Fascist constitution and Leopold III at its helm. Van Severen's movement, however, never commanded a mass following. The Flemings were not keen on Fascism, or any ideology that made the individual subordinate to the state. 'There is no place in the Flemish-Nationalist Party for people who defend dictatorship and absolutism,' Staf De Clercq, the party leader, said in his speech at the annual party conference in 1934. De Clercq's deputy, Hendrik Elias, declared that the party rejected 'the racial policies, the *Kulturkampf* and the authoritarianism of the Hitler regime.'[3] The Flemish-Nationalist *De Schelde* remained one of Europe's most outspoken anti-Fascist and anti-Nazi newspapers in the early 1930s. On more than one occasion it devoted its entire front-page editorial to 'Hitler's despicable anti-Semitism' and the

2   Leopold III 2, p. 27.
3   *Strijd*, 3 May 1936.

racial theories of the Nazis whose 'scientific value is nil, nothing but philosophical balderdash.'[4]

Nevertheless, the increase of Leopold's popularity in Flanders, and its simultaneous decline in Wallonia, was obvious. It turned the pattern of royalism around completely. King Albert had been the hero of the Francophones, his son became the hero of the Flemings. Ironically, Leopold came to be seen as someone who had fundamentally rejected his father's policy, although he was actually continuing it.

Unfortunately, Leopold was vain. Unlike his father, who always *suggested* to politicians what they should do, Leopold *ordered* them to do what he wanted. King Albert would have been careful not to announce the renunciation of the Franco-Belgian military treaty himself, leaving that task to a politician or to a general who could be dropped later if things went wrong. Leopold desperately wanted to show that the new policy was *his* policy. He even became angry when the Socialist leader Hendrik De Man tried to cover him. When De Man claimed that he had forced Belgium's international neutrality upon the King, Leopold sent the politician a photograph of himself out fishing, with the handwritten message: 'The King trying to catch a big fish called neutrality, not knowing that it had been already caught by you.'

Though De Man was reprimanded for stating that neutralism had been his idea, rather than Leopold's, Leopold might not have been able to renounce the Franco-Belgian treaty without the support of the BWP leadership. It was fortunate for the King that the first year of his reign coincided with a change of leadership in the Belgian Workers' Party.

The change was caused by the illness of the old BWP *patron*, Emile Vandervelde. His deputy, who gradually became the party's new strongman, was a brilliant intellectual in his late forties. Hendrik De Man was born and raised in Antwerp as the grandson of the Flamingant poet Jan Van Beers. As a teenager he had experienced the anti-Belgian and anti-militarist climate in the town. In 1905, the 20-year-old De Man left to study in Leipzig. There he joined the SPD, the powerful German Socialist Party. After the First World War, De Man emigrated to the United States, but he soon returned to Europe, dissatisfied with America's 'xenophobia and anti-Socialist witch hunts.'[5] He settled in Germany, where he became Professor of Social Psychology at Frankfurt University. Soon he was one of the most prominent and influential ideologues of the European Social Democrats. In May 1933, after the Nazis dismissed him from his Chair, De

4   *De Schelde*, 14 Aug. 1932 and 26 Jan. 1933.
5   Quoted in Claeys-Van Haegendoren, p. 127.

Man returned to Belgium where Vandervelde engaged him as head of the BWP think tank.

Barely six months later, in December 1933, De Man became the focal point of Belgian politics. He launched a constructivist scheme — the so-called *De Man Plan* — necessary, he claimed, to fight the high level of unemployment in Belgium. The Plan proposed the nationalisation of basic industries and a centrally planned economy. The idea of fighting capitalism by strengthening executive power in an authoritarian system, was consistent with the *Zeitgeist*. 'Planism' attracted many ambitious young anti-parliamentarian intellectuals to the BWP. Soon De Man teamed up with one of these, Paul-Henri Spaak, a Brussels Francophone barrister, of whom the French author Alfred Fabre-Luce would later write: 'By looking at this weathercock, one can always tell which way the wind of Europe is blowing.'

Spaak came from a well-to-do artistic family of actors and politicians. His father was the director of the Brussels opera, his mother a Liberal Senator and the sister of the Liberal Party leader Paul-Emile Janson. Spaak entered politics as a Communist revolutionary, 'delighted to lead rioting mobs.' He was still smashing windows as late as 1934, when he was already 35 years of age. The following year, however, Spaak, a chubby fellow with, as Count Capelle remarked, 'the hands of a woman,' became De Man's partner. They formed a brilliant team. Spaak ably translated De Man's theories into appealing political slogans.

In 1936, De Man and Spaak proclaimed that 'national socialism' was the central concept of the BWP's programme. This *socialisme national*, said De Man, was 'a socialism that recognises *l'importance primordial du fait national*. The primordial importance of the fact that one constitutes a single nation.'[6] Of course, De Man, who had been expelled from Germany, had not become a Nazi. In fact, his 'national socialism' was merely a pun. Belgium, as an artificial nation, did not really exist as a nation, and De Man knew this. The Belgian state was no more than the corporatist social welfare system run by the labour unions and other 'Social Partners.' Being a Belgian nationalist meant only that one was attached to the Belgian welfare state. 'What Spaak and I mean by national socialism is a socialism that attempts to achieve all that can be achieved within the national framework,' De Man explained in an interview in February 1937. He went on to state that the Belgian welfare system could — and should — eventually be replaced by a pan-European or even a global welfare system. 'I insist

6   *L'Indépendance Belge*, 17 Feb. 1937.

on being a good European, a good world citizen, as much as on being a good Belgian,' he said.[7] He reckoned that if one had to live in an artificial welfare state, it would be better to live in one on as large a scale as possible. The Belgian model had to be applied at a European level. Apart from being *'planists,'* 'national socialists,' and 'Europeanists,' De Man and Spaak were also neutralists. De Man believed that Germany had been badly treated at Versailles. This made a new war almost inevitable, as became clear when Hitler's troops marched into the demilitarised Rhineland in March 1936. Like Leopold, De Man felt that Belgium – urgently – had to detach itself from its military alliance with France.

De Man's ideas also attracted the Queen Mother. Elisabeth frequently invited the politician over. They became close friends. She confided to him that she always voted Socialist herself and encouraged her chamber maid to do so too. Elisabeth introduced De Man to her son, who appointed him as one of his personal counsellors, not only in political matters but also in private, and even intimate, ones as well. De Man soon discovered that the thing mostly on the King's mind was sex. In his private memoirs Leopold's secretary, Count Robert Capelle, wrote that his master was 'a weakling concerning sex, with various passionate adventures.' According to De Man, he had *'une sexualité très développée.'* Other characteristics included his stubbornness and 'his capricious mood swings.'

In March 1935, Leopold installed a three-party Cabinet of Catholics, Socialists and Liberals, led by the technocrat Paul Van Zeeland, with De Man as Minister of Employment and Public Works, and Spaak as Minister of Transport. One year later, in a cabinet led by Spaak's uncle, Paul-Emile Janson, De Man became Deputy Prime Minister and Minister of Finance, and Spaak Minister of Foreign Affairs. Leopold told Spaak that he was obliged to submit all important questions to him. Spaak was obedient. In May 1938, the grateful King made him Belgium's first Socialist Prime Minister ever.

De Man, who after Vandervelde's death became BWP President, did not return to the cabinet. His *'planism'* had left the state with a deficit of 2 billion francs. Leopold suggested that his friend become his *'maître des plaisirs,'* helping him to find prostitutes while 'gallivanting in Paris.' Once it had dawned on the Socialist leader that the King wanted to involve him in these affairs, he carefully avoided 'encouraging conversations of this type.'[8]

7   Quoted in De Schryver and De Wever, vol. II, p. 1995.
8   De Man 3, p. 38.

Apart from Brussels and Paris, Leopold's sexual escapades often brought him to Knokke, the new fashionable resort on the Flemish coast. In the early 1930s, Ostend was 'out,' and Knokke was 'in.' Knokke was a creation of Count Maurice Lippens, a former Governor-General of the Congo, who owned a huge tract of land in the dunes along the sea to the east of the old fishing village of Knokke. Lippens divided it into plots on which he built luxurious villas for fellow millionaires. In 1930, the shrewd Count donated one of his plots to Leopold. Once it was known that the King had a villa in Knokke, every member of the establishment wanted one as well. Leopold often went to his villa. It bordered on the golf course, where the handsome, sex-addicted King had ample occasion to meet willing women from Belgian 'high society'. Knokke is, of course, a perfect name for a place to meet willing women.

In April 1930, nearly six months before Baudouin, his first legitimate son, was born, Leopold became father of an illegitimate son, but there were also rumours of a daughter by a Swedish lady-in-waiting of the Queen. Women, however, were not Leopold's only obsession; fast cars were another. Unfortunately, he was a bad driver. On 29 August 1935, the 29-year-old Queen Astrid was killed in a car crash caused by her husband. While on a private vacation, Leopold's car crashed into an orchard near his Swiss home, the Villa Haslihorn on Lake Lucerne. The Queen died instantly, her head smashed against a tree; the King suffered a broken rib.

The Belgian State and Church propaganda portrayed Leopold as a deeply religious, mourning widower with three young children. Cardinal Van Roey wrote a hagiography about the royal marriage. In one Catholic publication, King Leopold, who in a period of 18 months had lost both his father and his wife in tragic circumstances, was compared to Christ. He was, the publication said, 'a broken man, who by his immortal love was crowned for the second time, and with thorns, as King of his People.'[9] To promote the message, the Church distributed post cards bearing a photograph of Leopold walking behind Astrid's hearse and shouldering a large cross that had been added by trick-photography: this was Jesus carrying his cross on the way to Golgotha!

Meanwhile, the conflict between Leopold and his brother Charles deepened. The Count of Flanders, still unmarried, spent most of his time in Raversijde near Ostend. His friends called him 'the Prince of Darkness' because he lived mostly at night. According to his biogra-

9   Denis and Ysabie, p. 9.

pher, 'Charles drank enormous quantities of milk mixed with even more whiskey, which he consumed not by the glass but by the bottle.'[10] In 1936, the Prince fell in love with the daughter of a wealthy Brussels pastry baker. When she became pregnant in 1938, he intended to marry her. As a member of the royal family, however, he needed the King's permission, but Leopold vetoed the marriage, arguing that he could not allow a baker's daughter to marry a prince. Charles never forgave his brother. He wanted nothing to do with the hypocrite again and struck up a friendship with another Saxe-Coburg outcast, Leopold II's son, Lucien, the Duke of Tervuren, who made a living as a travelling salesman of dental prostheses in the South of France.

A Work of Necessary Destruction

The second half of the 1930s saw a rapid succession of escalating conflicts between Leopold and his ministers. King Albert I had transformed Belgium into a corporatist regime where the powers running the state were politically unaccountable 'Social Partners,' like the trade unions. The agreement between the three major parties on this basic issue made Belgium, notwithstanding its ethnic division, a rather stable country, as Albert had intended it to be. Paradoxically, however, Belgium's governing cabinets were politically unstable, because Albert had, again deliberately, imposed an electoral system that resulted in weak coalitions. The ministers, who had nothing to say about the fundamental social and economic issues that the Social Partners dealt with, quarrelled about everything else. In the six years between Leopold's accession in 1934 and Hitler's occupation of Belgium, there were no less than nine different Belgian governments and 22 cabinet crises. These crises all arose from obscure party manoeuvres and intrigues, often over the assignment of government contracts or the appointment of leading civil servants.

None of the inter-war governments was brought down in Parliament. In fact, even today, Belgian governments hardly ever fall as a result of a direct vote in Parliament. The electoral system introduced after the Loppem Coup makes the individual deputies totally subservient to their party's ruling caucus. This politburo, where official representatives of the Social Partners of the party's ideological colour have their say, decides where a candidate is placed on the electoral list. It is his place on the list rather than the number of votes he receives that determines a candidate's chances of election. Conse-

10   De Lentdecker 2, p. 22.

quently, a Representative or a Senator who dares to disobey party directives commits political suicide. He can also forget the career opportunities of his sons and daughters in the civil service or in the many companies owned or controlled by the state or the 'Partners.' The Belgian system has a built-in tendency towards corruption: the more a politician submits to the system, the better off he and his family will be.

Unsurprisingly, Belgian politicians are more despised than their counterparts in neighbouring countries. In the late 1930s, Leopold tried to exploit these anti-political feelings. He blamed 'ministers who do not govern, but only obey the directives of their parties and cater to the trade unions.'[11] The King often acted the populist demagogue. It gained him the approval of many ordinary people and it helped prepare the ground for the more authoritarian regime he envisaged.

Meanwhile international tensions deepened. In March 1938, Germany annexed Austria — a move Spaak found 'only logical.' In July 1938, Spaak asked Czechoslovakia, which he considered to be 'an artificial state,' to 'stop its provocations of the Germans.'[12] Hendrik Borginon, the leader of the Flemish-Nationalist MPs in the Chamber of Representatives, disagreed with the appeasement policy of Spaak's government towards Berlin. In a speech on 26 October, Borginon remarked that it was impossible to deny that Nazi Germany had aggressive intentions. Germany had become a far bigger threat than France, he said. This 'pro-French' statement breached the official line of party president Staf De Clercq which stated as an axiom that 'for the Low Countries, France cannot be anything but a danger; Germany can become a danger; England will never be a danger.'[13]

Borginon, one of the founders of the *Front Partij*, was known to be anti-Hitler, as was Elias, the deputy president of the party. Other Flemish-Nationalist MPs, however, such as Reimond Tollenaere, declared that Nazi Germany was no threat to the West and that it was a bulwark against Communism. On 1 November 1938, Staf De Clercq settled the dispute between the two factions in an uneasy compromise. He came out in favour of strict neutrality, but warned against Nazism, which he implicitly compared with Communism. 'We reject Fascism and National-Socialism, we reject all totalitarian ideologies,' De Clercq wrote.[14] According to the *Sicherheitsdienst* (SD), the State Security Service of Nazi Germany, the Flemish-Nationalist party was

11   Leopold III 2, p. 18.
12   Quoted in Coolsaet, pp. 297–8.
13   Quoted in De Wever 3, pp. 195–6.
14   Quoted in Elias 2, vol. IV, p. 126.

divided into a pro-German group and 'a fervently Anglophile group around Borginon and Elias,' with De Clercq unable to choose sides.[15]

Dissatisfied with De Clercq's line, which they considered insufficiently critical of Nazi Germany, the local branch of the Antwerp *Front Partij* broke away from De Clercq's *Vlaams-Nationaal Verbond* (VNV, Flemish Nationalist Alliance), which was actually a federation of various local Flemish-Nationalist parties. In the 1938 municipal elections, the Antwerp *Frontists* supported the protest party of Leo Frenssen against the official VNV candidates. Frenssen was a Flamingant eccentric whose long hair and beard gave him a Rasputin-like appearance. He had spent the First World War in London, where he was a frequent visitor to Speakers' Corner in Hyde Park. After the war he tried to introduce this institution in Flanders. The Belgian authorities were not persuaded. Once, while 'speaking' at a Brussels street corner in August 1935, Frenssen was arrested and locked up in a lunatic asylum for nine days. Frenssen was also supported by *De Dag*, a tabloid founded in 1934, which rapidly became Antwerp's largest newspaper. Its journalists were mostly former Aktivists who, like its editor, had spent terms in prison after the First World War. *De Dag* was also the Jewish-friendliest of all Antwerp newspapers. Frenssen gained nearly fifteen per cent of the vote and six seats in the Antwerp municipal council, while the VNV had only one. The following year, in the 1939 parliamentary elections, Frenssen was elected as an Antwerp MP on a platform of pacifism, Flamingantism and hostility to racial prejudice. One of his political slogans was the rhetorical question: 'Who is most dangerous: the Jew or the Jew-hater?'[16]

When, on 15 March 1939, German tanks rolled into Prague, Hendrik Elias stressed that hitherto Germany had only annexed provinces inhabited by ethnic Germans, but that it had now started to violate the rights of other peoples. Even Van Severen, the former Flemish separatist who is generally considered to be the epitome of fascism in Flanders, instructed his followers to join the Belgian army in case of a German invasion.

Leopold III took an entirely different position. The Flemings were neutralist because they disliked France as much as they disliked Germany; the King was a neutralist for different reasons — he simply could not afford to run the risk of losing any war. Like the Flemish-Nationalists, Leopold's objective was to stay out of the war; but,

15   SD report, in De Wever 3, pp. 332 and 334.
16   Saerens, p. 420.

unlike them, he had to keep a second objective in mind as well: if Belgium was drawn into the conflict, it was vital that it end the war on the side of the victors or else it would disappear. Owing to the artificial nature of Belgium, Leopold had to be more than a neutralist; he had to be an appeaser of any would-be aggressor.

In February 1939, the Spaak cabinet fell. Spaak was succeeded as Prime Minister by Hubert Pierlot, a Catholic Walloon, while Spaak returned as Foreign Minister. Leopold was soon dissatisfied with his new Prime Minister, who refused to give in to Leopold's demands that he censor the Belgian press. 'We must create a neutralist mentality in Belgium,' Leopold said. 'The biggest threat for our country are France and Britain who want to force us to join the war on their side.'[17] Hence, the King intervened personally in October 1939 to prevent Belgium from recognising the exiled Polish government in London.

On 17 October, Karl Gebhardt, the Queen Mother's German physician, who had meanwhile been promoted to the rank of SS General, came to Brussels to complain about 'German-unfriendly remarks' in the Belgian media. 'The *Führer* is furious,' Gebhardt said.[18] Two days later, Spaak begged his colleagues in the cabinet 'to consider the possible consequences of the press campaigns against Germany.'[19] The Foreign Minister was under pressure to impose censorship, not only from the King, but also from Viscount Jacques Davignon, the Belgian Ambassador in Berlin. Davignon, the son of the Belgian Minister of Foreign Affairs from 1907 to 1915, demanded tight control of the press. 'Censorship would be ideal, but the government does not seem to dare,' he told Count Capelle. The King's secretary agreed and said that the cabinet consisted of '18 cowards.'[20]

In November 1939, Leopold made plans to replace Pierlot as Prime Minister by Count Lippens, the Knokke real estate investor, who had Fascist sympathies. Pierlot, unwilling to resign, decided to give in to the King's request for censorship. In December, an 'administrative censorship' was introduced: the distribution of a number of (foreign as well as Belgian) 'anti-German and unpatriotic publications' was prohibited, including the Flamingant *Het Vlaamsche Volk*, the British *Daily Express* and the French *Paris Soir*. On 9 January 1940, the German Ambassador to Brussels, Count Vicco von Bülow-Schwante, presented Spaak with an additional list of periodicals which he wanted to have outlawed as well. The government granted his request. All in all,

17   RAB SLIII nr. XV A13/60, Minutes Capelle, 16 and 27 Sept. 1939.
18   RAB SLIII nr. XV A13/95, Minutes Aspremont-Lynden, 17 Oct. 1939.
19   GSA microfilm 2030, Minutes cabinet meeting, 19 Oct. 1939.
20   SOMA PC24 nr. 1, pp. 43 and 63.

Belgium prohibited 61 publications, but the wayward Pierlot had added 7 pro-Nazi titles.

After Hitler's invasion of Denmark and Norway on 9 April 1940, London and Paris, convinced that a German attack on Belgium was imminent, asked Brussels for permission to station British and French troops on Belgium's territory. Leopold replied by sending Belgian troop reinforcements to... the Franco-Belgian border. They were under orders to shoot any French- or Englishman attempting to cross into Belgium. The French Prime Minister, Paul Reynaud, was scandalised. He felt insulted that Leopold should treat him on a par with Hitler. In Britain, Winston Churchill, the First Lord of the Admiralty, was equally infuriated. In 1944, he recalled that the Belgians had been 'the most contemptible of all the neutrals.'[21] Leopold, said Churchill, was 'a feeble specimen, thoroughly representative of the Belgian nation which vainly hoped to keep out of this war, no matter what they owed to those who saved them in the last war.'[22]

On 13 April, the King instructed the Belgian ministers to 'take swift action against Allied propaganda in Belgium.' The same day, he ordered Paul-Emile Janson, the Minister of Justice, and Robert De Foy, the head of the *Sûreté de l'Etat*, the Belgian secret service, to draw up lists of 'suspect Belgians and foreigners.' Those on the lists were to be arrested, extradited or 'placed in concentration camps' as soon as national security required. 'Be unyielding towards those who serve an anti-national cause over here,' Leopold said, adding that he 'refused to take sentimental considerations into account.'[23] The black lists of 'anti-national' Belgians included Flamingants and Communists. The 'foreigners from states which might become involved in war against Belgium'[24] included not only Germans and Italians living in Belgium, but also citizens from Allied countries. Most non-Belgians on the list, however, were Jewish fugitives from Germany and Poland.

Thousands of Jewish families had fled to Belgium in the late 1930s. They had not been welcome. After the German *Anschluss* of Austria on 11 March 1938, Charles du Bus de Warnaffe, the then Belgian Minister of Justice, ordered the Belgian Embassy in Vienna to deny visas to Jews. The Minister, a Walloon member of the Catholic Party, opined in Parliament that the Jews had 'for centuries constituted a problem in Europe' and that 'these criminals take our livelihood from

21 Churchill to Eden, 27 May 1944, in Keyes, p. 400.
22 Personal Minute Churchill, 8 Apr. 1945, in Keyes, p. 400.
23 SOMA PC24 nr. 1, pp. 147–50.
24 GSA microfilm 2081/1, Minutes cabinet meeting, 8 May 1940.

us.'[25] In an article Bus wrote that the Jews are an 'extremely unreliable' people; 'they have no word of honour and do not keep it.'[26] In May 1938, the anti-Semite hard-liner lost his ministerial post (to return after the war in 1945!), but King Leopold kept pressuring his government to stop the inflow of Jewish fugitives. 'The number of Israelites that have entered the country illegally since September 1939 is estimated to be 30,000,' he complained to Pierlot on 23 January 1940. 'Action against them cannot be harsh enough.'[27]

* * *

German troops crossed the Belgian border at 4 o'clock in the morning on Friday 10 May 1940. That same morning, Janson and De Foy ordered the police to round up the suspects on the *Sûreté's* black lists. Exactly how many people were arrested in this operation is unknown. Most documents relating to the arrests have disappeared. A German report written three months later states that in Antwerp alone 3,000 suspects were arrested. The majority of them were Jews, about 400 were (non-Jewish) German citizens and 50 were Flemish-Nationalists.[28] Many prominent Flamingants were gaoled, including the former Aktivist leader August Borms.

The Belgian authorities rounded up a considerable number of foreigners, often entire families. Most of them were people who had fled dictatorship in their home countries, such as East-European Jews, German political opponents of Hitler, and anti-Fascist Italians. Some Allied citizens were gaoled as well, probably by mistake through a mix-up of lists.

Meanwhile the Belgian army retreated. The Belgian and the Allied armies were no match for the *Wehrmacht*. Hitler's generals had developed a totally modern concept of warfare, the *Blitzkrieg*, which employed Panzer spearheads in close collaboration with fighter planes to deadly effect. Instead of an offensive over an extended front, the entire German army aimed its strength at a single target. This target was the French town of Abbeville on the Somme estuary. On 14 May, General Erwin Rommel's Panzer divisions broke through the French defences near Sedan to the south of the Belgian province of Luxemburg and rushed towards Abbeville and the English Channel.

25   Belgian Chamber of Representatives, Parliamentary Records, 22 Nov. 1938, pp. 52–3.
26   Quoted in Saerens, p. 212.
27   RAB SLIII, Leopold III to Pierlot, 23 Jan. 1940.
28   GRA 501/102, Wehrmacht Administration Activity Report nr. 7, 4 Aug. 1940, p. 49.

The German victory at Sedan decided the war. On the morning of 15 May, Paul Reynaud told Winston Churchill, the new British Prime Minister, that France was defeated.

In accordance with Article 68 of the Belgian Constitution, Leopold personally led the Belgian army during the war campaign. On paper it was a formidable army. Almost 900,000 men had been mobilised out of a population of eight million. However, 200,000 of them immediately fled to France, as did nearly 2 million civilians. Leopold, who had left Brussels for the army headquarters at Fort Breendonk to the south of Antwerp on the morning of 10 May, had appointed his friend Hendrik De Man, a Reserve officer with the rank of Captain, as personal aide-de-camp to the Queen Mother. The first night Elisabeth stayed at Laken, with De Man camping in front of her bedroom door. But when Belgian army and police units fired at each other under the Queen Mother's window — both groups supposing the others were German paratroopers that had landed in Laken Park — De Man decided to leave the Palace. One policeman was killed in the incident.

Elisabeth asked De Man to take her to the Villa Maskens at De Panne, where she installed herself on 14 May, the day of the fall of Sedan. 'Like my husband would have done, I will not leave Belgium,' she said.[29] On that same 14 May, the MPs of the VNV who were still in the country and had escaped arrest by the *Sûreté*, met in Brussels. The Flemish-Nationalists agreed that even if Hitler were to win the war, they would not collaborate with Nazi Germany. There was going to be 'no second Aktivism.' At that moment, however, they were unaware of the fact that Belgium had arrested many of their friends and party comrades and was deporting them to France. The *Sûreté* had decided to 'evacuate' all the 'suspect and unnational elements' it had arrested. The prisoners were stowed in railway wagons bound for France. One victim later recalled: 'It took our train seven days to get from Brussels to Orléans. Under a torrid heat, locked up with 40 people, including women and children, in a hermetically sealed wagon where we had to stay day and night, we suffered from hunger, a lack of air and especially from thirst. We were left for 43 hours without receiving even a drop of water. We were submitted to the brutality of the soldiers accompanying the escort and in many stations we were almost lynched by citizens who had been led to believe that we were parachutists and spies. Many people died *en route*.'[30] Most convoys arrived in the South of France before the fall of Abbeville. There, the prisoners were rounded up in Franco-Belgian concentration camps.

Late on the evening of 20 May, the first German Panzers rolled into Abbeville. The *Wehrmacht* had split the Allied armies in two and arrived at the Channel after less than two weeks of warfare. At De Panne, Elisabeth told De Man how glad she was. 'This war is in reality a Revolution,' she exclaimed. 'Hitler is a demon doing a work of necessary destruction. I firmly believe that a more socialist order will result from this.'[31]

Unfortunately, one wagon with 79 political prisoners from Belgium happened to be at Abbeville on the evening that the Germans arrived. The group was made up of 21 Belgians (including an agent of the British Intelligence Service) and 58 non-Belgians: 19 Jews, 15 non-Jewish Germans, 9 Italians (including at least 4 Communist opponents of Mussolini), 6 Dutchmen (including an 18-year-old girl with her mother and grandmother), 3 Luxemburgians, 2 citizens of neutral Switzerland, a Spaniard, a Dane, a Frenchman and an English-speaking Canadian. French soldiers gone berserk began to butcher the prisoners. They massacred 21 of them, including the Canadian, the Dutch grandmother, a German Catholic monk, a Hungarian Jew, a Czech Jew, a Communist Brussels town councillor and the Flemish politician George Van Severen and his deputy. Most were shot, but others, including the grandmother, were savagely stabbed to death with bayonets. The killings were interrupted by the rapid approach of the Germans who liberated the prisoners.

Thousands of civilians imprisoned by the Belgian authorities in France were released by the Germans in the course of the following weeks, including a large number of Jews. They were the only Jews ever liberated by Hitler's army. The *Wehrmacht* allowed them to return to Belgium. However, 3,537 Jews holding German and Austrian passports were kept imprisoned. This group later ended up in Auschwitz, where they were murdered. They were the only Auschwitz victims who had been arrested on the order of a Western government.

Upon his return to Antwerp, the old Flamingant Borms went to see the family of a Jew who had been imprisoned with him and who had not been freed, to offer financial assistance. Another Flamingant, the anti-racist MP Leo Frenssen who had also been imprisoned in the South of France, tried in vain to get Jewish co-prisoners released. Following the Abbeville massacre, *Wehrmacht* General Eggert Reeder

31   Quoted in De Man 3, pp. 76–7.

had Robert De Foy, the chief of the *Sûreté de l'Etat*, arrested. The SS, however, immediately ordered that De Foy be released. Reeder received the order personally by telephone from Reinhard Heydrich, head of the State Security Central Office of the *Reich*, the *Reichssicherheitshauptamt* (RSHA), in Berlin. It appeared that 'De Foy had in the months preceding the invasion closely collaborated with the RSHA and with Heydrich himself, to whom he had provided important material.'[32]

After the war, the Belgian authorities refused to investigate the matter of the deportations. Nor did anyone ever investigate how and on whose orders the Belgian secret service had assisted Heydrich before the war. Belgium never apologised for what happened, and never paid damages to the victims. It even refused to repatriate the bodies of the 21 victims in Abbeville.

How to Become a European

The Belgian army surrendered on 28 May. The 18-day campaign cost the lives of 8,000 Belgian soldiers and 12,000 civilians. Leopold and Pierlot had continuously quarrelled during the two-and-a-half weeks of the campaign. According to the government, France and Britain were Belgium's *allies*; according to the King they were using Belgium as a battlefield to fight the war *they* had declared on Germany in September 1939.

When the collapse of the Belgian front became imminent, Pierlot tried to persuade the King to follow the example of Queen Wilhelmina of the Netherlands and leave the country for England. Leopold refused. As supreme commander of the army, he could not abandon his troops, he said, because that would amount to desertion. There was a political reason for his refusal, as well, which he only revealed to confidents such as General Van Overstraeten: if he left, he would abandon the country to 'separatist tendencies,' but if he remained in German-occupied Belgium, his presence might 'deter the enemy from taking disastrous decisions.'[33] As Leopold wrote on 25 May, staying in Belgium was 'the only way to maintain Belgium's independence and the continuation of the dynasty.'[34]

Most Belgian government ministers had fled to the South of France before the fall of Abbeville on 20 May, but Pierlot and Spaak remained, trying to persuade Leopold to leave the country with them.

32   GRA 175/120, Reeder to Himmler, 20 Dec. 1943.
33   Van Overstraeten 1, p. 690.
34   *Verslag van de Commissie van Voorlichting,* Appendix 38, p. 269.

After a week of vain efforts, with the Germans rapidly closing in on the last remnant of Belgian territory, the ministers called upon Leopold for the last time at Wijnendale Castle near Bruges on 25 May, at five o'clock in the morning. Leopold was angry to be 'dragged from [his] sleep.'[35] No argument could persuade the stubborn King. Leopold almost succeeded in persuading Spaak to remain with him. When Pierlot saw that the Minister of Foreign Affairs began to waver, he took him by the hand and led him outside. The ministers departed for the coast, where they boarded a British boat. They arrived in London in the afternoon. Spaak had been weeping for hours. The next day, they travelled to France, where they joined their colleagues.

Leopold contacted the *Wehrmacht* on 27 May. At four o'clock the next morning (no sleep needed that night), he unconditionally surrendered himself and his army. Four hours later, the French Prime Minister Paul Reynaud gave a radio speech. He denounced the King as a traitor. Reynaud's radio speech was followed later in the day by one by Pierlot, who stressed that the Belgian government did not agree with the capitulation. He relieved all Belgian officers of their oath of allegiance to the King. 'Pierlot,' says Leopold in his memoirs, 'cowardly followed Reynaud and approved of the latter's disgusting radio speech. In doing so he trampled upon my honour, that of the dynasty and of the army.'[36]

The British were as angry as the French. On 29 May the *Daily Mirror* described the Belgian King as a 'regal Judas' who 'disgraced his father's splendid name' by his 'abominable desertion!' The *News Chronicle* called Leopold 'the unworthy son of a great father.' Former Prime Minister David Lloyd George opined that one would 'rummage in vain through the black annals of the most reprobate Kings of the earth to find a blacker and more squalid sample of perfidy and poltroonery.' The journalist Alexander Werth explained that he had 'heard say long ago' that Leopold had 'a German mistress provided by the Gestapo,' and added, somewhat prophetically as it soon turned out: 'I suppose he'll be back in the Royal palace complete with German girl-friend.'[37]

On 31 May, Pierlot and Spaak were in Limoges in Central France, where 143 of the 379 members of the Belgian Chamber of Representatives and the Senate, had gathered. The Limoges Parliament approved the Government's decision to continue the war on the

35   Leopold III 2, p. 56.
36   Leopold III 2, pp. 79 and 84.
37   Quoted in Keyes, pp. 365–6 and 388–9.

Allied side. In accordance with Article 82 of the Belgian Constitution, which stated that the ministers as a group take over the royal powers when the King 'is unable to reign,' the parliamentarians decided to transfer Leopold's authority to the Council of Ministers. In Belgium itself, however, the King's decision to surrender to the Germans was acclaimed by the majority of the people. The expectation was that France would soon surrender as well and that Britain would sign a peace treaty with Hitler, whose army had conclusively proved its superiority on the battle field.

The Germans escorted Leopold to Laken. Theoretically, he had become a Prisoner-of-War, like the rest of the Belgian army. *Wehrmacht* soldiers were posted in front of Laken Palace and Leopold was assigned a German aide-de-camp, Colonel Werner Kiewitz, an elegant former diplomat, who was under orders to make life agreeable for the King. Hitler intended to pamper the Belgian. According to Nazi Propaganda Minister Joseph Goebbels, the Führer paid Leopold 50 million francs as a reward for his 'strong sympathies for Germany.'[38]

It was not long before Leopold engaged Kiewitz as his *maître des plaisirs*. In Laken, Kiewitz discreetly provided call girls. Leopold also often travelled to his love nest in Knokke and, whenever he felt the urge to do so, Kiewitz took him on a 'pleasure trip' to Paris. The King could even rely on the German Secret Police to remove the traces of his erotic adventures. Once, he had been so stupid as to send naughty letters to the wife of the pianist Walter Rummel, an exalted young nymphomaniac who had the habit of opening her front door in the nude. The Gestapo paid Madame Rummel a visit 'in order to retrieve the personal letters that she had received from the King.'[39]

In Laken, Leopold was free to receive guests. The first visitor after his return home on 29 May was Cardinal Van Roey. Together they prepared a text which the Primate subsequently had read out as a pastoral letter from all the pulpits during Sunday Mass on 2 June. It explicitly approved the capitulation, stressed that, contrary to Pierlot's assertion, the King had 'in no way violated the Constitution' and called upon 'all Belgians to remain united and firm behind the King, the supreme personification of our Motherland in danger.' The pastoral letter contained not a word of criticism of the Germans. On the contrary, the Cardinal seemed to regard Hitler as an instrument of God: 'Be convinced that we are at this time witnessing an exceptional

38   Goebbels' diary, 30 May 1940, in Goebbels, vol. IV, p. 183.
39   Raskin, p. 104.

act of Divine Providence that reveals its power through great events before which we feel very small.'[40] These were Van Roey's words at the very moment that the Nazi war machine was wiping out the French army and the British were hurrying home from Dunkirk.

Another early visitor was SS Doctor Gebhardt. He came to see Leopold on 31 May to propose a meeting with the Führer. Hitler was due to arrive in Brussels the next morning on a 'tourist trip.' The German dictator wanted to show his architect the Brussels monuments of Leopold II. Hitler was especially fond of the *Palais de Justice* casting its dark shadow over the town.[41] Leopold agreed to receive Hitler, but asked for it to be an incognito meeting. The *Führer* was angered by this request and did not show up. The events of that week, especially the condemnation in Reynaud's radio speech and the convention of the Belgian parliamentarians at Limoges, had made Leopold cautious. He realised that De Man had been right in 1936: it was better for a King to have someone to screen off his political decisions. In future, Leopold would conduct his personal policy in secret and through the intermediation of his private secretary, Count Capelle. To start this new policy by making demands on Hitler, however, was an act of sheer stupidity which made Davignon, the King's advisor on foreign issues, despair. Gebhardt returned to Laken on 3 June to warn that, though the *Führer* was still positively disposed towards Leopold, it would be wrong to take this attitude for granted. Leopold at once asked to meet Hitler, but received no reply.

The King's main political aim was to dissuade Berlin from splitting Belgium up into a Flemish and a Walloon half. He wanted a significant group of staunch Belgicists to collaborate in order to convince the Nazis that it was in their interest to keep Belgium intact. One of these Belgicists was Robert Poulet, a Catholic Brussels journalist. Poulet was not very keen on working for the Germans but, during a meeting at Count Capelle's house, the King's secretary persuaded him to accept the editorship of *Le Nouveau Journal*, a newly established pro-German daily. Capelle asked Pierre Daye, another Belgicist journalist, to join Poulet. The Count told Daye: 'You would do well to collaborate with that newspaper, because if patriots such as you do not do it, then God knows who will gain control over the press.'[42] Interestingly, the Pierlot government also encouraged 'patriotic collaboration.' On 25 July, Justice Minister Janson wrote a letter from France to

40   Pastoral letter, 31 May 1940, in Bishops, pp. 138–9.
41   Speer, p. 54.
42   Quoted in Van Goethem and Velaers, p. 452.

Daye, saying: 'If you could contribute to the Brussels papers' retaining as much of their national character as possible, then you would be doing the country a great service. We encourage such attempts.'[43] The King and his aides also deemed it necessary to resume economic activity in the German-occupied country. In June 1940, Alexandre Galopin, the Governor of the SG, brought a committee together to run the economy. It included people like Jules Ingenbleek and Max-Léo Gérard, two former private secretaries of King Albert I, and Ernest-John Solvay, the owner of a Belgian company that was the fourth-largest chemical concern in Europe. Except for weapons and ammunition in the strictest sense, the Galopin Committee agreed to every kind of production for Nazi Germany, including engines and chemicals for the German army. This policy allowed SG subsidiaries to continue making profits during the war. In March 1941, Galopin paid a secret visit to Berlin to discuss Belgian deliveries with various Nazi ministries. Apart from Count Capelle and King Leopold, no one in Belgium, not even General Alexander von Falkenhausen, the head of the German administration in Brussels, knew about the visit.

Early in June 1940 Leopold was hoping that Hitler would establish him as a dictator in Belgium. He asked Paul Struye, an attorney at the *Cour de Cassation*, to work on a legal justification that would grant the King a period of twelve months in which he could rewrite the Constitution and all laws as he pleased. Before having himself proclaimed a dictator, however, Leopold wanted somebody else to do the preliminary 'dirty work.' As early as June 1940, he seems to have known, probably through Gebhardt, that the Nazis intended to purge Europe of the Jews. 'You know what I think of the Jews,' he told Capelle in November 1940. 'The damage which they have done is not sufficiently known. It is they who are responsible for all our problems.'[44] His anti-Jewish feelings, however, did not go so far that he wanted to become personally involved in the purge: 'I have no personal animosity towards the Jews; I have met many,' he stressed, 'but that does not prevent me from recognising the danger that they constitute.'[45] On 2 July 1940 he asked Capelle whether 'it would not be better that others than myself do the necessary works of purification that are needed in Belgium.'[46] Leopold did not wait for the Count's answer because already on 29 June he had told Kiewitz to ask the *Führer* to allow him to 'temporarily leave the country until the stabilisation of the new

43   Janson to Daye, 25 July 1940, in Van Goethem and Velaers, p. 449.
44   SOMA PC24 nr 2, p. 137.
45   SOMA PC24 nr. 2, pp. 216–7.
46   SOMA PC24 nr. 2, p. 68.

regime is completed.'[47] The King wished to go for a long holiday to the Bavarian Alps. He suggested that the Germans conceal this as a forced deportation, because that would not compromise him in the eyes of the Belgians.

The King's advisors feared that Leopold was committing another stupidity likely to earn him Hitler's contempt. Louis Wodon warned Leopold against the plan to 'retire for a few days in Bavaria,' a plan, he wrote, 'which Capelle seems to relate to the presumed initiative of the Germans for a purge in Belgium: arrests of Jews, of unwanted Belgians, etcetera.'[48] Kiewitz, who had not submitted the request to Hitler, was very anxious to know from Van Overstraeten whether Leopold had also put his request for a 'deportation to Germany' to Gebhardt.[49] The SS General had, indeed, returned to Laken on 29 June to meet the King. Whether Leopold repeated the request to him is unknown. On leaving the royal office, however, Gebhardt accidently bumped into De Man. The latter committed a stupidity as well: he told the German about Leopold's plan for installing a new government with De Man as Prime Minister. De Man seems not to have realised that the SS distrusted him, which was rather naive in someone whom the Nazis had expelled from Germany in 1933. Gebhardt returned to Berlin where he informed SS boss Heinrich Himmler of Leopold's plans for De Man.

Apart from Leopold's anti-Jewish diatribes, De Man and the King shared the same political opinions. On 28 June, the BWP president formally disbanded the Belgian Workers' Party. In a manifesto, which Leopold had approved beforehand, De Man wrote to the former BWP members: 'Do not resist the occupying force. Accept its victory. The war has led to the debacle of the parliamentary regime and the capitalist plutocracy in the so-called democracies. For the working-classes and for socialism, this collapse of a decrepit world, far from being a disaster, is a deliverance. The Socialist Order will thereby be established, as the common good, in the name of a national solidarity that will soon be continental, if not world-wide.'[50]

Leopold hoped that Nazi Germany would establish De Man's old dream of a 'United Europe.' He accepted that this would entail a certain loss of Belgian sovereignty, possibly even require that he take 'an oath of allegiance to Hitler;'[51] but he seemed prepared to accept this.

47   *Idem.*
48   Wodon to Leopold III, 4 July 1940, quoted in Van Goethem and Velaers, p. 385.
49   Van Overstraeten 2, p. 46.
50   Quoted in Claeys-Van Haegendoren, pp. 395–6.
51   De Man 3, p. 33.

'The freedom we had before the war was also a mere sham,' he told Capelle. 'Owing to the influence of internationalism, of the Jewry, of the freemasonry, of big business, we could only act insofar as Paris and London allowed us to.'[52] To Paul Struye, the King said in March 1941: 'There is a serious risk that we will no longer be independent after the war. But were we completely independent before the war, namely in the field of economics? To be frank: it is impossible to hesitate between German supremacy and English supremacy.' He told Struye that England was 'a social danger' and that he greatly admired the social-economic performance of the authoritarian German system.[53]

Leopold was strongly influenced by De Man's vision of a unified European welfare state under authoritarian leadership with one single economic policy, one foreign policy, and one defence policy. The chief goal on the political agenda in Laken was the integration of Belgium and its dynasty in a Federal Europe dominated by Germany. De Man expected much from Italy in this respect. The war had produced two victors on the Continent, he stressed: Germany *and* Italy. The Italian dictator Benito Mussolini was Hitler's partner in the so-called Berlin-Rome Axis. Hence, Hitler would have to take Mussolini's wishes into account when building the new Europe. De Man told Leopold that the need for a symbolic figure unifying the Axis would soon be felt, and that Leopold, a prince from Coburg whose sister was the Italian Crown Princess, held the best cards to be this figure. De Man had already discussed the idea of a dynasty for a Federal Europe with Mussolini's brother-in-law, the Italian Minister of Foreign Affairs, Count Ciano, in 1939. According to what De Man had heard from Ciano, the *Duce* favoured the idea of establishing Leopold as the monarch of such a Europe. In July 1940, De Man took the matter up with Otto Abetz, the German Ambassador in Paris. He, too, according to De Man, thought that someone of Leopold's capacities deserved a far higher position than that of King of Belgium. Perhaps, Abetz suggested, Hitler would even put Leopold on the British throne![54]

'A Ministering Angel Shall My Sister Be'[55]

Leopold's sister, Marie-José, the wife of the Italian Crown Prince Umberto, enjoyed the respect of Mussolini. For her sake, the Duce pleaded with the Führer on behalf of her brother. This explains why

52   SOMA PC24 nr. 2, p. 205.
53   SOMA PS4 nr. 1, p. 83.
54   SOMA PC24 nr. 2, pp. 93–4.
55   William Shakespeare, *Hamlet*, V. i. 263.

Hitler remained patient with Leopold and why he installed a relatively mild occupational regime in Belgium. It was a so-called *Militärverwaltung*, led by Conservative *Wehrmacht* generals, instead of a *Zivilverwaltung* of civilian Nazi party officials. The head of the *Militärverwaltung*, General Baron Alexander von Falkenhausen, was a Prussian aristocrat who sympathised with the titled Belgian nobility. Impressed as he was with royalty, he considered himself a partisan of the King and kept the Flamingants at bay.

In the weeks following Leopold's surrender, the Flemish-Nationalists in their political passiveness were being outmanoeuvred by the Belgicist circles around the King. Both Count Lippens and Hendrik De Man were setting up a government, each imagining himself as the future Belgian Quisling. When, on 3 June, Staf De Clercq heard that Lippens, De Man and other politicians, including the anti-Flamingant ex-minister Devèze, had already been received by the King, he wrote Leopold a letter to request an audience as well. The King flatly refused to meet the VNV leader. This persuaded De Clercq of the need to make his own political overtures to the Germans, lest the Flemings be overlooked in the Nazi-controlled Europe of the future. Indeed, a consequence of the intense political activity of the Belgicists was that many Flemish-Nationalists, who initially had decided against a 'second Aktivism,' soon felt obliged to collaborate with the Germans. De Clercq contacted Falkenhausen's deputy, General Eggert Reeder, a Catholic Rhinelander of far humbler stock than his superior, whom the Flamingants hoped to win over to their side.

By the end of June, it seemed as if *all* the Belgian politicians, including even Pierlot and Spaak, were anxious to resume their political careers in a German-occupied Belgium. After the French government had asked the *Reich* for the terms of capitulation on 19 June, the Belgian ministers and parliamentarians in the South of France had lost heart. Almost unanimously they asked Leopold's permission to return to Brussels. Camille Gutt, the Francophone Minister of Finance, however, decided to flee to Britain. Gutt was Jewish. In London, he met his colleague Albert De Vleeschauwer, the Minister of Colonial Affairs. De Vleeschauwer, who belonged to the Flamingant group within the Catholic Party, was the only minister who after the invasion had gone to England instead of France. He had offered his personal services plus the Belgian colony's resources to Churchill. 'It is a good thing you bring the Congo with you, because you are a bit thin by yourself,' Churchill had jested.[56]

---

56   Quoted in Stengers 6, p. 117. Also in Keyes, p. 432.

When Churchill heard that Pierlot and Spaak intended to surrender to the Germans, he was horrified. On 20 June Lord Halifax, the British Foreign Secretary, informed the Belgian government that, if it followed Leopold's example and capitulated, the British Prime Minister would renounce the solemn promise he had made in the House of Commons on 6 June to restore Belgium's independence after the war. The Belgian ministers were not impressed. They formally ordered the 200,000 Belgian soldiers who had fled to France to surrender to the Germans. Seven fighter pilots disobeyed and flew their planes to Britain. The government accused them of theft, had them court-martialled and dismissed from the army.

The vengeful Leopold, however, vetoed the return of Pierlot and Spaak. He had Falkenhausen issue a warrant for their arrest as soon as they crossed the border. This left the ministers no choice but to remain in Vichy, the capital of the unoccupied southern part of France, where Marshal Pétain had installed a Fascist puppet regime. The British Foreign Office tried to get Pierlot and Spaak over from Vichy to England, because it needed some Belgian Francophones. According to Roger Makins (the future Lord Sherfield), the leading civil servant for Belgian Affairs at Whitehall, it was 'totally unacceptable' that the government of Free Belgium in London 'should consist of a Jew and a Flamingot, without a single Walloon.'[57] De Vleeschauwer was sent to Spain to meet his colleagues on the border of Vichy France and to persuade them to come to London. But neither Pierlot nor Spaak believed in Britain's capacity to beat Hitler. They kept hoping for a reconciliation with the King, which would allow them to switch their allegiance to what they now clearly perceived to be the winning camp: Germany.

'M. Pierlot and M. Spaak are not deserving of much consideration,' Makins acknowledged. Nevertheless, 'however poor the material, one can only hope that they will improve. I therefore recommend that we bend all our efforts to extricate these miserable Ministers.'[58] Only after three months of waiting in vain for Leopold's permission to enter Belgium did Pierlot and Spaak finally depart for England. The two men arrived in London on 24 October 1940. There, together with Gutt and De Vleeschauwer, they formed a Belgian government-in-exile consisting of three Francophone Belgicists, who did not understand a single word of Dutch, and one Fleming. To many Flamingants in occupied Belgium, this overwhelmingly Francophone

57   Quoted in Keyes, p. 440.
58   Makins to Halifax, 29 Sept. 1940, in Keyes, p. 441.

government was an indication of what the Flemish position would be in post-war Belgium in case of a British victory. It convinced them that Flanders had not much to expect from the Allies.

* * *

While Pierlot and Spaak had been awaiting word from Leopold, the latter had been waiting for a reply from the *Führer* to his request for a meeting. The reply did not come. Leopold understood that Hitler was dissatisfied with him. When Gebhardt returned to Laken with the message that the Nazi regime distrusted De Man, Leopold decided to distance himself from his former friend. De Man's downfall presented an opportunity for his rival, Count Maurice Lippens. The latter suggested that the King appoint him Prime Minister and Viscount Davignon as Foreign Minister. But the *Führer* had enough of the political scheming in Laken. On 20 July, he forbade Leopold and his entourage to continue any political activities.

Following Hitler's veto on the installation of a Belgian collaborationist government, Leopold began to fear that Berlin was about to dissolve his kingdom. There were rumours that the Nazis were secretly negotiating with Vichy to offer Wallonia to France as recompense for the Alsace and Lorraine provinces that had been returned to Germany. Pétain's Prime Minister, Pierre Laval, was keen to have the Francophone Belgian provinces and established a special *Bureau des Affaires Belges* in Vichy. Its liaison was Georges Thone, a publisher from Liège, who led the *Ligue d'Action Wallonne*, an organisation of Francophiles prepared to collaborate with the Nazis if the latter allowed their country to join France.

Laken was greatly disturbed by the rumours that Belgium might be reduced to what Davignon called '*une terre flamande.*'[59] When a summit meeting was announced between Hitler and Pétain, the King lapsed into a deep depression. Marie-José decided to help. As Crown Princess of Hitler's Axis partner Italy, she had easy access to Hitler. She travelled to Laken late in September 1940. Apart from her brother and mother, she also met Lippens. He was, she noted in her diary, '*molto pro l'Axe.*'[60] With Falkenhausen and Kiewitz, she visited Dunkirk and its graveyard of battered British ships. From Belgium she travelled to Munich where she met Gebhardt on 16 October. The following day she was received by Hitler in his Alpine residence, the *Eagle's Nest* on the Obersalzberg above the Bavarian town of Berchtesgaden. The *Führer* succumbed to her charm. 'He took my

59   SOMA PC24 nr. 2, pp. 76–7.
60   Quoted in Petacco, p. 154.

hand,' she recalled later, 'and began to sing the praises of the Northern races: 'Do you know that you are the perfect incarnation of the Aryan princess? A living example of Aryan superiority.' And a whole litany about my figure, my fair hair, my eyes that have the colour of a Germanic sky.' Marie-José obtained from Hitler what she wanted: an invitation for her brother.

On 19 November, the King was received on the Obersalzberg. Hitler pampered his guest. The Gestapo even provided call-girls. According to Leopold, the very first thing the *Führer* said when he welcomed him was: 'I have a very great respect for you and for your dynasty, because your father has always treated Germany justly.'[61] Leopold asked Hitler to guarantee Belgium's integrity and independence. The *Führer* was not prepared to do this. He did, however, guarantee Leopold 'the continued existence of his dynasty.' This was a reassurance, not to Belgium, but to its royal family. Leopold did not know what to make of it. Could it be true, as De Man had told him, that Hitler had a greater Crown in store for him than that of Belgium? On his return to Brussels, Leopold could not resist the temptation to contact De Man and tell him the great news. According to De Man, the King enthusiastically told him 'that though no concrete results had been achieved during the meeting, he was deeply impressed with Hitler's personality. 'Only once in a thousand years a man of his stature is born,' he said.'[62]

This was one of the last conversations between De Man and Leopold. Early in 1941, De Man approved the marriage of his son to Marlene Flechtheim, a Berlin Jewess. The Queen Mother advised De Man to go into political hibernation. 'Play the dormouse,' Elisabeth said.[63] He subsequently left Belgium and retired to the Alps, at first in Vichy France, later in Switzerland, where he wrote a book about his European vision: *Au delà du Nationalisme* (Beyond Nationalism). Leopold never again replied to any of his letters. Though his political career was over, De Man's political legacy lasted, thanks to his one-time pupil Spaak, who, after the war, became one of the Founding Fathers of the European Union. Today this Union embodies De Man's great ideal of a 'Federal Europe with one single economic policy, one foreign policy, and one defence policy' which he hoped would 'establish the Socialist Order as the common good, in the name of a continental solidarity.' According to Spaak's 1969 memoirs, Hendrik De

---

61 Leopold III to Willequet, 22 Nov. 1976, in Willequet 4, p. 172.
62 De Man 3, p. 33.
63 De Man 3, p. 37.

Man was 'one of those rare men who on some occasions have given me the sensation of genius.'[64]

Soon after Leopold's return from Berchtesgaden, things went wrong again. The *Luftwaffe* proved unable to win the Battle of Britain. There was also the establishment of the Belgian government in London, which began to broadcast daily to Belgium through the BBC. Though only 20,000 Belgians remained outside the Belgian national territory after the repatriation of the Belgian fugitives from France, Pierlot claimed to be speaking for the entire Belgian population, as well as for the King. Leopold found this hard to take. To Paul Struye, he said: 'I have more freedom here than I would have in London.' Davignon told the American Ambassador in Berlin that it was 'ridiculous' to suppose that the King was a victim of Nazi propaganda and said that he was 'as free as anybody in Belgium.'[65]

Too many things, however, were slipping out of Leopold's control. The easiest problem to deal with were the Walloon Francophiles. They were silenced when Falkenhausen had Raymond Colleye, one of the most outspoken Walloon separatists, arrested. This allowed Colleye to pose as an anti-Nazi freedom fighter and a true Belgian patriot after the war. When the Francophiles realised that the Nazis were not going to allow Wallonia to join France, they switched their allegiance to the Allied camp and joined the armed resistance.

The Flemish separatists posed a far more serious problem. On 10 November 1940, two weeks after the announcement of Leopold's meeting with Hitler, Staf De Clercq had publicly and formally renounced the decision of his Flemish-Nationalist Party not to collaborate. The VNV had hesitated for a full six months about the question of whether or not to side with the Germans. However, with the Belgicists wooing Hitler and with the British backing a government-in-exile that was overwhelmingly Francophone, De Clercq announced in a radio speech that henceforward he would consider Germany as Flanders' ally. Anti-Belgian and pro-German sentiments ran very deep in Flanders since the deportations by the *Sûreté* and the Abbeville massacre. Indeed, according to the later Belgian Prime Minister Gaston Eyskens, the 'embitterment' caused by the arrests and deportations of the Flamingants by the Belgian authorities immediately after the German invasion on 10 May motivated 'many sorely tried Flemings to turn against Belgium and join the Collaboration.'[66]

64   Spaak, vol. I, p. 26.
65   Quoted in Van Goethem and Velaers, pp. 611 and 614.
66   Eyskens 3, p. 108.

There was, of course, the Jewish problem. Flemish Jews had always been very active within the Flamingant Movement. The Aktivist Marten Rudelsheim, who had died in a Belgian gaol in 1920, was revered by the Flemish-Nationalists as one of their greatest martyrs. Peter Tack, the President of the short-lived independent Flemish State that had existed from late December 1917 to early November 1918, had honoured his fellow Aktivist in 1933 as both a great Fleming and a great Jew, 'sacrificing his life for Flanders,' but also 'always remaining faithful to his Jewish race, the many talents of which were harmoniously embodied in his person.'[67] Another former Aktivist, the dentist Jan Laureys, a member of the Antwerp provincial council for the *Front Partij*, had personally helped Jewish fugitives from Nazi Germany before the war because, as he wrote in October 1936, anti-Semitism is 'inhuman, hateful, degrading.'[68] Elias, too, had always explicitly rejected 'the ideology of Fascist Nationalism; its ridiculous idolisation of everything that is supposed to be national, with xenophobia and a one-sided intellectual and military imperialism as its logical consequence.'[69]

Most Flemings in 1940 were unaware of the genocide Hitler had in store for the Jews. The Belgian government had censored anti-German articles in the press before the war, and the only Jews so far seen maltreated in the country, were those that were arrested by the Belgian authorities following the German invasion. In addition, during the first five months of the occupation the *Militärverwaltung* had not disturbed the Jews. Unlike the Netherlands and France, Belgium had experienced no discriminatory measures. Until January 1941 the Jews at the German prison camp of Fort Breendonk, near Antwerp, were treated no differently from 'Aryan' prisoners.[70]

An ironic consequence of De Clercq's public announcement of the VNV's willingness to collaborate with the Germans (while that of the King and his entourage had remained a secret) was that the vilest of all Belgian anti-Semites, the Belgicist Charles Somville, decided *not* to collaborate. Somville was the pre-war editor of a magazine preaching 'hatred against the Jewish race until this global enemy is eradicated,'[71] but his anti-Flamingant sentiments clearly outweighed his anti-Jewish feelings. After De Clercq decided to side with the Germans, Somville began to finance the partisans of the Belgian *Résistance*. Other

---

67 Quoted in Saerens, p. 160.
68 Quoted in Saerens, p. 308.
69 Quoted in De Wever 3, p. 75.
70 Waysblatt, pp. 457–8.
71 Quoted in Saerens, pp. 264 and 267.

right-wing Belgicists acted similarly. Hence, the artificial state of Belgium gave rise to a double paradox: while many Flemish democrats, who before the war had attacked Germany's racial laws, were led to collaborate with the Germans because they hated their own State so much that they automatically came to consider this State's invader as their friend, similarly, many anti-democrat Belgicists, who before the war had been sympathetic towards Nazism and anti-Semitism, joined the *Résistance*.

One important reason why the Flemish-Nationalist leadership ultimately decided to collaborate with the Germans was that they had teamed up with General Eggert Reeder, the second man in the *Militärverwaltung*. Reeder ran the German administration in Brussels while his boss drank champagne at the parties of the Belgian nobility. Reeder used the VNV to thwart the political ambitions of the SS in Belgium. The SS wanted the *Militärverwaltung* replaced by a *Zivilverwaltung* of Nazi party hardliners. Reeder needed the collaboration of a significant group of Belgians to be able to argue in Berlin that the *Wehrmacht* was perfectly capable of running affairs in Belgium and did not need the 'assistance' of the SS.

In the absence of a Belgian government, the ministerial cabinets in Brussels were led by senior civil servants, the so-called Secretaries-General. Reeder had two VNV politicians appointed amongst them. Victor Leemans became Secretary-General of Economic Affairs and Gerard Romsée received the highly influential post of Secretary-General of the Interior. Reeder had wanted Romsée at the head of the equally important Justice Department, but he was forced to accept a Francophone royalist there. Indeed, through Falkenhausen, the entourage of the King had its say in all the appointments. Romsée had to appear before an ad-hoc commission of Capelle, Davignon and Van Overstraeten, and got the job only because he was able to convince them that he was a royalist, too, whose ambition was restricted to achieving a form of Flemish autonomy *within* Belgium. Romsée and Leemans were frequently called to the royal palace during the war to receive 'instructions' from Capelle.

With Reeder on the side of the Flamingants, half the municipalities in Flanders soon had a VNV mayor — Antwerp being a notable exception — and, apart from Brabant, all the Flemish provinces had a VNV politician as Governor. The SS, however, tried to thwart the *Militärverwaltung*. It attempted to have the VNV outlawed directly by Hitler. SS publications described Staf De Clercq's policies as 'half-democratic-clerical, half-fascist party-hocus-pocus.'[72] Heydrich told Joachim Ribbentrop, the German Foreign Minister, that the leader of the VNV was a 'stupid Catholic anti-German marionette without any use for the German army.'[73] Himmler complained to Martin Bormann, Hitler's private secretary, that it was 'absolutely not in the Germanic and German interests to support this organisation.' He was appalled, he said, to discover that there were Germans who assisted the VNV 'in its resistance against pan-Germanic ideas.'[74] Ernst Ehlers, the head of the Gestapo *Judenabteilung*, wrote in January 1942: 'The VNV has so far shown not the least bit of understanding of the Jewish and racial question.'[75]

Though Hitler undoubtedly agreed with the SS, he felt obliged to keep the *Militärverwaltung* in charge in Brussels, because Mussolini insisted on it. All this, the *Führer* said, was the fault of Leopold with his close Italian connections: 'If only that accursed King had left the country, like the Queen of Holland, who fled and does not constitute a factor which one has to take into consideration.' 'If ever there was anyone I disliked, then it was that Belgian, that cunning scoundrel, that sly fox! However, his sister is the Crown Princess of Italy!'[76]

Leopold did his best to be in the SS's good books. He kept in close touch with Dr. Gebhardt. At the end of May 1941, he had Van Overstraeten complain to Otto Meissner, Hitler's *chef de cabinet*, about the 'anti-royalist attitude of the SS.' Meissner passed the message on to Himmler. A few weeks later the SS replied via Kiewitz that it was not at all hostile to the King. On the contrary, as Kiewitz told Van Overstraeten, the SS valued 'race' above all else, and so looked favourably on Leopold whom they admired for his 'physical type and moral character.'[77]

In the political strategy of the SS, however, there was no place for Belgium. Himmler aimed for the downright annexation of both Flanders and Wallonia by Germany. Each part of Belgium was to form a separate province of the *Reich*. To this end, Himmler established two SS chapters in the country. In Wallonia the pre-war Fascist party of Léon Degrelle, *Rex*, was integrated within the SS structures. In Flanders, the SS created a new political party, *DeVlag*, to fight the VNV. Flanders was the only country in occupied Europe where the Nazis could not rely on an existing political party. Having lost his political

72   *De SS-Man*, 1 Mar. 1941.
73   PAB Inland II g. Belgien 1940–1943, Heydrich to Ribbentrop, 29 Jan. 1941.
74   BAK NS 19 (Neu) 1544, Himmler to Bormann, 13 July 1942.
75   Ehlers, 31 Jan. 1942, in Steinberg 1, p. 139.
76   Hitler 1, p. 221; Hitler 2, pp. 302 and 341–2.
77   Van Overstraeten 2, p. 140.

significance, Leopold again lapsed into a deep depression. This worried the Queen Mother, who remembered her late husband's morose moods, which she knew to be a Saxe-Coburg family trait.

'Happy He With Such A Mother!'[78]

Lilian Baels was the prettiest girl in Belgium. Authors and journalists variously described the dark-haired girl in superlatives such as 'exotically beautiful,' 'as beautiful as a Greek night,' 'with eyes of fire' and 'as elegant as a beautiful cigar-girl from Andalusia.' It is hardly surprising that, as a regular visitor to the Knokke golf course in the late 1930s, she had attracted the attention of Leopold and there were rumours that they had slept together. Her father, Hendrik Baels, was a wealthy Flemish fish trader from Ostend. He was an ambitious and pompous man who had managed to become Governor of the province of West Flanders. Keen on mingling with the Belgian elite, he had raised his children in French and had bought a villa from Count Lippens' real estate company in Knokke. At the outbreak of the war, Baels and his family fled to Biarritz, the fashionable holiday resort in the South-West of France. In January 1941, the Queen Mother sent her chauffeur to Biarritz to fetch Lilian. Elisabeth judged that the 24-year-old constituted the perfect medicine for her son's despondence. It was her task, as Capelle says in his diary, to 'distract' the King. Soon, the Queen Mother discovered 'that the remedy was very mild and that the patient was not disposed to finish the treatment.'

The strong-headed Lilian demanded Leopold's exclusive attention. Her rival, Minime du Roy de Blicquy, *née* Baroness Marie-Louise de Fürstenberg, a former lady-in-waiting of the late Queen Astrid, who had remained at Court after the Queen's death, was told to pack her bags and leave. But Lilian was not content with the position of Laken's resident mistress; she wanted to be the King's wife. When Lilian got pregnant, Leopold gave in. He justified his decision to Capelle with the argument: 'When a woman gets under our skin, then nothing is able to curb this passion.' The marriage took place at Laken Palace on 6 December 1941. The following day, a Sunday, the Belgians learned of the royal marriage via a pastoral letter which Cardinal Van Roey had read out from the pulpit in all Catholic churches. The effect was devastating. It shattered the myth that Leopold was a Prisoner-of-War. The news could not have come at a worse moment, smack in the middle of the coldest winter in decades. The Germans were confiscating coal and potatoes to be shipped to Germany; the Belgians were suffering from cold and hunger and Allied bombings. The ordinary citizens had come to see Leopold as a martyr. They expected Leopold to live up to this image, because it mitigated their hardships: the King was to remain the poor widower of Astrid as well as the prisoner of Laken. Being neither widower nor prisoner, he had failed them twice. 'A double myth has been cruelly shattered,' General Reeder noted.[79]

'Send our prisoners a chick too,' someone painted on the wall of Laken Park. 'You have killed Astrid,' an anonymous letter to Laken said. The people nicknamed Leopold 'the son-in-law of Mr. Baels' and told saucy jokes about his affair with the daughter of a Flemish 'fishmonger.' Leopold's brother Charles was seething, too. Barely three years before, Leopold had forbidden him to marry his pregnant girlfriend because she was only a baker's daughter. 'Is the smell of shrimps so much more enticing than the smell of pastry?' Charles asked in a fit of rage.

Lilian had obtained her marriage with Leopold, but had she become Queen? In his pastoral letter of 7 December, the Cardinal wrote that the King had signed a deed which gave his second wife the title of 'Princess of Réthy,' expressly denying her the title of Queen, and depriving their children of any rights to the Belgian throne. The pastoral letter went so far as to say that Lilian herself had asked for such a deed as a condition to her marrying Leopold. The pastoral letter was a lie. 'The deed does not exist. I never drew one up,' the King told Capelle in March 1942.[80]

Sunday 7 December 1941, however, was to go down in history for a reason different from a shattered myth in Brussels. It was the day of the Japanese attack on Pearl Harbor and the American entry into the war. The balance of power gradually began to shift in the direction of the Allies. That same winter, Hitler, like Napoleon before him, was defeated in Russia by the forces of nature: freezing temperatures stopped the *Wehrmacht* within sight of Leningrad and Moscow. The following spring, the Germans launched an offensive towards Stalingrad and the oil fields of the Caspian Sea.

Nazi propaganda portrayed the struggle against the Soviet Union as a struggle between European civilisation and ungodly Communism, and called upon young men in the German-occupied countries to volunteer in this battle. Everywhere, national divisions of the so-called *Waffen-SS* were established. They had nothing to do with the

79   SOMA TB nr. 18, 1 Sept.–Dec. 1941.
80   SOMA PC24 nr. 3, p. 448/38.

'regular' SS, the *Allgemeine-SS*, but fought alongside the *Wehrmacht* on the Eastern Front. Belgium was given two *Waffen-SS* divisions, one for the Flemings and one for the Walloons.

Leopold regarded the battle on the Eastern Front as a fight, not between Christianity and Communism, but between Europe and Asia. He predicted that the Russians and the Japanese were about to ally themselves in a battle against the white race. 'This is only natural,' he explained to Capelle on 17 February 1942, 'because both the Russians and the Japanese are Asians. The greatest threat to the white race is the yellow menace.' Sometimes, the King could not sleep at night. 'I wake up in the middle of the night,' he confided to his secretary, 'and ask myself whether anything can still be done to avoid a catastrophe. Our civilisation will collapse, our race will be destr0yed.'[81]

Meanwhile, another race was being destroyed. The Nazis had lit the fires of the Shoah. Neither Cappelle nor any of the other royal advisors mention in their diaries or memoirs that the plight of the Jews kept Leopold from sleeping. Nevertheless, he was one of the first Belgians to receive detailed accounts of Nazi atrocities. Indeed, shortly after the royal marriage, SS Doctor Karl Gebhardt paid a visit to Laken. In Lilian's presence, Gebhardt, who was hanged after the war for conducting medical experiments on Jewish prisoners, gave a 'boastful account of the experiments he had carried out on human guinea-pigs.' The account left Lilian and Leopold 'frozen with horror,' as the King later recalled to his biographer Lord Keyes. After 'having sent Gebhardt packing,' he expressed his 'horror and disgust' to Kiewitz. The latter replied that 'there was no need for the King to receive Gebhardt in future and that he would keep him away.'[82] Unless Keyes made this story up, it proves that Leopold had already discovered during the war what the Nazis were doing to the Jews.

The history of the Nazi persecution of the Jews in Belgium has been well researched. When the Germans invaded Belgium, the country had about 64,000 Jewish inhabitants. More than 30,500 of them were deported to Nazi extermination camps. Of the latter group, only 1,821 survived. All in all, 45 per cent of the Jews living in Belgium were murdered, a far lower figure than the 80 per cent that died under the *Zivilverwaltung* in the Netherlands.

Only 3,000 of the Jews in Belgium had Belgian nationality. The others were predominantly '*Ostjuden*' — fugitives from Central and East

81   SOMA PC24 nr. 2, pp. 216–7 and 219.
82   Keyes, p. 359.

European countries. The Belgian authorities held that their responsibility was strictly limited to the Belgian Jews, most of whom, indeed, managed to survive the war. An example of this attitude is found in Cardinal Van Roey. Unlike Cardinal Verdier of Paris, Van Roey never protested against the persecution of the Jews in Germany in the 1930s. Worse, he disbanded the *Katholiek Bureau voor Israël*, an Antwerp Catholic organisation that tried to help the fugitives. During the war, too, Van Roey remained silent, unlike Cardinal Gerlier of Lyons and Archbishop De Jong of Utrecht, the Primate of the Netherlands, who had pastoral letters read from the pulpits of their dioceses, condemning anti-Semitism and encouraging the faithful to help the Jews. Van Roey wrote such letters only to defend the King and warn against anti-Belgian agitators. When the Bishop of Liège asked Van Roey for instructions about the Jewish problem, the Cardinal had his secretary reply that 'because the Germans have declared that they were only interested in the Jews of Greater-Germany, Poland, the Ukraine, Yugoslavia and Austria,' the Belgian Primate had decided 'to do nothing.'[83]

To Van Roey's credit, his secretariat did intervene with the German authorities during the war on behalf of 70 individual Jews. These were all either Belgian Jews or Jews who had converted to Catholicism. King Leopold's cabinet intervened in 80 cases involving only Belgian Jews, and the Queen Mother in almost 420 cases involving only Belgians or children. In 60% of these nearly 570 cases, their efforts were in vain: the Jews were deported to an extermination camp. This means that about 230 people can actually claim that their lives were saved by Cardinal, King or Queen Mother. The latter especially was hailed after the war as a heroine of the Jews.

Some leading Belgian collaborationists, whose names, unlike those of Van Roey and Elisabeth, do not figure on post-war lists of 'Friends of Israel,' were no less 'heroic.' In June 1943, the SS arrested 303 Belgian Jews. Elisabeth asked General Reeder to release them, which he did. In September 1943, the SS rounded up 794 Belgian Jews for transport to extermination camps in Germany. This time the Flamingant Secretary-Generals Romsée and Leemans intervened, and Reeder again set the prisoners free. During the final days of the German occupation, in August and September 1944, Romsée and Leemans were also able to halt a convoy of Jews (Belgian and non-Belgians) bound for Auschwitz. The two VNV politicians did at least as much for the Jews as the Cardinal, the King and the Queen Mother.

83   Max Vanden Berg to Mgr. Kerkhofs, 21 Sept. 1942, in Steinberg 3, vol. II, p. 201.

On 22 October 1942, Staf De Clercq died of heart failure. He was succeeded as leader of the VNV by the Anglophile Hendrik Elias. Elias wanted to reverse the party's previous policy of collaboration with the Germans. Gottlob Berger, the SS General supervising Belgian Affairs at SS headquarters in Berlin, reported to Himmler that Elias was the 'bitterest adversary' of the SS.[84] Berger at once phoned Reeder to annul Elias's appointment, but Reeder replied that he did not have the means to do so. Berger came to Brussels for a meeting with Reeder and Elias. He scolded Reeder and warned Elias that if the VNV mayors, governors and secretary-generals dared to resign their posts in protest of Nazi atrocities, 'five per cent of them will end up in concentration camps; and, lo and behold, the others will be only too pleased to be allowed to retain their posts!'[85] Elias was intimidated and for six months he did not dare to speak out against the SS. This was not to the liking of Father Jules Callewaert, a Dominican friar and one of the moral leaders of Flamingantism. He wrote to Elias on 3 April 1943, urging him to break with the collaboration policy. Callewaert called Nazism 'the return to complete paganism — something we as Catholics never can or will accept.' The Nazis, he continued, 'debase moral attitudes, principles and all values. It is no use saying: and what about Bolshevism? We must stand firm against everything that is evil.'[86] On 7 May, Elias sent an 'ultimatum' to Reeder, with a list of complaints about the SS. The VNV also stopped recruiting for the *Waffen-SS*. This open defiance of the SS was unique in the history of collaborationist movements in occupied Europe. Berger reported to Himmler that 'the VNV is an instrument of English propaganda' and suggested that Elias had received money from British agents and a promise from London for the political autonomy of Flanders after the war.[87] Elias expected that he would be arrested and sent to a concentration camp. Later, after the war, he confessed that if he had known at the time what a Nazi concentration camp really was, he would never have dared to challenge the SS.[88]

Father Callewaert, meanwhile, circulated copies of his letter to Elias. Soon Berger in Berlin had one on his desk. He had the text translated in German and passed on to Himmler suggesting that he 'put

84   BAK NS 19 (Neu) 1983, Berger to Himmler, 21 Oct. 1942.
85   BAK NS 19 (Neu) 1557, Berger to Himmler, 4 Nov. 1942.
86   For an English translation of Father Callewaert's letter, see Hermans, pp. 305–10.
87   BAK NS 19 (Neu) 1530, Berger to Brand, private secretary of Himmler, 30 Aug. 1943.
88   De Wever 3, p. 541.

this problem before the *Führer*.'[89] The SS was furious, but the *Militärverwaltung* in Brussels troubled neither Elias nor Callewaert. In August 1943, the friar wrote a report about the policies Flanders should follow after the war. This document, written early in August 1943, was widely copied as well. It proposed a political system based on Papal encyclicals. A copy ended up in London. The British Foreign Office thought that Callewaert, a Flamingant, had to be *by definition* pro-German, hence a 'Goth,' hence a collaborationist. A British report, referring to the friar as 'the Flemish Quisling,' consequently interpreted his text as a blueprint for the future Fascist regime in Belgium![90] Better informed Belgian politicians in London called it a 'Holy Water dictatorship.'[91]

On 3 January 1944, Hitler promised Himmler that the SS was to have its way in Belgium: the *Militärverwaltung* would be abolished and the country annexed to the *Reich*. The SS immediately began to prepare the ground for its take-over. Political adversaries of the annexation, including collaborators of the *Militärverwaltung* who were Belgian- or Flemish-Nationalists, were murdered. One of them, Alexandre Galopin, the Governor of the SG, was eliminated by an SS death squad on 24 February. The VNV was under fire from two sides. Many Flamingants were also killed by Belgicist or Communist partisans. 'We could expect to be assassinated any moment, either by the SS, or by the resistance,' Victor Leemans, the VNV Secretary-General for Economic Affairs, later recalled.[92] On 1 March, Constantin Canaris, the head of the Brussels SD, received a warrant signed by Himmler for Elias's arrest. All he needed was a phone call from Berlin to send the VNV leader to a concentration camp. Strangely enough, the phone call did not come. Perhaps the Nazis feared unrest in Flanders, a country strategically situated between England and Germany. Elias was not arrested until 3 January 1945. He was imprisoned in Austria until the end of the war.

* * *

King Leopold had spent the years following his marriage in domestic bliss. Prince Alexandre, his first child by Lilian, was born in July 1942. Life at Laken Palace was easy during the war. It was an island immune from the deprivations outside its walls. Though the fortunes of war had gradually shifted to the advantage of the Allies, and

89   BAK NS 19 (Neu) 842, Berger to Himmler, 28 May 1943.
90   SOMA microfilm FO 371/38872, p. 43, 18 Apr. 1944.
91   Huysmans, p. XXIV.
92   Quoted in Florquin, vol. VII, p. 128.

though the King had lost the protection of his Italian connection after the fall of Mussolini on 25 July 1943, Lilian kept Leopold too busy to care about his political future. On 30 July 1943, Hitler ordered the SS to monitor closely the King's movements. The *Führer* was afraid that Leopold would flee to Britain or lead a popular rising. He need not have worried. Leopold kept rejecting all attempts of the Pierlot cabinet in London to get in touch with him.

Pierlot was prepared to turn a blind eye to the 'patriotic collaboration' of the King. Already in July 1941, he had sent Robert Jourdain, a Jesuit priest, to Belgium with a reconciliatory message for the King. Father Jourdain was dropped by parachute in the Ardennes and succeeded in contacting Count Capelle. Leopold, however, refused to accept any message from Pierlot. On his return journey to England, Jourdain was arrested in Spain and imprisoned.

In March 1943, two months after the German defeat at Stalingrad, Capelle advised Leopold to distance himself publicly from the Nazis. The King refused, saying that he did not want 'to turn against a system of ideas of which I am inclined to approve.'[93] To General Van Overstraeten, Leopold said that a public protest against the Germans would amount to a statement of support for the Allied cause which he did not want to make. He was not prepared 'to support those from whom we need not expect gratitude.'[94]

In December 1943, Pierlot again sent an envoy to the King. This time François De Kinder, an Antwerp attorney whose sister was Pierlot's wife, was parachuted into Belgium. De Kinder succeeded in handing over Pierlot's letter to Cardinal Van Roey, but again Leopold would not accept it. Sadly, on his return journey, Pierlot's brother-in-law was arrested by the Germans and executed.

Early in 1944, Leopold began to take into account the possibility that Hitler might lose the war. He told Van Overstraeten on 24 January that there would be 'advantages' if the retreating Germans took him along as a prisoner. He toyed with the idea of having himself deported to Germany to boost his tarnished popularity in Belgium. He mentioned this so often that Van Overstraeten felt compelled to warn that if he was, indeed, ever deported, he would have to ensure 'this measure could not be attributed to his own request.'[95] A disadvantage of deportation, however, was that the King would not be in the country at the moment of the liberation. This worried Leopold

93   Quoted in Van Overstraeten 2, p. 221.
94   Quoted in Van Overstraeten 2, p. 230.
95   Van Overstraeten 2, p. 229.

because he wanted the Belgian people to know his instructions for post-war Belgium. Hence, he wrote the Belgians an Open Letter. He gave a copy of his 'Political Will,' as he called it, to Chief Justice Joseph Jamar to make it public after the liberation.

The 'Political Will' stated that pre-war politicians, such as Pierlot and Spaak, who had 'deserted and insulted' the King in May 1940, must not be allowed to hold any political office after the war 'so long as they have not regretted their error and granted the Crown complete and solemn redress.' Leopold told Van Overstraeten that he 'would not hesitate to join forces with the Communists.' He even discussed the possible inclusion of the Communists in a post-war Belgian government.[96] From the summer of 1944 onwards, the SG began to finance the Belgian Communist *Résistance*, for a total sum of 10.3 million francs (£3.4 million or $5.6 million at today's value).

Leopold made it very clear that he did not want to have anything to do with the Allies, whom he deliberately failed to thank for liberating Belgium. As he told Capelle in May 1944, he regarded the entry of the Allied forces as nothing more than 'the replacement of one military occupation by another.'[97] The 'Political Will' contained an explicit refusal to recognise the treaties with the Western Allies that the Pierlot cabinet had signed in London. According to the Belgian Constitution, all international treaties need a royal signature. Leopold indicated that he would not put his signature to any document tying Belgium to the Western Alliance.

On 7 June 1944, Leopold got what he wanted. One day after D-day, the landing of the Allies on the beaches of Normandy, Hitler ordered that the King be deported to Germany with his wife and children. The Germans brought the royal family to Hirschstein, a medieval castle in Saxony. Though Hirschstein Castle was a 'comfortable and well furnished' dwelling, Leopold asked Hitler to be lodged somewhere else, 'preferably in the Alps.' Lilian confided to Kiewitz that she feared that Hirschstein, 'a sombre building set in monotonous scenery,' would make the King 'depressed, a condition to which he is already disposed as it is, owing to his continuing ill fate in life.' She, too, asked to 'urgently assign them to a more pleasant residence.' Stressing that Leopold was 'loyal to the *Führer*,' she added that he could be 'of political service in the future, given that he knows the statesmen of the other side personally.'[98] Kiewitz put the request down in writing and

96   Van Overstraeten 2, pp. 292–4.
97   SOMA PC24 nr. 6, p. 35.
98   Quoted in De Jonghe 3, pp. 299–300.

passed it on to Berlin, but everything remained as it was, even after a friendly visit by Gebhardt.

The King remained in Saxony for almost nine months, until 7 March 1945, when his party was transferred to a villa on Lake Sankt-Wolfgang in the Austrian Alps east of Salzburg. The war was drawing to its end. On 8 May, the *Reich* unconditionally surrendered. Meanwhile, however, Belgium had already been liberated for over six months. British and Canadian troops had entered Brussels and Antwerp on 3 and 4 September 1944. On 9 September, one day after Pierlot's return to Brussels, Chief Justice Jamar handed the Prime Minister a copy of the King's 'Political Will.' Pierlot was stunned. He informed Spaak, who agreed to keep the document top secret and to act as if it did not exist. The British Prime Minister also received a copy. 'It stinks,' Churchill said. Anthony Eden, the British Foreign Secretary, called Leopold 'obstinate, even pig-headed.'[99] But the Belgian politicians could not do without their King. Belgium, as Achille Van Acker, the Socialist who succeeded Pierlot as Prime Minister on 12 February 1945, stressed, 'needs the monarchy like one needs bread.'[100] Hence, when the news reached the government that Leopold and his family had been liberated in Austria, the Belgian politicians decided to forget the past and welcome him back. On 9 May, Prince Charles, Prime Minister Van Acker, Minister of Foreign Affairs Paul-Henri Spaak, and other leading politicians left for Salzburg on a British plane to accompany the King home.

'Am I My Brother's Keeper?'[101]

The end of the war was the end of Hubert Pierlot's political career. When he returned to Belgium in September 1944, he was so unpopular that the American ambassador remarked that it was the Allied troops that kept him in place: 'The government is safe only so long as the military authorities are in the background. It will fall the minute that potential support is withdrawn.'[102] Hence, a more forceful government was installed with Allied backing in February 1945. It was a coalition of Belgium's three 'traditional parties,' the Catholics, the Socialists and the Liberals, plus the Communists.

Apart from Spaak, the politician with nine lives, who remained on Foreign Affairs, the new ministers had all spent the war years in Bel-

---

99   SOMA microfilms FO 123/593, p. 19, Eden to Churchill, 4 Oct. 1944.
100 Quoted in Stengers 8, p. 301.
101 Genesis, 4.9
102 DS 855.00/12-1244, Sawyer to State Department, 12 Dec. 1944.

gium. Prime Minister Achille Van Acker was a 46-year-old trade union leader from Bruges. When he assumed the leadership of the cabinet, he boasted to the press that his political motto was '*J'agis et puis je réfléchis*' (I act, then I think). He regretted some of his acts, though. In July 1940, Van Acker, hoping to become the leader of the collaborationist trade union in his home town, had asked Hendrik De Man to speak to the Germans on his behalf. He pursued De Man for months, until he noticed that the *Militärverwaltung* was favouring his local enemies of the Bruges VNV. After the war, Van Acker posed as a man of the *Résistance*. Only De Man could compromise him, and the pre-war Socialist leader had not yet returned from his exile in Switzerland.

The new Minister of Finance, Gaston Eyskens, a member of the Catholic Party, was a Flemish Professor of Economics from Leuven University. In lectures given during the war, Eyskens had praised the performance of the Nazi economy, 'made possible by the spirit of discipline and the application of the *Führerprinzip*.'[103] The new Minister of Justice, Charles du Bus de Warnaffe, had already been a cabinet member before the war, when he authored anti-Semite texts and systematically denied Jewish fugitives permission to enter Belgium. The new Minister of Education, Auguste Buisseret, a Liberal from Liège, had been a member of the *Ligue d'Action Wallonne*, the group that had been so eager to collaborate with the French Fascists in Vichy.

Each of these men had something to hide. Hence, they wished to distance themselves as far as possible from those who were accused of having collaborated with the enemy during the war. They dared not condemn the wave of terror that was being unleashed by the Communists against the so-called '*inciviques*', the French term for 'unpatriotic citizens'. Some even called for a more severe punishment of these 'traitors'.

The war had left deep scars: 90,000 Belgians had lost their lives, property had been destroyed, people had suffered deprivation, 3.5% of the population had been deported to Germany as forced labourers or concentration camp prisoners. In September and October 1944, following the German retreat, the anger and frustration which had accumulated during four years erupted. The mob descended on collaborationist families. Men were lynched, women raped, children abused, houses plundered. Self-declared 'patriots' rounded up suspects and imprisoned about 70,000 of them, often in appalling conditions. Hundreds were locked up in the cages of Antwerp Zoo.

103   Eyskens 1, p. 57.

Overnight the Nazi concentration camp of Fort Breendonk became a concentration camp for 'collaborationists.' Father Alfons Van Assche, the Abbot of the Benedictine monks of Steenbrugge, and a well-known Flamingant, was violently raped by his guards in gaol and died as a consequence.

In the immediate aftermath of the liberation, probably no government could have avoided excesses. Similar events happened in neighbouring countries during the first post-war days. Ten months after the liberation, however, on 17 June 1945, an inmate from Merksplas prison still complained to Cardinal Van Roey: 'Yesterday four women were brought in here. They had been tortured in an inhumane way: feet burned, a piece of the ear cut off, disfigured beyond recognition by beatings and kicks.'[104] The Cardinal received over 3,000 letters from prisoners and their families begging him for help. He turned down all requests, including one from his Flamingant first cousin.

Following the terror, the Belgian authorities organised a systematic purge of the *inciviques* with the intent of eliminating once and for all the anti-Belgicist enemies of the State. Flemish-Nationalist MPs who tried to reclaim their seat in Parliament were denied entry to the building. Belgicist collaborators, however, were left alone, with the exception of those who, like De Man, might compromise the new rulers. The Belgicists had collaborated, as Count Capelle explained, only 'to oppose German policies favouring the Flemish-Nationalists.'[105] Capelle, Lippens, Davignon, the business tycoons of the Galopin Committee, were not disturbed. Even Robert De Foy was allowed to resume his post as head of the *Sûreté de l'Etat*.

The Flamingants were not so fortunate. The authorities charged 405,067 citizens, almost five per cent of the entire Belgian population. Former Minister Albert De Vleeschauwer, the only Fleming of the initial war cabinet, was scandalised by the fact that Belgium 'was punishing about one million people directly or indirectly with a pointless repression.'[106] He took into consideration the suffering of the families of those charged. Others have calculated that the purge directly and indirectly hit 1.5 million of the 8 million Belgians. One *incivique*, Luc Desramault, had spent the entire five years of the war in Britain. Upon his return from London in May 1945, he was beaten up, arrested and imprisoned for 'collaboration with the enemy.' He had to remain in gaol until September. The reason, his attorney told him, was that he

104 Quoted in Van Roy 2, p. 25.
105 Quoted in De Bens, p. 337.
106 Quoted in De Lentdecker 1, p. 57.

had been a leader of a Flamingant scouts group and a member of the VNV before the war.[107]

One-quarter of those charged were formally punished by the authorities, although many more suffered repercussions in their daily lives, with jobs lost, careers broken or homes plundered by hooligans. Of those officially punished by the authorities, 57,254 Belgians received a sentence by a judicial court, while 43,093 others fell victim to the so-called 'civil purge.' The latter was a *government* decision that deprived people of their civil and political rights. Though the 'civil purge' was not a *court* decision, the *inciviques* were no longer entitled to vote or to stand for elections, nor were they allowed to work as civil servants. They were not entitled to reimbursements for war damages or pensions. They could not enroll at universities, nor participate in state examinations or start a business. One victim of the 'civil purge' was Prof. Cornelius Heymans of Ghent University, the 1938 Nobel Prize winner for Medicine. He had not been politically active during the war but was a Flamingant who during the 1920s and early 1930s had promoted the transformation of Ghent from a French-speaking university to a Dutch one. His lectureship was taken from him.

The Government deliberately aimed to disenfranchise as many 'enemies of the State' as possible. This became very clear in the weeks preceding the parliamentary elections of 17 February 1946, when thousands were listed on the register of the 'civil purged.' The 'civil purge' was also retro-active. Article 11 of the bill of 19 September 1945 stated that everyone who had 'not yet' been inscribed on the list, but had been a member of 'unpatriotic' political organisations (such as the VNV), was not allowed to vote. Posters at the entrances of the polling stations warned of severe penalties for anyone seeking to evade the new law: a prison sentence of six months and a fine of up to 5,000 francs (equalling £1,650 or $2,750 today).

The *inciviques* sentenced by judicial courts were also predominantly Flemish. Though the Flemings constituted 56% of the Belgian population, they made up 67% of those convicted for political collaboration with the enemy, 62% of those convicted for military collaboration (mainly volunteers on the Eastern Front) and 81% of those convicted for both political and military collaboration. Only for informing and for political collaboration combined with criminal offences, the Flemings scored low, respectively 32% and 52%. Political collaboration, however, or behaviour that was defined as such (it included 'mingling with Germanophiles, membership of the VNV, the acceptance

107   Vlaemynck 2, pp. 56–7.

of a German literary award' etc.), accounted for over 50% of all collaboration sentences.[108] One form of assistance to the enemy was not
punished: economic collaboration. This was explicitly exempted by a
bill of 25 May 1945. Most of the economic collaborators had been
Francophone Belgicists, such as steel baron Paul de Launoit. The most
important economic collaborationist was the SG. It had done business
with both sides during the war. 'The men connected with Société
Générale are playing both sides so that no matter which side wins, the
power and wealth of Société Générale will survive,' a report of the
Office of Economic Warfare in Washington D.C. had stated in September 1943.[109]

The Belgian courts sentenced 2,940 individuals to death, and executed 242 of these. In the Netherlands, where the Nazi occupational
regime had been far worse than in Belgium, only 123 collaborationists
were condemned to death and only 38 were executed. The Belgian
authorities wanted to set examples. The aged August Borms was executed in April 1946 because he had occasionally given farewell
speeches to Flemish volunteers setting out to fight on the Eastern
Front. Leo Vindevogel, the war-time Mayor of Ronse and an MP of the
Catholic Party, was executed in September 1945, one month after Van
Acker had formed his second cabinet: a left-wing coalition *without* the
Catholic Party. It is unclear why this father of eight had to die. He had
been neither a Nazi, nor a Flemish separatist.

The authorities also shot Stefan Laureys. He was the son of Jan
Laureys, the *Frontist* who before the war had been one of Antwerp's
most outspoken anti-racists and a helper of Jews. Stefan was an
anti-communist. In 1939 he had volunteered to fight in Finland
against the Soviet invasion. Later he joined the *Waffen-SS* on the Eastern front. In August 1944, when his regiment was transferred to the
Western front, Laureys deserted. He was in Antwerp at the moment
of the liberation, was arrested, sentenced to death and executed at the
end of February 1945. Another sad tale is that of 21-year-old Lucrèce
Vanbillemont, executed in February 1946 because she was the fiancée
of a Flemish member of the Gestapo. The latter was arrested in
Brussels two weeks after the liberation and found dead the following
morning in a Brussels pond with 21 bullets in his body. Vanbillemont
was accused of having given her boyfriend information, an allegation
she denied. Her parents tried in vain to find out where their daughter

---

108   Huyse and Dhondt, p. 192.
109   Quoted in Coolsaet, p. 349.

had been buried after the execution, but it has remained a secret to this very day.

Most death sentences, including that of VNV leader Hendrik Elias, but also those of real criminals, like Richard De Bodt, the hangman of the Breendonk Nazi concentration camp, were reduced to life imprisonment. Added to the 2,340 other sentences of life imprisonment, the total of those serving life sentences amounted to 5,038. This was as many as the annual average of *all* prisoners in Belgium before the war. In addition there were 3,366 *inciviques* who were sentenced to between 15 and 20 years in prison; 3,253 received a sentence of between 10 and 15 years (Father Callewaert, the author of the anti-Nazi letter that had enraged the SS, was condemned to 12 years of imprisonment 'for aid to the enemy, before [!] and during the occupation'); another 9,844 were sentenced to between 5 and 10 years of imprisonment; and 30,750 people received prison sentences of under 5 years.

One of the most famous *inciviques* was Hendrik De Man. He wrote to King Leopold and the Queen Mother to ask if he could reveal information relating to the Crown in his defence, but the royals never replied. De Man consequently decided to remain in Switzerland and not to show up for his trial. He was sentenced in his absence to 20 years, a fine of 10 million francs (£3.3 million or $5.5 million in today's value), the confiscation of his properties, the loss of his Belgian nationality and a prohibition to publish. In 1948, he received an additional sentence of two years and was fined one million francs for publishing his political memoirs. Copies of the book were confiscated in Belgium. De Man died under a train in an accident in Switzerland in 1953.

The purge removed all Flemish-Nationalists from the Belgian civil service. In 1991, Luc Huyse, a sociologist at Leuven University, described the post-war purge in Belgium as the settlement of the pre-war conflict between two political elites. The purge allowed the old Belgicist elite of the 'three traditional political clusters' around the Catholic, Socialist and Liberal parties to eliminate the anti-establishment VNV that in the 1930s had been gaining electoral momentum. 'The sentence actually concerned not so much the political collaboration with a foreign occupier, but the internal assault on the regime,' says Huyse.[110]

The purge of the Flamingants explains why extremist Francophones, who in the 1930s and during the war had conspired to establish an independent Wallonia or to join France, were ultimately recon-

---

110 Huyse and Dhondt, p. 267.

ciled to Belgium after the war. In September 1940, in a memorandum addressed to the Fascist French Vichy government, their leader, Georges Thone, had pleaded for the annexation of Wallonia by France, arguing that because 'Flemish domination in Belgium is growing, the entire structure of the Belgian State will gradually be transferred into Flemish hands.'[111] These Walloons were prepared to accept Belgium only if they could be sure that the Flemish majority would continue to be treated as if it were a minority. The purge meant that their nightmare of a Flemish-dominated Belgium would not come true in the foreseeable future. The Francophile separatists were even allowed to pose as loyal Belgians. Anti-Belgian Walloon separatism was not considered to be 'unpatriotic.' The Francophiles of Thone's *Ligue d'Action Wallonne*, who had offered their services to Vichy, were not prosecuted. On the contrary, Auguste Buisseret, Jean Rey and Fernand Dehousse became Belgian cabinet ministers after the war. Rey even presided over the European Commission from 1967 to 1970.

The political emancipation of the Flemings that had been achieved during the 1920s and 1930s was reversed after the war. In the first post-war government, less than one third of the cabinet ministers (6 out of 19) were Flemings. The result of the shift in the balance between the competing elites was reflected in the 1947 census in Brussels. Only 24% of the capital's population still considered it wise to declare itself predominantly Dutch-speaking, although 33% of the Brussels conscripts before the war had been Flemings.

The disenfranchisement of 3% of the Belgian electorate was a political handicap, not just for the Flemish-Nationalists, who did not regain a seat in Parliament until 1954, but also for the *Christelijke Volkspartij* (CVP, Christian People's Party), as the former Catholic Party was renamed after the war. At first the Christian-Democrats had welcomed the elimination of the Flemish-nationalist political elite. Soon, however, the CVP realised that the elimination of a large section of the conservative Flemish electorate strengthened the position of the extreme Left within the remainder of the political spectrum. In August 1945, Van Acker was able to form an extreme-left government of Socialists, Liberals and Communists. When the Christian-Democrats returned to power two years later, the list of the 'civil purged' was no longer extended.

* * *

111   Quoted in Van Goethem and Velaers, p. 1091, n. 121.

The period of the purge coincided with the most serious political crisis in Belgium's history: the so-called 'Royal Issue.' Because Leopold III was a captive in Germany when the country was liberated, Parliament declared on 20 September 1944 that the King was 'unable to reign' (Article 82 of the Constitution) and appointed his brother, Prince Charles, the Count of Flanders, as Regent. This was not to the liking of the Queen Mother, who wished to become the regent herself. But Spaak had warned the Allies that Elisabeth was 'a schemer with one half of her backside on the throne and trying to wriggle the rest on.'[112]

The Prince Regent was not much interested in politics. Charles lived mostly at night, when he indulged in whiskey and women. He duly put his signature to all the papers that his secretary, André De Staercke, laid before him. When he was later asked why he had agreed to the execution of the Catholic MP Vindevogel, though the latter could hardly be accused of collaborating, he replied that he did not recall having signed the execution order. Soon, De Staercke, who was only 32 years old, became the real man in power at the royal palace. Charles placed all his trust in him. Like many of Charles's friends and servants, De Staercke was a homosexual. Rumours had it that the Prince was extremely jealous and wanted to make sure that members of his entourage did not sleep with his girlfriends.

De Staercke organised the Prince Regent's daily schedule so that it left plenty of time for relaxation and pleasure. The Prince usually did not go to sleep before the early hours. Around noon, the servants propped Charles up and helped him recover from his hang-over. So long as Charles had not touched whiskey, he was amiable and charming, but when drunk he became aggressive. He destroyed furniture, hit his girlfriends and once even tried to strangle one of them. The Prince flitted from one woman to another and had a legendary sexual appetite. He also loved to visit ordinary brothels. Many whores in Belgium claimed to be 'the fiancée of Prince Charles.' One prostitute waxed poetic when recollecting her experience for Charles's biographer: 'He was one of those rare men who made you forget that our profession is all pretence,' she said. 'He was not a handsome man, but he had eyes that pierced you. I had the impression that he was trying to see inside my knickers and my heart at the same time.'[113]

Power being an aphrodisiac, Charles soon began to fancy his position as Regent. But could it last? When Leopold was set free in Austria

112   SOMA microfilm FO 123/599 p. 104, Lt. Col. Williams-Thomas to FO.
113   De Lentdecker 2, p. 94.

on 7 May 1945, the Prince and De Staercke accompanied the ministerial delegation that went to Sankt-Wolfgang to greet the King. Van
Acker was prepared to bring the monarch home, provided Leopold
promised to dismiss his wartime advisors and accept the international treaties that had been signed between the Pierlot government
and the Western Allies. Afterwards Van Acker told Sir Hughe
Knatchbull-Hugessen, the British Ambassador to Brussels, that the
King 'appeared to make no difficulty' regarding these conditions.[114]
Why, then, did the Sankt-Wolfgang meeting end in disaster?

Van Acker was not the first member of the Belgian delegation to
meet Leopold. On the evening of the delegation's arrival, 9 May, the
King and his wife received Charles in private. Within minutes they
were quarrelling. Charles ostentatiously refused to greet Lilian and
behaved as if she were not present. This made Leopold lose his tem-
per. The brothers began to quarrel. Charles left in anger. He paid his
brother a second visit the following morning. After barely a few minutes, he walked out, slamming the door. Meanwhile, Spaak and De
Staercke had persuaded the other members of the Belgian delegation
to demand of the King that he return to Brussels without his wife.
Leopold's subsequent talks with the delegation lasted three days,
while Lilian eavesdropped from an adjacent room. Spaak told a British Colonel, who had accompanied the Belgians to Sankt-Wolfgang,
that 'although the King had changed in appearance, he had not
changed his outlook — he was still a Fascist!!' Spaak was bent on
revenge. He conspired with De Staercke against the King. The Colonel
noted in his report that the events were truly 'Shakespearean' and
'shrouded in an air of the worst story book intrigue.'[115] Soon, it all
became too much for Leopold. He displayed the symptoms of a
nervous breakdown on 10 May and again on 11 May. The next morning, the King refused to resume the talks with the politicians. He said
that he was too ill to travel and that he would not be able to come to
Belgium for at least a month.

His refusal to leave Lilian temporarily behind in Austria and
accompany the ministers to Brussels cost him his throne. Upon their
return from Sankt-Wolfgang, Spaak and De Staercke handed the
Socialist newspaper *Le Peuple* damaging documents relating to
Leopold's actions during the war, including his telegram congratulat-
ing the *Führer* on his birthday in 1941. The paper published these,
along with vicious personal attacks on Lilian. On 28 May, politicians

114   SOMA microfilm FO 49012 p. 33, Knatchbull-Hugessen to FO, 3 Nov. 1945.
115   SOMA microfilm FO 123/595 pp. 47–8, Lt. Col. Williams-Thomas to FO.

from the Socialist, Communist and Liberal parties held a joint meeting in Brussels, where the Francophone Liberal MP Charles Janssens called Leopold 'the greatest *incivique* of them all.' The three parties of the Left said that Charles had to remain Regent until Leopold's eldest son Baudouin, the Duke of Brabant, was old enough to succeed his father. The three parties were overwhelmingly Francophone, while the Christian-Democrat Party was predominantly Flemish. The CVP spoke out in favour of the King, who, once he had been branded as an *incivique*, came to be regarded by many Flemings as yet another victim of an unjust purge.

On 15 June, Leopold announced from Sankt-Wolfgang that he was prepared to return to Brussels without Lilian. But it was too late. The Socialist Party called for a general strike and a march on Brussels to depose the King by force. The Liberal Ministers of the Interior and of Defence announced that they would refuse to order the police and the army to restore law and order in case of unrest. Knatchbull-Hugessen informed Churchill that Van Acker had warned him that there was a real danger of 'civil war.' Even if the Belgian authorities tried to restore order, the British Ambassador did not expect them to be able to do so, as they 'had few police and only one battalion of troops of doubtful reliability' at their disposition.[116]

Knatchbull-Hugessen feared that the situation could escalate into Belgium's falling apart. He argued that, given the 'long-term importance of Belgium as a factor in the European system,' the policy of non-intervention of British and American troops had to be reconsidered.[117] At the Foreign Office in London, Frederick Robert Hoyer-Millar (later Lord Inchyra) disagreed and advised on 26 June 'to keep out of this business as much as we possibly can.'[118] Two days later, Knatchbull-Hugessen wrote a letter to Eden's deputy, Oliver Harvey, in which he referred to 'French intrigue in Wallonia.' He said he was unable to measure the extent of it, but pointed out that Paris would not be 'deterred from pursuing the French separatist and annexationist ambitions by a desire not to displease us.' Indeed, it was 1830 all over again. The Ambassador pointed out that 'the whole existence of Belgium, not to mention the dynasty, rests largely on the fact that it is essential to our strategic and political interests on the continent.' He wanted to know whether, if Belgium broke up, London 'intended to

116 SOMA microfilm FO 371/49009 p. 71, Knatchbull-Hugessen to Churchill, 20 June 1945.
117 SOMA microfilm FO 371/49009 pp. 107–8, Knatchbull-Hugessen to Foreign Office, 23 June 1945.
118 SOMA microfilm FO 371/49009 pp. 104–6, Hoyer-Millar, 24–26 June 1945.

pursue the policy of abstention beyond the point where those interests, which have been permanent at all events since 1830 (without going back to Marlborough), would be sacrificed without any action on our part to defend them.'[119]

Harvey replied that the British reaction to a possible break-up of Belgium would 'depend on a large variety of factors, and in particular on whether the break-up came as the result of a bare-faced aggression on the part of the French, or as the culmination of a genuine separatist movement in Wallonia or through some combination of the two. Whichever way it came it would be rash to assume that our interests would oblige us to intervene with British troops either to keep the Walloons from seceding or to engage in conflict with the French.'[120] For the very first time since 1831, London refused to guarantee the existence of the artificial Belgian state. Harvey explicitly contradicted Knatchbull-Hugessen's assertion that the existence of Belgium was essential to Britain's strategic and political interests. He insisted that 'it would be more correct to say that the territorial integrity of Belgium has always been and will remain a paramount British interest so long as the alternative is the occupation of Belgium or of a substantial part of it by a country which there is good reason to fear might at some stage represent a military threat to this country.'[121] Splitting Belgium into two independent states would thus not necessarily be considered to be against British interests.

Moreover, the Americans did not mind if Belgium disappeared. In 1942, President Franklin D. Roosevelt had told Oliver Lyttelton (later Lord Chandos), a member of the British War Cabinet: 'In Belgium there are two communities. One are called Walloons and they speak French, the others are called Flemings and they speak a kind of low Dutch. They can't live together. After the war, we should make two states, one known as Walloonia and one as Flamingia, and we should amalgamate Luxembourg with Flamingia. What do you say to that?'[122]

The talk of violence, impending civil war and of his country's falling apart made Leopold postpone his return. On 14 July, he announced that he would not return until the Belgian people decided whether or not they wanted him back. The Christian-Democrats demanded that a referendum be held on the issue. In Belgium, two

119 SOMA microfilm FO 371/49010 pp. 27–8, Knatchbull-Hugessen to Harvey, 28 June 1945.
120 SOMA microfilm FO 371/49010 p. 31, Harvey to Knatchbull-Hugessen, 14 July 1945.
121 *Idem.*
122 Lyttelton, p. 309.

blocks now opposed each other: the Carlists and the Leopoldists. The former, predominantly Socialist and Walloon, the latter, predominantly Conservative and Flemish. The first round had been won by the Carlists.

The Grapes of Wrath

On 30 September 1945, Leopold left Austria, where he felt he was being watched by the Allied authorities. He hired a huge lakeside mansion, Château Le Reposoir, in Prégny near Geneva. From Switzerland, the King started a propaganda campaign to improve his record with the Belgians. His secretary, Jacques Pirenne, had friendly authors depict Leopold as a staunch anti-Nazi. Instead of being 'the greatest *incivique* of them all,' in Pirenne's version of the facts the King was the greatest hero of the *Résistance*. Pirenne, a Professor of History at the University of Brussels, created the 'Leopoldist' myth, in the same way that his father Henri Pirenne had created Belgicism: by *rewriting* history. If the facts did not fit, Pirenne simply denied them. 'He is a man of prejudice,' Leopold told Capelle, 'he has nothing of the historian in him; he wants to present history as he interprets it and refuses to take elements into account which contradict his version of the facts.'[123] Apart from Pirenne, Leopold could also count on the unwavering support of Cardinal Van Roey, who depicted the King's difficulty in regaining his throne as yet another thorn in the crown of his martyrdom. Children at Catholic schools were taught the prayer: 'Lord, bless our King Leopold. May his suffering and his sacrifice rise up to You, like the scent of incense.' Some Catholics even held speeches entitled 'My King, my Christ! My Leopold, my Jesus!'[124]

Not all Leopoldists were pleased with the lies and the exaggerations. Gaston Eyskens, the parliamentary leader of the Christian-Democrat CVP, thought the King's secretary was overdoing it. Pirenne was catering exclusively for the Francophone right-wing Belgicists, thereby undermining royal support in Flanders. At his press conferences, Pirenne spoke only French. Eyskens was perplexed that, notwithstanding the obvious contempt of the royal entourage for the Flemings, the latter remained so staunchly Leopoldist. In his memoirs he writes that Flemish public opinion did not have much 'political awareness.'[125]

The proposal of the CVP to hold a referendum about the King's return was not accepted by the other parties. The 'Royal Issue' became

123   SOMA PC24 nr. 3, Meeting with Leopold III, 26–28 Aug. 1948, p. 949/3.
124   Eyskens 3, p. 287.
125   Eyskens 3, p. 275.

the main issue of the 1946 elections. In Flanders the CVP improved 15% compared with its 1939 result, in Wallonia only 2%. In the country as a whole, the Christian-Democrats obtained 42.5%, the Socialists 31.6%, the Communists 12.7% and the Liberals 8.9%. In Flanders, the corresponding figures were 56.2%, 28.3%, 5.5% and 8.4%. Though the three parties of the Left did not have a majority in Flanders, they had a majority in Belgium as a whole. They formed a coalition cabinet led by Camille Huysmans, a Flemish Socialist and a convinced republican. Huysmans soon became a close friend of the Queen Mother, who had meanwhile converted from Nazism to Stalinism, and was sending personal messages to 'my dear Marshal Stalin.'[126] Only her anti-Americanism remained as fierce as ever. '*J'ai un culte pour Lenin*,' she told Huysmans. He confessed to her that he was an 'orthodox Marxist.'[127]

Elisabeth was not able to change Huysmans's opinion of Leopold, but she succeeded in making him less of a republican. 'If Leopold abdicates, then the path is clear for Prince Charles to take the throne − provided he is willing,' Huysmans told the press in October 1946. Charles was more than willing. De Staercke asked Winston Churchill to help get Charles on the throne. Churchill suggested that the Prince Regent marry his daughter Mary in exchange for British support. Preparations were made for a meeting between Mary Churchill and the Prince. Mary and her parents, however, got only as far as the British Embassy in Paris. There, to the annoyance of all, she fell in love with Christopher Soames, a young attaché, whom she married instead.

In March 1947, the Huysmans cabinet fell. Foreign Minister Spaak, irritated with his Communist colleagues, contacted Eyskens. Spaak and Eyskens agreed on most topics and formed a centrist coalition of Socialists and Christian-Democrats with 8 Flemish and 11 Francophone ministers. The CVP was still demanding a referendum about the King's return, while the Socialists wanted Leopold to abdicate, but Eyskens thought there were more important issues to deal with than arranging the return of a stupid stubborn king. Leopold complained to Capelle: 'Despite the presence of the CVP in the government, I do not receive a franc from the Civil List, and then they dare to pretend that I have their support!'[128] Since Charles had become Regent, the annual royal stipend of 12 million francs went to

---

126 RAB SAE nr. 617, Elisabeth to Stalin, 8 May 1945.
127 Quoted in Erauw, pp. 156 and 276, n. 238.
128 SOMA PC24 nr. 3, p. 1038/3.

him instead of to the King. Leopold was in financial trouble, caused by his luxurious way of life and his 'expensive' wife, whose wardrobe was widely commented upon in the Belgian papers. One of Lilian's cleavages even aroused emotions in Parliament, where MPs criticised her for showing 'her naked bosom' in public.

On 26 June 1949 new general elections were held in Belgium; the first ever in which women were allowed to vote. Again, the CVP made the King's return the central issue of the campaign. The Christian-Democrats progressed in Wallonia and lost in Flanders. On a national basis, the CVP gained 43.6% of the votes (+1.1); in Flanders, they obtained 54.4% (–1.8). The CVP were two seats short of an absolute majority in the Chamber of Representatives. They formed a coalition with the Liberals, who agreed to hold a referendum about the King's return. The new government, led by the Fleming Eyskens, counted eight Flemings on a total of seventeen cabinet ministers, an improvement on the previous post-war governments.

The long-awaited referendum was held on 12 March 1950. In Belgium as a whole, 57.7% voted for Leopold's return. While in Flanders, however, 72.0% of the electorate declared itself in favour of Leopold's return, in Wallonia only 42.1% and in Brussels only 48.1% did so. The Francophones took to the streets and started rioting. André Renard, the young and charismatic leader of the Socialist Trade Union in Liège and the publisher of the newspaper *La Wallonie,* said that the Walloons wanted 'to rid themselves of the servile northern bigots' in Flanders. 'The very existence of our people is threatened by the demographic advantage of the Flemings,' he wrote. 'Incited by their religious and economic leaders, the Flemings use Belgian centralism to oppress the numerically weaker Walloons.'[129]

Renard made it clear that the Flemings had to back down, or he would proclaim an independent Walloon Socialist Republic. 'We deliberately stirred up passions,' Joseph Coppé, the editor of Renard's newspaper, admitted forty years later: 'At the office, floor plans of army and police barracks were distributed and the *Marseillaise* was sung.'[130] During a meeting on 24 March, Renard's mentor, Joseph Merlot, a Socialist MP and the Belgian Minister of the Budget in the Huysmans and the Spaak-Eyskens cabinets, reminded the Liégeois of the decisive role which volunteers from the Walloon capital had played in 1830. The Belgian Revolution, intended to merge Belgium and France, had not been carried through to the end, Merlot

129   *La Wallonie,* 24 Mar. 1950.
130   Anthierens, p. 54.

said, and had to be completed. He suggested organising a Walloon national convention to install a provisional revolutionary government, with himself as Prime Minister and Renard as Minister of Defence. The French Consul in Liège participated in preparatory meetings.

Following the referendum, Leopold and Lilian seem to have been confident that they would soon return to Brussels. They decided to have a second child. By May, Lilian was pregnant. Leopold's optimism shows that he did not know the history of his country. Just as in 1912, when the Walloons refused to accept the decision to introduce school vouchers, although it had obtained a majority in Belgium as a whole, they now threatened to tear the state apart if the majority did not give in to them. As in 1912, the government backed down for the sake of national unity. The Christian Trade Union with its huge vested interests in both Flanders and Wallonia, did not want Belgium to fall apart. Because the trade union guaranteed Eyskens and his colleagues their eligible places on the electoral list of the CVP, the ministers were forced to save the Belgian Union, even at the cost of sacrificing a fundamental democratic principle. 'The president of the United States can be elected with a majority of one vote,' Eyskens said, 'but not a king.'[131]

The Eyskens cabinet resigned. New general elections were called for 4 June 1950. In public, the CVP campaigned under the promise that, no matter what the consequences might be, the King had to come back. The party knew it would derive electoral benefit from this stance. Eyskens later explained: 'There is always a difference between what politicians say and what they mean. To the electorate the CVP leaders said "We will put the King on the throne again," but to me they added, "so that he can abdicate honourably." The first part of the sentence was meant for the masses, the second part only for certain people.'[132]

Flanders and Wallonia again voted differently. The CVP's pledge to bring Leopold back brought it additional votes in Flanders, but lost it some in Wallonia. In the country as a whole, the Christian-Democrats obtained 47.7% of the vote; in Flanders, they received 60.4% of the vote. For the first time since the 1912 general elections, the Christian-Democrats gained an absolute majority in Parliament, winning 108 seats on a total of 212. The CVP could now govern alone. The new Prime Minister was the Walloon Christian-Democrat Jean

131 Eyskens 2, pp. 65–6.
132 Eyskens 2, 67–8.

Duvieusart. 'Given the situation in Wallonia, it had to be a Walloon,' Eyskens later explained.[133]

Six weeks after the elections, on 20 July 1950, Parliament lifted the King's 'inability to reign' and ended the Regency. Defiant Walloon MPs sang the *Marseillaise* in protest against what they perceived to be a Flemish victory. Two days later, early in the morning, like thieves in the night, Leopold and his sons, Baudouin and Albert, left Geneva. The King arrived at the military airport of Evere near Brussels at 7:18 a.m. He was driven the short distance to Laken Palace along streets guarded by 5,500 soldiers and policemen but otherwise eerily empty.

As soon as the news spread that the King had returned, a general strike erupted in Wallonia. Heavy riots followed, pro- and anti-Leopoldists fought in the streets of Brussels — the latter under the personal command of the middle-aged Spaak, who had rediscovered the revolutionary fervour of his youth. The Brussels riots left two people dead. In Wallonia local mayors prevented the municipal police from restoring order. In Liège a parallel police force of Socialist trade unionists was formed. Flanders, however, refused to go on strike and remained peaceful, apart from Ghent where Socialists beat a tram driver to death for refusing to go on strike. The murderers were never punished.

On 30 July, rioters attacked a group of policemen in Grâce-Berleur, a suburb of Liège. When hooligans tried to grab a policeman's gun, the police fired. Three men were killed on the spot, a fourth one died a few days later. Wallonia now had its martyrs; Renard could trigger his revolution. He mobilised for a huge protest demonstration in Brussels on 1 August.

Leopold was prepared to fight for his throne. The Government, however, did not want to take responsibility for a civil war. With the exception of one single minister, Albert De Vleeschauwer, the 'Flamingoth' of the London wartime cabinet, all the ministers privately asked the King to step down. If he did not abdicate, they would resign. In his memoirs, the King writes that the Christian-Democrats begged him not to reveal to the public that it was the CVP that was taking his crown from him: 'One of them, Theo Lefevre, even asked me, on his knees, not to blame the CVP. These gentlemen had decided my fate, but were afraid to take up their responsibility before the public.'[134] Late in the evening of 31 July, the Government told the King that it would not call in the army to maintain law and order in

Brussels when the anti-Leopoldists entered town the next morning. It was the last thorn in his crown.

At six o'clock on the morning of 1 August, the King signed a letter of abdication in favour of his son, the Duke of Brabant. The Socialists cancelled their march on Brussels. Less than a fortnight after his return to Laken, Leopold's reign had come to an end. He had truly reigned only from February 1934 to May 1940 and during the last ten days of July 1950. His brother Charles, who was Regent from September 1944 to July 1950, had ruled nearly as long as he.

Queen Fabiola and Baudouin I, Fifth King of the Belgians

Chapter 6

The Saint (1950–1993)

'Great Princes Have Great Playthings'[1]

It was a tall, stiff, myopic and shy 19-year-old with spectacles who appeared in a General's uniform before the joint houses of Parliament on Friday 11 August 1950. As soon as he raised his arm to take the constitutional oath, the Communist deputy Julien Lahaut and his comrades shouted '*Vive la République.*' A week later, two men rang the doorbell of Lahaut's house in Seraing near Liège. When the politician opened the door, he was shot. His murderers were never found.[2]

Baudouin resented the politicians who had made him rob his father of his crown. He felt he had to make amends to Leopold. On his uniform, he wore the sign of the Leopoldists: a 'III' enclosed by two 'L's. He had his father, stepmother and siblings live with him in Laken Palace. At home, the former monarch was seated at the head of the dinner table. Leopold and Lilian also slept in the royal bedroom, while Baudouin insisted on retaining his boyhood room. In the evenings, he went through the events of the day with his father and Jacques Pirenne, Leopold's secretary. In 1952, Baudouin granted Pirenne the hereditary title of Count.

Young Baudouin also adopted Leopold's grudges. When his uncle Charles sent him a telegram of congratulations after his accession to the throne, he did not acknowledge it. During a horse show in the Ardennes in December 1950, Baudouin noticed that Pierlot was standing in line to shake his hand. He greeted the person in front of

---

1   William Cowper, *The Task*, V. 177.
2   In December 2002, the Belgian press revealed that one of Lahaut's murderers was the late François Goossens, a Belgicist extremist. This was confirmed by Goossens' son.

the former Prime Minister, ostentatiously skipped the latter, and passed on to the next person. Baudouin behaved in a hostile fashion towards most politicians. When an aide advised the young King that it was wiser to smile at an opponent than show him one's disdain, Baudouin snapped: 'Am I not the master of my own smiles?!'

The Belgians now had a king who never seemed to smile. The press called him *'le roi triste.'* Royalists explained to the people that Baudouin was sad because of his unhappy youth. Yet Claude De Valkeneer, head of the royal press service from 1953 to 1983, wondered whether his master was 'really sad or was he only sulking?'[3] After a visit to an Antwerp school in April 1953, a witness complained to Prime Minister Jean Van Houtte about the 'marble indifference' which the King had displayed, and his lack of response to the public's enthusiasm.

In February 1952, King George VI of Great Britain died. Baudouin refused to attend the funeral because England had insulted his father. Consequently, all Western heads of state were in London except Belgium's. Only Huysmans made a fuss about the affair in Parliament. The other politicians remained silent. According to Eyskens, 'one did not want to restart the Royal Issue all over again. Everyone was tired.'[4] In May 1960, Baudouin turned down an invitation to the wedding of the British Princess Margaret. Initially, he also refused to attend Winston Churchill's funeral in January 1965, but Spaak persuaded him to swallow his pride and go.

In April 1954, the Socialists won the general election. The voters were disappointed in the CVP. It had not delivered its promise to bring Leopold III back. In addition, the Socialists had promised to reduce military conscription from 24 to 18 months. The CVP lost its absolute majority in Parliament and fell from 47.7 to 41.1% of the Belgian electorate. In Flanders, it fell from 60.4 to 52.0%. Achille Van Acker returned as Prime Minister. He formed a left-wing coalition of Socialists and Liberals. This coalition had no majority in Flanders, but no one seemed to care. The Flemings were also underrepresented in Parliament, where a Flemish seat required 48,000 votes, while 34,000 votes sufficed to obtain a Walloon seat. Van Acker showed Baudouin the list of his new cabinet members. It included Charles Janssens, the Francophone Liberal who in 1945 had called King Leopold 'the greatest *incivique* of them all.' Baudouin vetoed him at once. He told Van Acker that he would not sign the government's appointment if

3   Quoted in Koninckx and Lefèvre, p. 57.
4   Eyskens 2, p. 87.

Janssens was a cabinet member. Van Acker gave in. He, too, was 'tired.'

The Belgian politicians, who had expected to have an easy time with the young king, discovered that arguments, threats and promises had no impact on him. Baudouin told them that he was prepared to *suffer* the consequences of his obstinacy if need be. The politicians had no answer to such an attitude. All Baudouin's predecessors had been obstinate and stubborn, but this King also had principles. How utterly un-Belgian! How did he get to be like this?

Baudouin had had a dismal childhood. The death of his mother the week before his fifth birthday had deeply scarred the Duke of Brabant. The genetic inclination of the Saxe-Coburgs to moroseness and depression was soon visible in the small boy. He was also very pious. He placed medals of saints under his pillow, and every night, he said a prayer for his Mummy's soul. For months on end, he woke up in the middle of the night, afraid that his mother 'was burning in hell or purgatory'.

Baudouin's schooling was the responsibility of his Governor, Viscount Gatien du Parc Locmaria. While King Leopold lived in Laken and Knokke with his mistresses, his three children spent most of their time at Ciergnon Castle in the Ardennes. Parc Locmaria and his family lived there with them. The Viscount had seven children and he treated the three princes as if they belonged to his own crowd. The Viscount was very devoted to Baudouin. He was also a devout Catholic. The example of his religious life may have helped the young depression-prone boy to sublimate his moroseness into a deep religiosity. The Parc Locmarias also served as an example of conjugal fidelity.

In July 1942, after Lilian had given birth to Prince Alexandre, Leopold called the three children from his first marriage back to Laken. He had been asked to do so by Lilian. Thanks to Lilian, life at Laken came to resemble the life that the Parc Locmaria children had with their own parents. Never before had a Belgian Crown Prince had the privilege of living so close to his father. Baudouin could recover from the scars on his soul. His parents had time for him. His stepmother went swimming with him in Laken's private swimming pool and they played tennis together. Leopold developed his son's riding skills and taught him to play golf. He also taught him the family myths. To Baudouin, Leopold I, the bigamist who had founded the Belgian dynasty, became the incarnation of Wisdom; the tyrannical Leopold II was the Genius who had donated Belgium the Congo, which the Anglo-Saxons were forever trying to steal; the double-faced

Albert was the Hero, without whom the Allies would never have been able to beat the *Kaiser*; and Leopold III, of course, was Father, who in his person combined all the Wisdom, the Genius and the Heroism of the world.

The quiet life within Laken's walls, where the war seemed far off, continued for two years, until June 1944, when the Germans deported the royal family to the *Reich*. In the final weeks of the war, during the *Götterdämmerung* of the Nazi regime, Leopold feared that Hitler might have him murdered together with his wife and children, in the same fashion as the Bolsheviks in 1917 had slaughtered the Tsarist family in Jekaterinenburg. On the sensitive 14-year-old boy, his father's outspoken fear must have left a deep impression. The ties binding Baudouin to his father and stepmother became even closer in those agonising months of early 1945.

The following five years of exile in Prégny reinforced these ties even further. Belgian politicians who visited the King in Switzerland noticed that 'while Leopold talked, Baudouin sat looking at him in admiration.' What the politicians did not know was that the adolescent knelt down every morning and evening to pray. 'Lord,' he wrote in his diary in 1948, shortly before his 18th birthday, 'send me a saint to guide me in my spiritual life and to educate me.'[5]

In the early 1950s, Baudouin and his stepmother conspired to restore Leopold III to the throne. The latter was still in his prime, while his son loathed the royal job that had been bestowed on him. Leopold himself thwarted their plans. He was no longer interested in resuming the functions of a monarch but reckoned that his political influence through Baudouin was sufficient. The Liberal journal *Le Flambeau* even wrote that Belgium was a 'diarchy,' instead of a monarchy. To Leopold, this situation offered the additional advantage that he had more freedom and privacy, while he also received an adequate income without having to work for it. When Baudouin succeeded him, the Civil List was set at 44 million francs (£3.7 million or $6.1 million at today's value): 30 million for the young King, 6 million for his father, 4 million for Uncle Charles, and 4 million for Elisabeth, the Queen Grandmother.

Lilian felt let down. Leopold was often away on foreign trips — alone. The former King was interested in wildlife and ethnology as well as photography. He combined these interests by going on photo and film safaris to primitive tribes in the Asian, African and South-American rainforests, engaging Ernst Schäfer to help him. Schäfer

5   Quoted in Suenens 2, p. 28.

was a former SS officer who in 1938–39 had led a much publicised
expedition to Tibet on a quest to investigate the origins of the Aryan
race. After the war, he moved to Venezuela.

Leopold also travelled around Europe. These were expeditions in
search of a different kind of 'wildlife.' For a while Leopold had an
affair with a voluptuous British assistant producer of nature documentaries, whom he met at a dinner in London. The ex-king was,
however, careless with his erotic correspondence. He left a number of
compromising letters and pictures in a borrowed car, which the Belgian Ambassador in Britain was ordered to retrieve. After the affair
ended, the young woman's London flat was broken into and the
saucy letters stolen. Later Leopold had a relationship with a young
French woman who was 34 years his junior. Around 1960, Lilian, then
44 years old, found a letter from the 25-year-old *Française* inviting the
59-year-old Leopold to accompany her to Bangkok. Lilian suddenly
felt very old. 'There is talk of a divorce,' wrote the Socialist leader Van
Acker, a meticulous chronicler of court gossip, in June 1961: 'The
affair with the *Française* has been going on for two and a half years.
Leopold has spent 11 million francs on her.'[6] Was this lady the same
woman whom Roger Frey, the French Minister of the Interior, warned
the Belgian Ambassador in Paris against? Frey told the Embassy that
Leopold was having an affair with a communist spy.

While the ex-king travelled, his wife was in Laken with the young
King. Soon, the 'diarchy' consisted of Baudouin and Lilian. 'The former king does not interfere any longer. He is no longer interested,'
Van Acker wrote in his diary on 21 December 1951. 'Unfortunately,
Baudouin sees *the woman* every day.' On 21 November 1952, an
alarmed Van Acker noted: 'The King has left Brussels for Tyrol
together with Lilian. They are travelling in the same sleeping com-
partment.' Five days later, Van Acker returned to the affair: 'It is very
annoying. The information that they share the same *couchettes* is correct. The cabinet fears that the news will leak out.' Three months later,
on 29 January 1953, the 22-year-old King and his 36-year-old stepmother were about to leave for the Côte d'Azur. 'In a special train, but
in what conditions?' Van Acker panicked. 'It is becoming a real
"enchantment." They tell each other over the phone: "*Je suis à toi.*" He
will lose everything. "*Je te quitte jamais.*" The whole matter seems lost
in case of a marriage.'

Since the publication of excerpts of Van Acker's diary in 1998, there
has been much speculation about the nature of the relationship

6   For the extracts from Van Acker's diary, see Falter.

between Baudouin and his stepmama. It need not have been a sexual affair as Van Acker suggested. Maybe it was just a genuine deep friendship. Lacking social contacts, Baudouin could only look for friends within his own family circle. Hence, he only had his brother Albert and his stepmother to be close to. The diatribes in the press against Lilian occasionally made Baudouin cry. Once, he was so upset that he had to cancel all his appointments for the day. There was shock as well on 21 July 1957, when Lilian barely escaped death. She was seated next to Leopold in a brand new sports car when her speeding husband missed a bend at Cortina d'Ampezzo in Italy. The roofless car landed upside-down in a ditch. Leopold and his wife suffered only minor bruises. The former king, who never seemed to learn from experience, had almost made Baudouin's stepmother another Astrid.

* * *

The Christian-Democrats won the general elections of 1 June 1958, leaping from 41.1 to 46.5% of the votes in Belgium as a whole, and from 52.0 to 56.5% in Flanders. To help the CVP, the bishops warned the Flemings not to vote for the *Volksunie*, the new Flemish-nationalist party. Emile-Joseph De Smedt, the Bishop of Bruges, wrote a pastoral letter, which was read from the pulpits. It declared that 'to vote for the *Volksunie* is a mortal sin' and 'to vote for the CVP is a matter of conscience.'[7] Paradoxically, the CVP remained below its 1950 figure in Flanders, but in Wallonia, where episcopal influence was limited, the party did better than ever since the introduction of general suffrage in 1919. A great number of Francophone left-wing voters defected to the Christian-Democrats because the CVP out-promised the Socialists. Gaston Eyskens vowed to reduce military conscription from 18 to 12 months and presented an economic plan, the so-called *Key Plan*, somewhat similar to Hendrik De Man's pre-war scheme. Eyskens promised to raise the Belgian Gross Domestic Product by 40% in ten years and threw money at various groups of the electorate in order to buy their adherence. He promised free health care and free education, plus one billion francs in subsidies to the farmers. 'Nobody knew what to do with that money,' he admitted many years later, 'but we went to all the country towns and said: "We'll give you a billion francs, one thousand million." It was a stupendous propaganda stunt.'[8]

Eyskens formed a coalition with the Liberals and became the new Prime Minister. Like his predecessor Van Acker, he was worried by

7   Pastoral Letter, 22 May 1958, in Bishops, pp. 166–8.
8   Eyskens 2, p. 99.

the close relationship between Baudouin and his stepmother. In the spring of 1959, he discussed it with his Liberal coalition partners and with the Socialist opposition. The leaders of the three traditional parties sent Eyskens to Leopold with the request that he move out of Laken and settle in Argenteuil House near Waterloo. Lilian, however, was opposed to the move, and she had her way. 'Lilian still decrees,' Van Acker confided to his diary, 'if she does not have her way, she starts sulking.' In October Van Acker went to see Baudouin to persuade him to have his parents move out, but the King retorted that 'the smear campaign' against his stepmother had to stop. He told Van Acker that journalists and politicians made her life 'into such a hell that some would commit suicide in a similar situation.'

According to the politicians, the only way to get rid of Lilian would be for Baudouin to marry. The Belgicist politicians hoped for a marriage with an English princess. This would mend the strained relations between the Belgian and the British branches of the Saxe-Coburg family and once again promote London into the foremost protector of the interests of the Belgian dynasty, and, hence, of Belgian national unity. Princess Margaret, the daughter of George VI, was considered to be a suitable bride. She was the same age as Baudouin. When Baudouin refused to attend George VI's funeral, however, it was clear that a romance between the two was out of the question. In 1956, *Het Volk*, the newspaper of the Christian-Democrat trade union, wrote that Baudouin was about to become engaged to the 20-year-old Alexandra of Kent, a first cousin of British Queen Elizabeth II. The article was based entirely on wishful thinking.

Perhaps Baudouin did not want to marry? On 19 April 1958, over six thousand guests, including eighteen kings and other heads of state, attended a ball at the royal palace. It was the first ball at the Belgian Court since January 1934. Baudouin opened the ball with Crown Princess Beatrix of the Netherlands (to please the Flemings), had a dance with Isabelle of Orléans (to satisfy the Walloons) and retired around midnight. He was visibly disinterested and bored. The ball went on. The day after, the cleaning party discovered many lost objects, including jewels, that were later reclaimed by their rightful owners, and three pairs of ladies' knickers, that were not.[9] It was the last royal ball of Baudouin's reign. He preferred more solitary pastimes. There were rumours that he was considering resigning in favour of his brother Albert to enter a monastery.

9   Lobkowicz, p. 144.

On 9 April 1953, Baudouin's eldest sister Joséphine-Charlotte — nicknamed 'Jo-Jo' — married Prince Jean of Bourbon-Parma, the heir to the throne of Luxemburg. Baudouin left the church arm in arm with Lilian to make it clear to everyone that as far as he was concerned she was the uncrowned Queen of Belgium. This message was reinforced at the Laken ball of April 1958, when Lilian wore a diamond tiara that had belonged to Queen Astrid. This caused a new row in the family, because Jo-Jo thought that she was more entitled to her mother's tiara then Stepmama. Speaking of family quarrels, something else was remarkable about Jo-Jo's wedding: the whole family was there, except Uncle Charles. The Count of Flanders was also absent when his mother celebrated her 80th birthday in 1956. He was not even present at Elisabeth's funeral in November 1965.

The vendetta between Charles and his family had deepened further since 1950. In 1955, Charles demanded the split of the remainder of his father's inheritance that had so far been managed by a family trust. This added stocks worth at least 140 million francs (£11.6 million or $19.3 million at today's value) to the Count of Flanders' portfolio, as well as one-third of the 4,000 hectares (9,600 acres) of the royal domain near Retie. Charles sold his share for 75 million francs. According to his attorney, Georges Bricmont, this was far below the actual value, but the vengeful Uncle wanted to show his 'Leopoldist' relatives that he was disinheriting them by virtually giving his possessions away.

Prince Charles gave 50 million francs to Isabelle Wybo, his illegitimate daughter, and spent the rest lavishly on whores, mistresses and friends. In 1980, however, the Prince took Bricmont to court. The attorney had sold property belonging to the Prince and had transferred money and stocks to anonymous bank accounts and phantom companies in Liechtenstein. One of the Liechtenstein companies was called *Volpone*. Volpone is an old childless man in an Italian tale, who constantly receives visits from relatives who are hoping to get hold of his inheritance. Charles said that Bricmont had robbed him. On 15 February 1982, the Brussels court acquitted Bricmont. The judge stated in his verdict that much was unclear in the case and that it was certainly possible that Bricmont had enriched himself at the expense of the Prince. It was, however, not the accused who had to prove his innocence, but the accuser who had to prove the guilt, which he was unable to do. Moreover, the judge stressed, 'His Royal Highness has helped to forge documents. If certain said embezzlements cannot be proved, the Prince himself is to blame.'

The case was brought before the Brussels Court of Appeal in November 1982. 'I had no idea that Prince Charles was so rich. I am astonished by this juggling with millions and all kinds of phantom companies,' the President of the Appeal Court said during the proceedings. The Public Prosecutor, however, declared that he was convinced that Bricmont had robbed the Prince of at least one-quarter of his 'immense patrimony,' but added that 'respect for his privacy and discretion render it impossible for me to disclose the exact amount of the Prince's patrimony.' On 9 March 1983, the attorney received an effective prison sentence of five years and was ordered to pay 1.5 million francs in damages to the Count of Flanders. 'It is clear,' the verdict said, 'that the Count of Flanders wished to keep his patrimony hidden from the fiscal authorities, from his debtors and from his legal heirs. Bricmont has used the Count's wishes to steal from him and this to his own enrichment.' Nevertheless, the Court admitted that much of what had really happened with Charles' money remained a mystery. Contrary to the normal procedure, Bricmont was not arrested in the court room and was allowed to go home. The next day, he fled to Canada.

Charles died three months later, on 1 June 1983, at the age of 79, in an Ostend hospital. He was buried in the royal crypt in Laken on 7 June. His brother Leopold refused to attend the funeral. The public interest for the former Regent's demise was also limited, even amongst the Walloons who had once wanted him on the throne. King Baudouin walked behind the hearse, as did his brother Albert, the Prince of Liège. The latter had quite liked his uncle. He had often visited old 'Volpone' in Raversijde during the 1970s. Charles's fortune has mysteriously disappeared, together with the memoirs that he is said to have written.

'Mumbo-Jumbo Is Dead In The Jungle'[10]

Prince Charles was not the only embarrassment to Belgium. So was his mother, the Queen Grandmother. After the war, Elisabeth became the patroness of a prestigious music contest, the *Concours Musical International Reine Elisabeth*. It gave her a perfect alibi to travel extensively in the Eastern Bloc. In 1955, she went to Warsaw to attend the International Chopin Contest. It was the very year in which the Warsaw Pact was established. Her visit, the first by a royal to the Communist World, greatly embarrassed the Belgian government. Foreign Minister Spaak tried to persuade her not to go, but she went anyway and publicly congratulated the Polish President because his country had 'wisely

10   N. Vachel Lindsay, *The Congo*, 3.

chosen its own way.'[11] Asked by a Polish journalist whether she had encountered difficulties in entering the Democratic [Communist] World, she answered: 'No, but I did have difficulty getting out of the West.'

In 1958, the Queen Grandmother attended the Tchaikovsky Music Contest in Moscow and went to place flowers at the Lenin mausoleum. The next year, she travelled to Belgrade to meet Marshal Tito. It would be wrong, however, to conclude that Elisabeth admired all dictators. She no longer wanted to have anything to do with the 'Fascists.' 'What are a dictator's promises worth,' she asked of Spain's General Franco in 1960.[12] Equally dangerous were the Americans, who, she said, 'threaten the world if one allows them to continue with their criminal game and their self-seeking vanity that will lead to the suicide of mankind.' The American politicians, she wrote to the Nobel Peace Prize winner Albert Schweitzer in 1961, 'should be locked up in a lunatic asylum.'[13] She was referring to John F. Kennedy.

In the autumn of 1961, the 85-year-old red granny, together with her daughter Marie-José, the former Queen of Italy, travelled to the People's Republic of China, a state not then officially recognised by any Western country or by the United Nations. On the way to China, the two ex-queens made a stop-over in Moscow to dine at the Kremlin. In China, they met Chairman Mao and together with him inspected the troops parading on Tiananmen Square on 1 October, the anniversary of the Communist Revolution. Elisabeth subsequently gave a speech, in which she said: 'The Belgian patriots are opposed to the absurd policy that excludes China from the United Nations. From your great example the Belgian people will learn how to fight every injustice.'[14] She returned home with a huge portrait of Mao, which adorned the hall of her residence from then on.

In the spring of 1962, she paid another visit to Moscow together with Marie-José. They both stayed in the Kremlin and on 1 May inspected the military parade with Khrushchev and Brezhnev. She received the Soviet Medal of Peace, which she often wore afterwards. Again, *la reine rouge* went to Lenin's tomb. 'I have a great respect for Lenin. He has done very much for the Russian people; everyone, even

11   RAB SAE nr. 620E, Elisabeth to President Zuwacki, 24 Dec. 1956.
12   RAB SAE nr. 620, Elisabeth to Father Bouliez, 18 Oct. 1960.
13   Maison Albert Schweitzer, Gunsbach, Schweitzer Correspondence, microfiches 102–01 and 102–02, Elisabeth to Schweitzer, 10 Dec. 1957 and 23 Nov. 1961.
14   *Le Peuple*, 25 Nov. 1965.

those who do not share his views, must dare to admit this,' she said in an interview in a Belgian newspaper.[15]

In the autumn of 1965, her friend, Camille Huysmans, was arranging a visit for her to East Germany. 'I believe it would be a good thing for you to journey to the GDR. You will like its political views,' he wrote to her. 'The population is unanimously satisfied with its government's politics and economic policy. Everyone is happy there, even those who still adhere to a religion.'[16] She answered: 'Everything which you tell me is true and I greatly admire it all.'[17] But she died on 23 November 1965, at the age of 89, before being able to visit East Berlin and shake hands with Erich Honecker, the man who had built the Berlin Wall. 'We shared many ideas,' Huysmans wrote in an obituary. 'We were both democrats. That is why she went to the Soviet Union and to China to examine the positive achievements of these regimes. She came back greatly satisfied with what she had seen and intended to go to East Germany in the spring.'[18]

* * *

While his grandmother dabbled in foreign politics, Baudouin did the same. In May 1955, the 24-year-old monarch visited Belgium's Congo colony. Baudouin was thrilled by the almost physical adoration of the natives. He entered Leopoldville (known today as Kinshasa) under a bamboo arch atop of which barebreasted girls waved. Exuberant Congolese flocked to greet him in large numbers. They gave the young man in his white uniform, whom they called 'Mwana Kitoko' (the nice boy), the warmest welcome he had ever received.

The infatuation did not last, however. On 4 January 1959, riots erupted in Leopoldville after the Force Publique, the colonial army, banned a meeting organised by Joseph Kasa-Vubu, a local politician. There were over 500 deaths. 'We have only used one-hundredth of our strength,' General Emile Janssens, the commander-in-chief of the Force Publique threatened. 'Let these deaths be a lesson to those who were lucky enough to escape the bullets. And if they do not keep quiet, then we are ready to play this game again.'

The Leopoldville massacre made Baudouin realise that his kindhearted 'second people' was not as contented as he had supposed. He felt the need to regain his position as its 'Nice Boy' and make some

15   *De Nieuwe Gazet*, 22 May 1962.
16   RAB SAE nr. 654, Huysmans to Elisabeth, 13 Sept. 1965.
17   Archives Museum of Flemish Cultural Life Antwerp, Huysmans Papers f/127/350, Elisabeth to Huysmans.
18   *Le Peuple*, 25 Nov. 1965.

amends. On 13 January 1959, the King spoke about the riots on Radio-Brussels. It was, according to the historian Jean Stengers, 'probably the most important act of Baudouin's entire reign.'[19] It certainly had the most dramatic impact. In his speech, Baudouin announced: 'It is our firm resolve to lead the Congolese peoples, without a hesitancy which might prove fatal, but also without inconsiderate precipitation, to independence in prosperity and peace.' The speech was a blunder, because it was a lie. The King promised independence, but was not prepared to give it: he hoped that by promising independence, the blacks would stop demanding it. The speech had been the King's own initiative. In fact, the Government had formulated its own declaration, which was far more cautious: 'Belgium intends to organise in the Congo a democracy capable of wielding the prerogatives of sovereignty and deciding about its independence,' it said. The Government had its own message broadcast on the Congolese radio, and not the King's, but the news soon spread in the colony that *Mwana Kitoko* was about to grant full independence.

In an attempt to undo the momentum that he himself had created, Baudouin wrote to Eyskens: 'It is imperative that we safeguard in the Congo the imprescriptible rights that our pioneers have created for us. If, God forbid, we lose the incomparable patrimony which the genius of Leopold II has donated us, Belgium would suffer immeasurable moral and material damage and those responsible for giving it up would be decried by all.'[20] The King blamed Eyskens for a situation that was rapidly getting out of control.

There now was political unrest all over the Congo. Kasa-Vubu was no longer the most radical of the Congolese leaders. In Stanleyville (today Kisangani), the capital of the East Province, a charismatic and ambitious young radical, Patrice Lumumba, had organised his own party, the *Mouvement National Congolais* (MNC). When Pierre Leroy, the Governor of the East Province, imprisoned Lumumba on 1 November 1959, the Belgians committed a second major blunder. They made Lumumba into a martyr and a nation-wide popular symbol.

On 16 December, Baudouin committed the third blunder. He departed for the Congo, convinced that he could calm the natives. He only made matters worse. The Congolese were convinced that *Mwana Kitoko* had personally come to release Lumumba from gaol and put him at the helm of an independent state that Baudouin would proclaim on the spot. When they realised that this was not the case, they

19   Stengers 8, p. 177.
20   Baudouin to Eyskens, 4 Sept. 1959, in Stengers 8, p. 177.

threw stones at his car. The hawkish Pierre Leroy told the King that if he were authorised to take 'special measures,' order could be restored. 'Go ahead,' Baudouin said, 'I will cover you.'[21]

Eyskens, however, realised better than Baudouin and his advisors that Belgium could not hold on to the Congo. He was extremely sceptical when General Janssens of the *Force Publique* boasted that he had 'the mightiest and best disciplined army in the whole of Africa.' The General said that he only had to make *'une promenade militaire au Congo'* to solve all the problems, but Eyskens doubted whether Janssens' army of 25,000 men — all Congolese except for 1,000 Belgian officers — could put the genie back in the bottle. Moreover, Belgian public opinion would not support a war waged to hold on to a colony it had never wanted in the first place.

Eyskens proposed to grant the Congo full independence within six months by installing a class of docile blacks who were prepared to keep the existing economic and military structures intact. It could not be very difficult to do so: One only needed to *buy* the current Congolese leaders and corrupt them. Lumumba was released from prison on 25 January 1960 and flown over to Brussels where other Congolese politicians had already been gathered for a Round Table conference with the Belgians. 'They were terribly impressed by what they experienced over here,' Eyskens later recalled: 'They could visit brothels and have as many white women as they liked.'[22]

On 20 February, an agreement was reached: in exchange for independence on 30 June 1960, the blacks accepted that the ministries of Defence and Foreign Affairs would remain exclusively in Belgian hands (even the army would retain its white officers) and all existing property rights of the Belgian companies and entrepreneurs would be upheld. This was an agreement that the two main powers in the Congo — the SG and the *Force Publique* — could accept. For them, nothing would change.

After the Congolese parliamentary elections of May 1960 in which Lumumba's MNC won 41 of the 137 seats and became the biggest party, it was decided that Kasa-Vubu would become the country's president, a mostly ceremonial function, and Lumumba prime minister. Unfortunately, the Congolese Prime Minister ran into a major conflict with the Belgians almost immediately. The cause was, again, a blunder by Baudouin — the greatest blunder of them all.

21   Leroy, p. 116.
22   Eyskens 2, p. 117.

In his speech during the independence ceremony of the young Congo Republic on 30 June 1960, the King sang the praises of the genius of Leopold II, who had 'delivered the Congo basin from the odious slave trafficking that decimated its people eighty years ago.' He stressed the 'grand work' of 'Leopold II who did not come to you as a conqueror but as a civiliser.'[23] Lumumba felt compelled to give a rebuff. He recalled the 'humiliating slavery' that had been imposed on the Congolese by Leopold II. 'Our wounds are still too fresh and painful for us to banish them from our memory,' he said. Baudouin listened in anger. He was raging. 'I am leaving. We return to Brussels at once,' he told Eyskens. That evening, after having placed flowers at Leopold II's statue in the Congolese capital, a still furious Baudouin flew back to Brussels.

Lumumba's rebuff became his death warrant. He had said something that greatly disturbed the *Société Générale*: 'Our land was taken from us in the name of so-called legal documents which only recognised the right of the strongest.' The SG concluded that Lumumba was questioning the legality of the land ownership by the Belgian companies. With such a man governing the Congo, the SG's immense economic interests were at risk.

The *Union Minière*, the SG's mining subsidiary, controlled the mineral-rich Katanga province in the south of the Congo. There 22,000 blacks, supervised by 2,200 whites, extracted over 300,000 tons of copper per year, making the Congo the fourth-biggest copper-producing country in the world. Copper was the linchpin of the UM's wealth. But the Katanga also made the UM the world's major supplier of strategic minerals such as cobalt (75% of world production) and uranium. In addition there was an abundance of more 'ordinary' minerals like gold and coal. The UM had 34,000 square kilometres in concession. In the 1950s it made an annual net profit of between 2.5 and 4.5 billion francs. In the southern part of the adjacent province of the Kasai, another SG subsidiary controlled the diamond trade. Congo was the SG's treasure-house: 44% of the SG's worldwide profits were generated in the country.

The SG began to mastermind a plan against 'Satan,' as the Congolese Prime Minister was nicknamed in the Belgian diplomatic telex messages. The UM told Moise Tshombe, the President of the Katanga Provincial Government, that it would support him if he proclaimed Katangese independence. Tshombe, whom the Belgian secret telexes referred to as 'the Jew,' decided to grab his chance. All he needed was an opportunity to get into action. *The Jew* did not have to wait very long. The opportunity was soon provided by another of *Satan*'s adversaries, General Janssens, the Commander-in-Chief of the *Force Publique*. Janssens said of Lumumba that he was 'more devil than man.'[24] No doubt he had decided that the time had come for some *exorcism* in the Congo.

On 5 July, there was a mutiny of the *Force Publique* in Thysville (today Mbanza-Ngungu) in the Lower Congo Province, 175 kilometres to the south of Leopoldville. Black privates rebelled after General Janssens had deliberately provoked his men by calling them together and writing on a blackboard: 'Before independence = after independence,' thereby indicating that nothing would change with regard to racial discrimination in the army. When the news of Janssens' provocation reached Thysville, furious soldiers attacked the compounds of their white officers and raped their wives. The rebellion soon spread to army barracks in the capital. Fifteen Belgians, five other Europeans and an unknown number of blacks were killed. Lumumba was able to restore order on the evening of 8 July by 'Africanising' the army. He promoted a number of sergeants, the highest rank that Congolese had so far achieved, to colonel. One of them, Joseph-Désiré Mobutu, was appointed Commander-in-Chief in place of Janssens.

The major figures of the SG in Brussels concluded that the fact that Lumumba had 'Africanised' the army, in spite of the Belgo-Congolese agreement that the *Force Publique* would remain under Belgian control, indicated that he was about to 'Africanise' the economy, as well. On 9 July, following deliberations between Eyskens, Baudouin and Paul Gillet, the Governor of the SG, Belgian soldiers were flown to Elisabethville (today Lubumbashi), the capital of the Katanga, even though there had been no troubles there yet. Brussels announced that it was sending 10,000 paratroopers and other soldiers to the Congo to 'evacuate' all Europeans who wanted to flee from 'danger.'

Ten days later, Belgian paratroopers stormed the port of Matadi. Twenty Congolese soldiers and policemen were killed in the attack. The Belgians also attacked the barracks of Kolwezi, the Katanga's mining centre, killing 13 soldiers of Lumumba's army, while Tshombe proclaimed the independence of the Katanga. Lumumba called on the United Nations and the United States for help. On 14 July, the UN Security Council decided to send UN troops to the Congo to restore order.

24 Quoted in Geerts, p. 116.

Meanwhile, Belgium began to run the Katangese state, where Tshombe was surrounded by Belgian advisors. The informal Belgian embassy at Elisabethville was known as *Mistebel*, the *Mission Technique Belge*. The head of *Mistebel* was Count Harold d'Aspremont-Lynden. His assistant was a young scion of an important Belgicist family, Viscount Etienne Davignon, the son of Jacques Davignon, the former Belgian Ambassador to Nazi Germany.

The next phase in the Belgian plan was the *reconquista* of the diamond area of the southern Kasai. General Charles-Paul de Cumont, the commander of the Belgian troops in the Congo, ordered his men on 14 July 'to assure that the Kasai Province imitates the Katanga.' On 8 August, the southern part of the Kasai formally seceded under Albert Kalonji, the Speaker of the Congolese House of Representatives. With Belgian backing, Kalonji installed himself at Bakwanga (today Mbuji-Mayi) as 'Albert I' of the 'Kingdom of the Kasai.'

In Brussels, Baudouin blamed Eyskens for the troubles in Africa. Baudouin was convinced that if it had not been for the soft-heartedness and the improvisation of Flemish politicians, his dynasty would still own *its* Congo. He decided that the Eyskens cabinet had to be replaced by a 'strong, competent and independent' government of national unity. The King secretly summoned Paul Van Zeeland, the president of the *Banque Belge d'Afrique*, and NATO Secretary General Spaak. He wanted them to form a new government. On 9 and 10 August, vicious editorials in the leading Francophone Brussels newspapers attacked Eyskens, who was blamed for his 'monstrous naivety, ignorance and stubbornness.'

Baudouin told Eyskens that, as he had clearly lost public support, he had to resign. The Prime Minister, however, refused to step down so long as he had a parliamentary majority. The crisis lasted for two weeks, until the King and Eyskens reached a *modus vivendi*. The politician remained Prime Minister but would only deal with Belgian affairs, while the cabinet would be extended to include a Minister of African Affairs, who would have a free hand in the Congo. This man was Laken's confidant, Count Aspremont-Lynden.

The Count and the King shared the same vision on the Congo, which was voiced on 2 October in a single phrase by Baudouin's brother, Crown Prince Albert, to a journalist of Associated Press: 'The Congolese crisis can be reduced to one single person: Patrice Lumumba.' Aspremont-Lynden told his collaborators: 'Our single most important goal is the definitive elimination of Lumumba.'[25] The

25 Aspremont-Lynden to Mistebel, 6 Oct. 1960, in De Witte 2, p. 117.

Count had his own intelligence service, led by Major Jules Loos. He worked on three different plans for the assassination of Lumumba, either by having him poisoned, kidnapped by soldiers from the Kasai, or murdered by a prostitute. These were not the only murder plans. The UM had also contacted professional killers to rid them of *Satan*. There were so many killers around that they even got in each other's way. One of them, Edward Pilaet, complained of this in a report to Lieutenant-General Raymond Dinjaert, the head of the military desk at the Belgian royal palace.

Congolese leaders, including former 'Lumumbists,' like Chief of Staff Mobutu, were bribed. Aspremont-Lynden even managed to corrupt Kasa-Vubu. He had him depose Lumumba on 5 September. Pilaet tried to persuade Mobutu to assassinate Lumumba. Mobutu, who still had a certain loyalty towards Lumumba, felt he could not do this. 'The problem with Mobutu,' Pilaet reported to his contacts in Brussels, 'is that he is too much of a pacifist.' His conscientious objections were soon smothered with Belgian money. Mobutu was offered 20 million francs for the arrest of Lumumba. On 16 October, Kasa-Vubu met Tshombe in Elisabethville. They agreed that the Congolese Prime Minister had to be 'completely neutralised (if possible physically).' A report of the meeting was sent to Baudouin's *chef de cabinet*, who passed the report on to the King.[26]

Lumumba was arrested on 1 December and imprisoned in Thysville. On 4 January 1961, he managed to smuggle a political statement out of prison. The Belgians, he wrote, 'have corrupted some of our countrymen; others they have bought; they have contributed to the distortion of the truth and the besmirching of our independence.' On 17 January, Lumumba was flown over to the Katanga in a Belgian DC 4, together with two other prisoners, the Congolese Minister of Youth and the Speaker of the Senate.

During the six-hour flight, the three men were severely abused. The plane arrived at Elisabethville shortly before five o'clock in the afternoon. From the airport, they were brought to a house on the outskirts of Elisabethville. There, they were tortured for four hours by Katangese policemen while Belgian officers looked on. Later that evening, the three men were thrown in a car and driven to a place in the bush some 50 kilometres from Elisabethville, where they were executed by Katangese soldiers under Belgian command. Tshombe and some of his ministers were present at the execution. One of the blacks,

---

26   RAB K, Weber to Lefébure, 19 Oct. 1960, in De Vos, Gerard, Gérard-Libois and Raxon 2, p. 26.

remembering the lessons learned from Leopold II, suggested chopping off the hands of the three men and sending them to Leopoldville. This suggestion was turned down by a Belgian officer.

On 9 February, a Belgian plane flew a second load of Congolese politicians to their death. This time the destination was Bakwanga in Kalonji's 'Kingdom of the Kasai.' During the four-hour flight, the prisoners had been almost literally kicked to pieces. One of them had his jaw beaten to bits; it was dangling loose from his head. He had also been blinded. The six died a horrible death at the hands of Kalonji.

With General Mobutu firmly in power in Leopoldville, the SG now opted for the reunification of the Congo. In September 1962, Kalonji's 'kingdom' was reintegrated into the Congo. In January 1963, the independence of the Katanga formally ended. Baudouin was never reminded of *Satan* again, except for one incident during a visit to Trinity College in Dublin in May 1968. Irish students shouted 'Lumumba' as the King passed by. He pretended not to hear.

A Marriage Made in Heaven

On 2 July 1959, Baudouin's younger brother, Crown Prince Albert, married the daughter of an Italian prince. To Baudouin's annoyance, Eyskens was a nuisance again. He objected to the official announcement of 14 April 1959 whereby 'Their Majesties the King and King Leopold' had approved the marriage of Albert without bothering about Article 60 of the Constitution which required that the marriage of a Crown Prince be approved by the King *and* the Government. Eyskens insisted that things be done by the book. Hence, a new preliminary royal approval — by Baudouin, not by his father — was given on 24 June, to which the signatures of both Eyskens and his Minister of Justice were added.

His brother's marriage set Baudouin thinking about his own future. He came to the conclusion that being a king was very similar to being a priest. The main difference was that a priest was called to celibacy, while a king had a duty to procreate and provide an heir to the throne. If God wanted him to be king, He had to help him find a queen who shared his ideas about priestly kingship.

Early in February 1960, Baudouin met an ambitious cleric, the 55-year-old Leo-Joseph Suenens, a Professor of Philosophy at the Catholic University of Leuven and the Auxiliary Bishop of Brussels. Suenens had been invited to Laken by Leopold and Lilian, in his capacity as Deputy President of Leuven University to discuss the prospects of Baudouin's 17-year-old halfbrother, Prince Alexandre, whose parents wanted him to obtain a university degree.

After discussing Alexandre's future with his parents, Suenens was introduced to Baudouin. They took a short stroll through Laken Park. Suenens was a perceptive man. He noticed Baudouin's mystical inclination and, guessing what was on the King's mind, he wrote him a letter the next day. It was full of implicit hints which, as Suenens must have realised, gave the young man the impression that the cleric had been sent to him by Divine Providence. Suenens said in the letter that he was writing to Baudouin because he had been struck by 'your ability to listen.' This is 'an art,' the flattering Suenens continued, 'which you also clearly exercised during your visit to the Congo and which is part of the rhythm of your daily life.' After the praise, the bishop played on Baudouin's self-pity. 'How lonely you must be. This struck me as we walked in the park.' Suenens, however, underlined that, thanks to this loneliness, Baudouin was 'better able to judge people and circumstances' — which was again flattery — and it was also a highway to God. 'I allow my pen to randomly follow my musings about all kinds of things,' Suenens added, as if he had not carefully considered all that he was writing but was acting on an impulse that came not from himself but from another source. 'I would like very much to help you answer your magnificent vocation: God's dream for your life.' He concluded by hinting that it might be God himself who was speaking through the letter: 'I feel deeply involved in your life through a warm affection. If the Lord wishes to use this deep affection to speak to you now and again, then I would love to be his spokesman.'[27] A few days later, Suenens sent Baudouin a book by a French Jesuit, Father Jean-Pierre de Caussade, entitled *L'Abandon à la Providence Divine*.

As envisaged, the King reacted by inviting Mgr. Suenens over again. Their second meeting took place on 28 February. Baudouin confided that he had recently gone on a pilgrimage to Lourdes in the South of France, to 'ask Our Lady to solve the problem of my marriage.' Suenens replied that he had a friend in Brussels, an Irish woman named Veronica O'Brien, who had a privileged relationship with Our Lady. Miss O'Brien, a 55-year-old nun, was the chairwoman in Belgium and France of the Legion of Mary, a Catholic organisation that had been founded in Ireland in the 1930s. Baudouin immediately expressed his wish to meet this nun. Suenens said he would arrange a

---

27   Suenens to Baudouin, 12 Feb. 1960, in Suenens 2, pp. 18–21.

meeting, confirming to the King that such a meeting 'brings a special grace, prepared for you by Our Lady of Lourdes.'[28]

Baudouin received Veronica O'Brien in Laken on 18 March. They talked for more than five hours. In 1991, Baudouin referred to his first meeting with O'Brien in a diary entry which reads as follows: '43 years ago [in 1948], I asked you, Lord, to send me a saint to guide me in my spiritual life and to educate me. Twelve years later [in 1960] Grace entered my life, dressed in green. At that moment You reminded me of the prayer I uttered as a young man of 18 years [1948].' Baudouin often referred to people in codes, usually with religious connotations. Lumumba was *Satan*, O'Brien *Grace*, and Suenens *Michael* [the Archangel].

The King told O'Brien that he would like to marry a devout, Catholic, 'preferably Spanish,' aristocratic girl. He referred to this woman of his heart as *Avila*, after the Spanish mystic Saint Theresa of Avila. The problem was that he did not know any devout Spanish aristocratic families. The following morning, O'Brien reported that during the night she had heard a voice from Heaven which said: 'Go to the King and suggest that you go to Spain, to prepare the way for him.' Baudouin, *Grace* and *Michael* were thrilled: the Virgin Mary herself had taken it upon her to be the royal matchmaker. O'Brien at once cancelled a series of lectures in the United States and, to the amazement of her friends, cut all her ties with the Legion of Mary. On Good Friday 15 April, she boarded a plane to Madrid. Two days later, on Easter Sunday, Suenens wrote Baudouin: 'I rejoice in what the Holy Virgin is doing. You need only to close your eyes, place your hands in hers and trust her completely.'[29]

Upon her arrival in Madrid, O'Brien went to see the Papal Nuncio. She carried a letter, written by Suenens, asking assistance in contacting Catholic aristocratic circles. The Nuncio sent the nun to the headmistress of a renowned Madrid high school for girls from wealthy Catholic families. The headmistress referred her to one of her former pupils, Fabiola Mora y Aragón, an unmarried lady of noble birth who lived on her own and spent many hours in church. At the age of 32, Fabiola was already considered an old spinster in Spain, but she knew many aristocratic families with teenage daughters.

Fabiola was a tall woman with brown eyes, dark hair and a fine-boned Goyaesque face with a high forehead under a billowing hairdo. She was the sixth of the seven children — three boys and four

28 Suenens to Baudouin, 29 Feb. 1960, in Suenens 2, p. 23.
29 Suenens to Baudouin, 17 Apr. 1960, in Suenens 2, p. 35.

girls — of Gonzalo Mora y Fernández, 4th Marquess of Casa Riera and 2nd Count of Mora. Her father, who died in 1957 at the age of 70, had been one of the largest landowners in Spain. The family lived in a palace in downtown Madrid, with 17 domestics who all had to be bachelors and were obliged to join the Moras when they prayed the rosary on their knees every evening. By the mid-1950s, all Fabiola's siblings had married and left their parents' home. Fabiola had a relationship with a young aristocrat for a while, but she did not consider him serious enough. She broke off the relationship, decided to settle for a life of her own and bought herself a single person's apartment. Every evening, she returned to the Mora Palace to have dinner with her parents. After her father died in surgery following a fall, she assisted her mother in leading the evening prayer with the servants. Every evening 19 people went on their knees to say the rosary — one widow and 18 spinsters and bachelors.

The Mora residence came to resemble a convent. Mother and daughter turned it into a shrine to the deceased count. Everyone had to wear black; television, radio and gramophone were forbidden; the clock was stopped at the hour of Count Mora's death; the telephone wire was cut so that it would never ring again; the magazine which the count had been reading was left opened on his desk on the page he had reached; his coat was left on the hook; his walking stick by the door. The beautiful garden, however, was transformed. After Count Mora's death, his widow could freely indulge in her passion for dogs. The servants were ordered to take in stray dogs. Soon, there were over fifty of them. When a television crew visited the place in 1960, they saw 'an impressive multitude of dogs let loose on an uprooted lawn.'[30]

It was this somewhat dull and presumably not very happy lady whom Veronica O'Brien went to visit at the end of April 1960, to ask for the references of some decent Catholic girls. On meeting Fabiola, 'good-looking and striking,' O'Brien heard a voice say: 'This is *Avila*.' On 30 April, she sent Baudouin a letter to tell him that 'a miracle' had happened: 'It brings tears to my eyes. If I am so touched, what feelings must rise in the Virgin Mary's heart. You cannot imagine what wonderful dreams Jesus and Mary have of you and what a source of pride and comfort you are to them already.' However, she warned: 'Satan is near. He will try to persuade you to long for something other than that which you already have.'[31] But, no, Baudouin did not want 'anything

30   Putman, p. 8.
31   O'Brien to Baudouin, 30 Apr. 1960, in Suenens 2, pp. 41–2.

other than that which he already had.' He liked all he heard about
Fabiola. Like her, he attended Mass every day and prayed the rosary
every evening. He asked *Grace* to invite *Avila* to come to Brussels to
meet him. The nun handed Fabiola a letter from Suenens in which the
latter explained that she had been chosen by Heaven to marry the
King of the Belgians. The letter ended with a call 'to walk on the water
and to believe in the love of God and of Mary, and not to exclude mir-
acles.'[32] Fabiola went to Belgium to meet Baudouin. They liked each
other and met again in July in Lourdes.

Soon they were engaged. In Madrid, Fabiola gave an interview to
the Catholic weekly *Vida Nueva*. 'King Baudouin is a saint,' she said.
'If you could only see how he prays. I assure you that even the nuns
and priests admired how he prayed. It would not be surprising if at
his death, many years from now, he were to ascend into Heaven.'[33] On
15 December 1960, they were married in Brussels. Baudouin's wedding led to a political reconciliation. Britain's Princess Margaret was
among the 4,200 guests. Fabiola persuaded her husband to resume
friendly relations with Buckingham Palace. The efforts culminated in
a State Visit by the Belgian royal couple to Great Britain in 1963, when
Baudouin was made a Knight of the Garter and an honorary Marshal
of the RAF.

Where one quarrel ended, however, another began. Fabiola disliked Baudouin's stepmother on sight. The dislike was mutual. The
two women had nothing in common. Lilian was flashy and mundane;
Fabiola was exactly the opposite. As Herman Liebaers, who was
Baudouin's *Grand Maréchal*, or head of the ceremonial office, wrote in
his memoirs: 'Baudouin did not enter a monastery; the monastery
came to him in the person of Fabiola.'[34]

With the arrival of Fabiola, there was one woman too many at
Laken Palace. Lilian felt that she was about to lose her position as
Baudouin's best friend. Their relationship came to a very abrupt end.
When the newlyweds returned to Laken from their honeymoon on 29
December 1960, they found the palace empty. Lilian, Leopold, and
their three children were gone. They had moved to Argenteuil House
near Waterloo… and they had taken the furniture and paintings with
them. 'It was a sight that I will never forget,' Eyskens recalled in his
memoirs: 'When I entered the hall of the great rotunda, I saw the

32   Suenens to 'Avila,' in Suenens 2, p. 51.
33   Quoted in Fralon, p. 227.
34   Liebaers, p. 95.

Queen standing among the suitcases. The King was sitting on a wooden trunk.'[35]

Baudouin never forgave Lilian for this humiliation. He would never again meet his stepmother, except at the funerals of the Queen Grandmother Elisabeth in 1965 and of his father in 1983. For many years, Baudouin and his brother, Crown Prince Albert, who sided with him, also refused to speak to Leopold, who was not even allowed to meet Albert's children. According to Gaspar Vuylsteke, Leopold's aide-de-camp, in order to have pictures of his grandchildren, he had 'to cut them out of magazines.'[36] In the late 1970s, the brothers met up with their father for the first time in almost two decades, but the encounter was not a happy one. They had little to say and Leopold ridiculed Baudouin's piety. After that meeting, Baudouin would occasionally telephone Leopold, but they felt no need to see each other. Leopold died at the age of 82 on 25 September 1983. Lilian survived Baudouin, and died, aged 85, in 2002.

Sadly, the joys of parenthood were not granted to Fabiola and Baudouin. In June 1961, after the royal couple visited the Vatican, Pope John XXIII announced to the Vatican press how happy he was that the Queen was expecting a baby. The Belgian press reacted in surprise, as it had not yet been informed. John XXIII was a great admirer of Baudouin. 'Once, I saw him kiss a telegram that he had received from the King on the occasion of the feast of his patron saint,' Suenens, who became the new Belgian Primate and Cardinal in 1961, relates in one of his books.[37] Unfortunately, Fabiola miscarried two weeks after the visit to Rome.

In February 1962, the Queen was pregnant again. A visit in Lausanne to Professor Rochat, a renowned Swiss gynaecologist, brought terrible news: 'Owing to a physiological defect you have only a ten per cent chance of carrying a baby to full term, and barely a five per cent chance of surviving the birth,' Rochat said.[38] A few weeks later, the Queen was delivered of a stillborn child after a four-month pregnancy. In August 1963, a new pregnancy was announced. Again, the Queen miscarried. In March 1966, the royal couple visited Pope Paul VI to receive the papal blessing over their fourth pregnancy. Fabiola made a pilgrimage to Assisi, where she crawled to the shrine of Saint Francis on her knees. In July, however, the baby died in her womb, while the Queen had to undergo urgent surgery and nearly

35   Eyskens 3, p. 626.
36   Vuylsteke in *Dag Allemaal*, 25 Feb. 1995.
37   Suenens 1, p. 96.
38   Séguy and Michelland, p. 103.

lost her own life as well. Early in 1968, Baudouin and Fabiola were in Lourdes to pray for a safe birth for their fifth unborn baby. By March, this child, too, had died in the womb. Again, the Queen had to undergo surgery. The doctors warned that every new pregnancy would endanger Fabiola's life. Baudouin and Fabiola became resigned to the fact that they would never have children.

Their grief gained them the sympathy of many Belgians. In a sense, this is a paradox because it is usually the royal children that make a monarchy popular. Laurence Van Ypersele, who studied Baudouin's popularity, has pointed out, however, that he and Fabiola were turned into a symbol of parenthood precisely because they had no children. Their image was that of 'a king-father and a Queen Mother, who were always and completely available for their subjects, as parents are for their children.'[39] To a certain extent this image had been constructed by the propaganda experts at the royal palace, but the fact that Baudouin genuinely felt like a 'king-father' and openly talked about it made their work easy. 'You know that we are childless,' the King said in a speech to a group of youngsters in 1979. 'For many years we struggled to fathom the meaning of this sorrow. But gradually we came to understand that, having no children ourselves, we have more room in our hearts to love all, truly all children.'[40]

The Fattest Lady that Ever Walked

When Baudouin succeeded to the throne, Flanders was still the poorest region of the country. Three-quarters of the Belgian unemployed lived in Flanders. Early in 1951, eleven of the seventeen Flemish administrative districts had an unemployment rate of over 10%. Wallonia, on the other hand, enjoyed full employment. Indeed, in the early 1950s, there were hardly any people out of work anywhere in Western Europe, with the exception of Flanders, which served as a permanent labour pool for Wallonia. Many Flemings had to commute. Some were away from home for more than fourteen hours a day. They had no alternative: three-quarters of Belgium's industrial activity was located along the axis of the Samber and Maas rivers in the Francophone part of the country.

Demographically, however, Flanders was becoming ever more important. In the early 1950s, it counted 183,000 families of four children or more, against only 86,000 in Wallonia. Between 1950 and 1970, the Belgian population (foreigners included) rose from 8.7 to 9.7 mil-

39   Van Ypersele 2, p. 256.
40   Laken, 19 May 1979, in Baudouin, vol. II, p. 956.

lion. This was entirely attributable to Flanders, where the number of inhabitants had grown from 4.4 to over 5.4 million, while in Wallonia it had only grown from 3.0 to 3.1 million. The bilingual district of Brussels even witnessed a drop from 1.3 to 1.1 million. The Belgian authorities refused to take this demographic shift into account in the assignment of the seats in the Chamber of Representatives. Constitutionally, there should have been one representative for every 40,000 citizens. However, 542,000 Belgians were not represented in Parliament in 1957, of whom almost 475,000 were Flemings.

The economic situation changed dramatically from the 1950s onwards, when American companies discovered the Flemish labour pool and the fact that Belgium had the lowest corporate taxes in Europe. As American companies made Flanders their base on the European continent, the Flemish commuters found jobs nearer home and were no longer prepared to work in Wallonia. Owing to this 'Anglo-Saxon interference,' the share of the Belgian economy controlled by the SG gradually fell from about 40% to 20% by the late 1970s. By 1968, 18% of Belgium's active population worked for foreign (mostly American) companies. Less than a decade later, the figure had risen to 33%.

At about the same time, the Walloon economy was running into serious problems. Oil was rapidly replacing coal as a fuel. In order to keep the Walloon coal mining competitive, the Belgian government had to give heavy subsidies. By 1958, several billions of Belgian francs were being spent annually on subsidies to the mines of the Borinage region around Mons and the Centre region around Charleroi. There coal was extracted at a real cost of 1,037 francs a ton, while it had to be sold on the market at 835 francs. The difference was made up by the Belgian taxpayers. Thanks to these subsidies, which were defended both by the SG shareholders and the trade unions, the mines worked on. After the Flemish miners had left to work for the American companies recently established in their own home towns, they were replaced by Italian immigrants.

In the 1960s and '70s, the steel works along the Brussels-Charleroi Canal and around Liège also ran into problems. They had become completely outdated and were situated too far inland, while new hyper-modern steelworks were established by the Luxemburg steel group *Arbed* along the Sea Canal to the north of the Flemish city of Ghent. More state subsidies were diverted to Wallonia in order to keep its steel production going, although the price for producing one ton of steel was a quarter higher in Wallonia than in Ghent.

From the late 1960s onwards, thousands of Moroccans were called over to work in the subsidised Belgian steel industry. As the latter came from a former French colony, they had the additional effect of strengthening the Francophone element in Belgium. By the early 1970s, Belgium's immigrant population had risen to 720,000. Some 220,000 of them made up 7.2% of the active population. The arrival of the Moroccans in the Brussels area led to serious 'racial' problems. Traditionally, the Brussels upper class had been Francophone, while the lower and middle classes consisted of Flemings. Because of the frenchification process since 1830, the middle class had gradually become Francophone as well, while the lower classes had remained Dutch. The Moroccans settled in lower class neighbourhoods, like Kuregem, Molenbeek and Schaarbeek, that were the last vestiges of Flemish culture in Brussels. The gradual transformation of these neighbourhoods into North-African ghettos drove the Flemings out. By the mid-1990s, the Dutch language in the Belgian capital was all but dead. Brussels, though situated geographically in Flanders, had become an almost entirely Francophone enclave. Moreover, its North-African Muslims, speaking French in public and Arabic or Berber at home, were extremely hostile to the efforts of Flamingant politicians to maintain Dutch as an official language in the capital. The latter came to regard the immigrants as a fifth column, a 'Trojan horse of Belgicism.'

Another Trojan horse was Europe. The European integration process started in the early 1950s with the establishment of three organisations for supranational cooperation: the *European Coal and Steel Community* (ECSC), *Euratom* (for the development of peaceful applications of nuclear energy) and the *European Economic Community* (EEC). In 1957, the three organisations were combined in the *European Communities* (EC), which, in 1993, after the *Maastricht Treaty*, was transformed into the *European Union* (EU), as an embryo for a pan-European state.

One of the 'founding fathers of Europe' was Paul-Henri Spaak. Though the Belgian Foreign Minister was generally considered to be an opportunist, he always remained loyal to Hendrik De Man's vision of Belgium as a multi-cultural social-corporatist welfare state that had to be elevated to the European level. Spaak realised that such a European superstate would sooner or later become a competitor of the United States. Hence, he saw Europe as a neutralist 'third power' alongside the Soviet Union and the United States, which (since Germany had been defeated and Britain was 'Anglo-Saxon' like the Americans) France was to lead. In March 1947, Spaak told the Russian

Ambassador in Brussels that Belgium would never join an alliance against the Soviet Union.[41]

Consequently, in the summer of 1948, he tried to thwart the establishment of the North Atlantic Treaty Organisation (NATO) by adopting an uncooperative attitude in the Working Group that convened to set up the Atlantic alliance. American diplomats complained that 'the contributions of the French and Belgian members of the Working Group have so far been exactly zero. They have come forward with no positive or constructive idea whatsoever, nor have they had anything to say about ideas that have been put forward by other people that contributed in any way to their development.'[42] The Canadian Ambassador to Belgium also noticed 'Spaak's well-known friendly attitude towards Russia.'[43] The State Department in Washington supposed that Spaak was hesitating between an Atlantic Europe and Europe as a third way because America did not sufficiently stimulate European unification.[44] Belgium's reluctance to send troops to fight in Korea in 1950 led to renewed American criticism of Brussels, but the situation greatly improved after the Americans decided to support fully Spaak's leadership of the European Movement.

The Belgian Foreign Minister chaired the Intergovernmental Conference whose conclusions were published in April 1956 in the so-called Spaak Report and which laid the foundation for the Treaty of Rome the following year. It recommended the creation of a European Common Market as a step towards political unification. 'Public opinion was indifferent,' Spaak said: 'The work was done by a minority who knew what they wanted.'[45] The British Labour leader Clement Attlee, a socialist like Spaak, but a democrat and not a corporatist, clearly perceived what was at stake when he called the ECSC 'a body appointed by no one and responsible to no one.'[46]

There was a strange consequence of Britain's initial refusal to become involved in the European integration process. The territories of the six original members of the EC (Belgium, the Netherlands, Luxemburg, West Germany, France and Italy) corresponded closely with that of the 9th century Empire of Charlemagne. According to Henri Pirenne and the Belgicists, this was the same Empire whose remnant had been Belgium. The Belgicists regarded the European

41   Coolsaet, pp. 361–2, 378–9.
42   Quoted in Reid, p. 116.
43   Quoted in Coolsaet, p. 384.
44   NAW 855.00/2–1649, Young to Secretary of State, 16 Feb. 1949.
45   Spaak, vol. II, p. 71.
46   Quoted in Eyskens 3, p. 378.

unification as a process to reassemble the pieces of Carolingian Europe and establish a 'Greater Belgium' with the Germans in the position of the Flemings and the French in that of the Walloons. The Belgian Constitution did not allow a transfer of sovereignty to a supranational level, but the Belgian politicians transferred power to 'Europe' without bothering to change the Constitution. They did not consider their country to be transferring power; it was just expanding.

In May 1957, two months after his victory in Rome, Spaak left the Belgian government, where he was replaced as Foreign Minister by his friend Victor Larock, the editor of the Socialist Party newspaper *Le Peuple*. With American backing, Spaak moved on to become Secretary General of NATO, which, according to Eyskens, he wished to transform from a military into a political and economic organisation as well. To his frustration, he did not succeed.

* * *

In the autumn of 1960, Prime Minister Gaston Eyskens's government coalition of Christian-Democrats and Liberals concluded that it was madness to continue subsidising the Walloon mines. The latter had already devoured 120 billion francs. Eyskens announced a bill, the so-called *Loi Unique* (Single Act), which abolished most subsidies, even though he had won the 1958 elections, especially in Wallonia, with a promise of big spending. According to André Renard, the charismatic leader of the Socialist Trade Union in Liège, the Francophones were the victims of 'reactionary Flemings.' Renard called for a general strike. 'We will strike your government down,' former minister Victor Larock told Eyskens.[47] During five weeks in December 1960 and January 1961, Wallonia came to a complete stand-still. Renard followed the same script as during the 1950 strike when he had forced King Leopold to abdicate: he threatened with a Walloon secession if the Fleming Eyskens did not resign. Some 700,000 Walloons joined the strike, which became violent and turned to insurrection when Socialist mayors prevented the municipal police from restoring law and order. Gangs of 'Renardists' ordered all shops and petrol stations to close down, except those holding a licence from the Socialist trade union. Railway stations were stormed, buses and trams set ablaze, trains derailed. People who refused to obey what one Minister called 'Renard's dictatorship' were beaten up and landed in hospital. According to a report by the Interior Ministry, 1,500 acts of sabotage and violence were committed. Hundreds of people were wounded and four were killed in riots.

In Flanders there were few disturbances. It was as if the Flemings and the Walloons were living in different countries. This greatly upset the Belgicist establishment, including the King. They wanted Eyskens to back down. 'I was pressured, apparently with the approval of the Court, to give in,' he says in his memoirs. If, however, the choice had to be made between Belgian unity or democracy, Eyskens knew what to choose. 'I will never give in to street violence,' he said: 'The essence of democracy is that only Parliament can bring a Prime Minister down.'[48] In the chapel at Laken, Baudouin and Fabiola prayed on their knees for national reconciliation, asking God for Eyskens' resignation. But Baudouin did more than just pray. He lent God a helping hand.

In his insistence on the primacy of Parliament, the Prime Minister risked tearing down the corporatist fabric that underpinned the Belgian state. Eyskens was, indeed, refusing to acknowledge the main principle introduced at the Loppem Coup half a century earlier. In other words, socio-economic issues should be dealt with, not by the elected politicians, but by a consensus of the so-called 'Social Partners,' that is by the three officially-recognised trade unions and the Belgicist Federation of Employers. By not recognising corporatist consensus politics, Eyskens was, in the opinion of Baudouin and the establishment, a dangerous revolutionary; it was he who had 'provoked' the Walloons to go on strike.

In her analysis of the crisis of January 1961, the historian Gita Deneckere states that Baudouin 'clearly favoured the "neo-corporatist" consensus model between the Social Partners.'[49] Taking the decisions 'outside the "normal" parliamentary procedures' allowed the King to play a prominent role behind the scenes. Baudouin 'solved' the conflict on 4 January by summoning a dozen men to the royal palace. Amongst this small group of power-brokers were August Cool, Louis Major and Armand Colle, the leaders of the Christian-Democrat, Socialist and Liberal trade unions; as well as the representatives of the three major financial-industrial conglomerates: Paul Gillet, the Governor of the SG, Count Paul de Launoit of the holding Cofinindus-Brufina, and Baron Jean-Charles Snoy et d'Oppuers of the Lambert holding. The King asked two Francophones — Franz De Voghel, the Deputy Governor of the central bank, and Professor Henri

48   Eyskens 2, p. 133.
49   Deneckere 2, p. 190.

Janne, a Socialist Senator — to defuse the situation. They succeeded with ease. Louis Major of the Socialist trade union agreed to drop Renard and call an end to the strike if the CVP dropped Eyskens and formed a left-wing goverment coalition with the Socialists in order to undo Eyskens' measures. August Cool of the Christian-Democrat trade union, who was the real boss of the CVP because he assigned the eligible places on the electoral lists of most CVP parliamentarians, accepted. De Voghel and Janne wrote a six-point basic programme for the new coalition, which was handed to the King on 15 January by the Socialist Party leader Leo Collard. All this political manoeuvring happened in secret. Nothing was known about it until Deneckere published her study in 1998.

To maintain an appearance of democracy, the 'Social Partners' allowed the Single Act to be voted on in Parliament. It passed on 13 January with 115 votes against 90 and one abstention. But Eyskens's fate had been sealed. Three weeks later, the government fell over the refusal of his own CVP to accept his proposal for redistributing the seats in Parliament according to the new demographic situation. Eyskens wanted to increase the number of MPs by at least ten additional Flemings. According to Karel Van Cauwelaert of the Christian-Democrat trade union, such a measure was not appropriate 'after the wounds which the strike against the Single Act had left in Wallonia.' Eyskens realised that he had been trapped: 'Behind my back the Christian trade union had prepared a change of the coalition.' A general election was called. The CVP did not want to have Eyskens at its electoral meetings. He was told that he was 'a provocateur.'[50]

The elections of 26 March 1961 resulted in heavy losses for the CVP. It fell from 46.5 to 41.5% of the Belgian electorate. In Flanders, it still had an absolute majority with 50.9%, although 5.6% of the Flemish voters had deserted. Seats were gained both by the Flemish-Nationalist *Volksunie* and by the Communists. They each obtained five of the 212 seats in the Chamber of Representatives — the latter exclusively in Wallonia, and the former in Flanders.

Though both the CVP and the Socialists had lost seats in the elections, they formed a left-wing coalition led by the Flemish Christian trade unionist Theo Lefevre. The Socialist heavyweight in the new cabinet, which no longer included Eyskens, was Spaak, who became Deputy Prime Minister and Minister of Foreign Affairs. Two weeks before the elections, he had resigned his function as NATO Secretary

50 Eyskens 3, pp. 636–42.

General to 'help the democrats bring Eyskens down and prevent his return to power.'[51] The first measure of the new government was the proclamation of an amnesty for everyone who had been involved in riots during the strikes. Some of the leading 'Renardists' became prominent cabinet ministers. Behind the scenes, André Renard greatly influenced the new government. Renard's unexpected death, in July 1962, at only 51 years of age, prevented his return to the political limelight in Wallonia, but his disciple, André Cools, a young MP from Liège, replaced him.

The Lefevre-Spaak cabinet undid the measures taken in the Single Act. The subsidies to money-losing industries were reintroduced. Some Walloon industries, however, had become too outdated and, hence, too expensive to keep going. In those cases, André Cools demanded that the Flemish commuters be sacked first. 'I have not been elected as a representative of the Flemish labourers,' Cools said.[52] He cared exclusively about Wallonia. Walloons who lost their jobs were taken care of by the public sector. If they joined one of the three establishment parties and/or unions, the latter gave them jobs, often in the municipal administration. Political patronage became a necessity, even for an ordinary charwoman. From the lowest to the highest levels all jobs were distributed by the governing parties on the principle of proportionality. Three decades later, 40% of Wallonia's working population was employed by municipal, provincial, regional or national government, against 'only' 25% in Flanders. Moreover, unemployment benefits — which in Belgium are financed by the state but distributed by the three 'official' unions of the Christian-Democrats, Socialists and Liberals — were raised to a level where it became rewarding *not* to have a job. By being officially unemployed and working on the sly (doing odd jobs for relatives, neighbours, friends and friends' friends), some unschooled labourers were able to earn a higher income than by being regularly employed. Belgium became the country with the highest percentage of social beneficiaries in the world; the only country with more people receiving benefits from the state than working for a living. The so-called 'dependency ratio' reached 107% in 1997, compared to 94.1% in France, 88.3% in Germany, 79.4% in Britain, 77.5% in the Netherlands, 70% in Japan and 50.8% in the United States.[53]

51   Spaak in *Le Peuple*, 4 Mar. 1961.
52   Quoted in Ruys 2, p. 197.
53   Figures provided by the Belgian Ministry of Social Affairs, in *De Standaard*, 19 Nov. 2001.

During the Golden Sixties, when the Belgian economy was booming with an annual average growth of 5.4%, the state was able to pay these generous 'social benefits,' although taxes were raised substantially to fund them. As the economic growth was mainly generated in Flanders, great flows of money, the so-called 'social transfers,' passed from Flemish taxpayers to Wallonia in the form of subsidies and welfare benefits. Corporate tax went up, as did income tax. The latter rose so drastically that the government included a provision in the tax bill stating that the amount of income tax an individual had to pay should not exceed 50% of his total income.

The Belgians had not wanted this to happen. Indeed, the 1965 elections dealt a severe blow to the Lefevre-Spaak cabinet, while the opposition parties — the Liberals as well as the Flemish-Nationalist *Volksunie* — gained votes. At the national level, the CVP fell by 6.0% to 34.5% of the electorate. In Flanders, it lost its absolute majority, dropping to 44.3%. The Socialists lost 8.4% of the national electorate and ended at 28.3%. The Liberals gained 9.3% of the national vote and jumped to 21.6%. The *Volksunie* more than doubled to 6.7% of the Belgian electorate (and 11.2% of the Flemish).

As in 1961, however, the losers teamed up to form a new coalition, continuing the policies that the electorate had rejected. The same thing happened after the 1968 elections, when the CVP and the Socialists lost again; they simply continued as if they had received a new mandate. Belgians had become used to this pattern since the 1918 Loppem Coup. In fact, only 9 of the 57 20th-century cabinets which were formed since that coup marked the beginning of the corporatist regime in Belgium reflected the verdict of the voters. Most coalitions simply departed from the rule that they had to include the biggest party in Flanders (which was the CVP) and the biggest party in Wallonia (the Socialists). This was also what the King preferred.

All the while, the tax burden continued to grow. By 1978, the level which an individual's total income tax was not allowed to exceed had been raised to 67.5% of his income. Indeed, with a marginal tax rate at 80%, there were people whose after-tax income was only 32.5% of the sum they had actually earned. Belgium had become, as one minister later acknowledged, 'a fiscal Himalaya.'[54] In the late 1990s, the marginal tax rate was brought down to 55%. Corporate tax stood at 40.17%.

---

54 Mark Eyskens, Belgian Minister of Finance, in *The Wall Street Journal Europe*, 14 Oct. 1986.

The Flemish economy continued booming until 1973, when it caused the Belgian GNP to grow by 6.5%. Then, the party was over as a result of the international recession. By 1975, Belgium's economic growth had fallen to 1.8%; by 1981, it stood at 1.9%. The economic crisis led to additional unemployment, which the government countered by employing additional civil servants. Government spending went up from 34% of GNP in the mid-1960s to 42.7% in 1973, and to 50% in 1976. The 1970s saw the creation of 200,000 new jobs in the public sector. Finally, by 1985, Belgium, with its 10 million inhabitants and a labour force of 4.2 million, had 500,000 people on the dole and 830,000 working for the government — which meant that the income of more than 1.3 million Belgians (or 20% of the voting population) was being provided directly by the state. Belgium had ended up with as many state employees as the Netherlands (15 million inhabitants) and one of the largest public sectors in Western Europe. With 7.7 employees in state educational services for every 100 Belgians up to 24 years of age, compared to 6.9 in Britain, 4.3 in the Netherlands and 2.7 in Germany (West). With an annual state subsidy of $12,000 for each employee in the mining industry, as opposed to $3,000 in Germany (West). With an annual government subsidy of $385 million for the postal services, compared to only $65 million in Germany (West). With a government subsidy of 8.3 Belgian francs for every kilometre travelled by every railway passenger, compared with 2.7 francs for the Netherlands, 2.4 francs in Britain and 1.7 francs in Switzerland.

In late November 1985, a 32-year-old Fleming, Guy Verhofstadt, became Deputy Prime Minister and Minister of the Budget. Like Gaston Eyskens 25 years earlier, in an apparent fit of political iconoclasm, he attempted to abolish the subsidy mechanism and began to rock Belgium's corporatist boat. 'The Flemings are being dragged down by the South, by the paralysis of its leading establishment — the Francophone Socialist trade union, the *Parti Socialiste* and the Walloon Employers,' he wrote.[55] As Verhofstadt belonged to the Liberal Party, the coalition's junior party, his position was, however, not as strong as Eyskens' had been. As soon as rumours spread, in the spring of 1986, about Verhofstadt's plans to cut government spending, the trade unions went on strike. Again, as in 1961, Flanders remained relatively calm, but Wallonia was brought to a standstill by a general strike of state employees in May 1986.

Verhofstadt was at once toned down by the Christian-Democrat Prime Minister Wilfried Martens and by the Minister of Social Affairs,

---

55   Verhofstadt, p. 38.

Jean-Luc Dehaene, the watchdog of the Christian Trade Union in the cabinet. The union ordered his removal from the government. King Baudouin agreed. He told Martens to form a government with the Socialists instead of continuing with the Liberals. 'Personally I would have preferred to continue with Verhofstadt,' Martens later said, 'but I could not refuse the King's request.'[56] He resigned and put together a new cabinet, this time one of the CVP and the Socialists. It continued the old tax-and-spend policies. Verhofstadt remained in opposition for twelve years, until he had lost his revolutionary fervour and had accepted Belgium's corporatist structure. He became Prime Minister in 1999 in a leftist coalition of Liberals, Socialists and Greens, which increased the government subsidies to the three official trade unions within its first year in office.

* * *

The failure of the young Verhofstadt to abolish the 'social transfers' forced the Belgian government not only to raise taxes even further, but also to borrow money on a scale that was unprecedented anywhere in the Western world. Belgium's annual budget deficits were twice as high as the EC average. In July 1981, Budget Minister and Deputy Prime Minister, Guy Mathot, a Walloon Socialist, told his party conference that he could not care less: 'The deficit appeared by itself, it will also go away by itself.' But, unfortunately, it did not. On the contrary, the record deficits (12.4% in 1982) added up to a gigantic government debt. In 1985, the total debt of the Belgian State exceeded the amount the Belgians earned over the whole year. Indeed, the 1985 public debt was 5.07 trillion francs, or 101% of that year's GNP. A *Wall Street Journal* leader-writer referred to Belgium as 'the fattest lady that ever walked.'[57] At the end of 1988, the national debt had reached 114% of GNP. It peaked at 138.8% — the highest figure in any Western country — in 1993, the year of Baudouin's death, before the government was able to stop it from growing any further. The fat lady collapsed under her own weight as most tax revenues were devoted to paying off interests on old debts, while essential public services were rapidly deteriorating for lack of capital.

Unwilling and unable to cut back its 'social' expenditure, the government had for decades neglected the state's primary duty: the protection of its citizens. Since the mid-1970s, the police and the judiciary had no longer been given the necessary funds to function adequately.

---

56 Quoted in De Ridder, Hugo 3, p. 236. Also Martens in *Humo*, 24 August 2004.
57 *The Wall Street Journal Europe*, 16 Oct. 1985.

Underpaid and understaffed, with out-dated equipment and infrastructure and poor working conditions, caught up in a patronage system where the support of an establishment party and/or union is
more important than competence for the advancement of one's
career, police officers and judges lost their motivation. The signs were
there for all to see when in the 1980s the country fell victim to waves of
extremely violent crime. In 1982, 60 post offices were raided; in 1984,
the figure had risen to over 200; in 1985, almost 300 offices were
raided, before the government assigned the postal services the money
to protect its offices, staff and clients. In a series of 14 raids (mostly in
broad daylight) on stores and supermarkets between August 1982
and November 1985, the so-called 'Crazy Brabant Killers' shot dead
29 people. The police were unable to catch the culprits. The affair
remains the greatest unsolved murder case in Western Europe.

In September 1989, Roger Van Camp, the highest-ranking prosecut-
ing magistrate in the Court of Appeals in Antwerp, complained that
his court had a backlog of over 18,500 civil lawsuits. He called it 'a
qualified form of refusal to do justice on the part of the State, and there
is nothing we can do about it.' Antiquated methods and bad conditions slowed down the legal machinery. They also hampered investigations and prosecutions in criminal cases. Van Camp warned that
'very serious white collar crime, several cases of criminal violence,
thefts and even crimes involving drugs' were going unpunished
because the authorities lacked the means to do anything about it.[58]
Not surprisingly, a decade later Antwerp was a centre of Albanian,
Russian, Georgian and Chinese mafia organisations and triads, smuggling diamonds, weapons and drugs.

In the absence of a strong police and judiciary, Belgium became a
cornucopia of scandals with a high incidence of administrative and
political corruption, money laundering, graft, kickbacks in high
places, and even political assassination. In July 1991, the Socialist
Party leader André Cools was murdered execution-style on a parking
lot in Liège, possibly because he was blackmailing a party member,
Alain Van der Biest, the Belgian Minister of Pensions. Van der Biest
committed suicide in March 2002, before he could be brought to court.
The authorities discovered, however, that Cools himself was
involved in the Agusta and Dassault corruption cases, dealing with
the purchase of military helicopters and aircraft in the late 1980s. It
emerged that the Socialist Party had been bribed in both cases. One of
the other top politicians in the Agusta case was King Baudouin's

---

58   Quoted in *The Wall Street Journal Europe*, 16 May 1990.

favourite politician, the Belgicist Fleming Willy Claes, the then Minister of Economic Affairs, who had to resign as NATO Secretary General in 1995 because the Belgian judiciary wanted to prosecute him. Claes, found guilty of taking bribes, was 'slapped' in September 1998 with a three-year suspended prison sentence and a fine, which his party paid for him. He remained a respected 'elder statesman' and contrived to have his daughter succeed him in Parliament. One army General closely involved in the Dassault affair, Jacques Lefebvre, died in mysterious circumstances in a Brussels hotel room in March 1995.

Also found guilty of corruption in these or similar cases were Etienne Mangé, the head of the Belgian Postal Services and the treasurer of the Socialist Party; and the so-called 'three Guys:' Guy Coëme, the former Minister of Defence, Guy Mathot, a former Deputy Prime Minister, and Guy Spitaels, the President of the Socialist Party and also a former Deputy Prime Minister. Mathot was involved in numerous erotic 'adventures' as well. He was a womaniser, who, as his party leader Spitaels pointedly remarked, '*montre son zizi à tout le monde*' (shows his willy to everyone).[59]

The Christian-Democrats had their crooks, as well. The most notorious was Paul Vanden Boeynants. When this former Prime Minister was convicted in 1985, the judge called him 'an incorrigible swindler.' He did not have to serve his three-year gaol sentence, however, because of 'the services he had rendered to the country.' Yet, he felt he had been done a great injustice: 'I have stolen from no one, except the state,' he said.[60] His voters loved him for it. They considered Vanden Boeynants to be one of them, because, like them, he looked upon the State as a vehicle for personal enrichment. He was their role model.

Worst of all was the corruption of the ordinary man. The 'social transfer' mechanism inevitably led to the corruption of Wallonia. In effect, its politicians told the electorate: if you vote for us, we guarantee that the State will never check whether you really need the social security handouts you receive or not. In return, the electorate allowed the politicians to do whatever they wanted. Four decades after the 1960–61 strike against the Single Act, Caroline De Gruyter, a journalist from the Netherlands, visited the Borinage region in the Hainaut province. She was amazed to meet several families that had been on the dole for three generations and did not have a single relative officially with a job. The families concerned were very pleased with this situation: 'Once the miners were exploited by the state; now we

59   Quoted in Ruys 2, p. 199.
60   *De Standaard*, 13 Jan. 2001; *Knack*, 17 Jan. 2001.

exploit the state,' one of the unemployed told her. They all voted for the Socialist Party, because it guaranteed that nothing would change and that Flemish money would keep on flowing to Wallonia. They described the attitude of Flemish-Nationalists 'who do not want to pay taxes to support the Walloon jobless' as 'unsocial behaviour!' One of the things that struck De Gruyter was the fact that the people of the Borinage admitted to lacking all sense of shame. It prompted her to call them 'a Community beyond Shame.' Many even boasted that the paedophile Marc Dutroux, who acquired international notoriety in the late 1990s, was one of them.[61]

Eager for ever more money, in June 2000 the Walloon authorities asked for additional subsidies from the European Union to support their region with its unemployment rate of 16% (compared with only 6% in Flanders). The unemployment rate was over 30% in the Borinage and some other parts of Hainaut. Between 1994 and 2000, Hainaut had already received 60 billion francs (£900 million or $1.5 billion) from the European reconstruction funds, and an additional 50 billion (£750 million or $1.25 billion) had been promised until 2006. At the same time, however, entrepreneurs from the adjacent province of West-Flanders were complaining that they were unable to fill up their job vacancies because the unemployed from nearby Hainaut were *refusing* to work in Flanders. The Walloon Socialist Minister of Employment declared on the latter's behalf that 'notwithstanding the free traffic of employees within Europe, no one can be forced to go and work across the linguistic border.'[62]

In 2003, Flanders, with 58% of the Belgian population, financed 64.3% of Belgium's social security benefits and received only 57.6% in return. During the 1990s, it paid the Francophones an annually increasing sum, equalling 3.5% of Flemish GDP in 1990, 3.8% in 1999 and 4.2% in 2003. Paradoxically, these 'solidarity payments' proved to be exactly the reason why Flanders could not fill up its 30,000 job vacancies: the 250,000 unemployed in Wallonia refused to accept Flemish jobs because the Flemish taxpayers were already providing them with a handsome income for doing nothing.

The Great Leap Forwards

A puzzling question is why the Flemings have accepted this permanent drain on their national resources. The answer is *federalism*. The latter has made it constitutionally impossible to abolish the 'social

61   *NRC-Handelsblad,* 5 May 2001; *De Standaard,* 12 May 2001.
62   Marie Arena in *De Standaard,* 26 Aug. 2000.

transfers' and the 'solidarity payments.' Between 1970 and 1993 Belgium was transformed, through four revisions of the Belgian Constitution, into a federal state where democratic majority rule was neutralised. The process was completed a few weeks before King Baudouin died of heart failure in July 1993.

The 1960–61 strike against the Single Act had focused on more than the reintroduction of the subsidies to the mines. André Renard, the leader of the strike, made political demands as well. He saw federalism as a means towards preventing the Flemings from meddling in Wallonia's affairs and 'suffocating its social experiment and anti-capitalist reforms.' The Belgian Federation would have to provide the money, but Wallonia would be free to decide what to do with it.[63]

Renard was a political genius — probably the greatest one that Belgium ever had apart from Leopold I, Emile Waxweiler and Hendrik De Man. He perceived that the emancipation of Belgium's Dutch-speaking majority within a unitary state would inevitably lead to 'reactionary Flanders' imposing its will on Wallonia. Therefore, he proposed to turn Belgium into a federal union of a Flemish and a Walloon state, with both states assuming an equal status at federal level. This would give the Francophones a 50% say in government instead of the 40% that they would eventually end up with in a unitary Belgium. If Brussels were also to become a constituent state of the federation, the Francophones would even have a permanent majority position of two-to-one, as Brussels was now overwhelmingly Francophone.

One of the architects of federalism in Belgium, Wilfried Martens, explained in January 1972 what it was all about: 'Flanders is not allowed to dominate Belgium because this will cause the country to explode. The federal construct is designed precisely to prevent this happening. This implies that Flanders yield its power.'[64] Martens was an ambitious 35-year-old politician. In his youth he had been a Flamingant, opposed to the yielding of Flemish power. By 1972, however, the cynical Martens had allied himself with the Belgian establishment.

At first, the 'Renardist' idea of federalism, which after Renard's death in 1962 had been adopted by the powerful Liège branch of the Socialist Party, did not receive the support of the Belgicist establishment nor of the King. They feared that federalisation would be a first step towards the unravelling of the country. But, by 1968, the establishment had been traumatised by a number of incidents that convinced them that Belgium was growing into a Flemish-dominated

63   Meynen, pp. 207 and 244.
64   Quoted in De Ridder, Hugo 4, p. 75.

state — an '*état belgo-flamand*.' This began with two huge protest demonstrations in the streets of Brussels, in which over 100,000 Flamingants participated. The first occurred in October 1961, the second in October 1962. The demonstrations forced the government to take a number of pro-Flemish measures such as the delineation of language boundaries and of Brussels' city limits and the acknowledgement that in Flanders, with the exception of bilingual Brussels, Dutch was the only official language.

But the real traumatic experience for the Belgicists was the conflict over Leuven. The pride of this Dutch-speaking town was its university, the oldest in the Netherlands, which had been established in 1425 by Duke Jan IV of Brabant. The university was run by the Catholic bishops. Originally the academic language had been Latin, but in the course of the late 19th and early 20th centuries, Latin had been replaced by the vernacular, which in Leuven according to the bishops was... French. Gradually, some courses had been organised in Dutch as well, resulting in the 1930s in a bilingual university. In 1966, the students demanded that their university based in Flanders should become a Dutch university. Cardinal Suenens reacted in the fashion of his predecessors Van Roey and Mercier. In an authoritarian pastoral letter, the bishops 'ordered' the professors and students to accept that Leuven be partly French, and warned that they would 'not tolerate' any dissent. Times had changed, however, since the days of Van Roey and Mercier: the rigid Belgicist commands of the bishops were no longer accepted. The pastoral letter led to widespread indignation. The students went on strike, backed by the majority of the professors and Flemish public opinion. The Leuven letter caused the bishops to lose much of their authority in Flanders, not only on political, but also on religious and moral issues. Some Flamingants even went so far as to argue that the Flemish submissiveness to the Catholic Church in the past had been Flanders' undoing. When the Flamingant banker Lode Claes became a Senator for the *Volksunie* in 1968, Baudouin invited him to dinner in Laken. Asked by the King why the Flemings had protested so little against their humiliations since 1830, Claes answered: 'Because they are Catholics, Your Majesty. If only 15 per cent of them had been Protestants, then the whole history of Belgium would have been different. Their Catholic meekness plays them false.' At this Fabiola abruptly put down her knife and fork and left the room in silence but visibly angry, and did not return.[65] Lode Claes was never again invited to Laken.

---

65   Pauwels and Verstraete, p. 11.

In the spring of 1968, after months of student agitation and numerous protest demonstrations, the bishops finally gave in. All Francophone courses at Leuven University were abolished. The Belgian establishment suddenly realised that it could no longer count on the Church, the institution that had so far been its most forceful ally in keeping the Flemings in check. The shock was so great that the Vanden Boeynants government fell over the Leuven affair after Flemings and Walloons within the cabinet started quarrelling, and the political parties split along linguistic lines. For the very religious Baudouin, Leuven came as a double shock. It was a sign of Flemish rebellion against both Catholicism and Belgicism. The old Belgium — *la Belgique de papa*, as it came to be called — was dead. It was time to design a new one.

The following summer, Vanden Boeynants negotiated a coalition of Christian-Democrats and Socialists with André Cools and other leading Renardists. They agreed to rewrite the Belgian Constitution in a federalist sense. The 1970 Constitution confined the borders of Brussels to 19 urban municipalities. The Flemings insisted on confining Brussels, because the outward movement of wealthy Francophones from the capital to the surrounding green countryside of Flemish Brabant was causing the number of Francophones there to rise steadily. Francophones who moved out of the 19 municipalities would have to accept that they were moving into Dutch-speaking Flanders. In the capital itself, where by 1970 the number of Flemings had dwindled below 30%, half the top jobs in executive functions and the public services were set aside for Flemings. In return, Flanders accepted the application of the same principle at national level. In future, half the Belgian cabinet would consist of Francophones. The same 'parity principle' applies for judges in the Supreme Court, army officers, Belgian diplomats and leading civil servants. The Flemings regarded this as a victory because, until 1970, the Francophones held more than half the top jobs, even though they comprised only 40% of the population.

The parity rule also came to apply with regard to government infrastructure investments. As a result, Wallonia — larger than Flanders in area and less populous — boasts a great number of highways that are hardly used. The oddest trade-off happened in 1979 when in return for Wallonia allowing the Flemings to establish a Dutch-language primary school in the village of Komen, a 10 kilometre strip of highway was constructed between the Walloon villages of Pecq and Armentières. In 2001, the Francophone Socialist leader Elio Di Rupo vetoed the construction of a new railroad in the harbour of Antwerp because the state did not have the money for equivalent works in Wallonia. When Flanders proposed to pay for the Antwerp railroad exclusively with Flemish money, Di Rupo remained unmoved. He believed that even this arrangement would undermine the parity or 'solidarity' principle that not a single franc was allowed to be spent in the north if the south did not (or could not) spend one as well.

Another novelty of the 1970 Constitution was the so-called 'bolt mechanism.' This implied that for all future changes to the Belgian institutional framework, not only an overall two-thirds majority in Parliament was needed, but also a 50 per cent majority in every language group. This bolted the door to democratic majority rule in Belgium. In order to ensure that a measure did not pass, it was sufficient that 44 of the 87 Francophones amongst the 212 delegates in the Chamber of Representatives voted against it, even if the other 168 MPs were all in favour of it. The Constitution of 1970 turned Belgium into a country dominated by the majority within the minority — in other words, by the Renardist Left in Wallonia. The Flemings accepted this because they had been able to define the borders of Brussels and guarantee for themselves half the political power in the capital. But the latter proved to be a Pyrrhic victory, because of the two Trojan horses of Belgicism that were beginning to enter Brussels in the early 1970s: the immigrants and Europe.

The integration of thousands of Moroccan immigrants in Brussels was severely hampered by the fact that these North-African newcomers did not see the point of learning Dutch in a city that was predominantly Francophone. The bilingual status of Brussels, however, meant that most jobs required at least a basic knowledge of Dutch. Soon, the Flamingants were blamed for blocking the upward social mobility of the immigrants. Under the pressure of immigration, the Flemish politicians were compelled to renounce the protected status of Dutch in Brussels. In 2001, the parity in Brussels was abolished, although at national level it was not.

The Belgian capital also became the capital of the European Community. This led to another type of immigrant: thousands of well-to-do European civil servants. Many of these Eurocrats preferred to live outside the 19 Brussels municipalities and settled in villas in the nearby Flemish countryside. As most of them spoke French but no Dutch, their presence strengthened the frenchification process. The pressure to extend bilingual Brussels into six or more Flemish suburban municipalities steadily grew. Even in 1958, Wilfried Martens — then still a Flamingant — had warned that the Belgicists would 'use the status of Brussels as the capital of Europe to keep the Flemings out of power.'[66] Paul-Henri Spaak, the EC's Founding Father, seems to have realised this. The expansion of Brussels was the political goal of the last years of his life. He joined a newly established political party, the *Front des Francophones* (FDF), that fought for an enlargement of Brussels beyond the 19 municipalities. After Spaak's death in 1972, his daughter Antoinette Spaak became the FDF party leader. Many members of the Belgian establishment sympathised with the FDF. One of the FDF leaders was Jean Van Ryn, the attorney of former king Leopold III. Viscount Etienne Davignon, the Belgian European Commissioner from 1977 to 1985, was also close to the FDF.

In the 1971 general elections, the FDF gained 28% of the votes in the constituency of Greater-Brussels (the 19 Brussels boroughs plus 35 surrounding municipalities of Flemish Brabant). The government could no longer resist its demands when in the 1974 general elections it obtained an absolute majority in the 19 municipalities. Brussels became a de facto third region of Belgium, next to Flanders and Wallonia. The logic of Belgian politics pressured Prime Minister Leo Tindemans, a CVP politician from Antwerp, to accept the FDF in his government coalition. Formerly, when Belgium only consisted of two regions — Flanders and Wallonia — the golden rule had always been that a cabinet had to be formed with representatives of the biggest parties from both regions. Now, however, Brussels had been added as a separate district. Consequently, the coalition had to be one of CVP, Socialists *and* FDF.

In October 1978, however, in a dramatic political kamikaze attempt in front of the television cameras, Tindemans brought down his own government in order to thwart an arrangement between the CVP party leader Wilfried Martens, the Socialist leader André Cools and FDF leader Antoinette Spaak to institute bilingual status far into Flemish Brabant. 'It was the only honourable option,' Tindemans later declared, complaining about the arrogance of Cools: 'He was extremely brutal. You were his servant, or you were destroyed.'[67] Tindemans was destroyed. Though he became Flanders' most popular politician and the only one who succeeded in leading his party to an electoral victory in the second-half of the 20th-century, Tindemans never returned as Prime Minister because of a veto from the King and the Walloon Socialists. On 27 January 1979, Baudouin and Cools agreed that they would have Martens, the Flamingant-turned-Belgicist who had become the figurehead of the Christian-Democrat

66 Quoted in De Ridder, Hugo 4, p. 193.
67 Tindemans in *De Standaard*, 10 Mar. 2001.

trade union in the CVP, form a new coalition. Even though the Flemish voters had rejected it, a new cabinet of CVP, Socialists and FDF was put together.

Martens was a godsend to Baudouin. He became the King's loyal servant, complying with his every wish, leading nine cabinets of varying composition in a twelve-year period. In 1991, Jean-Luc Dehaene, another confidant of the Christian-Democrat trade union, succeeded him after the CVP had been severely beaten in the elections that marked the breakthrough of the first openly secessionist Flemish party since the war, the *Vlaams Blok*. In his 12 years in office, Martens quadrupled the Belgian government debt from 2,000 to over 8,000 billion francs and brought his party down from 48.1% of the Flemish electorate (the 1979 European elections won by Tindemans) to 26.9% (1991 general elections). Eight years of the same policies under Dehaene further raised the debt to 11,000 billion francs and reduced the votes of the CVP to 22.2% (1999 general elections).

Though Belgium had 21 different government cabinets between 1970 and 2000, the regime was not unstable. The governments mostly fell over minor issues and were soon patched up again with the same politicians. Ministerial careers of 5 to 8 years were common. Dehaene, Tindemans and Vanden Boeynants were cabinet members for 18 years; Mark Eyskens (the son of Gaston) for 16 years; Martens and Willy Claes for 12 years; André Cools for 10 years. The champion was Jos Chabert of the CVP. He was a minister for 24 years. Nepotism was another characteristic of Belgian politics. The Christian-Democrats Eyskens, Nothomb and Aspremont-Lynden; the Socialists Anseele, Van Acker and Tobback; the Liberals Janson, Vanderpoorten and Michel are but a few names of families with a minister in two, sometimes even in three, generations. The list of parliamentary dynasties is even longer. Nowhere in the world does the phenomenon of ministerial careers spanning almost two decades and ministerial and parliamentary careers passing from one generation to another exist to the same degree as in Belgium. With the 21st-century approaching, nepotism became even worse. In 1999, Louis Michel, Belgium's Foreign Minister, had his son Charles appointed Walloon Minister of the Interior. The boy was barely 23 years old and became a cabinet member upon leaving university.

In corporatist Belgium, all decisions are taken by a small circle. Ministers can only survive if they are subservient to the real powers of corporatism — the Crown and the 'Social Partners.' The *Belgian disease* is an appalling system of patronage and nepotism that stifles all transparancy, democratic control and economic development. The

Christian-Democrat trade union grew immensely rich thanks to its loyal CVP politicians. When the Belgian franc was devalued by 8.5% in February 1982, that decision had been taken by a small group of four: the trade union's chief economist Alfons Verplaetse, the chairman of the trade union's bank Hubert Detremmerie, Prime Minister Wilfried Martens, and the latter's *chef de cabinet* Jacques Van Ypersele de Strihou, a financial wizard who had previously presided over the European Monetary Committee. The Governor of the Belgian central bank, who was opposed to the devaluation, was not informed. Verplaetse succeeded him a few years later.

It has often been suggested that Detremmerie's bank used inside information about the impending devaluation for its own profit. This claim has never been investigated. In his memoirs Leo Tindemans writes that it is curious that a trade union leader and a private banker can decide a devaluation. He says that such practices 'cast doubt on the meaning of elections, on respect for the institutions and their competences, and on the significance of the elected politicians in a democracy.'[68] It has also been said that the Belgian royal family sold its Belgian financial assets and transferred its fortune to the United States shortly before the devaluation.[69] Following the devaluation, Ypersele, Martens's 'financial wizard,' was employed by Baudouin as his own *chef de cabinet*.

The Christian-Democrat trade union also made a fortune on real estate in Brussels' Leopold Quarter. It bought large parts of the neighbourhood at low prices in the 1980s, a few weeks before Martens publicly announced that the Belgian government intended to build the new offices of the European Parliament in the Leopold Quarter. The Belgian press hardly questioned these practices. Most newspapers were either linked to one of the traditional political parties or owned by the 'Social Partners.' Moreover, the papers all received government subsidies making them subservient to the regime they were supposed to scrutinise. 'Belgians know that the Belgian press is not a good place to look for information about what's going on in Belgium,' an American journalist based in Brussels wrote in 1990: 'In the popular image, the Belgian press is a network of private clubs dominated by political parties. What the politicians don't want said, isn't said.'[70] Laken, too, bought itself the adherence of the press. Some editors,

---

68 Tindemans, p. 446.
69 Polspoel and Van Den Driessche, p. 228.
70 *The Wall Street Journal Europe*, 11 Apr. 1990.

such as Frans Verleyen of the leading Flemish magazine *Knack*, were even invited to accompany the King on private holidays abroad.

Martens and Dehaene led Belgium through three further revisions of the Constitution (those of 1980, 1988–89 and 1993) while Verhofstadt added yet another (in 2001). These bestowed upon Brussels virtually the same status as Flanders and Wallonia, reduced the official representation of the Flemings in Brussels to 20 per cent (while retaining the parity system at national level) and saddled the country with extremely complicated institutional structures.

Belgium is an asymmetrical federal state, consisting of two types of member states on two different levels. The Belgian Federation is made up of three so-called 'Communities' — Flemish, Francophone and German-speaking — and three 'Regions' — Flanders, Wallonia (which includes nine German-speaking municipalities) and Brussels. Broadly speaking, the Communities deal with 'people-related matters,' such as culture, education, youth protection, etc., but not with social security nor health care, because there the 'solidarity principle' must prevail. The Regions deal with 'territory-related matters,' such as urban planning, environment, economic development, employment, public works, transport, etc., but not with matters that are regarded to be of strategic importance such as the railroads, the postal services and Brussels international airport, which is located in Zaventem in Flanders.

The Communities and the Regions all have their own parliaments and governments, but those of the Flemish Community and the Flemish Region overlap, while the others do not. Hence, Belgium boasts six different legislatures and six executives: apart from the federal parliament and government, there are also the Flemish, the Walloon, the Brussels, the Francophone and the German-speaking parliaments and governments.[71] The federal level decides about constitutional matters, foreign and defence policy, justice, the maintenance of law and order, economic and monetary policy, and social security plus health care. Because the welfare departments are federally organised, the

---

71   In 1985, the Fleming Toon Van Overstraeten got elected into the Walloon Parliament. Amongst his voters were inhabitants of formerly Flemish municipalities, like Waterloo, which since Belgian independence had been frenchified and transferred to Wallonia while retaining a Flemish minority of some 15 per cent. The other members of the Walloon legislative body unanimously refused to allow Van Overstraeten to participate in their meetings and excluded him. Christian Van Eyken, a Francophone elected in the Flemish Parliament in 1995, was, however, allowed to take his seat because the Flemish Parliament did not consider it correct to ban someone who had been democratically elected.

'social transfers' keep flowing from the Flemings to the Franco-phones. Fiscal issues have also remained at federal level, because, as the Walloon Socialist leader Elio Di Rupo, said, 'lowering taxes in Flanders is dangerous for the Belgian Union. This will jeopardise the Belgian economic and monetary union. Moreover, it is absurd to introduce divergences in taxation between Flanders and Wallonia at a moment when a fiscal harmonisation process is going on between the member states of the European Union.'[72] The Communities and the Regions receive most of their money from the Belgian Federation according to a proportional stipend, with Flanders receiving 55% from the Community pool and 57.5% from the Regional provisions, although according to its tax contributions it is entitled to 64%.

* * *

The institutional complexity of asymmetrical federal Belgium made its institutions almost impregnable. Political responsibility became very difficult to pin down, leaving the real Powers of Corporatism more room for manoeuvring behind the scenes. Baudouin realised that this allowed the Crown to strengthen its own position. He also took the les-son from his grandfather King Albert I to heart: the monarchy had to ally itself to the Francophone Socialists. No wonder their leader Guy Spitaels could triumph in his May Day speech of 1988: 'We, Francophones, we, Walloons, have won. Brussels will be a state on a par with Flanders and Wallonia, and the national solidarity mechanism will be to our advantage.'[73] Two months later, in a televised speech to the nation, Baudouin stressed that the Belgian federal system had to 'promote unity, maintain solidarity between the various member states, and reject any form of separatism, overt or covert.'[74]

The King did not want the Flemings to question the 'social trans-fers.' He considered the 'solidarity' between the Belgians to be a moral imperative. 'You can see that Wallonia is an economic sham-bles,' he told a Flemish politician, 'you, Flemings, who control every-thing, must not act so greedily.'[75] When the journalist Hugo De Ridder was appointed the chief editor of the leading Flemish newspa-per *De Standaard*, Baudouin received him at the royal palace and inter-rogated him about his views. 'I have already frequently stressed that we had better not calculate the exact amount of the transfers, because

72   Quoted in *De Standaard*, 27 June 2000.
73   Quoted in De Ridder, Hugo 3, p. 180.
74   21 July 1988, in Baudouin, vol. II, p. 1295. An English translation of this speech can be found in Hermans, pp. 447–9.
75   Quoted in Polspoel and Van Den Driessche, p. 82.

otherwise Flemish public support for the social security system risks disappearing,' De Ridder said. 'I have just heard a wise man,' the King replied.[76]

The official figure of the 'social transfers' from Flanders to Wallonia — 6.6 billion euros or 4.2% of Flanders' GDP in 2003 — is generally regarded as being deliberately underestimated. Bart De Wever, the leader of the New Flemish Alliance, a group of Flemish separatists elected in the Flemish Regional Parliament on a platform with the Christian-Democrats, claimed that the real 2003 figure amounted to 11.3 billion euros or 7.2% of Flanders' GDP. For Wallonia this constitutes a bonus to its budget of almost 20% of its own regional GDP.

In his speeches to the nation, Baudouin invariably referred to the need for intra-Belgian 'solidarity.' His speeches were highly political statements wrapped in moralistic phrases. Contrary to other Western-European monarchies, like Britain and the Netherlands, royal speeches in Belgium emanate from the King, not from the Government. Since the early 1980s the King annually addressed the nation via the media on at least three occasions: somewhere in late January, on the national holiday of 21 July, and on Christmas Eve. His speeches sounded like sermons, which in a sense they were. Since the bishops no longer issued pastoral letters, the *King-Priest* did. Baudouin was genuinely convinced that the existence of Belgium was part of God's plan. He had been raised in the tradition of Belgicist Catholicism. In his opinion, Belgicism and Catholicism were of the same order: unifying elements that bind people of different languages and cultures together into something '*katolikos*' — something *universal*. Belgium had to show the world that a universal supra-national federal state was a possibility. It had to be a beacon to the world.

Baudouin's prayer intentions were often political, but he prayed with the intensity of a saint. Cardinal Suenens frequently came to join him. He was the King's closest advisor. According to Grand Maréchal Liebaers the King saw Suenens more frequently than his ministers. 'Lord, Thou knowest the fear I carry with me,' Baudouin prayed: 'The situation in Belgium worries me. What shall happen to Cockerill-Sambre [the biggest Walloon steelworks]? Jesus, watch over my country.'[77] He was convinced that God had made him King precisely for the purpose of praying and suffering for Belgium. The country needed him because it was so precious and fragile that he had to watch over it as a father over a sick child. 'Belgium is a *pays*

76   Conversation on 14 July 1989, in De Ridder, Hugo 7, p. 139.
77   Quoted in Suenens 2, p. 92.

d'incertitude,' Professor Roger Lallemand, a longtime Francophone Socialist MP, wrote in 1998; 'it is a state marked by uncertainty. Nobody can guarantee that the country will last. Belgium is a discontinuity that perpetuates itself. Today, it perpetuates itself in a vague consensus and a permanent state of constitutional reform.'[78]

Out of Africa, into Europe

Baudouin once confided to a friend that he was king 'to love his people, to pray for his people, to suffer for his people.'[79] His love for his country strengthened him in his physical suffering from sciatic pains and backaches. Sometimes the pain forced him to walk on crutches. The King's private life was ascetic. He did not smoke, he drank no alcohol and lived very frugally. Prince Serge of Yugoslavia, who visited Laken frequently as a child, thought the Belgian royals odd. 'Baudouin seemed to have an ocean of immobility surrounding him. He always spoke in a compassionate tone and asked boring questions about our studies, like a Father Jesuit talking to his students. We had the impression that he floated as he walked. An unreal being. In Laken Park, a little wooden chalet had been built where the royal couple led a life of *petits-bourgeois*. Fabiola cooked and Baudouin washed up. She adored him as if he was a living god on a pedestal. They both had a halo above their heads.'[80]

Politically the King of the Belgians is the most powerful of all Western monarchs. Unlike his colleagues in Britain, the Netherlands, Spain and the Scandinavian countries, Baudouin personally chose his country's prime ministers. He entrusted the politician of his liking with the task of forming a coalition government by appointing him *formateur*. Apart from Vanden Boeynants (twice) and Dehaene (once), who set up a cabinet for another candidate of the King, all *formateurs* who succeeded in forming a cabinet subsequently became Prime Minister. Representatives of the SG sat in on the coalition talks to assure that the politicians did not agree on measures that would go against the holding's interests, such as levying a tax on its electricity subsidiary Electrabel.[81] The King also had a say in deciding who were appointed ministers. Sometimes Laken directly appointed its favourites. In 1985, the Flemish Liberal Belgicist Herman De Croo 'received a phone call from the palace at two o'clock in the morning. They abso-

78   Lallemand, p. 232.
79   Quoted in Suenens 2, p. 95.
80   Quoted in Serrou, pp. 23–4.
81   Karel Van Miert in *Humo*, 23 Jan. 2001.

lutely wanted me to become a minister. I was even allowed to choose my department.'[82]

In the mid-1970s Cardinal Suenens introduced Baudouin and Fabiola to the Charismatic Renewal, a Roman-Catholic variety of Pentecostalism. Strangely enough, this exuberant form of Christian devotion greatly appealed to the royal couple. Perhaps it was a welcome change from the strict formality of Laken. At the palace, the King surrounded himself with Charismatics. One of them, Jacques Van Ypersele de Strihou, nicknamed 'Spirou,' became the King's *chef de cabinet* in 1983. *Spirou* held his position for over two decades — longer than anyone since Jules Van Praet in the 19th century. Together with the royal couple and Suenens, he initiated a Charismatic prayer group at the palace. When not praising the Lord with raised hands, he kept a watchful eye on the King's financial and business interests. Baudouin was afraid of losing his financial perks. 'Who will do the mending that my palace needs if the country falls apart?' he is reported to have asked a minister once.[83]

Spirou played an important role in Belgian politics by controlling the King's schedule. Only the Prime Minister had direct access to the King, while even the ministers had to go via the royal *chef de cabinet*. When Luc Van den Brande, the Premier of the Flemish Executive, fell out of royal favour because he was too much of a Flamingant, the Christian-Democrat was no longer invited to the Palace for the annual coffee on Flanders Day. Van den Brande blamed 'some Yperseles and others who have no constitutional or democratic mandate but practise an undemocratic form of closet politics.'[84] But *Spirou* had the last laugh: he politically outlived the Flemish Premier. A royal *chef de cabinet* can only be called to account by the King and not by the Government or by Parliament.

Early in April 1990, Baudouin made headlines by his refusal to sign Belgium's Abortion Act. Belgium was late in legalising abortion. Together with Ireland, it was the only country in Europe where abortion had remained illegal. This did not mean, however, that Belgian women could not obtain abortions. Their abortions were even reimbursed by the sickness funds. Doctors only had to register the foeticide as a curettage. It was estimated that in Belgium 20,000 abortions were performed each year, compared with 100,000 births. The judicial authorities, having other priorities, did not trouble the abor-

82   De Croo in *Humo*, 5 June 2001.
83   Van Den Driessche, p. 17.
84   Van den Brande in *Knack*, 15 Dec. 1999.

tionists. Still, Belgium's Socialists and Liberals insisted that abortion be legalised because theoretically the possibility of prosecution always existed. Parliament approved the legalisation of abortion on 29 March 1990. For a law to take effect, the Belgian Constitution requires that the King sign the bill. Baudouin refused to sign the Abortion Bill because the Catholic Church forbids its members to facilitate abortions. He told Charismatic friends a few months before the bill was voted that he would 'sooner abdicate than sign.' In the end, however, he did not abdicate but told Prime Minister Martens that the government had to find 'a legal solution in which the necessity of a well functioning parliamentary democracy can be reconciled with the King's right not to act against his conscience.'[85] André Alen, a Professor of Constitutional Law who was Martens's advisor, came up with a 'creative interpretation' of Article 82 of the Constitution. That article states that 'should the King find himself unable to reign,' a regent is appointed. To avoid the appointment of a regent, Alen combined Article 82 with Article 79, which states that after the death of a monarch and before his successor has taken the oath, the 'Ministers assembled in Council' temporarily assume the royal prerogatives. The King wrote to Martens to confirm his agreement with the solution that Parliament declare him 'unable to reign' and vote him back into office after the 'Ministers assembled in Council' had signed the abortion bill in his place.

On 4 April, the Belgians were informed that, because of conscientious objections, Baudouin was 'unable to reign.' The following day, all the ministers, including those who were opposed to abortion, signed the bill. Enormous pressure was exerted on the Catholic members of the cabinet in order not to have them raise conscientious objections as well: Article 79 required that they *all* sign. The next day, Parliament, with the exception of the Vlaams Blok, voted the King back into office. Baudouin was grateful for Professor Alen's 'creativity' and granted him a Baron's title.

Paradoxically, the abortion affair enhanced Baudouin's popularity, even among pro-abortionists. The contrast between the corrupt Belgian politicians who did not give a jot for the Constitution because they had no principles, and a man who put his conscience above it out of principle, amazed the Belgians. The same phenomenon which occurred with respect to his grandfather and father in the 1930s applied to Baudouin, too. The King, though he bore a personal responsibility for maintaining and expanding the corporatist Belgian

85   Quoted in Van Den Driessche, p. 26.

regime which *by its very nature* corrupted the political class, came to be perceived by the public as a paragon of virtue. The more the public came to loath the politicians, the louder it applauded when the King spoke out against them. The royal spin doctors took advantage of this. The King became a living myth; he was depicted as a defender of the weak and the meek, the poor, the unborn, the handicapped, immigrants, prostitutes, AIDS sufferers. Baudouin played his role with enthusiasm: he began publicly to criticise the politicians because they did not do enough for the underprivileged. From 1990 onwards, when he celebrated his 60th birthday and the 40th year of his reign, Baudouin figured prominently in the press. Not a week went by without a televised programme about the King. According to researchers Maud Bracke and Christine Denuit-Somerhausen, there was 'a direct link between the orchestrated mobilization of sympathy for the King in 1990–91, and the spontaneous condolence shown by the populace at the time of his death.'[86]

In 1992, Baudouin launched a crusade against prostitution and the abuse of women. With the press in his wake, he visited *Payoke*, a shelter for prostitutes in Antwerp run by Patsy Sörensen, a Trotskyite feminist. In her book *De maskers af! Over socialisme, prostitutie en mensenhandel* (Take off the Masks! On Socialism, Prostitution and the Trafficking of Humans), Sörensen recalled the royal visit on 28 October 1992: 'His visit to Payoke was a political act of great consequence. It was a very clear signal to the ministers.'[87] Baudouin convened the political and judicial authorities in Antwerp's Town Hall and lectured them about their duties. The King ordered the police to release one of Sörensen's protégées who had just been arrested as an illegal immigrant. Roger Van Camp, the head of the Antwerp judiciary, was strongly rebuked when he dared to contradict the King by saying that illegal immigrants had to be extradited.

Sörensen gained direct access to Laken. She began to ring up the King about specific girls who lacked a visa to stay in Belgium. Baudouin subsequently ordered the ministers to do something for them. Soon he became a kind of ombudsman for asylum seekers. 'When asylum seekers were involved, the law was of no importance to him,' a Minister said.[88] Sörensen's political career was also launched with the King's support. In 1994, she became the first ever

86   Bracke and Denuit-Somerhausen, p. 70.
87   Sörensen, p. 27.
88   Van Den Driessche, pp. 34 and 39.

Trotskyite alderman in Antwerp City Council, before being elected a Member of the European Parliament for the Greens in 1999. Baudouin had personally lobbied the Green Party to give Sörensen an eligible place on the electoral list.

The King's loyal paladin Wilfried Martens not only helped Baudouin by federalising Belgium and taking the blame for the malfunctioning of the Belgian regime, but he also protected the foreign interests of the Saxe-Coburg family. Even after the Congo's independence, these interests were vested mainly in Central Africa. Thanks to Field Marshal Joseph-Désiré Mobutu, the Congo's strongman from 1961 to 1997, the Belgian royal family retained its huge stake in the former colony. The fact that President Mobutu changed the name of his country to *Zaire* was just political cosmetics. Though the Zairean dictator nationalised the copper mines of the *Union Minière* in 1967, he continued to pay the SG a share of the copper profits. The King also personally interfered with Mobutu to protect Belgian (and personal) business interests in the former colony. One such instance occurred in 1972 when he lobbied for a participation of the Walloon electricity company ACEC, a subsidiary of the SG, in the Inga II dam.

The importance of Zaire to the royal family, however, began to diminish as copper production in the Katanga plummeted. From an annual 470,000 tons in the early 1960s it had fallen to 30,000 tons by the early 1990s. In December 1988, Mobutu, dissatisfied with the King's apparent loss of interest in Zaire, launched a personal attack on Baudouin. He told television journalists that he owned a letter by the King requesting him to favour certain Belgian companies. In Laken, Baudouin exploded with anger. He ordered the government 'to do nothing for Zaire anymore.' All aid programmes and economic assistance to the former colony had to be stopped.[89]

As Zaire fell out of favour, Baudouin's attention shifted to Rwanda, another part of the Belgians' former African empire. The King regarded the Rwandan president Juvénal Habyarimana as his political and religious pupil. Habyarimana, who had seized power in a military coup in 1973, had been introduced to Charismatic spirituality by Baudouin and Fabiola. Whenever the Belgian royals met the President and his wife, the four of them went on their knees and prayed together. Habyarimana belonged to Rwanda's ethnic majority, the Hutu. When early in October 1990, 2,500 rebels of the Tutsi minority marched on the capital Kigali, Habyarimana begged Baudouin for help. The King wrote to Martens that it was Belgium's 'duty' to send troops. He also rang up a number of ministers to persuade them. These were emotional calls; Baudouin even wept whilst speaking to one of the ministers. The Cabinet gave in and sent 530 Belgian paratroopers to defend the Hutu regime.

The Tutsi threat prompted the *Akazu*, the clan of Habyarimana's wife, to plan a systematic genocide of the Tutsi. The Akazu, led by the first lady, four of the President's brothers-in-law and his eldest son Jean-Pierre, was a criminal organisation. It made fortunes smuggling gold, drugs and gorillas and is also suspected of having murdered the American biologist and gorilla-protector Diana Fossey in December 1985. In preparation of a Tutsi genocide, the Akazu distributed 20,000 rifles, 20,000 hand grenades and 25,000 machetes amongst extremist Hutu during 1992 and 1993.

All this was occurring at a time when Baudouin decided that he had to bring about a 'national reconciliation' between Rwanda's two ethnic groups. He undoubtedly thought that he had the expertise to do so, considering that he had transformed Belgium into a federal state. His efforts resulted in negotiations between Hutu and Tutsi representatives under the supervision of the Belgian Ambassador. Baudouin put pressure on Habyarimana, entreating him to guarantee the Tutsi a say in Rwanda. The new Belgian Constitution clearly served as a source of inspiration for the proposal to introduce a parity rule for top civil servants and army officers. On 4 August 1993, an agreement was signed between Habyarimana and the Tutsi rebels in the Tanzanian town of Arusha. Belgium's interference in the Arusha peace process, however, made it very unpopular with Hutu radicals, including the Akazu.

It is indicative of the naivety of the do-gooders in Laken that, despite their close personal contacts, they did not notice that their 'Charismatic friends' were preparing a genocide. On 1 February 1994, Johan Scheers, Habyarimana's Belgian attorney, warned the royal entourage of his fears for the Belgian paratroopers who were based in Rwanda as part of a UN force. 'Kigali is a barrel of gunpowder. I know that our boys are there and that it can explode any moment,' Scheers said. Habyarimana had told Scheers that he was 'trapped in the nets of the Akazu.' Scheers also warned Willy Claes and Leo Delcroix, the Belgian Ministers of Foreign Affairs and Defence. Wilfried Martens, however, saw 'nothing alarming' when he visited Rwanda later that month. Neither did Delcroix and Marie-Johane Roccas, the head of the King's press office, when they toured Rwanda in March.[90]

Barely three weeks later, Habyarimana was assassinated together with Cyprien Ntaryamira, the president of neighbouring Burundi. Their plane exploded above Kigali airport late on 6 April. The following morning ten Belgian paratroopers guarding the residence of the Rwandan Prime Minister were attacked by members of the Presidential Guard. The Belgian soldiers surrendered and were cruelly butchered. The murder of the paratroopers was the signal for the start of the genocide. All over Rwanda, the long-prepared plans were put into action and Hutu extremists began to kill Tutsi and moderate Hutu. The death of the ten Belgians caused the politicians in Brussels hastily to pull back all their troops, thereby abandoning thousands of frightened Tutsi who had sought refuge near the Belgian barracks. During the following three months, between 500,000 and 800,000 Tutsi and moderate Hutu were shot, burned alive or hacked to pieces. The killing spree only ended when Tutsi rebels, aided by Uganda, conquered Kigali and installed a Tutsi regime.

The African adventures of the Belgians and their kings started with Leopold II's genocide in the Congo and ended with the genocide in Rwanda. Belgium's international reputation was served badly by its African record. On the home front, too, Belgium did little to improve its international reputation during the last decades of the 20th century. The country remained the dithering, utterly unreliable ally that it had always been. In March 1985, Brussels refused until the last minute to deploy 16 cruise missiles on its territory, even though, like its NATO partners Britain, France, Italy and the Netherlands, it had agreed in 1979 to deploy American missiles if the Soviet Union did not destroy its SS-20 arsenal. During the Gulf War of 1990–91, Brussels refused to sell ammunition to Great Britain because, as Martens said, 'we do not want to have anything to do with military actions.'[91]

* * *

The last years of Baudouin's life were marred by increasing ill health. The King suffered more frequently from the sciatic pains in his back and in 1980 he began to have heart trouble as well. In 1983, he underwent surgery of the spinal column. In 1991, he was operated on for prostate cancer; in 1992, he had to undergo open-heart surgery.

Meanwhile, Flemish-Nationalists were becoming more radical. The Vlaams Blok became a curious alliance of orthodox Catholics and self-declared 'pagans' of the New Right, of conservatives and liberals, of Eurosceptic Atlanticists and anti-American neutralists, of free-marketeers and ecologists. What united them was their dissatisfaction with the Belgian federal and corporatist system which forced the socialist paradigms of the Walloon political class upon Flanders. Especially in Antwerp, the Flamingants became outspokenly anti-monarchist. During a royal visit to the Flemish capital in 1980, protest demonstrators vastly outnumbered the monarchists in the crowd. The King and his staff panicked and fled the city at full speed — an unprecedented event. Liebaers describes it in his memoirs as 'a wild flight' and a 'sinister hurried ride through the empty depots along the River Scheldt.'[92] In the municipal elections, the Vlaams Blok became the biggest party of Flanders' largest city. All other parties, the three establishment parties plus the Greens and Baudouin's Trotskyite friend Patsy Sörensen, were forced to form a coalition with the sole purpose of preventing the Vlaams Blok from taking over the municipal administration.

At the general elections of 24 November 1991, the Flemish secessionists jumped from 2 to 12 seats in the Chamber of Representatives and from 3.0% to 10.3% of the Flemish electorate, mainly at the expense of the CVP, who dropped from 31.6% to 26.9%, and the Flemish Socialists, who dropped from 24.6% to 19.9%. In his 1991 Christmas speech, Baudouin warned that the 'spectre of racism and intolerance' was haunting Belgium. As racist incidents in Belgium were rare, it could only be an implicit reference to the electoral victory of the Vlaams Blok. 'We have to eradicate this cancer,' the King said.[93]

Baudouin began to suffer increasingly from moroseness. According to two of his closest collaborators, Claude De Valkeneer and Jean-Marie Piret, he suffered both mentally and physically because of the growing tensions between Flemings and Walloons. By the early 1990s, Baudouin, though only in his early 60s, was old. He felt worn. Only rarely did he enjoy his royal 'profession.' One of the few occasions he enjoyed was the compiling of the annual list of new nobles. Every year, Baudouin promoted a number of Belgians to the nobility. Together with Britain and Spain, Belgium is the only country where people still receive titles. Unlike the British and Spanish monarchs, however, the Belgian King can appoint new aristocrats as he pleases. This is a royal prerogative over which the Government has no say. In the 43 years of his reign, Baudouin created 5 princes, 49 counts, 18 viscounts, 310 barons and 169 knights. Like his predecessors, Baudouin used the titles to buy adherence and loyalty to his House and to the

92   Liebaers, p. 360.
93   Royal speech, 24 Dec. 1991, in Baudouin, vol. II, p. 1407.

ideology of Belgicism. Usually the titles were personal for the life of the receiver, but, if Baudouin had been greatly pleased, he granted a hereditary title or changed a personal title into a hereditary one. Another support for Baudouin, which brought him much joy and relief in his difficulties, was his private think tank, the King Baudouin Foundation. This *Fondation Roi Baudouin*, established in December 1975 as a gift of the nation to its monarch on the 25th anniversary of his accession to the throne, had been an idea of Grand Maréchal Liebaers. He saw it as an instrument supporting the King 'as the ultimate guardian of public morality.' The think tank was to promote ideas that were dear to the King, such as environmentalism, the protection of the young, the equality of men and women, and the pluricultural society. 'Multiculturalism is Belgium's national asset,' said Liebaers. 'We feared that this asset would deteriorate, as economic and social contrasts along with institutional reforms would lead to mono-cultural and monolinguistic models.'[94]

The Foundation became an extension of the King's political and economic cabinet. It started with capital of 1.3 billion Belgian francs. Being a gift from the nation, over 500 million francs came from the sale of special gold and silver commemoration coins and postage stamps, while an equal sum had been collected by the National Lottery (a state-owned institution holding the monopoly to organise lotteries in Belgium) and some companies. Successful entrepreneurs eager for a noble title had been told that the donation of a few millions would help. The public had also been asked for donations, but these contributions only amounted to a meagre 15 million francs. In the years that followed, the National Lottery contributed the bulk of the Foundation's annual budget. By the mid-1990s, this budget exceeded 750 million francs, 400 million of which came from the National Lottery and the rest from donations by ambitious businessmen and from interests on the Foundation's capital which had grown to 5 billion francs. In 2000, its capital amounted to over 8.3 billion, the budget stood at 1.5 billion and the Foundation employed more than 100 people. The first Secretary General of the Foundation was Baudouin's half-brother, Baron — later Count — Michel Didisheim, an illegitimate son of Leopold III. The Foundation, housed behind the royal palace in the buildings that had once been the government offices of Leopold II's Congo Free State, became a means of providing royal favourites with jobs, of sponsoring Belgicist journalists and academ-

94 Liebaers, p. 319.

ics through scholarships and prizes, and of supporting projects in line with the ideology of Laken.

In former days, these activities had been taken care of by the SG. By the late 1970s, however, the once so powerful holding had run into serious difficulties. It had lost most of its African assets, while many of its industrial activities in Belgium had become outdated and unprofitable, though the SG daughters Electrabel and Distrigas retained the monopoly on the supply of electricity and natural gas in Belgium, and its bank, the *Générale de Banque* or G-Bank, was still the country's largest. The value of one SG share dropped from 3,342 francs in 1972 to 852 francs in 1979. The situation would have been worse if the SG had not had the state to cover most of its losses. One way of doing this was by merging virtually bankrupt daughters, such as ACEC, with profitable daughters. The latter then deducted the losses of the former from their taxes. The idea for this mechanism of 'fiscal recuperation' came from the government itself, keen to prevent the bankruptcy of ACEC, which would lead to social unrest in Wallonia. Other loss-making daughters, such as the steelworks Cockerill-Sambre, were sold to the state. By 1981, the state had been saddled with 81% of the Walloon steel industry, while the SG owned no more than 1.9%. The Walloon steelworks cost the Belgian taxpayers 300 billion francs, and the SG continued to pay huge dividends to its shareholders. The state also financed the clean-up of zinc and cadmium pollution by SG companies in the provinces of Antwerp and Limburg.

In 1990, the King Baudouin Foundation was asked to work out a programme for positioning Belgium in the European Union. Prime Minister Wilfried Martens had launched an ambitious project to present Belgium to the world as 'the prototype of the European Community.'[95] According to Martens, Belgium could serve as a model for Europe: 'The Federal Belgian State is a prefiguration of a Europe of Peoples, brought together in their organised diversity.' Martens was convinced that Europe needed Belgium, but also that Belgium needed Europe: 'A country which is federalised in the way Belgium is, must have a transcendent project to commit itself to, otherwise it becomes very difficult to keep it together. For me that project is: Europe.'[96] The King shared this opinion. He had already made 'Europe' his top political priority.

95   *De Standaard*, 18 Dec. 1989.
96   Martens in De Ridder, Hugo 4, p. 193.

In his televised speech of 21 July 1987 Baudouin told the Belgians that he hoped that 'our country would be the living proof that differing cultures can develop and bloom together within one political entity. For Belgium this would guarantee peace and prosperity, while at the same time it would constitute an important contribution to the development of a United Europe.' In his Christmas sermon of 1988 he said: 'If we accept this challenge, we will show Europe in which direction its unification must proceed. Belgium can and must become the cradle of a federal Europe.'[97]

Gradually he came to see himself as the king of a federal Europe rather than a federal Belgium. In a sense — with Brussels as the capital of both NATO and the European Commission — Baudouin, who systematically invited all the international politicians and bureaucrats passing through Belgium on NATO and EU business over to his royal palace, was the obvious monarch of a united Europe. European symbolism became ever more important in the royal speeches. In his speech for the national holiday of 21 July 1992, he talked more about Europe than about his own country. He also promoted the concept of a Federal Europe abroad. In a speech in Oxford in October 1987 he warned against 'individual and collective selfishness' and called for 'a unified economic and social space, and the organisation of a common European defence within a European Union.' In November 1992, he told French President François Mitterrand in Paris: 'You know, Mister President, that we try to put into practice in our own country, the federal option which we propose for Europe.' In May 1993, in Amsterdam, he said: 'Within Belgium we take the same option as we take within Europe.'[98]

In his last televised speech, ten days before his death, Baudouin again stressed the importance of 'the European construction.' He told his compatriots: 'It is necessary to proceed with a truly federal Europe. That is exactly the kind of Europe that can best help us to combat the economic crisis, to defend employment, resist the temptation of egotism and narrow and disastrous nationalisms.'[99] This was once again a warning against Flamingantism. According to Baudouin only the latter was 'selfish, narrow and disastrous,' while Belgicism and Europeanism, because they are multicultural, he considered to be by definition altruistic, broad and beneficial. Moreover, in their universality Belgicism and Europeanism resemble Baudouin's Catholi-

97   Baudouin, vol. II, pp. 1256 and 1302.
98   Oxford, 20 0ct. 1987, in Baudouin, vol. II, p. 1259; Paris, 30 Nov. 1992, in Baudouin, vol. II, p. 1436; Amsterdam, 11 May 1993, in Baudouin, vol. II, p. 1453.
99   21 July 1993, in Baudouin, vol. II, p. 1465.

cism. He never understood that what is required of religion is not necessarily required in the realm of politics.

The King died of a heart attack on the evening of 31 July 1993, not yet 63 years old. Fabiola found him dead on the terrace of Villa Astrida, their holiday home in the Spanish town of Motril, when she went to call him in for supper. 'The Belgians have become orphans,' *La Libre Belgique* wrote on 2 August. During the days preceding the funeral the Francophone press especially was very emotional. After one week, *Le Peuple* felt it was time for some irony: 'After all that has been written and said, we are surprised that he has not risen on the third day,' it commented on 10 August.

A melodramatic funeral service was held on 7 August. The head of the Belgian Commissariat for Immigrants, an AIDS doctor, and a prostitute came forward to bear testimony to the King's support for their causes. The service was attended by many heads of state, including the Japanese Emperor and the British Queen Elizabeth II. It was the first time ever that a Japanese and a British monarch attended a funeral abroad. Baudouin's stepmother Lilian was not present. Nor was President Mobutu of Zaire, who was denied a visa to enter Belgium. Mobutu was represented indirectly, however, by Britain's Prince Philip. His uniform displayed the riband of the Zairean Order of the Leopard (a creation of Mobutu's). It looked very garish compared to the sober purple of the Order of Leopold, Belgium's most prestigious decoration, as worn by everyone else.

In his sermon, Cardinal Godfried Danneels, Archbishop of Mechelen- Brussels, said that Baudouin had been 'more than a king: like David, he was the shepherd of his people. As a good shepherd, he gave his life for his own.' Danneels also said that Belgium now had 'an intercessor beside the throne of the Lamb.' With this remarkable statement, he implied that the King had gone straight to Heaven, hence, that he was a saint. On the Sunday following the royal funeral, the Belgian bishops had a pastoral letter read from the pulpits to emphasize Baudouin's exemplary life as a Christian. One year later, in an interview in *La Libre Belgique*, Danneels declared: 'I honestly think that the King was a saint. He was a man of prayer and of incredible patience. He cared for every individual, but especially for those that Christ loved most: the children, the humble, the poor, the sinners, the prostitutes, the AIDS sufferers.'[100] Danneels' predecessor as Belgian Primate, Cardinal Leo-Joseph Suenens, who died in 1996, almost 92 years old,

100   *La Libre Belgique*, 5 May 1994.

devoted the last three years of his life to the cause of persuading Rome that Baudouin was truly holy. He seems to have had some success. When Pope John Paul II visited Belgium in June 1995, the Holy Father went to pray on Baudouin's grave — something which a Pope normally reserves for martyrs and saints. And he praised the late king for 'his faith, his piety and the example of his life which he has left as a legacy to Europe.'[101]

---

101 Quoted in Van den Berghe 4, p. 160.

Albert II, Sixth King of the Belgians,
and Queen Paola

Chapter 7

Bread of Tears
(1993 and after)

Dolce Far Niente

The sixth King of the Belgians took the constitutional oath on 9 August 1993. The 59-year-old Albert II scrupulously followed in his brother's footsteps. 'Belgium must show that different cultures can live together harmoniously in the same country,' he said in his maiden speech as King. 'There is only one means for combating the threat of individual and collective egotism: solidarity. This is what we should aim for in the European Community through the establishment of a dynamic and social Federal Europe.'[1] He also retained Jacques Van Ypersele de Strihou — 'Spirou' — as the royal *chef de cabinet*.

There had never been political or personal disagreements between Baudouin and Albert, but their characters were very different. Baudouin had been an ascetic, serious and depression-prone bigot. Albert, whose physiognomy was rounder, was an easy-going, decadent *bon-vivant*. The new King was said to be downright lazy. According to some, *Spirou* took advantage of this laziness to expand his own power. He even came to be referred to maliciously as the 'Viceroy.' This was not doing him justice because Van Ypersele, one of Belgium's leading financial experts, had made his own personal interests totally subservient to those of the dynasty.

When Baudouin succeeded Leopold III in 1950, Parliament had set his Civil List at 36 million Belgian francs and the stipends for other

1   Baudouin, vol. II, pp. 1471–2.

members of the royal family (his father Leopold, his uncle Charles and his grandmother Elisabeth) at a total of 14 million. His brother Albert, the Prince of Liège, received nothing until his marriage in 1959 when he was assigned a yearly allowance of 3.5 million. On the occasion of Baudouin's marriage in 1960, the King's Civil List was increased to 42 million. Since 1965, the Civil List had been automatically index-linked to the rising costs of living. When Baudouin died, it amounted to 273.3 million francs (£4.9 million or $8.2 million at today's value): 248.2 million for the King; 11.8 million for Albert; and 13.3 million for Lilian, their father's widow. Parliament decided to award the new king the same amount his late brother had received, while his eldest son, Prince Philippe, the new Duke of Brabant, got 13.7 million. Baudouin's widow, Fabiola, got 45.5 million, and Lilian retained her 13.3 million. This meant that the Civil List went up by 47.4 million. Laken did not consider it enough and lobbied for a stipend for Albert's other children, Astrid and Laurent. By 2001, the royal family had achieved its goal.

In 1999, when the Duke of Brabant married, his allowance was more than doubled, to 31.8 million, and he also received a one-off marriage grant of 10 million francs. That same year, Parliament agreed to grant Astrid her own annuity of 11 million. Albert's youngest son, Laurent, had already been receiving an income of 9 million francs per year since 1994. In theory, this was in payment for his work as chairman of the Royal Institute for the Protection of the Environment and Clean Technologies. In reality, however, this institute had been set up especially to provide the Prince with an income and a staff. Over half the Institute's budget went to its royal chairman, who was consequently the best-paid of all Belgian civil servants.

Laurent, however, felt he was being discriminated against: his siblings did not have to pay income taxes on their allowances as the Civil List was tax-exempt, while he was taxed at the prohibitive rate of 55% that applied to every Belgian earning an annual income of 2.4 million francs (£36,000 or $60,000) or more. The Prince publicly complained that the State was confiscating half his income. He told the media that he was the only member of the royal family who had to pay taxes; this was unfair because he worked as hard as the others. Consequently, in June 2001 Prime Minister Guy Verhofstadt decided to grant Laurent a tax-free allowance of 11 million francs as well, plus reimbursements of expenses totalling 700,000 francs a year.

Laurent's allowance increased the Civil List from 273.3 million francs when Baudouin died in 1993 to a total of 419.2 million (£6.3 million or $10.5 million) by 2001. Apart from the Civil List, the Belgian royals also enjoy the usufruct of the *Donation Royale*, the huge real estate possessions that Leopold II had illegally bestowed on the Belgian State to disinherit his daughters. The *Donation* consists of castles and mansions that serve as homes for the various members of the royal family, but it also owns large sites in the centre of Brussels where, from 1956 onwards, office buildings were erected. These are let to the European Union and to the Belgian Ministries of Finances and Justice. The *Donation* also owns a portfolio in shares, bonds and cash, which in January 1999 was worth 1.3 billion francs (£19.5 million or $32.5 million).

The primary function of the Civil List is to allow the royal family to employ a staff in accordance with its status. In Belgium, however, most palace employees are paid directly by the state and do not cost the king anything at all. He is allowed to pick his collaborators amongst army officers, diplomats and civil servants. Even *Spirou* was technically a director-general of the Belgian Treasury, even though he never worked at the Treasury. A staff of 30 domestic servants is kept at the expense of the *Donation Royale*, which also employs over 100 civil servants paid by the federal or regional governments. In addition there is the King Baudouin Foundation, the royal think tank, which in 1998 donated 100 million Belgian francs to a newly established institution, the Prince Philippe Foundation, in order to provide the Crown Prince with a free political cabinet of his own. As a consequence, the dynasty can divert a significant part of the Civil List to its private fortune.[2]

No one knows how rich the Belgian royals are. According to the July 1999 issue of the British magazine *EuroBusiness* the Belgian royals possess 2,255 million euros (£1.4 billion). This makes the Saxe-Coburg family by far the richest family in Belgium, far ahead of the Janssen family, heirs of the business empire of Ernest Solvay and worth 1.2 billion euros. The royal families of Liechtenstein (5.0 billion euros), Luxemburg (4.7 billion euros), Britain (4.2 billion euros) and the Netherlands (4.1 billion euros) are, however, a lot richer. In their 2001 book about the power of the Belgian monarchy, journalists Guy Polspoel and Paul Van Den Driessche estimated the fortune of the royal family at only 12 billion francs (297 million euros).[3] This puts the Saxe-Coburg family in 25th place on the list of the richest Belgian families and at the bottom end of the royal houses of Europe. Surprisingly, Laken reacted to the book by Polspoel and Van Den Driessche with a

2   Ilegems and Willems, p. 84.
3   Polspoel and Van Den Driessche, pp. 227–9.

press release stating that the private fortune of King Albert consists of financial assets of 'less than five per cent of the figure mentioned,' plus a yacht, the *Alpa*, in the harbour of Antibes and a villa in the French village of Châteauneuf-de-Grasse, not far from Cannes.

* * *

Albert had always regarded life as a long holiday which, unfortunately, had to be interspersed occasionally with short periods of work. He did not want to alter his lifestyle when he became king. He continued to live at cosy Belvédère House rather than move into nearby Laken Palace. He continued to spend as many days as possible in *Le Romarin*, his villa in the South of France. When in Belgium, he tried to devote as much time as possible to his hobby of touring the country on his powerful motorbike. Whenever the Belgians encountered a group of speeding, muscular and armed motorists, these could either be Hell's Angels or the King and his bodyguards.

Like Baudouin, Albert was not very intelligent. He had only finished secondary school. In the military, he had joined the Navy. According to Joseph Luns, the Dutch Secretary General of NATO in the early 1980s, Albert 'is, indeed, an admiral, but I do not think that he would have passed an exam for a corporal.'[4] He was, however, in charge of his own affairs. Unlike his father, whose marriage had been arranged by the latter's parents, and his brother, whose marriage had been arranged in Heaven, Albert picked his own bride — an achievement which was unprecedented in the annals of the Belgian dynasty. What is more, she was pretty, she was partly Belgian, and he could even say that indirectly he had to thank the Pope for her.

The 24-year-old Prince of Liège had been sent to represent Belgium at the coronation ceremony of Pope John XXIII on 4 November 1958. Whilst in Rome, he met Paola, the seventh and youngest child of the late Fulco VI Ruffo di Calabria, 6th Duke of Guardia Lombarda and 17th Count of Sinopoli. The Ruffos were one of the most noble families in Italy. In the Middle Ages they provided Constantinople with two empresses. Though they probably descend from a red-haired Norman thug who usurped an estate in the southernmost tip of Italy in the late 11th century, the Ruffos claim to descend from the Ancient Romans, in particular from the *gens Rufa*, whose mythical ancestor was said to have been the Trojan hero Aeneas, the son of the Greek Goddess Aphrodite, known to the Romans as Venus. On seeing the 21-year-old princess, Albert must have undoubtedly believed the latter story to be true. Paola, whose family arms included shells, resembled Sandro Botticelli's Venus rising from the sea on a giant shell. She was slender and tall, with golden hair and deep green eyes. Her face, as pretty as a mermaid's, had almost perfect features. She had the freshness of a young starlet, but lacked the sophistication of Albert's stepmother Lilian. With her looks, however, a girl did not need brains to succeed in life or become Queen of the Belgians.

Albert discovered a kindred soul in Paola. They were both unintelligent, hedonistic young people, who took life easy and tried not to get tired during the day in order to be able to dance the night away. Paola was born in 1937 as a welcome though probably unplanned baby. She came seven years after the nearest of her six siblings, when her mother, Princess Luisa *née* Countess Gazelli di Rossana, was already 41 years old. Her three elder sisters and her *Mamma* spoilt her to bits. She hardly knew her father, a member of Mussolini's Fascist Senate. Prince Fulco VI died of heart failure in 1946, at the age of 62. Paola never knew her paternal grandparents either. Prince Fulco V (d. 1901) had been the Lord Mayor of Naples. His wife, Laure Mosselman du Chenoy (d. 1925), was the daughter of a rich Francophone Belgian banker, Theodore Mosselman, the grandson of an 18th-century mayor of Brussels who came from a long line of Flemish butchers. Theodore's wife was Isabelle Coghen, the daughter of Count Jacques Coghen, the first Finance Minister of independent Belgium. The ambitious Coghen was the son of a Brussels hatter. He had made it to the position of commissary of the holding *Algemeene Maatschappij* in 1830, when he switched sides, from King Willem to the Belgian revolutionaries, and helped to sell the holding out to the new regime. It subsequently changed its name to *Société Générale* (SG). The grateful Leopold I made Coghen a Count. Hence, Paola's Belgian ancestor had helped Albert's family acquire much of their wealth.

Albert and Paola were married in Brussels on 2 July 1959, a blustery, cold and wet Thursday. The newlyweds settled in Belvédère House opposite Laken Palace. The surrounding domain, originally 3 hectares in size, was quadrupled to 12 hectares (29 acres) by incorporating part of Laken's municipal park into it. The whole complex was walled to protect the sunbathing princess from the admiring gazes of her new countrymen. Paola did not make herself loved. 'She was not the ugly, but the dumb duckling,' the otherwise royalist journalist Louis De Lentdecker said. He admitted that he had 'no esteem for Paola.'[5] His indignation was caused by the fact that Albert and Paola

5   De Lentdecker in *Dag Allemaal*, 16 Feb. 1999.

unashamedly pocketed the 50 million francs (£3.75 million or $6.25 million in today's value) that the public had donated to them as a wedding present, while tradition required them to use the money for charity.

Paola also insulted the Flemings by flatly refusing to learn Dutch. She did not see the point of learning a language which she found ugly. The fact that the majority of the Belgians would not be able to converse with her was lost on the princess. She just smiled and never said a word. Very soon her ceremonial duties began to bore her. During official meetings and ceremonies she did not hide the fact that she would rather be somewhere else. She ostentatiously looked at her watch, yawned unashamedly, or asked Albert in a loud voice: 'When are we leaving?' She refused to accept flowers from a little girl during an official visit, fell asleep during a speech, could not retrieve her shoes after she had taken them off under the table during a banquet, had conductor Herbert von Karajan and his orchestra wait half an hour before she arrived at a concert and was denied entry into Rome's Saint Peter's Basilica because her skirt was too short. 'She seems to enjoy upsetting the Belgians,' the German tabloid *Bild* wrote.[6]

Only fashion designers loved her. During a three-day visit to Luxemburg, she was seen wearing twelve different dresses. Paola was also a favourite target of the paparazzi. She was the first royal to show the world her legs, dancing bare-footed in nightclubs, wearing hot pants, skimpy miniskirts or dresses with deep slits. One has to admit that she had beautiful legs. In 1961, she was also the first princess ever to be photographed in a bikini. Like her colleagues, Caroline and Stephanie of Monaco and Diana of Wales, twenty years later, Paola sunbathing was an attractive sight. The British photographer Reginald Davis said that 'with her classical beauty and elegance, she could have made fortunes as a model and a cover girl.'[7]

Paola did, however, fulfil the most important duty expected of a royal princess: to procreate. On 15 April 1960, she gave birth to Prince Philippe. Two years later, on 5 June 1962, Princess Astrid was born. On 19 October 1963, she had a second son, Prince Laurent, who was named after her Belgian grandmother Laure Mosselman. The fact that she had provided the dynasty with its next generation made Paola feel superior to 'the barren queen.' When she was asked to take over some of Fabiola's duties, she sneered at her childless sister-in-law: 'She has nothing better to do. If she had three children, like I have, she

6   *Bild am Sonntag*, 5 Oct. 1969.
7   Davis in *De Post*, 13 Sept. 1987.

would not have time for it.'[8] Her husband had even less time. Like all Saxe-Coburgs, with the exception of Baudouin, he had children on the wrong side of the blanket. One of them, the foxy Delphine Boël, born in 1968 of an affair between Albert and the wife of the Walloon industrialist Jacques Boël, became an avant-garde sculptor, designing giant penises in the Belgian national colours and frogs adorned with crowns.

Paola was hurt by her husband's promiscuity. So was her mother, a fierce Italian *donna*, who, during a family dinner on the occasion of Albert and Paola's tenth wedding anniversary, confronted her son-in-law with an embarrassing picture. It showed Albert leaving a Paris nightclub in the company of a 'babe' who was *not* Paola. It was not long before Paola was seen with other men. There was talk of an impending divorce, but King Baudouin threatened Paola that if her marriage broke up, she would lose her children, her royal title and her allowance. Paola and Albert each went to live in a separate wing of Belvédère House. She also had an apartment of her own on Brussels' smart Avenue Louise, where she could invite friends over privately.

According to gossip in the late 1990s, one of Paola's lovers is the real father of Prince Laurent. *Het Nieuwsblad*, an otherwise serious Flemish newspaper, brought the news under the headline '*Laurent is een bastaardzoon,*' while *P-Magazine*, a glossy Flemish weekly, referring to the many bastards of the Saxe-Coburgs in Belgium since 1831, exclaimed with glee: 'We are probably all royals! Except Laurent.' The leading Francophone Brussels paper *Le Soir* warned: 'All this is part of a Flemish conspiracy to attain independence.'[9]

Sliding Into Gomorrah

In 1962, Albert became president of the Belgian Institute for Foreign Trade. This meant that he accompanied delegations of Belgian businessmen on promotional trips abroad. It was assumed that doors opened more easily to Belgian trade missions if these included the Crown Prince. Albert accompanied three, sometimes four, of these trade missions a year — some one hundred over a thirty-year period. Each trip lasted about eight days, which meant that he was away from home three to four weeks a year. The trips allowed the Crown Prince to enjoy exotic sexual adventures. His staff had a code phrase for this, which was soon also known to journalists: 'The prince is off for some nature exploration.' Albert's *chef de cabinet*, Baron (later Count) Michel

---

8   Quoted in *Point de Vue*, 25 May 1973.
9   *Le Soir*, 21 Oct. 1999.

Didisheim, was said to be the fruit of some 'nature exploration' by Albert's father, Leopold III.

One trade expedition was to haunt Albert for decades to come. On 14 June 1976, *Eurosystem Hospitalier* (ESH), a subsidiary of the SG, entered into a mammoth contract worth 36.3 billion Belgian francs (currently £1.36 billion or $2.27 billion) with the Saudi authorities to build and exploit hospitals for the Saudi National Guard in Riyadh and Jeddah. The contract was the result of a trade mission to Saudi Arabia led by the Prince of Liège in October 1975. Albert's presence played a pivotal role in convincing Prince Abdullah bin Abdul Aziz, halfbrother of King Khaled and the head of the Saudi National Guard, to have the Belgians build the hospitals instead of an Anglo- American consortium. The contract was arranged, as it was said, 'prince-to-prince'.

Shortly after work had started, a Mexican subcontractor of the Belgians went bankrupt. As a result, the building works ran up serious delays, the Saudis stopped their payments and the underfunded ESH got into financial difficulties. Albert personally intervened with his Saudi 'colleague,' Crown Prince Fahd, in April and October 1978 to solve the problems, but to no avail: ESH went bankrupt the following year. This was an embarrassment for the SG because at the same time another subsidiary, Sybetra, had run into problems in Iraq, where in Alka'im, a spot in the middle of the desert, it was building the world's largest plant for phosphate-containing fertilisers. In order to keep Sybetra going, the Belgian government, feeling that it could not allow a second Belgian project in the Middle East to collapse, decided to participate in the Sybetra project for 300 million francs. The money was wasted, because in 1981 Sybetra ceased to exist, after having cost the SG 5 billion francs. A decade later, it was discovered that the Belgians had provided Iraq with the technology for extracting yellow cake out of phosphate. Yellow cake is an ingredient used in the production of nuclear arms. The plant in Alka'im, which was actually part of the Iraqi nuclear arms programme, was destroyed by the Allies during the 1991 Gulf War.

The latter never interested the Belgian media much, but the debacle of Eurosystem Hospitalier kept the papers busy for years. After the ESH bankruptcy, it was discovered that in order to obtain the Saudi contract, the company had paid a staggering 8.5 billion francs (currently £319 million or $530 million) — or almost a quarter of the contracts' value — in bribes. Part of this money, at least 200 million francs, though some sources even mention 1.5 billion, had been paid to Belgian intermediaries. It has never been discovered who they were. Was Prince Albert one of them? The question was hinted at some Belgian newspapers, but Parliament never investigated the matter.

Some of the bribes were paid in kind. The public relations director of ESH ran a ring of prostitutes to pamper clients and business partners. This PR director, a pretty Egyptian of Dutch nationality, whose full name was Fortunato Habib Israel, but whom everyone knew as 'Tuna,' was a prostitution expert. *Madame Tuna* had settled in Brussels in 1968 after her divorce from her Dutch husband. The perceptive lady had noticed that the 'capital of Europe' lacked a network of luxury call-girls. Hence, she established one. Her speciality was the organisation of multi-partner sex orgies or 'pink ballets'. Through her work, Tuna met the Belgian billionaire Roger Boas, owner of the arms company Asco, one of the companies involved in the ESH project. Boas made Tuna the head of public relations at ESH. Her job was, as she told the Brussels police on 26 February 1979, 'finding girls who would agree to keep the Prince and his companions company on their trip abroad. These girls were prostitutes.'[10] Tuna employed up to 200 prostitutes and provided services, including pink ballets, to ESH business partners world-wide. Sometimes, work even had to be sub-contracted, in particular to her friend, Lydia Montaricourt, who had bought over Tuna's Brussels escort service when the latter went to work for ESH. Tuna also offered girls two-year contracts as 'nurses' in Saudi Arabia.

After ESH went bankrupt, some of its former managers asked Prince Albert's support for obtaining new contracts in Saudi Arabia. Henri Simonet, the Belgian Foreign Minister, felt compelled to warn King Baudouin that his brother was getting involved in a new deal to win the Saudis over with 'commissions and intermediaries.' In a strongly worded rebuttal, probably written by Didisheim, the Prince threatened to resign as president of the Belgian Foreign Trade Institute. He wrote Simonet on 27 September that neither he nor Didisheim had ever insisted on departing on any trade missions. The initiative had always come from the government. He also denied that he had ever received any benefits in return. 'You will understand,' he wrote, 'that I am somewhat embittered after the attacks in the press and the insinuations about me. In this case, as in all projects where my support has been requested — and there are many — I have done my best to defend Belgium's interests.'[11]

---

10   Quoted in Belgian Chamber 3, 573/9–95/96, appendix III, p. 86, n 204.
11   Albert to Simonet, 27 Sept. 1979, in De Ridder, Hugo 6, pp. 154–5.

Prime Minister Martens came to Albert's rescue. He declared in Parliament that no member of the royal family could be accused of any wrongdoings in the ESH affair. Other scapegoats had to be found. Some directors of the bankrupt company were brought to court for mismanagement, but the case took so long that in 1989 it was precluded by lapse of time. The only 'victim' of the affair seems to have been Didisheim, who resigned as Albert's *chef de cabinet* and was appointed Secretary-General of the King Baudouin Foundation instead. Initially, the police also went after the prostitutes. Tuna Israel was questioned, but, though she confessed to having run a prostitution network, she was not bothered again. She left the country and settled in Malta where she became the executive secretary of a local company belonging to her friend, the arms dealer Roger Boas. Lydia Montaricourt, however, was arrested. She, too, confessed that she was a pimp. During a search of her Brussels apartment on 19 February 1979, the police confiscated her diary, lists of clients going back to the years that Tuna ran the prostitution ring, letters, photos taken during pink ballets, a dildo and a vibrator, and 200,000 Belgian francs.

The confiscated list of clients was political dynamite. Not only did it include an 'Albert,' but also a 'Beaurire,' whose phone number matched the private number of Lieutenant-General Fernand Beaurir, the head of the Belgian *Gendarmerie*, and the big boss of the investigating policemen. In one of the pictures, the policemen recognised their chief, stark naked! One of the ring's prostitutes, 30-year-old Maud Sarr, who was questioned on 19 March 1979, told the police that some clients of the network were also furnished with minors. The officers and magistrates researching the case soon ran into problems. Vital evidence, such as the picture of the naked Beaurir, the diary of Montaricourt and the list of clients, mysteriously disappeared from the police files. The officers were transferred to other departments and the investigation was discontinued.[12] Montaricourt, who had remained silent about her clients, was convicted on 2 May 1979, barely three months after her arrest, to 15 months of imprisonment. No case had ever been dealt with so quickly by the Belgian judiciary. After the verdict, she was released at once without having to serve her sentence. She was given back her confiscated 200,000 francs, her dildo and vibrator, and emigrated to France.

No one denies that the pink ballets, the orgies organised by Tuna's prostitution ring in the 1970s between consenting adults, actually took place. But apart from these 'genuine' pink ballets, there are also

12   Belgian Chamber 3, 573/9–95/96, appendix III, p. 86.

the so-called 'false' pink ballets: orgies involving sex with children. Whether the latter really existed, no one knows for sure. Some people, the 'believers,' think they did; others, the 'non-believers,' do not.

In 1979, a Brussels psychiatrist, Dr. André Pinon, divorced his wife Josiane Jeunieau. Pinon asked a private detective, Bob Louvigny, to shadow his ex-wife. A few weeks later Louvigny informed him that Jeunieau frequently attended '*partouzes*' or sex parties. Rumours had it that children were drugged and abused there. The minors were said to be supplied by a judge of the juvenile court of Nivelles, a Walloon town not far from Brussels. Other participants in the orgies were said to be two ministers, an arms dealer, a General of the *Gendarmerie*, and a royal prince. The non-believers argue that the whole story was made up with elements of what Pinon, Louvigny or others may have heard from frustrated policemen who had been removed from the investigation into the Tuna ring. In September 1979, Pinon went to the police with the allegations. The police, suspecting that Pinon wanted to take revenge on his wife and the judge who had assigned Pinon's children to his wife rather than to him, did not take the matter seriously.

A few months later the psychiatrist met Christine Doret, who told him that she had been a *partouze* participant. Doret said that the orgies had already cost three lives. Two children had committed suicide after being abused, and a woman had a fatal car accident after leaving a *partouze* drugged and drunk. Pinon got into touch with Jean-Claude Garot, the editor of the Radical-leftist magazine *Pour*, who agreed to meet Doret. On 18 June 1981, they met for an interview which was taped by Garot. Doret said that Deputy Prime Minister Vanden Boeynants and Crown Prince Albert had participated in some of the parties. Two weeks later, the office of *Pour* was the scene of a burglary and arson attack. On 5 July, Garot handed a copy of the Doret tape to the police investigating the attack. An officer duly put down a transcript of the tape in his report. The police, however, did not see the point of investigating this any further because it had soon found the culprits of the arson attack: a group of extreme right-wing hooligans of the Francophone Belgicist *Front de la Jeunesse*. The leader of the raid, Jean-Philippe Van Engeland, escaped to Paraguay and was sentenced in his absence to five years of imprisonment in November 1982.

Two years later, however, a new chapter was added to this saga. On 24 April 1984, Paul Latinus, a friend of Van Engeland's, committed suicide. An official inquiry concluded that he had hanged himself. His mother and his girlfriend were convinced that Latinus had been murdered. He was not depressed, they said, and the telephone wire that he is said to have used could only carry a weight of 40 kilos. Moreover, Latinus had informed the police on 28 October 1983 that he had received death threats because he possessed the 'Pinon file.'

In 1984, a Brussels magistrate conducted an investigation to establish whether the *partouzes* involved minors or not. He ordered a couple of young female police officers to infiltrate the orgies and look for children. The investigation was a farce. The young women, who had only recently joined the police force, had no undercover experience and were not prepared to join in the fornicating. 'Our girls ran away after half an hour,' one senior police officer said. 'This was only normal. Either you join in, or you don't.'[13] Even the believers were not surprised that with such an amateurish investigation no children were found. The police discovered nothing: no drugs, no politicians, no minors, only group sex between consenting adults, which is not illegal. The police also took down hundreds of car license plates of the attendants of sex parties in the years 1984 and 1985. According to a newspaper article many years later, in 1996, a car from the royal court figured on this list.[14] True or not? No further investigation was conducted into the matter, however, because partner-swapping is not a criminal offence. Moreover, the police had more urgent things to do.

In the early 1980s, Belgium was terrorised by the Crazy Brabant Killers. This gang killed 29 people apparently randomly in a series of raids, mostly on supermarkets. The Killers seemed to be doing it for fun: they hardly stole anything. On 8 January 1986, Jean Bultot, the deputy-director of Saint-Gilles prison, the largest Brussels prison, fled to Paraguay. Some said that Bultot, who was suspected to have recruited gangsters in gaol, knew more about the Crazy Killers. A few years later, Freddy Troch, a Flemish magistrate investigating the gang, contacted Bultot in Paraguay. Bultot advised Troch to look into the Pinon case. The raids on the supermarkets were only pretexts, he said. What it was all about was the elimination of witnesses. Sensational stories appeared in the press: Bultot had supplied boys for the *partouzes*; both Jacques Fourez, murdered with his wife during a raid of the gang on a supermarket in Nivelles on 17 September 1983, and Leon Finné, murdered in a supermarket in Overijse on 27 September 1985, knew incriminating facts about the pink ballets; the widow of a restaurant owner murdered by the Crazy Killers in Ohain had told the police that her husband knew that Lieutenant-General Beaurir and minister Guy Mathot were *partouzeurs*.

13   Belgian Chamber 2, testimony Audenaert, 4 Mar. 1997, in Janssens, Stef, p. 77.
14   *De Financieel-Economische Tijd*, 5 Oct. 1996.

Troch was very sceptical about all this. His staff had already been the target of deliberate disinformation and manipulation attempts to get the investigation into the Crazy Brabant Killers on the wrong track. Nevertheless, he was willing to investigate the possibility of a link between the murders and the pink ballets. Soon, however, he ran into problems with the Brussels judicial police, led by Chief Superintendent Frans Reyniers, who refused to give information and boycotted his investigation. 'I have had nothing but conflicts with Mr. Reyniers,' Troch later said. 'Hence, it is only logical that I distrusted the Judicial Police of Brussels.'[15] In December 1990, after an escalating series of conflicts between different sections of the police, Troch was taken off the case.

Reyniers, however, had problems with his own subordinates as well. In 1989, two Brussels policemen, Jean-Paul Peelos and Alain Etienne, acting on their own initiative, had reopened the investigation into the Pinon case and the Tuna and Montaricourt prostitution rings. They had not informed Reyniers because they knew him to be a friend of arms dealer Roger Boas. As part of their freelance investigation, Peelos and Etienne even had their boss, Reyniers, shadowed. The two men also questioned Maud Sarr again. She was one of Lydia Montaricourt's former girls, who — unlike ten years earlier — was willing this time to provide the names of some participants of the pink ballets. She mentioned the ministers Vanden Boeynants and Mathot, and a number of businessmen and high-ranking police officers and magistrates. She added that Montaricourt had secretly filmed them having sex with minors. 'Lydia told me that she had the judiciary in her power because of these tapes. Personally I think Lydia was released so soon after her arrest to prevent her from dropping a bombshell. Someone whose career is at risk because he can be seen practising sodomy with minors will want to avoid any scandal,' Sarr said.[16] The videos were probably used to blackmail people. A Brussels real estate developer close to Vanden Boeynants is said to have paid a staggering 140 million francs for a tape in which he 'starred.' Peelos suspected that the video had been sold by a couple murdered by the Crazy Brabant Killers.

It did not take long for their superiors to discover that Peelos and Etienne were secretly conducting their own private investigation. They were disciplined and their documents were confiscated by

---

15 Belgian Chamber 2, testimony Troch, 25 Apr. 1997, in Janssens, Stef, pp. 110 and 112.

16 A copy of the *procès-verbal* was leaked to the newspaper *La Dernière Heure* that published it on 14 February 1990.

Benoît Dejemeppe, the Chief Public Prosecutor of Brussels. Dejemeppe locked everything away in his drawer. 'There were no new elements there,' he said.[17] On 13 February 1990, Maud Sarr gave a prime time interview on the private Flemish television network VTM. She explicitly named former Prime Minister Paul Vanden Boeynants, Commander Léon François, the former head of the National Drug Squad (who had meanwhile been exposed as being a drug dealer himself), and two judges as *partouzeurs*. 'They inhaled cocaine at a fearful rate, drank unlimited quantities of champagne, and indulged in perverse acts, including sex with boys of thirteen or fourteen,' Sarr said.

Many papers, however, questioned Sarr's reliability when it was discovered that she had made VTM pay 20,000 francs for her testimony and that the two judges she had named had previously convicted her for providing a false alibi to a gangster involved in an armed robbery. Similarly, the credibility of Jean Bultot, the fugitive deputy-director of Saint-Gilles prison, was questioned when a video turned up showing a naked Bultot rollicking and frolicking with a bunch of prostitutes in a bath of jam in the Brussels sex club, *le Jonathan*. Freddy Troch's team had previously discovered that Frans Reyniers also frequented *le Jonathan*, but they did not make much of it. The jam parties were no *partouzes*, Troch's people said, only some 'topless wrestling' in strawberry jam.[18]

Two weeks later, on 1 March, former Colonel Herman Vernaillen of the Belgian *Gendarmerie* said on state television in the Netherlands that in the early 1980s, when he was investigating the drug trafficking of Commander François, he had seen photos of the pink ballets, showing naked men abusing children. Two days later Vernaillen (who, together with his family, had barely escaped a terrorist attack in 1981 — an attack that was never solved and that he suspected may have come from within the *Gendarmerie* itself) told the Flemish newspaper *De Standaard*: 'There were six, seven perhaps eight of these photos. As far as I recall there were no women in the pictures.' The Belgian papers also revealed that Chief Superintendent Reyniers had confirmed the existence of videos of sex parties to the members of a parliamentary inquiry committee investigating the malfunctioning of the police and the judiciary. Reyniers said nothing about the contents, however, which meant that, if no children had been present, probably nothing illegal had happened. When asked by parliamentarians

---

17   Dejemeppe in *De Standaard*, 20 Feb. 1990.
18   Belgian Chamber 2, testimonies Sack, Collewaert and Van Rie, 28 Apr. 1997; testimony Sack, 20 June 1997, in Janssens, Stef, p. 115.

about the content, one police officer (also generally supposed to be Reyniers) told them behind closed doors that he was not allowed to say anything 'so as not to embarrass the Crown.'[19]

Six years later, in June 1996, when the investigation into the Crazy Brabant Killers had still not produced the slightest result, the Belgian Chamber of Representatives appointed a second parliamentary inquiry committee to investigate the malfunctioning of the police and the judiciary. Again astonishing things were revealed. Peelos and Etienne told the parliamentarians that in March 1990, as a penalty for their freelance investigation into the pink ballets, the Minister of Justice, Melchior Wathelet, had suspended them for a period of 17 months. In this period, all their files had vanished. Two other police officers, Gerard Bihay and Frans Balfroid, said that they had also been taken off the case of the Crazy Killers when they started investigating the pink ballets. Bihay and Balfroid claimed they had tried to find out who the *gendarmes* were who had been made to stand guard outside the establishments where Lieutenant-General Beaurir was attending sex parties in the late 1970s. The officers also confirmed that the picture of 'Beaurir as God made him' had mysteriously disappeared from the police files.[20]

Even Georges Marnette, Reyniers' deputy and someone who did not believe that criminal offences (drug abuse and sex with minors) had been committed during the orgies, told the parliamentarians that 'the police investigation into the pink ballets was sabotaged from within.'[21] Marnette also said that Paul Latinus had not committed suicide, but had been murdered. Bruno Bulthé, a magistrate and, like Marnette, a 'non-believer,' confirmed that vital pieces of evidence, such as the diary of Lydia Montaricourt, had disappeared from the cellars of the Brussels *Palais de Justice*. 'To make those documents disappear, one has to know where they are. Those cellars, or rather catacombs, are like the cave of Ali Baba.' Bulthé added that his superior, Chief Public Prosecutor Benoît Dejemeppe, had forbidden him to consult the file relating to arms dealer Boas. Bulthé was 'convinced' that some people mentioned in that file 'could possibly be the victims of blackmail.'[22] In order to blackmail someone, it was not necessary for him to have committed criminal offences; for a high-ranking person the fact that he had engaged in acts that were generally perceived to be immoral, such as recreational sex outside matrimony, might suffice.

19   *Het Laatste Nieuws*, 16 May 1990.
20   *Het Laatste Nieuws*, 22 Feb. 1997.
21   *Het Volk*, 5 Mar. 1997.
22   Belgian Chamber 2, testimony Bulthé, 4 Mar. 1997, in Janssens, Stef, pp. 70–1.

A team of academics, who had been asked to assist the parliamentary inquiry committee, concluded that though the sexual abuse of children could not be proved, there had been a staggering number of 'anomalies' in the investigation into the call girl network of Montaricourt, Tuna Israel and Eurosystem Hospitalier. 'Possible protection of high-ranking people cannot be excluded,' they said.[23] In its report of 14 October 1997, the inquiry committee wrote that the police investigations into the Montaricourt, Israel, ESH and Pinon cases 'have not been dealt with in a normal way.' According to the parliamentary committee these cases had been 'sabotaged from above.'[24] The parliamentarians particularly criticised the fact that Tuna Israel had not been prosecuted in 1979. Since then, however, eighteen years had passed and it was too late to remedy it. Moreover, what sensible Belgian magistrate would jeopardise his career by bringing to court a madam who had publicly confessed that it had been her job to provide prostitutes to the former Crown Prince and present King?

'On Horror's Head Horrors Accumulate'[25]

The remarkable unwillingness of the police and judiciary to investigate the pink ballets and the nervousness of the authorities when this case was mentioned in the press and in Parliament, gave rise to many urban legends. Soon Belgium was rife with stories about drugged children being abused by perverted high-ranking businessmen, generals, magistrates, ministers and princes. There was talk of satanic rituals in which children were raped, maimed and murdered. These stories were reinforced by a series of suspicious disappearances involving children in the early 1990s. The missing children were mostly girls in their early teens, such as the Flemish Nathalie Geijsbregts and the Walloon Elisabeth Brichet.[26] In December 1992, an anonymous social worker told a newspaper that there were criminal networks in Belgium that specialised in abducting children, drugging them and putting them to work as prostitutes. After a while, he stated, the children 'are killed with planned overdoses because they have become too old and have become dangerous witnesses.' He said that 'the pink ballets continue as before among the high society' and that Belgian criminals even provided chil-

---

23   *De Financieel-Economische Tijd*, 1 Oct. 1997.
24   Belgian Chamber 3, 573/7–95/96, p. 31.
25   Shakespeare, *Othello* III. iii. 371.
26   The Brichet case was solved in July 2004, when the wife of French serial killer Michel Fourniret, who lived in Belgium, confessed that her husband had abducted and killed Elisabeth Brichet in December 1989. Police found her corpse in France in the garden of Fourniret's château.

dren to prostitution rings abroad.[27] Had Belgium become the world's entrepot for white slavery? In August 1993, Albert became the sixth King of the Belgians. For a short while, this diverted the attention of the public to something other than the disquieting number of disappearing children, the stupendous government debt, the collapse of 'the fat lady' and the consequent incompetence of the inefficient, understaffed and demoralised police forces and judiciary.

Paola and Albert seemed to have overcome their marital problems. When they succeeded to the throne, they were a middle-aged couple with grandchildren. The newspapers wrote that, thanks to their children, there had been a marital reconciliation. Still, rumours that Albert used the service of prostitutes had not died down. In April 1998, the King's cheque book was stolen in Cannes. The culprit was said to be a French call-girl. Paola and Albert no longer quarrelled openly, however, and led a quiet life. Very quiet, indeed, because, even as king, Albert made sure he worked no more than a few hours a week. He frequently retired with Paola to the South of France, where she devoted her time to gardening and he went for spins on his motor bike. Albert was no control-freak; he was confident that his *chef de cabinet* and other members of the Belgicist establishment would take care of his kingdom and his business interests without him constantly looking over their shoulders. Nothing escaped the all-seeing eye of Van Ypersele de Strihou. In August 1998, the King's cabinet reprimanded the town of Sint-Niklaas for providing some minor logistics for a memorial service for August Borms, the Flamingant leader from the first half of the century, who was born there in 1878. But *Spirou* was most useful to Albert in financial matters.

In 1997–98, the managers of Belgium's biggest bank, the *Générale de Banque* or G-Bank, wanted to merge their bank with ABN-Amro, the biggest bank of the Netherlands. The entire Belgian establishment, including the 'Social Partners,' was mobilised to thwart this project. It reminded the Belgicists too much of the Kingdom of the United Netherlands which the Belgian revolutionaries had ripped apart in 1830, while the 'Social Partners' feared that the corporatist culture of the Belgian companies would not survive a merger with a foreign company run on market principles.

Their alternative was to have G-Bank, which was 30% owned by the SG holding and 70% by institutional and private investors, absorbed by Fortis. The latter was the insurance company of Maurice Lippens. Fortis owned a 12% stake in the SG, while the SG in turn owned 20% of Fortis. In this way Lippens and Viscount Etienne Davignon were on a par. Davignon was chairman of the SG and vice-chairman of Fortis; Lippens was chairman of Fortis and vice-chairman of the SG.

On 10 December 1997 Alfons Verplaetse, the confidant of the Christian-Democratic trade union and the Governor of Belgium's central bank, ordered Fred Chaffart, the general manager of G-Bank, to surrender his bank to Lippens. 'You will not escape us,' Lippens's deputy, Herman Verwilst, a former Socialist Senator and *chef de cabinet* of Deputy Prime Minister Willy Claes, told G-Bank's managers.[28] On 12 December, King Albert in person received Lippens to discuss the take-over of the bank by Fortis. The King himself telephoned Baron Paul-Emmanuel Janssen, the chairman of G-Bank's board, to pressurise him. When Janssen replied that he and Chaffart would like to meet the King to explain the bank's position, Albert told him that this was impossible as he was ringing on his mobile from the South of France. As it happened, the management never got to see the monarch. The request by Jan Kalff, the president of ABN-Amro, for an audience with the King was also turned down. Even Van Ypersele de Strihou refused to meet Kalff and hear his arguments.

ABN-Amro made a take-over bid that was 15% higher than the offer made by Fortis. Kalff wanted to acquire at least 60% of G-Bank. The Dutchman had not taken into account, however, that in corporatist Belgium market laws do not apply. The Belgian Commission for Banking and Financial Business (CBF), a government institution which has to approve take-over bids, was told by *Spirou* that it had to guard 'higher national interests.'[29] Moreover, the Belgian law regulating take-overs had been co-authored by Lippens's lieutenant Verwilst while he was still in Willy Claes's cabinet, and fitted the needs of the Belgicist establishment: it was complicated and full of gaps which the CBF could fill with self-made jurisprudence. Soon, the ABN-Amro lawyers were complaining about the 'unclear legal framework' in Belgium. Kalff even came to call this a *'terra incognita.'*

During a chaotic and highly irregular meeting of the Board of G-Bank, stage-managed by Viscount Davignon, on the night of 5 to 6 June 1998, the bank's capital was raised by 10%. The new stocks went to Fortis, bringing its share to 43%. Some journalists described it as 'a carefully-planned coup against the chairman of the board and the

28   Quoted in Michielsen and Delvaux, p. 163.
29   Michielsen and Delvaux, p. 178.

management.'[30] Neither Baron Janssen nor Chaffart knew of the plans beforehand. Prior to the meeting, many independent members of the board had been summoned to the royal palace where *Spirou* told them they were expected to vote in favour of Fortis. Those who did not could give up all hope of ever acquiring a Baron's title. The reluctant Baron Paul Buysse, the Flemish chief executive manager of the British group Vickers, who had recently received his title and been made president of the Prince Philippe Foundation, was told that he 'had to take up his responsibility.'[31] Buysse did what he was asked to do, as did the other hesitant board members. Maurice Lippens promised them that if their vote for Fortis would make them personally liable to claims for legal damages from ABN-Amro or from G-Bank shareholders, Fortis would pay everything.

Baron Paul-Emmanuel Janssen was disgusted; he showed his contempt by ostentatiously addressing all the board members during the meeting by their noble titles. He resigned after the meeting. Refusing to be called a Baron any longer, he had his title removed from his stationery. Others rejoiced. Lippens told the press that the decision of the G-Bank's board to tip the balance in favour of Fortis was 'a birthday present for the King.' The decision had, indeed, been taken on 6 June 1998, Albert's 64th birthday. One present being worth another, King Albert made Maurice Lippens a Count six weeks later. So far, only Lippens's eldest brother, Leopold, had been a Count, as the title of the Lippens family had been one of primogeniture. Maurice, however, got the title for himself and *all* his descendants in perpetuity. 'I am very proud of this,' he said. 'It is a great honour to receive such a title for oneself and one's heirs. My daughters are now countesses and my son is a count.'[32] There also was a title for Alfons Verplaetse, the Governor of the central bank, who became a Viscount.

When the Vlaams Blok asked questions in Parliament about the King's role in the G-Bank affair, Prime Minister Dehaene replied: 'As far as I know no action was undertaken in the political sense of the word.'[33] He explained that he could 'not allow the actions of the King and his collaborators to be questioned in Parliament, as this would undermine the Belgian political system.'

* * *

30   Michielsen and Delvaux, p. 200.
31   Michielsen and Delvaux, p. 196.
32   Lippens in *Humo*, 16 May 2000.
33   Belgian Chamber of Representatives, Parliamentary Records, 9 June 1998, C 590, p. 5.

Meanwhile, however, the Belgian citizens were worried about more serious matters than the 'birthday presents' which the establishment was giving Albert II. The whole world was in shock since learning of Marc Dutroux, who in 1996 became the most notorious Belgian ever. Dutroux was born in 1956 and grew up in Roux, a destitute suburb of the Hainaut industrial centre Charleroi. He started out as a petty criminal, involved in car theft and fraud. This probably brought him into contact with some of the mafia clans that control society along the Walloon industrial axis. These clans, whose power extends into the judiciary and the police, may have protected him against the law.

One night in June 1983, Dutroux broke into the house of an old woman, tortured and raped her and stole her money and jewels. In January 1985, he kidnapped an 18-year-old girl in Obaix. He raped her in his van and took pornographic pictures of her. Then, offering her 100 francs, he released her. In June, together with Jean Van Peteghem, an accomplice, he kidnapped an 11-year-old boy in the Charleroi suburb of Gilly. The child was raped in Dutroux's van and the vile act was photographed. Dutroux proudly showed the pictures to his wife Michelle Martin. In October, a 19-year-old girl was subjected to the same ordeal in Binche. In December, Dutroux, Van Peteghem and Martin abducted an 18-year-old girl near Namur. She was raped frequently and violently, while everything was filmed. Two days later, the same thing happened to a 15-year-old girl. Like the other victims, she was dropped near her home the next morning.

In February 1986, Dutroux, Van Peteghem and Martin were arrested. Dutroux was given a gaol sentence of 13 years and six months. He should have been in prison until August 1999, but was released early, on 6 April 1992, by Justice Minister Melchior Wathelet, a Walloon Christian-Democrat, ignoring negative advice from the prison authorities. Michelle Martin, convicted to five years, had already been released after two years in 1988.

At this point the story gets a specifically Belgian twist. Barely three days after his release from prison, Dutroux was generously granted 'invalid' status by the Socialist Sickness Fund. This meant that henceforward, Dutroux and Martin received 80,000 francs (currently £1,440 or $2,400) a month in welfare benefits. He was said to have suffered psychological damage during his years in prison and was thus unable to work for a living.[34] With a monthly social security cheque and loads of free time, Dutroux had the opportunity to put his plans into action.

---

34   Belgian Chamber 4, pp. 40–1 and 213.

He bought a number of houses throughout the province of Hainaut and began to build dungeons in the cellars.

He also resumed his swindle in cars. One of his contacts was Jean-Michel Nihoul, a Brussels 'businessman' who had already spent some time in gaol for fraud. In the 1980s, Nihoul was involved in the organisation of *partouzes*. Nihoul never denied this, though he has always stressed that there had never been minors present at his orgies. Dutroux frequently made trips to Slovakia where he hired prostitutes and committed perversions which he videotaped. Nihoul advised Dutroux to film sado-masochist acts as this made a lot of money. 'Of course, I assumed that Dutroux only intended to involve adults,' Nihoul later specified.[35]

In November 1992, Dutroux was questioned by the Charleroi municipal police because he had tripped up little girls on the local ice rink on purpose, touching their genitals as he helped them up. Although he had a criminal record for violent sexual abuse, the police did not charge him for these indecencies. In October 1993, the *Gendarmerie* in Charleroi received disturbing news from an informer. He told the police that Dutroux was building cells in the cellars of several of his houses 'to keep children there as they awaited transport to foreign countries.'[36] The police searched the cellars of Dutroux's houses and discovered that there were, indeed, 'tunnelling works' in progress. Dutroux told the officers that he was about to enlarge his properties. The police accepted this.

On 24 June 1995, two 8-year-old girls, Julie Lejeune and Melissa Russo, were abducted in Grâce-Hollogne near Liège. They were locked up in a cellar of Dutroux's in Marcinelle and subjected to acts of horrible sadism. Though Marc Dutroux ought to have been an obvious suspect, he was never questioned by the police. This is extremely puzzling because a confidential report of 10 August 1995 to the head of the Charleroi *Gendarmerie* mentions that the police had been approached the week before by two informers who, independently from each other, said that Dutroux was in the business of trafficking little girls. One informer declared that Dutroux had asked him to assist him in catching children. The other said that Dutroux had told him that 'the sale of young girls brings in between 100,000 and 150,000 francs per girl.'[37]

35   Nihoul in *Der Spiegel*, 16 Oct. 2001.
36   Belgian Chamber 4, p. 42.
37   Belgian Chamber 4, p. 47.

On 23 August, Dutroux kidnapped two Flemish girls, the 17-year-old An Marchal and the 19-year-old Eefje Lambrecks, at Bredene, a coastal resort near Ostend. His accomplice was Michel Lelièvre, a 21-year-old drug addict whom Dutroux supplied with heroin. An and Eefje were raped and imprisoned on the first floor of Dutroux's home in Marcinelle, while Julie and Melissa still languished in the dungeon below. A few days later, the two Flemish girls were brought to the house of Bernard Weinstein, another accomplice, in the Charleroi suburb of Jumet. As it happened, the police were watching Weinstein's house in the course of an investigation into car thieves. They either failed to notice the arrival of the two young women or did not find this suspicious. An and Eefje were tortured, murdered and buried in Weinstein's back yard.

Two weeks after the abduction (at that time An and Eefje may still have been alive), the Belgian police received a letter from Jeannine Lauwens, Dutroux's mother. She wrote that two girls between 16 and 18 years old had been staying in her son's house. 'Given that more and more young girls are disappearing, I think the least I can do is inform you of the passage of these unknown girls,' Dutroux's mother wrote. The police... did nothing. In late November 1995, Dutroux and Weinstein quarrelled. Weinstein was drugged and buried alive in the garden of Dutroux's house in Sars-la-Buissière.

On 22 November, a school girl was abducted in Obaix, the village where Dutroux's mother lived. The girl was raped in a van, her throat was slit with a knife but she managed to escape. 'This is the *modus operandi* of Dutroux,' a local officer concluded. Two weeks later, on 6 December, Marc Dutroux was arrested. However, not for the Obaix assault nor for child abduction, but for the imprisonment of two men and a woman, whom he suspected of cheating him. The three managed to escape and accused Dutroux and Weinstein. On 13 December, while Dutroux was in gaol, the police searched his house in Marcinelle. They did not find the two 8-year-old girls, who may still have been alive after seven months behind a hidden wall in Dutroux's cellar. During the search, a number of items were confiscated, including chloroform, a speculum and vaginal ointments, and videotapes. The officers did not view the tapes, but copied them and sent the originals to Brussels. It is hard to believe, but both the original tapes as well as the copies mysteriously disappeared.[38]

On 20 March 1996, the Charleroi judiciary decided not to prosecute Dutroux for the imprisonment of the three adults. Instead, he was set free 'on humanitarian grounds' because Michelle Martin had just given birth to their third child. Upon arriving home, Dutroux discovered that Julie had starved to death in the dungeon. He claims Melissa died the following day. Martin had only brought the girls food once, shortly after Dutroux's arrest. He buried the little corpses next to Weinstein.

On 28 May, Dutroux and the heroin addict Lelièvre abducted the 12-year-old Sabine Dardenne in Tournai as she was cycling to school. Sabine was imprisoned in the cellar in Marcinelle. On 9 August, Dutroux and Lelièvre abducted the 14-year-old Laetitia Delhez when she was returning home in the evening from the municipal swimming pool in Bertrix, not far from Neufchâteau in the Belgian province of Luxemburg. A student, who learned car number plates by heart as a hobby, told the police that he had noticed a white van not far from the pool. The van was Dutroux's. On 13 August, Michel Bourlet, the Chief Public Prosecutor of Neufchâteau, and his deputy, investigating magistrate Jean-Marc Connerotte, arrested Dutroux, Martin and Lelièvre. Two days later, in the late afternoon of 15 August, Connerotte and his men freed Sabine and Laetitia from their dungeon in Marcinelle. Over 7,000 videos were confiscated from the house. In the following weeks the bodies of Julie, Melissa, An, Eefje and Weinstein were discovered. On 17 August, Jean-Michel Nihoul, the Brussels 'businessman,' was arrested as an accomplice. He had phoned Dutroux a couple of times prior to the abduction in Bertrix and had handed Lelièvre a large quantity of xtc-pills the day after the abduction.

'If I am allowed to, I will get to the bottom of this case,' Michel Bourlet declared on Walloon television. 'Everyone whom we recognise on the videos will be prosecuted.' The Dutroux affair gave Belgium one of its greatest traumas ever. Suddenly, ten million Belgians discovered that they were living in a morally bankrupt, totally incompetent state. They noticed how Bourlet and Connerotte were not allowed to get to the bottom of the case. On 14 October, the *Cour de Cassation*, the highest judicial authority in Belgium, ruled that Connerotte's presence at a fundraising spaghetti dinner for the families of the missing children cast doubts on the impartiality that was required of him in the investigation against Dutroux. The magistrate was taken off the case and replaced by Jacques Langlois. Unlike Bourlet and Connerotte, Langlois did not believe that Dutroux was a mafia protégé working for a larger network.

On 20 October 1996, the Sunday after the so-called 'spaghetti ruling,' 300,000 Belgians took to the streets of Brussels in response to an appeal for a 'white march' by the mother of Elisabeth Brichet, a teenager who had been missing since 1989. The people walked through Brussels in silence, many of them with their children, holding white balloons. It was the greatest protest demonstration ever in Belgium's history, but the politicians of the Belgian corporatist regime were not impressed. According to Louis Tobback, the leader of the Flemish Socialist Party, the marchers showed their political impotence by carrying white. 'It symbolised innocence and virginity,' he explained five years later, 'but it also meant that their message was blank. I was not afraid of that.'[39]

King Albert seemed less at ease at the time. He returned earlier than usual from his summer holiday and received the parents of the murdered girls in audience, as well as those of a dozen other abducted children. More than one year after the disappearance of their daughter An, Paul and Betty Marchal received a phone call from the King. For months the Belgian authorities had cold-heartedly insinuated that An had run away. Now, with her murderer arrested, late one night, when the Marchals were already in bed, the phone rang. A voice told the Flemish couple, in French, that the *'Palais du Roi'* was at the other end of the line. Then the King came to the phone and invited Paul and Betty over for a personal meeting.

Some parents, such as those of little Melissa Russo, had misgivings about the royal invitation. The previous winter, the Russos had run out of money in their search for their child. In despair, they had asked the royal couple for help. On 20 December 1995, Queen Paola's office answered that the Queen only gave financial assistance 'on the basis of a file drawn up by a welfare office.' On 24 January the King's secretary wrote that the Russos should not question the competence and willingness of the police to find Melissa: 'All possible traces are being investigated by the relevant authorities. Rest assured that each person in his place is doing his best to complete the investigation in a satisfactory way.' Further letters from the Russos were left unanswered.[40] Despite their disappointment in the King, however, the Russos, too, accepted Albert's invitation. Between 4 and 16 September, he and Paola received fifteen couples. Only Elisabeth Brichet's father turned down the royal invitation.

On 18 October, two days prior to the white march, the King organised a round table conference in the Throne Hall of the royal palace. Over seventy parents of abducted children, government ministers and academics attended the meeting, which was chaired by Albert. It

39   Tobback in *Knack*, 11 July 2001.
40   Danneels, pp. 256–7.

was a huge media event. The King severely admonished the Belgian authorities: 'The complete truth must be revealed concerning this tragedy, its origin and its ramifications, and this must be done within a reasonable time limit,' he declared. The monarch even called upon the people to participate in the white march 'as a sign of solidarity,' and 'in a constructive spirit, with respect for our democratic institutions.' Albert regarded the fact that Flemings and Walloons were marching through Brussels in a single protest demonstration as an indication of Belgian national unity. 'This may sound terrible, but it was fortunate that there were Flemish as well as Walloon victims,' Tobback acknowledged eight years later.[41]

In December 1999, Paul Marchal voiced his disappointment: 'We have been used by those who wanted to show how much they cared for the nation. Today it is clear that these people do not even keep their promises. The King literally told me that I could always contact him when there was a problem. When I tried to do so, I was unable to get hold of him. Afterwards, I had to learn from the newspapers that I had violated court protocol. Do not tell me that the illustrious gentlemen have ever cared for anything more than appearances.' Another year later, in 2000, Marchal said: 'I no longer believe that justice will be done. Oh yes, Dutroux will be convicted, but only as an *Einzelgänger* who acted entirely on his own. The authorities do not want to investigate whether there was a network of paedophiles or not. What they do not wish to seek, they will not find.'

Meanwhile, the Dutroux investigation had fallen apart. The case was weighed down by conflicts between Langlois and Bourlet. Langlois refused to carry out investigations requested by Bourlet which he considered unnecessary and time-consuming, such as DNA tests on 6,600 human hairs that had been discovered in Dutroux's houses. The investigators also failed to view the confiscated videotapes until four years later, in 2000, when it emerged that some of the tapes… were nowhere to be found. The trial against Dutroux, Martin and Lelièvre, which was originally planned for 1998, was postponed to 2000, then to 2002, then to 2003, then to March 2004. The trial ended on 22 June 2004 with the conviction of Dutroux to life imprisonment, his wife to 30 years, Lelièvre to 25 years and Nihoul to 5 years.

* * *

After Dutroux's arrest, the Belgian Chamber of Representatives had appointed a parliamentary inquiry committee to investigate why the

41   Tobback in *De Morgen*, 28 Feb. 2004.

police, despite the abundance of clues, had not been able to find the child-murderer sooner. The findings of the Committee, as published in its first report on 14 April 1997, indicated several individuals who had committed serious professional errors. One of these was Benoît Dejemeppe, the Chief Public Prosecutor of Brussels: 'The committee believes that Mr. Dejemeppe does not meet the requirements needed to head his corps,' the text said. Dejemeppe's behaviour, as the reader may recall, had already been questioned by a previous parliamentary committee investigating the bungling of the case of the Crazy Brabant Killers. Despite the harsh words about Dejemeppe's manifest incompetence, no action was taken against the Brussels Chief Public Prosecutor. He remained in function as if nothing had happened and was promoted in 2002 to the position of councillor at the *Cour de Cassation*, Belgium's supreme court.

A second report of the parliamentary committee, published in February 1998, indicated that the malfunctions in the Dutroux case were possibly not just a matter of incompetence, but may have been organised deliberately to cover up a larger conspiracy linking Dutroux and Nihoul to the notorious pink ballets. 'The circles of the sex parties which Nihoul frequented in the eighties provided a source of contacts from whom he would later obtain all kinds of favours and interventions,' the report stated. In order to research possible networks of child trafficking, Michel Bourlet, the Neufchâteau Public Prosecutor, opened a so-called 'green line' where people were guaranteed absolute anonymity when they supplied information about paedophile crimes. This initiative yielded many horrific testimonials. Some were, undoubtedly, made up by deranged people. Others were, however, taken seriously by Bourlet. Six women and a male transvestite were asked to give further information. They received a code — an 'X' and a number.

'X1,' who later revealed herself to the media as Regina Louf, was a young Flemish woman who claimed to have been the victim of a network which operated between 1970 and 1990, abusing, raping, torturing and killing children. Police officers Patrick De Baets and Aimé Bille, who interrogated X1, believed her because she provided some correct information, unknown to the general public, relating to an unsolved murder case twelve years earlier. Louf said that as a little girl she had witnessed the assassination of the 16-year-old Christine Van Hees, whose corpse, burned and cruelly sexually mutilated, was found on 13 February 1984 in the Brussels suburb of Oudergem. Louf also mentioned a villa in Knokke where *partouzes* with children were held in the 1980s.

The other 'Xs' had similar stories, but were less detailed. A significant part of Belgian public opinion, the 'non-believers,' think that the stories were made up by traumatised people or lunatics. Others, the 'believers,' are convinced they are genuine. The truth will never be known. The investigations into the Xs were aborted after X3 accused 'a royal prince' of having been a participant in the *partouzes*. X3's declarations caused panic amongst the investigators. The penal immunity of the royals meant that the policemen could not continue their inquiry. Jean-Luc Decker, one of X3's interrogators, explained to judge Etienne Marique, who acted on behalf of the parliamentary inquiry committee, that investigating magistrate Jacques Langlois had stressed that no officer was allowed to record allegations against the royals. 'Concerning the declarations of X3 discrediting the royal family, it should be known that these have not been included in the records, by order of Mr. Langlois,' Decker specified to his superiors of the *Gendarmerie*. 'I have told Judge Marique that no officer of the Neufchâteau unit has conducted investigations against people enjoying immunity or privilege of jurisdiction.'[42]

The investigations into all seven Xs were stopped because X3 had referred to the royal family. The Belgian authorities feared that 'by enhancing the credibility of the Xs — for example by solving an old murder — they would set off a constitutional time bomb.'[43] Officers De Baets and Bille, who were checking X1's declarations about the murder of Christine Van Hees, were taken off the case. Though X1 had never made any declarations about a member of the royal family, De Baets and Bille were officially accused of falsifying the X1 testimony. Two years later, in January 2000, a judge ruled that the officers had committed no irregularities, but they were not allowed to resume the investigation.

Various members of the parliamentary committee were indignant. Patrick Moriau, a Walloon Socialist, said that he feared that the criminal networks extended into the highest levels, including the royal palace.[44] The large majority of the Belgian media, however, depicted the Xs as hysterical lunatics. The believers were said to be paranoids obsessed with the theory of a Grand Conspiracy. The press even launched vicious attacks against 'Bourlet and his insinuations.'[45] King Albert called for calm and national reconciliation. In his speech on the

---

42   Decker to Major Guissard, 23 Sept. 1997, in Bulté, De Coninck and Van Heeswyck, p. 325.
43   Bulté, De Coninck and Van Heeswyck, p. 325.
44   Kalisz and Moriau, p. 311.
45   *Knack*, 11 July 2001.

occasion of the national holiday on 21 July 1997, he said that children in Belgium were now well protected, and that 'all the diverse insinuations must stop.'

In 2001, Jean Nicolas, a Luxemburg journalist, authored a book, *Dossier Pédophilie: Le scandale de l'affaire Dutroux*, summarising all the allegations that had been made against the King over the years. He offered it to the renowned Parisian publisher Flammarion. Despite an intervention by the Belgian Ambassador to persuade Flammarion not to publish Nicolas' book, it was released in September 2001. The King and the Belgian government took Flammarion to court for the 'libellous accusations expressed by fantasists and sensationalists.' Initially, they demanded that a statement be inserted in every copy, declaring that the allegations 'had been proved unfounded after thorough judicial, parliamentary and journalistic investigation.' Vlaams Blok parliamentary leader Gerolf Annemans, who had been a member of both parliamentary committees, pointed out that this was a blatant lie, as the parliamentary investigations had concluded that the judicial investigations had not proceeded in a normal fashion owing to manifold irregularities. When Annemans announced that he would question the Minister of Justice in Parliament to discover exactly where and when the allegations had been found 'unfounded,' Albert's lawyers backed down, demanding only that each copy of Nicolas's book carry an insertion stating that 'the King of the Belgians and the Belgian Government formally deny the allegations.' On 18 October 2001, a court in Paris ordered Flammarion to insert this declaration in every copy.

Nicolas, however, was not the first foreign journalist to point out the irregularities in the Dutroux investigation. In January and February 2001, two German television chains, WDR and ZDF, broadcast documentaries about a series of suspicious deaths. Hubert Massa, the Public Prosecutor from Liège, who dealt with the Dutroux case, shot himself through the head in July 1999. Other suspicious deaths include that of the scrap dealer who had made the van disappear that Dutroux is said to have used to abduct Julie and Melissa, and about a dozen others, including Simon Poncelet, a young inspector investigating a traffic in stolen cars. On 21 February 1996, Poncelet was executed behind his desk during a nightly raid by criminals on the Mons police office where he was working late. Poncelet was the son of the Public Prosecutor of Tournai. His murderers were never found. According to Nicolas, he was assassinated by the mafia as a warning to his father, who was investigating the alleged paedophile activities of Elio Di Rupo, the leader of the Walloon Socialist Party.[46]

Di Rupo, a promiscuous homosexual, who was said to make no secret of the fact that he visited gay bars of ill repute,[47] was accused by former minister Herman De Croo, an MP of the Liberal opposition, of having slept with underage boys. When in 1999, the Liberals formed a coalition with Di Rupo's Socialists, De Croo became Speaker of the Belgian Chamber of Representatives. As Di Rupo's immunity from prosecution had to be lifted by the Chamber before the police were allowed to charge him, the Di Rupo file became De Croo's direct responsibility. De Croo refused to act because he had now become Di Rupo's political ally. Questioned by a journalist in June 2001, the Speaker acknowledged: 'Yes, there is a file about Di Rupo waiting on my desk. I have not wanted to look at it yet. So I do not know what it contains.'[48]

The Hinge of Europe

The Dutroux affair resulted in a complete loss of confidence on the part of the Belgians in their judicial system. As many as 72 per cent of the Belgians had no faith in it, according to an international survey in 2000.[49] Also many of those working for or within the system lost faith in it. 'I am no longer active in Francophone Belgium. That is simply impossible,' Carine Hutsebaut, a psychotherapist and expert in the behaviour of psychopaths, said.[50] Even Eliane Liekendael, the Public Prosecutor at Belgium's highest court, the *Cour de Cassation*, felt compelled to declare: 'I do not know whether the Constitutional State and the Rule of Law in which I have believed for half a century, will be able to survive much longer.' The King resented her for this statement, which she made on 14 October 1998 during the Agusta corruption trial. Two months later, when Mrs. Liekendael retired, she did not get the Baron's title which all previous public prosecutors of the high court had received upon retiring. She also received no more invitations to society events at the royal court, such as the wedding of Crown Prince Philippe, while politicians convicted for corruption in the Agusta trial, such as the Socialists Guy Spitaels and Willy Claes, did.

---

46   Nicolas and Lavachery, p. 176.
47   De Ridder, Hugo 7, p. 249.
48   De Croo in *Humo*, 5 June 2001.
49   *Le Monde*, 1 Feb. 2000.
50   Hutsebaut in *De Morgen*, 16 June 2001.

Meanwhile, Belgium tried to prop up its severely battered image abroad. In his speech for the national holiday on 21 July 1998, Albert proclaimed the restoration of Belgium's international standing to be the highest priority of Belgian politics. Very soon, Brussels became the world's leading moralist. It began to pose as the world's conscience on the basis of a Universal Jurisdiction Act allowing the prosecution in Belgium of all crimes against humanity committed anywhere on the globe. By voting this bill, Belgium became the only country in the world where any stranger could bring his own or any other head of state to court. Only one head of state enjoyed immunity of prosecution: Belgium's own King. Any judicial investigation in which there is the slightest possibility that the Belgian monarchy may be discredited is automatically discontinued. The so-called Feluy corruption case was never brought to court, a newspaper revealed in 2002, 'because there was some indication, not even proof, that a member of the royal entourage was involved. Not even as a party, but as the possible owner of a suspicious bank account.'[51] As a result, all the culprits went free.

By 2004, Belgian magistrates had opened investigations or were considering allegations against Augusto Pinochet, Ariel Sharon, Yasser Arafat, Fidel Castro, Saddam Hussein and some 30 other foreign political leaders. Even British Prime Minister Tony Blair, U.S. President George W. Bush as well as his father, the first President Bush, and other leading members of the U.S. government and army had 'war crimes' complaints lodged against them at the Federal Prosecutor's office in Brussels. The same year, however, the Belgian Parliament changed the universal jurisdiction bill, restricting its application to instances where it is not possible for charges to be brought against someone in their own country. The bill was changed because the United States had threatened to move NATO headquarters out of Belgium, and Brussels hotels, restaurants and taxi drivers had warned that this would entail a considerable financial loss.

Belgium also presented itself to the world as the most hospitable country on earth. In May 2000 it introduced the so-called 'Quick Citizenship Bill,' granting hassle-free Belgian citizenship virtually upon demand to every individual who has lived in the country for three (in some cases only two) years. The bill was seen by the Belgicists as an instrument for creating an electorate (voting is compulsory for Belgian citizens) whose allegiance is to a 'multicultural' Belgium rather than to 'nationalist concepts' such as Flanders. The 'Quick Citizenship' policy caused thousands of asylum seekers to flock to Belgium. While their number fell in the European Union, it rose in Belgium by 19.3% in 2000. There were 42,691 asylum seekers, or 4.2 per thousand Belgians. This was an EU record, compared with 1.8 in Britain, 1.0 in Germany, 0.8 in France and 0.9 in the EU as a whole (0.2 in the United States). In that same year, 61,980 foreigners became Belgians, or 6.2 per thousand citizens — an absolute world record. Instead of a multi-cultural Utopia, however, Belgium became a safe haven for international criminals, whose newly-acquired Belgian passports enabled them not only to vote in Belgium but also to travel freely throughout all the European countries of the Schengen group and without a visa to the United States. In February 2001, an MP of the Flemish Secessionists objected to the policy of granting citizenship upon demand without investigating the applicants. Claude Eerdekens, the chairman of the Naturalisation Commission of the Belgian Chamber of Representatives and a leading Walloon Socialist, replied that it was only normal that the 'Flemish racists' should object, given that half the applications were made in Brussels and that 98.8% of these were filed in French. 'Our Commission does more for the frenchification of Brussels than the Flemings can ever do to prevent it,' he boasted.[52] In Antwerp, too, the Socialist Mayor Leona Detiège defended the policy of granting citizenship (and the subsequent right to participate in elections) to as many immigrants as possible, on the grounds that 'the Vlaams Blok is currently overrepresented as the immigrants are not allowed to vote.'[53] Father Johan Leman, a Dominican priest and the director of the Centre for Equal Opportunities and the Fight against Racism (CEOFR), a government agency working for Prime Minister Verhofstadt, commented: 'What will "our own people" still mean in fifteen years from now? We will get so many new Belgians that this slogan becomes meaningless. The Vlaams Blok is a thing of the past.'[54] The Belgicist line of reasoning was taken up by the Muslim extremist Dyab Abu Jahjah, a 'new Belgian' born in Lebanon in 1971, where prior to his arrival in Flanders in 1991 he had been a member of the radical Hizbollah. 'Some say that I am not loyal to Belgium. Have I ever burned the Belgian flag or demanded that the country be split, like the Vlaams Blok does?' Jahjah asked.[55] His followers staged violent demonstrations in Antwerp, burning not Belgian, but Flemish, Israeli and American flags.

52   Eerdekens in *Le Matin*, 9 Feb. 2001.
53   Detiège in *Knack*, 13 Sept. 2000.
54   Leman in *De Standaard*, 15 Jan. 2000.
55   Abu Jahjah in *P-Magazine*, 3 May 2002.

Equally 'loyal to Belgium' were the Russian and Georgian criminals who became Belgian citizens in 2000 after paying half a million Belgian francs (£7,500 or $12,500) to Abraham Melikov, the godfather of the Georgian mafia in Belgium. Melikov, who despite ten years of criminal activities in the country had had no difficulty in becoming a Belgian citizen himself, bribed a civil servant working for the parliamentary Naturalisation Commission (and probably also some MPs, though the Belgian judiciary was not able to discover who they were) to have at least sixteen 'clients' made into Belgians. According to the Belgian press, 'the entire leadership of the Russian mafia' acquired Belgian citizenship in this fashion.[56] 'One can also look at it this way,' Herman De Croo, the Speaker of the Chamber of Representatives, commented: 'While some Flemings despise their Belgian nationality, other people are prepared to pay millions for it.'[57]

Many terrorists also used the Quick Citizenship Bill to become Belgians. One of them was Tarek Maaroufi. He masterminded the murder on 9 September 2001 of Ahmad Shah Massood, the leader of the anti-Taliban forces in Afghanistan. Born in Tunisia in 1965, Maaroufi arrived in Belgium in the late 1980s. Twice, in 1992 and 1996, Tunisia asked the Belgian authorities to extradite him. Twice Brussels turned the request down. When in March 1995 the Belgian police arrested twelve members of the *Groupe Islamique Armé* (GIA), Maaroufi was one of them. By September 1997, however, the twelve had all been set free. The unwillingness of the Belgian authorities effectively to imprison some of the most dangerous terrorists, prompted Charles Pasqua, the then French Interior Minister, to criticise Belgium for its lack of resolve in the fight against international Islamic terrorism.[58] France had been a main target of GIA attacks, including the bombing of the Parisian Saint-Michel metro station on 25 July 1995 which killed seven people. The Belgian authorities have always categorically denied it, but it was rumoured at the time that Brussels had made a deal with the terrorists, agreeing to turn a blind eye to conspiracies hatched on Belgian soil in exchange for immunity from attack. In a GIA statement, addressing the Belgian King but posted to the French Embassy in Brussels in June 1999, the terrorists explicitly referred to such a deal dating from the summer of 1996.

In January 2001, the American secret services discovered a plot to bomb the U.S. Embassy in Rome. According to the CIA, the attack was

56   *De Standaard,* 13 Oct. 2001.
57   De Croo in *Knack,* 17 Jan. 2001.
58   Committee I, p. 87.

planned by an al-Qa'eda unit linked to Maaroufi, who had by now become a Belgian. As such, he could travel freely to Italy. The CIA informed the Belgian authorities that it would like to question Maaroufi, but Belgium did not comply. Three months later, the Italian police rounded up an al-Qa'eda cell in Milan. The Milanese cell had been in regular contact with Maaroufi. On 18 April, the Italian authorities asked Belgium to arrest and extradite him. Again, Brussels refused, arguing that it did not extradite Belgian citizens. Meanwhile, Maaroufi had recruited two men to murder Massood. One of them was Abdesattar Dahmane. Born in 1962 in Tunisia, he, too, had become a Belgian citizen. After receiving training as suicide bombers, the two men travelled to Afghanistan. Posing as Belgian journalists, they applied for an interview with Massood. Once they were in his presence, they detonated the explosives which they carried on their persons.

The Massood assassination preceded the al-Qa'eda attacks of 11 September 2001 on New York and Washington by two days. But even after 9/11, Washington had to pressure Brussels for three months to have Maaroufi arrested. The Belgian authorities replied that they could not initiate an investigation for crimes committed abroad. Brussels angered the Americans even more by declaring that, if al-Qa'eda leader Osama bin Laden were ever arrested in Belgium, he would not be extradited to the U.S., as Belgium does not extradite prisoners to countries that have not abolished the death penalty. Brussels had previously refused to extradite GIA leader Ahmed Zaoui to Algeria and the Turkish terrorist Fehriye Erdal to Turkey for exactly the same reason.

In May 2002, an inquiry ordered by a parliamentary commission to ascertain what the Belgian secret service had done to screen Islamic extremists in Belgium revealed that the *Sûreté de l'Etat* had remained passive because there were no indications that the terrorists would attack Belgian targets. According to the report, the *Sûreté* had allowed the Belgian Muslim community — numbering over 350,000 members — to become heavily infiltrated by fundamentalist extremists. Thirty of Belgium's 300 mosques, the report said, were run by fundamentalist clerics and had become radical centres.[59] Terrorists were being recruited amongst Muslims in schools, prisons, hospitals and sports centres. The biggest mosque in Belgium, the Great Mosque of Brussels, built in the Jubilee Park with Saudi money on a piece of land donated by the late King Baudouin, operated its own 'Islamic police,' supervising certain Brussels neighbourhoods with a large concentration of Muslims. It even organised paramilitary training. The report referred to sermons at the Great Mosque calling Brussels 'the capital of the infidels,' openly supporting Osama bin Laden, and admonishing the faithful to prepare for *Jihad*.[60]

According to the report, Brussels had become the ideal logistics centre for international Islamic terrorist groups because of Belgium's open-door immigration policy, the deliberate hands-off policy of the authorities towards the mosques, the geographical position of Belgium in the heart of Western Europe, and the fact that French is an official language in Brussels, which makes the city attractive to North Africans.[61] After nearly 175 years of Belgian rule, Brussels had totally lost its original Flemish identity. It had been left with an identity vacuum, which was now being filled up by another identity that was not even a European one.

* * *

The Belgian authorities regarded Islamic terrorism as less dangerous than the growing popular appeal of Flemish secessionism, which, though democratic and non-violent, threatened the survival of Belgium and the perks of all those on the Brussels' gravy train. The electoral appeal of the separatist Vlaams Blok (VB) had slowly, but gradually grown since its establishment in 1977. From 3% of the Flemish vote in the general elections of 1987, it had jumped to 10.3% in 1991, 12.3% in 1995, 15.8% in 1999, 18.2% in 2003, and 24.1% in the regional elections for the Flemish Parliament in June 2004, when it became the biggest party in Flanders, surpassing the three establishment parties of the Christian-Democrats, the Socialists and the Liberals. Moreover, the VB also became the largest party in Belgium, supported by 981,587 voters, while the *Parti Socialiste*, the biggest party in Wallonia and Brussels, got only 878.577 votes. Its surge caused the Belgicists to panic. On 9 November 2004, less than five months after the VB became the country's major party, the *Cour de Cassation* declared the party a racist organisation, thereby forcing it to disband.

Ever since its first electoral breakthrough in 1991, the establishment had been trying to counter the Vlaams Blok. The 'Social Partners' began to expel all trade union members whom they discovered to be VB sympathisers. The three mainstream parties established the so-called *'cordon sanitaire.'* This is a French veterinary term referring to a quaran-

---

60   Committee I, pp. 113, 119, 126–7.
61   Committee I, p. 103.

tine zone around contagious animals. In Belgian politics, it refers to an agreement to isolate the VB and never to cooperate with it, not even at the municipal level. VB representatives were excluded from boards such as those of Ghent University. The party was not allowed to propose candidates for major functions in the judiciary and the diplomacy, where all posts are traditionally assigned by the political parties in accordance with their political weight, and VB politicians were excluded from participating in most radio and television shows.

Shortly after the 1991 elections, the Centre for Equal Opportunities and the Fight against Racism (CEOFR) was established. This agency, funded by the government, included representatives of all political parties, except the VB, on its board and was given the authority to prosecute for 'racial discrimination.' According to the Belgian Anti-Racism Act, discrimination is each form of distinction or preference 'which has or may have as its aim or consequence that the recognition, the enjoyment or exercise on an equal footing of human rights and fundamental freedoms in the political, economic, social or cultural sphere or in other areas of social life, is destroyed, affected or restricted.' Contrary to the European anti-discrimination treaties, the Belgian bill not only prohibits distinctions that have restrictions as their aim, but also distinctions that *may have* these as their consequence. Hence, every preference is a form of discrimination. The Act also states that whoever 'cooperates' (in whatever way) with racists, commits a criminal offence, even if he does not commit racist acts.

In 1993, the CEOFR brought the son and son-in-law of VB leader Karel Dillen to court on the charge of cooperating with the VB. The Brussels Penal Court let the two off the hook by declaring itself incompetent to issue a verdict in the case. Meanwhile the Belgian Parliament voted a series of new laws, including a bill outlawing all private funding of political parties. Henceforward, they would be financed by the state in accordance with their number of votes in the last elections. They can, however, be deprived of their subsidies by a simple parliamentary majority in case of a conviction for racism. As other funding is illegal, such a decision would in fact kill a party.

In October 2000, the CEOFR brought three non-profit organisations of the VB to court on the charge of cooperating with the VB. In order to prove that the VB was a racist organisation, CEOFR director Father Leman submitted 16 texts published by local VB chapters between 1996 and 2000 on immigration issues. Though some texts contained rude comments about immigrants abusing welfare programmes, others were mere quotes of official statistics on crime and social expenditure and one was an article written by a female Turkish-born VB member about the position of women in fundamentalist Muslim societies. Again, the Brussels Penal Court refused to issue a verdict, arguing that it is up to the electorate to decide the fate of political parties. The CEOFR took the case to the Brussels Court of Appeal, which reaffirmed the previous ruling, whereupon the CEOFR took the case to the *Cour de Cassation*. The latter overruled the Brussels verdict and sent it to the Court of Appeal in Ghent, a stronghold of Socialists and Liberals. This court granted the Belgian regime what it had been asking for and sentenced each of the three VB organisations to paying the CEOFR 12,400 euros in damages. The verdict was read out by Alain Smetryns, a Belgicist judge from Ghent, who chaired the Francophone section of the local Lions Club. According to judge Smetryns, what the VB wrote in the 16 texts was not necessarily untrue, but constituted a criminal offence because it was published with 'an intention to contribute to a campaign of hatred.' On 9 November, the *Cour de Cassation*, with as many Francophone as Flemish judges, upheld the Ghent ruling. The conviction forced the VB to disband. Indeed, the ruling was a precedent, allowing the prosecution by the CEOFR of every individual VB party member and everyone who has ever cooperated, in whatever capacity, with the party. The Ghent verdict literally stated: 'Rendering punishable every person who belongs to or cooperates with a group serves as an efficient means to suppress such groups, as the lawmaker intended. Rendering punishable the members or collaborators of the group or society inherently jeopardises the continued existence or functioning of the group.'

It was the first time in the history of Western Europe that a country banned its largest party. Five days later, however, the former VB politicians established a new party, the *Vlaams Belang* (Flemish Interest). This move was at once denounced by King Albert's son, the 44-year-old Crown Prince Philippe, who lashed out in an interview: 'Some people and parties, such as the Vlaams Belang, oppose Belgium and want to tear our country to pieces. I can assure you that they will have to deal with me first. And do not underestimate me: I can be tough when I need to. I won't let anyone walk over me. Anyone who harms Belgium will find me in their way.'[62] It was a warning not only for the Vlaams Belang, but for all Flamingants, including the New Flemish Alliance, a small but likewise separatist party, elected on a platform with the Flemish Christian-Democrats, that had joined the Flemish regional government in June 2004.

* * *

Upon approaching its 175th anniversary, Belgium was finding it increasingly difficult to maintain the image of a normal liberal democratic nation state, governed by the consent of the people. At the heart of its hybrid, unrepresentative and largely unaccountable regime is a democratic deficit that is there for the whole world to see. The Belgian politicians do not seem to care, however. Despite its failings, the authorities in Brussels continue to propagate the 'Belgian federal model,' which, according to Crown Prince Philippe, 'can be an inspiration for the European Union.'[63] The heir to the Belgian throne perceived the striking parallels between Belgium and Europe as an artificial state in the making. Like him, many members of the Belgian political class feel perfectly at home in the European institutions. Familiar with Belgium, the 'discontinuity perpetuating itself in a permanent state of constitutional reform,'[64] they function better than anyone else in a scenario that is constantly changing. 'There are all kinds of interesting parallels between Belgium and Europe,' Belgian Prime Minister Guy Verhofstadt said. 'Belgium is the laboratory of European unification. Foreign politicians watch our country with particular interest because it can teach them something about the feasibility of the European project.'[65]

Like 'Europe,' that other gravy train in Brussels, Belgium has never been based on a sense of national unity. It has been held together by a political class prepared to subvert democracy to its own ends. The Belgian regime, because it could not be based on a real nation, could never tolerate a democratic form of governance. Ironically, in the early 21st century, the Belgian model, the ideal of the 20th-century welfare state corporatists, came to fascinate an entirely new group of intellectuals and artists. These so-called 'neo-Belgicists' began to sing the praises of Belgium as the world's first post-modern or post-national nation, unaware that they were actually applauding a post-democratic model. In 1985, in his book *De afwezige meerderheid* (The Absent Majority), the Flamingant philosopher Lode Claes had pointed out that Belgium is characterised by an 'identity of non-identity.' This was repulsive to Claes, who argued that without identity and a sense of genuine nationhood, there can also be no democracy and no morality. The neo-Belgicists, however, regard the absence of identity as the supreme morality. On 6 March 1998, they published the Open Letter *Gedaan met nationalistische dwaasheid* (Let's Stop

63   Philippe in *De Standaard*, 19 May 2001.
64   Lallemand, p. 232.
65   Verhofstadt in *Humo*, 29 July 2003.

Nationalistic Foolishness) in which they stated that they do not believe in the existence of 'national identity' and are not prepared to march behind any national flag, except the Belgian flag 'because the latter does not represent anything.' An identity is nothing to be proud of, their message read, but Belgium is something to be proud of exactly because it is nothing. As Belgium does not stand for an identity, it is 'an antidote against nationalism.'[66]

Moreover, because it stands for nothing, Belgium can easily be replaced by a larger 'non-identity concept' such as Europe. In the early 1940s, Hendrik De Man had already said that one had to proceed *beyond nationalism*. In a speech in Antwerp on 20 April 1941 (Hitler's birthday), De Man told his followers that it was necessary to 'transform Belgium, not abandon it,' through 'an *Anschluss* to Europe.' What was needed, he said, 'was as much federalism and as little separatism as possible,' so that 'Belgium, exactly because it is not based on a unique national sentiment, can become the vanguard of the European Revolution; the principle on which the new European Order hinges.'[67] De Man's ideal was echoed by the neo-Belgicist intellectuals and artists.

Even though, or perhaps exactly because, it stands for nothing, Belgium needs a tangible symbol. Without the civic glue that binds countries with a genuine national identity, Belgium, as we have seen, could not have already survived for six generations were it not for two basic elements: its corporatist social welfare system that has corrupted a substantial section of the electorate, and its royal family that has given it an element of mystique and a semblance of unity. 'The monarchy is the only way to keep an artificial country such as Belgium together. In a homogeneous country, I would be a republican, but not in Belgium,' the Socialist Party leader Louis Tobback said in December 2001.[68] According to the Walloon Socialist Claude Eerdekens 'the King is the last bulwark against the continuing advance of Flemish imperialism.'[69]

Perhaps Europe, in order to become a viable federal European state, needs an institution no Europhile has yet considered: a common dynasty. This may even be more fundamental than a common social policy, a common currency, a constitution, a flag and an army. Would the Belgian Saxe-Coburgs not be the most likely candidates to become the monarchs of such a 'post-national, non-identity' state, precisely

66   *De Standaard*, 6 Mar. 1998.
67   De Man 3, pp. 218–20.
68   Tobback in *Gazet van Antwerpen*, 29 Dec. 2001.
69   Eerdekens in *l'Echo*, 3 June 2000.

because they are nothing: not British, not French, not German, not Italian, not Danish, not Spanish, not even Flemish or Walloon? Being nothing, they are the only 'true' Belgians, the only 'true' Europeans.

This would imply, however, that all European citizens would have to become Belgians. And that is a nightmare which these citizens, if they watch Belgium as carefully as Belgian Prime Minister Verhofstadt says their politicians do, will want to avoid. The history of Belgium confirms that, without a sense of national identity, democracy and public morality wither away. The Flemings and the Walloons have had to pay a heavy price for the artificial, 'non-identity' state that the international powers bestowed on them in 1830. The reader must ponder the question of whether all that has happened in Belgium could also have happened in any other country. Or is the 'Belgian disease' unique to Belgium because Belgium itself is unique? If so, how long will it continue to be unique? Will the 'Belgian disease' soon become the 'European disease?' Will Europe, like Belgium, become a federal state which fails in the basic duty of a state: to guarantee law and order, provide a fair judicial system, and protect its citizens and their children? In a few decades from now, will Europeans, like Belgians today, be obliged to say of their pan-European — supra-national, or rather post-national and post-democratic — state: *Thou feedest us with the bread of tears* (Psalm 80:5)?

The future of the European continent depends to a large extent on the reader and on the decisions he allows his politicians to take. It is not inevitable that all Europeans will be Belgians, with the British in the position that the Flemings have occupied for the past 175 years. Perhaps — and what an irony that would be — the people of Flanders, citizens of a nation designed to deny nationality, will become the forerunners of the countermovement, bringing down the Belgian construct and thereby proving that Europe as a federal superstate is a non-starter — the non-starter that Belgium, but for the Saxe-Coburgs on their gravy throne, would have been.

Abbreviations

Abbreviations used in the text

ABIR	Anglo-Belgian India Rubber Company
ACEC	*Ateliers de Constructions Electrique de Charleroi*
AIA	*Association Internationale Africaine*
AIC	*Association Internationale du Congo*
BWP	*Belgische Werklieden Partij*: Belgian Workers' Party
CBF	*Commissie voor Bank- en Financiewezen*: Commission for Banking and Financial Business
CEOFR	Centre for Equal Opportunities and the Fight against Racism
CFS	Congo Free State
CVP	*Christelijke Volkspartij*: Christian People's Party
DeVlag	*Deutsch-Vlaemische Arbeitsgemeinschaft*: Flemish Nazi party
EC	European Communities
ECSC	European Coal and Steel Community
EEC	European Economic Community
ESH	*Eurosystem Hospitalier*
EU	European Union
FDF	*Front des Francophones*
GDR	German Democratic Republic
Gestapo	*Geheime Staatspolizei*: Nazi German secret police
GIA	*Groupe Islamique Armé*: Algerian terrorist group
MNC	*Mouvement National Congolais*
NATO	North Atlantic Treaty Organisation
RSHA	*Reichssicherheitsdienst Hauptamt*: Headquarters of the Nazi State Security and Secret Police
Sabena	*Société Anonyme Belge d'Exploitation de la Navigation Aérienne*: Belgian national airlines
SD	*Sicherheitsdienst*: State Security Service of Nazi Germany
SG	*Société Générale*
SPD	*Sozialdemokratische Partei Deutschlands*: German Socialist Party
UN	United Nations

UM	*Union Minière (du Haut-Katanga)*
VB	*Vlaams Blok*
VNV	*Vlaams-Nationaal Verbond*: Flemish-Nationalist Alliance

Abbreviations used in the footnotes

AQO	Archives of the Quai d'Orsay (the French Foreign Ministry), Paris
BAK NS	*Bundesarchiv Koblenz Nationalsozialismus*: German National Archives of the Nazi period, Koblenz
DS	Archives of the US Department of State, Washington DC
FO	Archives of the British Foreign Office, Kew (London)
GRA	German Records of Alexandria, the German World War II documents in the US National Archives, Alexandria, VA
GSA	General State Archives, Brussels
HHS	*Haus- Hof- und Staatsarchiv*: State Archives, Vienna
MFA	Archives of the Belgian Ministry of Foreign Affairs, Brussels
NAW	US National Archives, Washington DC
PAB	*Politisches Archiv des Auswärtiges Amtes Bonn*: Archives of the (West) German Foreign Ministry 1945–1990, Bonn
PRO	Public Record Office, Kew (London)
RAB	Royal Archives Brussels, Brussels
RAB FC	*Fonds Congo*: Congo archives of Leopold II
RAB FG	*Fonds Goffinet*: Private archives of Leopold I and Leopold II
RAB FG AQL	Archives of Queen Louise
RAB FG PSDB	Archives of the private secretariat of the Duke of Brabant (later Leopold II)
RAB FH	*Fonds Havre*: Correspondence between Albert I's cabinet and the Belgian government 1914–1918
RAB FLI	*Fonds Leopold I*: Archives of the secretariat and cabinet of Leopold I
RAB K	Congo archives, 1960–1961
RAB KAD	King Albert I's Diary
RAB SAE	Archives of the secretariat of Albert I and Queen Elisabeth
RAB SLIII	Archives of the secretariat of Leopold III
RAM	Royal Army Museum, Brussels
RAM WC	Wilmet Collection
RAW	Royal Archives Windsor, Windsor
RAW QVJ	Queen Victoria's Journal
RMCA	Royal Museum of Central Africa, Tervuren
SAC	*Staatsarchiv Coburg*: State Archives Coburg, Coburg
SAP MP	State Archives Pilsen, Pilsen (Czech Republic), Mensdorff-Pouilly Papers
SOMA	*Studie- en Documentatiecentrum Oorlog en Hedendaagse Maatschappij*: Study and Documentation Centre of World War II and Contemporary Society, Brussels
SOMA PC24	Capelle Papers
SOMA TB	*Tätigkeitsberichte*: Daily reports of the German Military Administration in Brussels, 1940–1944

Bibliography

For unpublished and archival sources, newspapers and periodicals:
See footnotes

Published Sources

Aanvullende Nota op 8 October 1947 gepubliceerd door de Commissie van Voorlichting ingesteld door Z.M. Koning Leopold III op 14 Juli 1946. Brussels: Goemaere, 1947.

Adriaenssen, Agnes. *Marie José: Laatste koningin van Italië.* Leuven: Van Halewyck, 1999.

Albert I [King of the Belgians].
1. *Les Carnets de Guerre d' Albert Ier Roi des Belges.* Ed. Raoul Van Overstraeten. Brussels: Charles Dessart, 1953.
2. *Le Roi Albert au travers de ses lettres inédites 1882–1916.* Eds. Marie-Rose Thielemans and Emile Vandewoude. Brussels: Office International de Librairie, 1982.
3. *Albert Ier: Carnets et correspondance de guerre 1914–1918.* Ed. Marie-Rose Thielemans. Louvain-la-Neuve: Duculot, 1991.

Anstey, Roger. *King Leopold's Legacy: The Congo under Belgian rule 1908–1960.* London: Oxford University Press, 1966.

Anthierens, Johan, ed. *Brief aan een postzegel: Kritisch Koningsboek.* Leuven: Kritak, 1990.

Aron, Robert. *Léopold III ou le choix impossible.* Paris: Plon, 1977.

Aronson, Theo. *The Coburgs of Belgium.* London: Cassell, 1968.

Ascherson, Neal. *The King Incorporated: Leopold II in the Age of Trusts.* London: Granta Books, 1999 (first published in 1963).

Ashdown, Dulcie M. *Victoria and the Coburgs.* London: Robert Hale, 1981.

Asselberghs, Herman, and Dieter Lesage, eds. *Het museum van de natie: Van kolonialisme tot globalisering.* Brussels: Yves Gevaert, 1999.

Bachmann, Gertraude.
1. *Die Reise der Coburger Erbprinzessin Auguste Caroline Sophie an den Hof der Zarin Katharina II. in St. Petersburg 1795.* Coburg: Coburger Landesstiftung, 1992.
2. *Herzogin Marie von Sachen-Coburg und Gotha geborene Herzogin von Württemberg 1799–1860.* Coburg: Historische Gesellschaft Coburg, 1999.

Banning, Emile.
1. *L'Afrique et la conférence géographique de Bruxelles.* Brussels: Muquardt, 1877.
2. Les traités de 1815 et la Belgique. Brussels: G. Van Oest & Cie, 1919.
3. Les origines & les phases de la neutralité belge. Ed. Alfred De Ridder. Brussels: Librairie Albert Dewit, 1927.
4. *Mémoires politiques et diplomatiques.* Brussels: Renaissance du Livre, 1927.
5. *Les textes inédits d'Emile Banning.* Ed. Jean Stengers. Brussels: Académie Royale des Sciences Coloniales, 1955.
Baroche, Madame Jules, née Céleste Letellier. *Notes et souvenirs.* Paris: Les Editions G. Crès et Cie, 1921.
Baudhuin, Fernand. *Histoire économique de la Belgique 1914-1939,* 2 volumes. Brussels: Bruylant, 1944.
Baudouin [King of the Belgians]. *Wij, Boudewijn, Koning der Belgen: Het politiek, sociaal en moreel testament van een nobel vorst,* 2 volumes. Ed. P.J. Vic Neels. Balen: Eurodef, 1996.
Bauer, Karoline.
1. *Verschollene herzensgeschichten: Nachgelassene Memoiren von Karoline Bauer,* 3 volumes. Ed. Arnold Wellmer. Berlin: Louis Gerschel Verlag, 1880-1881.
2. *Aus meinem Bühnenleben: Eine Auswahl aus den Lebenserinnerungen der Künstlerin.* Ed. Karl von Hollander. Weimar: Gustav Kiepenheuer Verlag, 1917.
Bauer, Ludwig. *Leopold: der ungeliebte König der Belgier und des Geldes.* Amsterdam: Querido Verlag, 1934.
Baumont, Maurice. *La faillite de la paix 1918-1939,* 2 volumes. Paris: Presses Universitaires de France, 1967-1968 (first published in 1945).
Beauharnais, Hortense de [Queen of Holland]. *Mémoires de la Reine Hortense,* 3 volumes. Eds. Prince Napoléon and Jean Hanoteau. Paris: Plon-Nourrit, 1927.
Belgian Chamber of Representatives.
1. Doc. 59/8-1988 [Report of the Parliamentary Inquiry Committee into the Crazy Brabant Killings], 30 Apr. 1990.
2. Unpublished minutes [of testimonies before the Second Parliamentary Inquiry Committee into the Crazy Brabant Killings], Mar.-June 1997.
3. Docs. 573/7-95/96 to 573/12-95/96 [Reports of the Second Parliamentary Inquiry Committee into the Crazy Brabant Killings], 14 Oct. 1997.
4. Doc. 713/6-96/97 [Report of the Parliamentary Inquiry Committee into the Dutroux-Nihoul Case], 14 Apr. 1997.
5. Doc. 713/8-96/97 [Second Report of the Parliamentary Inquiry Committee into the Dutroux-Nihoul Case], 16 Feb. 1998.
Belgian Senate.
1. Unpublished minutes [of testimonies before the Senate Inquiry Committee into the Rwanda Massacre], Apr.-June 1997.
2. Doc. 1-611/7 1997-1998 [Report of the Senate Inquiry Committee into the Rwanda Massacre], 6 Dec.1997.
Beyens, Baron Eugène. *Le Second Empire vu par un diplomate belge,* 2 volumes. Bruges/Paris: Desclée de Brouwer/Plon-Nourrit, 1924-1926.
[Bishops of Belgium]. *Herderlijke brieven over politiek 1830-1966.* Ed. Karel Van Isacker. Antwerp: De Nederlandsche Boekhandel, 1969.
Boigne, Comtesse de, née Eleonore Adèle d'Osmond. *Mémoires de la Comtesse de Boigne, née d'Osmond, publiés d'après le manuscrit original,* 4 volumes. Ed. Charles Nicoullaud. Paris: Plon-Nourrit, 1907-1908.

348   *A Throne in Brussels*

Boudart, Marina, Michel Boudart and René Bryssinck, eds. *Modern Belgium.* Palo Alto: Society for the Promotion of Science and Scholarship, 1990.

Boudens, Robrecht. *Kardinaal Mercier en de Vlaamse Beweging.* Leuven: Davidsfonds, 1975.

Bracke, Maud. 'Het persoonlijke leven van koning Boudewijn.' In Koninckx and Lefèvre, below.

Bracke, Maud, and Christine Denuit-Somerhausen. 'De representatieve functie van de koning.' In Koninckx and Lefèvre, below.

Braive, Gaston, and Jacques Lory, eds. *L'église et l'état à l'époque contemporaine: Mélanges dédiés à la mémoire de Mgr. Aloïs Simon.* Brussels: Facultés Universitaires Saint-Louis, 1975.

Brialmont, Henri-Alexis. *Brialmont: Eloge et mémoires.* Ed. Paul Crokaert. Brussels: A. Lesigne, 1925.

Brion, René, and Jean-Louis Moreau. *De Generale Maatschappij van België 1822–1997.* Antwerp: Mercatorfonds, 1998.

Bronne, Carlo.
1. *Léopold Ier et son temps.* Brussels: Goemaere, 1942.
2. *La conspiration des paniers percés.* Brussels: Goemaere, 1959.
3. *Albert Ier: le roi sans terre.* Paris: Plon, 1965.

Bruffaerts, Jean-Michel. 'Voorrang aan het hart of aan het staatsbelang? Huwelijken en erfenissen aan het Belgische hof ten tijde van Leopold I en Leopold II.' In Janssens and Stengers, below.

Buchanan, James M., Robert D. Tollison, and Gordon Tullock, eds. *Toward a Theory of the Rent-Seeking Society.* College Station: Texas A&M University Press, 1980.

Buchanan, James M., and Gordon Tullock. *The Calculus of Consent: Logical Foundations of Constitutional Democracy.* Ann Arbor: University of Michigan Press, 2001 (first published in 1962).

Buffin, Baron Camille. *La Jeunesse de Léopold Ier, roi des Belges.* Brussels: Henri Lamertin, 1914.

Bülow, Bernard, Fürst von. *Denkwürdigkeiten,* 4 volumes. Berlin: Ullstein Verlag, 1930.

Buls, Charles.
1. *Esthétique des villes.* Brussels: Sint-Lukasarchief, 1981 (first published in 1894).
2. *Het dagboek van C. Buls.* Ed. Marcel Bots. Ghent: Liberaal Archief, 1987.

Bulté, Annemie, Douglas De Coninck and Marie-Jeanne Van Heeswyck. *De X-dossiers: Wat België niet mocht weten over de zaak-Dutroux.* Antwerp: Houtekiet, 1999.

Buraggi, G.C., and others. *Belgio e Piemonte nel Risorgimento Italiano.* Turin: G. Chiantore, 1930.

Cailliau, Maurits, ed. *Joris van Severen: Jaarboek 5.* Ieper: Studie- en Coördinatiecentrum Joris van Severen, 2001.

Caine, Hall, ed. *King Albert's Book.*London: The Daily Telegraph, 1914.

Capelle, Count Robert.
1. *Au service du Roi,* 2 volumes. Brussels: Charles Dessart, 1949.
2. *Dix-huit ans auprès du Roi Léopold.* Paris: Fayard, 1970.

Capron, Victor.
1. *Le mariage du Comte de Flandre.* Brussels: Victor Capron, 1991.
2. *La descendance naturelle de Léopold I, Roi des Belges.* Brussels: Victor Capron, 1995.

Carlier, Donat. 'Du tabou nationaliste à l'approfondissement démocratique.' *La Revue Nouvelle,* 11 (2000): pp. 10–8.

Carton de Wiart, Edmond. *Léopold II: Souvenirs des dernières années 1901-1909*. Brussels: Goemaere, 1944.

Cattier, Félicien. *Etude sur la situation de l'Etat Indépendant du Congo*. Brussels: Larcier-Pedone, 1906.

Cecil, Lord Robert. *A Great Experiment: An Autobiography*. New York: Oxford University Press, 1941.

Ceulemans, P. *La question arabe et le Congo*. Brussels: Académie Royale des Sciences Coloniales, 1959.

Charlotte [Princess of Great Britain and Hanover]. *Letters of Princess Charlotte 1811-1817*. Ed. A. Aspinall. London: Home and Van Thal, 1949.

Claes, Ernest. *Jeugd*. Antwerp: Standaard Boekhandel, 1940.

Claes, Lode.
1. *Het verdrongen verleden: De collaboratie, haar rechters en geschiedschrijvers*. Beveren: Orbis en Orion uitgevers, 1983.
2. *De afwezige meerderheid*. Leuven: Davidsfonds, 1985.
3. *De afwendbare nederlaag*. Leuven: Davidsfonds, 1986.

Claeys-Van Haegendoren, Mieke. *Hendrik de Man: Een biografie*. Antwerp: De Nederlandsche Boekhandel, 1972.

Colenbrander, Herman Theodoor.
1. *Gedenkstukken der Algemeene Geschiedenis van de Nederlanden 1795-1840*, 10 volumes in 22. The Hague: Rijks Geschiedkundige Publicatiën, 1905-1922.
2. *Willem I: Koning der Nederlanden*, 2 volumes. Amsterdam: Nederlandse Historische Bibliotheek, 1931-1935.
3. *Willem II: Koning der Nederlanden*. Amsterdam: J.M. Meulenhoff, 1938.

Collins, Robert O. *King Leopold, England and the Upper Nile 1899-1909*. New Haven: Yale University Press, 1968.

Committee I [Standing Committee Monitoring the Intelligence Services]. *Jaarverslag 2001: Rapport van het onderzoek naar de manier waarop de inlichtingendiensten aandacht hebben voor extremistische en terroristische islamitische activiteiten [Annual Report 2001: Report of the Inquiry into the Ways in which the Intelligence Services Screen Extremist and Terrorist Islamic Activivities]*. Brussels: Vast Comité van Toezicht op de Inlichtingendiensten, 2002.

Conrad, Joseph. *Heart of Darkness*. London: Penguin Books, 1999 (first published in 1899).

Conway, Martin. *Collaboration in Belgium: Léon Degrelle and the Rexist Mouvement 1940-1944*. New Haven/London: Yale University Press, 1993.

Cookey, S.J.S. *Britain and the Congo Question 1885-1913*. London: Longmans, Green & Co, 1968.

Coolsaet, Rik. *België en zijn buitenlandse politiek 1830-2000*. Antwerp: Van Halewyck, 2001.

Coppieters, Bruno, and Michel Huysseune, eds. *Secession, History and the Social Sciences*. Brussels: VUB Press, 2002.

Corti, Egon Caesar.
1. *Leopold I von Belgien: Sein Weltgebaüde Koburger Familienmacht*. Leipzig: Rikola Verlag, 1922.
2. *Maximilien et Charlotte du Mexique 1860-1867*, 2 volumes. Paris: Plon-Nourrit, 1927 (first published in German as *Maximilian und Charlotte von Mexiko* in 1924).

Corti, Egon Caesar, and Camille Buffin. *Léopold Ier: Oracle politique de l'Europe*. Brussels: Librairie Albert Dewit, 1926.

Cottenier, Jo, Patrick de Boosere, and Thomas Gonnet. *De Generale 1822–1992*. Berchem: EPO, 1989.

Crombois, Jean-François. *Camille Gutt: Les finances et la guerre 1940–1945*. Gerpinnes: Quorum-Ceges, 2000.

Cunliffe-Owen, Sidney. *Elisabeth: Queen of the Belgians*. London: Herbert Jenkins, 1954.

Danneels, Mario. *Paola: Van 'la dolce vita' tot koningin*. Leuven: Van Halewyck, 1999.

Dantoing, Alain. *La 'collaboration' du Cardinal: L'Eglise de Belgique dans la Guerre de 40*. Brussels: De Boeck-Wesmael, 1991.

Daye, Pierre. *Léopold II*. Paris: Fayard, 1934.

De Belgische expansie onder Leopold I (1839–1865): Verzameling studies. Brussels: Koninklijke Academie voor Overzeese Wetenschappen, 1965.

De Bens, Els. *De Belgische dagbladpers onder Duitse censuur 1940–1944*. Antwerp: De Nederlandsche Boekhandel, 1973.

De Bie, Mark. *De Coburger: Leopold I, een monoloog als zelfportret*. Tielt: Lannoo, 1990.

Deboosere, Sabine, Ria Van Alboom and Mark Van den Wijngaert. *Monarchie en macht: België en zijn koningen*. Brussels: BRTN, 1992.

Declercq, Raf, and Jos Rondas. *9 februari 1946: Lucrèce Vanbillemont terechtgesteld in Brugge*. Kortrijk: Groeninghe, 2001.

De Jonghe, Albert.
1. *De taalpolitiek van Willem I*. Sint-Andries-bij-Brugge: Darthet, 1967.
2. *Hitler en het politieke lot van België 1940–1944: De vestiging van een Zivilverwaltung in België en Noord-Frankrijk: Deel I Koningskwestie en bezettingsregime van de kapitulatie tot Berchtesgaden (28 mei–19 november 1940)*. Antwerp: De Nederlandsche Boekhandel, 1972.
3. 'De laatste boodschap van Kiewitz namens koning Leopold III voor Hitler (15 juni 1944).' *Belgisch Tijdschrift voor Filologie en Geschiedenis*, LXV, 2 (1987): pp. 274–300.
4. 'Aspekten van de de wegvoering van koning Leopold III naar Duitsland (7 juni 1944).' *Bijdragen-Cahiers Navorsings- en studiecentrum voor de geschiedenis van de Tweede Wereldoorlog*, 11 (March 1988): pp. 5–120.

Delathuy, A.M. [Marchal, Jules].
1. *E.D. Morel tegen Leopold II en de Kongostaat*. Berchem: EPO, 1985.
2. *Jezuïeten in Kongo met zwaard en kruis*. Berchem: EPO, 1986.
3. *De geheime documentatie van de onderzoekscommissie in de Kongostaat*. Berchem: EPO, 1988.
4. *De Kongostaat van Leopold II: Het verloren paradijs 1876–1900*. Antwerp: Standaard Uitgeverij, 1988.
5. *Missie en staat in Oud-Kongo (1880–1914): Witte paters, scheutisten, jezuïeten*. Berchem: EPO, 1992.
6. *Missie en staat in Oud-Kongo (1880–1914): Redemptoristen, trappisten, norbertijnen, priester van het H. Hart, paters van Mill Hill*. Berchem: EPO, 1994.

De Lentdecker, Louis.
1. *Requiem voor Leopold III*. Brussels: Grammens, 1983.
2. *Prins Karel*. Brussels: Grammens, 1987.

Deleu, Jozef, ed. *Encyclopedie van de Vlaamse Beweging*, 2 volumes. Tielt: Lannoo, 1973–1975.

Delforge, Paul, Philippe Destatte and Michel Libon, eds. *Encyclopédie du Mouvement Wallon*, 3 volumes. Mont-sur-Marchienne: Institut Jules Destrée, 2000–2001.

De Man, Hendrik (Henri).
1. *Cahiers de ma montagne*. Brussels: Editions de la Toison d'Or, 1944.
2. *Persoon en Ideeën: Autobiografie*. Ed. Mieke Claeys-Van Haegendoren. Antwerp/Amsterdam: Standaard Wetenschappelijke Uitgeverij, 1974.
3. *Le 'Dossier Léopold III' et autres documents sur la période de la seconde guerre mondiale, réunis, présentés et édités par Michel Brélaz*. Ed. Michel Brélaz. Geneva: Editions des Antipodes, 1989.
De Man-Flechtheim, Marlène. *Geschiedenis van mijn leven: Een tijdsdocument*. Ed. Mieke Van Haegendoren. Leuven: Acco, 1993.
De Meulder, Bruno. *De kampen van Kongo: Arbeid, kapitaal en rasveredeling in de koloniale planning*. Amsterdam/Antwerp: Meulenhoff/Kritak, 1996.
Demoulin, Robert. *Guillaume Ier et la Transformation économique des provinces belges (1815–1830)*. Liège/Paris: Faculté de Philosophie et Lettres/E. Droz, 1938.
Deneckere, Gita.
1. 'De kerk in het midden: De koningen en de binnenlandse politiek.' In Janssens and Stengers, below.
2. 'Koning Boudewijn en de modus vivendi op sociaal-economisch gebied: Casusanalyse van een discrete koninklijke interventie tijdens de staking van 1960-61.' In Koninckx and Lefèvre, below.
Denis, Jean, and Reinier Ysabie. *Koningin Astrid*. Leuven: Erasmus, 1935.
De Potter, Louis-Antoine, *La révolution belge 1828 à 1839: Souvenirs personnels avec des pièces à l'appui*, 2 volumes. Brussels: Jamar, 1840.
De Preter, René. *De 200 rijkste families: Geld en macht in de wereld van de holdings en miljonairs*. Amsterdam/Berchem: Ekologische Uitgeverij/EPO, 1993.
Deprez, Kas, and Louis Vos, eds. *Nationalisme in België: Identiteiten in beweging 1780–2000*. Antwerp: Houtekiet, 1999.
De Ridder, Alfred.
1. *Le mariage du roi Léopold II*. Brussels: Albert Dewit, 1925.
2. *La crise de la neutralité belge de 1848: Le dossier diplomatique*, 2 volumes. Brussels: Librairie Kiesling & Cie/M. Weissenbruch, 1928.
3. *Fragments d'histoire contemporaine de Belgique*. Brussels/Paris: Librairie Nationale d'Art et d'Histoire, 1931.
4. *Les projets d'union douanière franco-belge (1836–1843)*. Brussels/Paris: Maurice Lamertin, 1932.
De Ridder, Hugo.
1. *De keien van de Wetstraat*. Leuven: Davidsfonds, 1983.
2. *Geen winnaars in de Wetstraat*. Leuven: Davidsfonds, 1986.
3. *Sire, geef me honderd dagen*. Leuven: Davidsfonds, 1989.
4. *Omtrent Wilfried Martens*. Tielt: Lannoo, 1991.
5. *De strijd om de 16*. Tielt: Lannoo, 1993.
6. *Jean-Luc Dehaene: Mét commentaar*. Tielt: Lannoo, 1996.
7. *Geen blad voor de mond: Notities voor een biografie*. Tielt: Lannoo, 2001.
De Schaepdrijver, Sophie. *De Groote Oorlog: Het koninkrijk België tijdens de Eerste Wereldoorlog*. Amsterdam-Antwerp: Atlas, 1997.
De Schryver, Reginald, and Bruno De Wever, eds. *Nieuwe Encyclopedie van de Vlaamse Beweging*, 3 volumes. Tielt: Lannoo, 1998.
De Staercke, André. *Tout cela a passé comme une ombre: Mémoires sur la Régence et la Question Royale*. Brussels: Racine, 2003.
Destrée, Jules. *Wallons et Flamands: La querelle linguistique en Belgique*. Paris: Plon, 1923.

Dethomas, Bruno, and José-Alain Fralon. *Les milliards de l'orgueil: L'affaire de la Société Générale de Belgique.* Paris: Gallimard, 1989.

De Volder, Jan. *Benoît XV et la Belgique durant la Grande Guerre.* Brussels/Rome: Institut Historique Belge de Rome, 1996.

De Vos, Luc, Emmanuel Gerard, Jules Gérard-Libois and Philippe Raxon.
1. *Nota van de experts [Notes for the Parliamentary Inquiry Committee into the Lumumba Assassination].* Unpublished document, 6 June 2001.
2. *Koning Boudewijn en de Congo-crisis [Report for the Parliamentary Inquiry Committee into the Lumumba Assassination].* Unpublished document, 5 Nov. 2001.

Dewachter, Wilfried.
1. *Besluitvorming in Politiek België.* Leuven: Acco, 1992.
2. *De regering rechtstreeks verkiezen.* Leuven: KUL Afdeling Politologie, 1998.
3. *De mythe van de parlementaire democratie: Een Belgische analyse.* Leuven: Acco, 2001.
4. *Van oppositie tot elite: Over macht, visie en leiding.* Leuven: Acco, 2003.

Deweerdt, Denise. 'Arbeiderstoestanden van 1850 tot 1876.' In Dhondt, below.

De Wever, Bruno.
1. *Staf De Clercq.* Brussels: Grammens, 1989.
2. 'De Vlaams-nationalisten in de parlementsverkiezingen van 1936.' *Belgisch Tijdschrift voor Nieuwste Geschiedenis,* XXIII, 3–4 (1992): pp. 281–353.
3. *Greep naar de macht: Vlaams-nationalisme en Nieuwe Orde: Het VNV 1933-1945.* Tielt-Gent: Lannoo/Perspectief, 1994.

De Witte, Ludo.
1. *Crisis in Kongo: De rol van de Verenigde Naties, de regering Eyskens en het koningshuis in de omwerwerping van Lumumba en de opkomst van Mobutu.* Leuven: Van Halewyck, 1996.
2. *De moord op Lumumba.* Leuven: Van Halewyck, 1999.
3. *Voor koning en vaderland [Report for the Parliamentary Inquiry Committee into the Lumumba Assassination].* Unpublished document, Oct. 2000.

Diedrich, Karlheinz. *Die Belgier, ihre Könige und die Deutschen: Geschichte zweier Nachbarn seit 1830.* Düsseldorf: Droste, 1989.

Discailles, Ernest. *Charles Rogier (1800-1885) d'après des documents inédits,* 4 volumes. Brussels: Lebègue & Cie, 1893–1895.

Dhondt, Jan, ed. *Geschiedenis van de socialistische arbeidersbeweging in België.* Antwerpen: Ontwikkeling, 1960.

Dino, Duchesse de, née Dorothée de Courlande. *Chronique de 1831 à 1862: Souvenirs de la duchesse de Dino,* 4 volumes. Ed. Princesse Radziwill, née Marie de Castellane. Paris: Plon et Nourrit, 1909–1910.

Dufoux, Georges. *Les Saxe-Cobourg-Gotha: Un destin royal et tourmenté: Histoire et descendance (1778–2000) masculine et féminine, légitime et illégitime, en 58 tableaux assemblables et commentés.* Fontainebleau: Dufoux, 2000.

Dumoulin, Michel, and Eddy Stols, eds. *La Belgique et l'étranger aux XIXe et XXe siècles.* Louvain-la-Neuve/Brussels: Collège Erasme/Nauwelaerts, 1987.

Duparc, Frederik Jules. *Willem II, België en Luxemburg.* The Hague: Albani, 1934.

Elias, Hendrik.
1. *Geschiedenis van de Vlaamse Gedachte 1790-1914,* 4 volumes. Antwerp: De Nederlandsche Boekhandel, 1963–1965.
2. *25 jaar Vlaamse Beweging 1914/1939,* 4 volumes. Antwerp: De Nederlandsche Boekhandel, 1969–1972.

Emerson, Barbara. *Leopold II of the Belgians: King of Colonialism.* London: Weidenfeld and Nicholson, 1979.

Entretiens sur la Belgique contemporaine. Brussels: Larcier, 1904.

Erauw, Willem. *Koningin Elisabeth: Over pacifisme, pantheïsme en de passie voor muziek.* Ghent: Stichting Mens en Kultuur, 1995.

Esmeralda [Princess of Belgium]. *Léopold III: Mon père.* Brussels: Racine, 2001.

Eyskens, Gaston.
1. *Les fondements de la politique économique de l'Allemagne et de l'Italie.* Leuven: KUL, 1941.
2. *Het laatste gesprek: Herinneringen aan 40 jaar politiek leven.* Ed. Jozef Smits. Kapellen: Pelckmans, 1988.
3. *De Memoires.* Ed. Jozef Smits. Tielt: Lannoo, 1993.

Falter, Rolf. ''Je te quitte jamais:' Het koningshuis in de aantekeningen van Achiel van Acker.' *Standaard Magazine,* 3 Apr. 1988: pp. 18–21.

Fetter, Bruce. *L'Union Minière du Haut-Katanga 1920–1940: La naissance d'une sous-culture totalitaire.* Tervuren: Les cahiers du CEDAF, 1973.

Fishman, Joel. *Diplomacy and Revolution: The London Conference of 1830 and the Belgian Revolt.* Amsterdam: CHEV, 1988.

Florquin, Joos. *Ten huize van...*, 18 volumes. Leuven: Davidsfonds, 1962–1982.

Fraden, Denise. *Baudouin: L'éducation d'un roi.* Strombeek-Bever: Le Scorpion, 1975.

Fralon, José-Alain. *Baudouin: L'homme qui ne voulait pas être roi.* Paris: Fayard, 2001.

Fraser, Flora. *The Unruly Queen: The Life of Queen Caroline.* London: Macmillan, 1996.

Franck, Christian, and Claude Roosens. 'Koning Boudewijn en de buitenlandse politiek.' In Koninckx and Lefèvre, below.

Frateur, J. Léopold. 'La notion de race à la lumière des données de l'hérédité expérimentale.' *Bulletin des Séances: Institut Royal Colonial Belge,* 8 (1937): pp. 567–601.

Freddy, G. *Léopold II intime.* Paris: Félix Juven, 1905.

Fris, Victor. *'t Jaar 30: een volksboek.* Ghent: Vuylsteke, 1905.

Galet, Emile Joseph. *S.M. le roi Albert: Commandant en chef devant l'invasion allemande.* Paris: Plon, 1931.

Gan, L.H., and Peter Duignan. *The Rulers of Belgian Africa (1884–1914).* Princeton: Princeton University Press, 1979.

Garsou, Jules.
1. *Alexandre Gendebien: Sa vie, ses mémoires.* Brussels: Van Sulper, 1930.
2. *Les débuts d'un grand règne: Notes pour servir à l'histoire de la Belgique contemporaine,* 2 volumes. Brussels: L'Eventail, 1931–1934.
3. 'Léopold II et les partis politiques.' In Stinglhamber and Dresse, below.
4. 'Le cabinet du roi.' In Stinglhamber and Dresse, below.
5. *Un grand soldat: Le Général Chazal (1808–1892).* Brussels: Office de Publicité, 1946.
6. *Les relations extérieures de la Belgique (1839–1914).* Brussels: Editions Universitaires, 1946.

Garsou, Jules, and Gustave Stinglhamber. 'Léopold II et la défense nationale.' In Stinglhamber and Dresse, below.

Geerts, Walter. *Binza 10: De eerste tien onafhankelijkheidsjaren van de Demokratische Republiek Kongo.* Ghent: Story-Scientia, 1970.

Gerard, Emmanuel. 'Boudewijn, de regering en de binnenlandse politiek.' In Koninckx and Lefèvre, below.

Gérard, Jo.
1. *De dames van Laken: Het leven van vijf Belgische koninginnen.* Ghent: Het Volk, 1978.
2. *Chronique de la Régence 1944–1950.* Brussels: J.M. Collet, 1983.
3. *Léopold II: Le pharaon des Belges.* Brussels: J.M. Collet, 1984.
4. *La lionne blessée: Marie-Henriette, Reine des Belges.* Brussels: J.M. Collet, 1986.
5. *Albert II et sa famille.* Braine l'Alleud: J.M. Collet, 1993.

Gérard-Libois, Jules, and José Gotovitch.
1. *L'An 40: La Belgique occupée.* Brussels: CRISP, 1971.
2. *Léopold III: De l'an 40 à l'effacement.* Brussels: POL-HIS, 1991.

Gerretson, C. *Muiterij en Scheuring 1830,* 2 volumes. Leiden: Sijthoff, 1936.

Geyl, Pieter. *Geschiedenis van de Nederlandse Stem,* 6 volumes. Amsterdam/Antwerpen: Wereldbibliotheek, 1961–1962 (first published in 1930–1958).

Gille, Bertrand, ed. *Lettres adressées à la Maison Rotschild de Paris par son représentant à Bruxelles,* 2 volumes. Louvain/Paris: Nauwelaerts, 1961–1963.

Gilmour, David. *Curzon.* London: John Murray, 1994.

Giscard d'Estaing, Antoine. *Léopold III: Un Roi dans la tourmente.* Brussels: Editions Racine, 1996.

Goebbels, Josef. *Tagebücher 1924–1945,* 5 volumes. Ed. R. Reuth. Munich: Piper, 1992.

Goemaere, Pierre. *Albert Iᵉʳ: Loin des Foules.* Grenoble: Arthaud, 1935.

Goris, Jan Albert. *Lof van Antwerpen.* Antwerp: Lions Club Antwerpen-Centrum, 1994 (first published in 1940).

Gossart, Ernest. *Emile Banning et Léopold II 1867–1892.* S.l.: Librairie Maurice Lamertin, s.a.

Greville, Lord Charles. *The Greville Memoirs,* 8 volumes. London: Longmans, Green and Co., 1896.

Grey, Lt.-Gen. Charles. *The Early Years of H.R.H. the Prince Consort, Compiled Under the Direction of Her Majesty the Queen.* London: Smith, Elder & Co., 1869.

Haag, Henri. *Le Comte Charles de Broqueville, Ministre d'Etat, et les luttes pour le pouvoir 1910–1940,* 2 volumes. Louvain-la-Neuve/Beauvechain: UCL/Nauwelaerts, 1990.

Hannes, Juul. 'Met de fiscale bril bekeken: Vlaanderen in België 1830–1914.' In Verhulst and Pareyn, below.

Hardie, Frank. *The Political Influence of the British Monarchy 1868–1952.* London/New York: Harper & Row, 1970.

Harry, Gérard. *Léopold II.* Turnhout: Brepols, 1920.

Haslip, Joan. *Imperial Adventurer: Emperor Maximilian of Mexico.* London: Weidenfeld & Nicholson, 1971.

Hasquin, Hervé. *Les séparatistes wallons et le gouvernement de Vichy (1940–1943): Une histoire d'omerta.* Brussels: Académie royale de Belgique, 2004.

Hayek, Friedrich A., von.
1. *Law, Legislation and Liberty,* 3 volumes. London: Routledge & Kegan Paul, 1973–1979.
2. *The Fatal Conceit: The Errors of Socialism.* Chicago: The University of Chicago Press, 1988.

Helmreich, Jonathan E. *Belgium and Europe: A Study in Small Power Diplomacy.* The Hague/Paris: Mouton, 1976.

Hennebicq, Léon. 'L'expansion économique et la patrie belge.' In *Entretiens sur la Belgique contemporaine,* above.

Hermans, Theo, ed. *The Flemish Movement: A Documentary History 1780-1990*. London/Atlantic Highlands, NJ: The Athlone Press, 1992.

Hibbert, Christopher.
1. *George IV*. London: Allen Lane, 1975.
2. *Wellington: A Personal History*. London: Harper Collins Publishers, 1997.

Hitler, Adolf.
1. *Hitlers Tischgespräche im Führerhauptquartier 1941-1942*. Ed. Henry Picker. Stuttgart: Seewald Verlag, 1965.
2. *Monologe im Führerhauptquartier 1941-1944: Die Aufzeichnungen Heinrich Heims*. Ed. Werner Jochmann. Hamburg: Knaus, 1980.

Hird, Frank. *Stanley: The Authorized Life*. London: St. Paul & Co, 1935.

Hochschild, Adam. *King Leopold's Ghost*. London: Papermac, 2000 (first published in 1998).

Holden, Angus. *Uncle Leopold: A Life of the First King of the Belgians*. London: Hutchinson & Company, 1936.

Horne, John, and Alan Kramer. *German Atrocities 1914: A History of Denial*. New Haven: Yale University Press, 2002.

Huizinga, J.H. *Mr. Europe: A Political Biography of Paul Henri Spaak*. London: Weidenfeld & Nicholson, 1961.

Huyse, Luc, and Steven Dhondt. *Onverwerkt verleden: Collaboratie en repressie in België 1942-1952*. Leuven: Kritak, 1991.

Huysmans, Camille. *Camille Huysmans: Geschriften en Documenten – Volume VII: Camille Huysmans in Londen*. Eds. Herman Balthazar, and José Gotovitch. Antwerp: Standaard Wetenschappelijke Uitgeverij, 1978.

Huyttens, E. *Discussions du Congrès National de Belgique*, 5 volumes. Brussels: Société Typographique Belge, 1844.

Hyde, H. Montgomery. *The Mexican Empire: The History of Maximilian and Carlota of Mexico*. London: MacMillan, 1946.

Hymans, Paul. *Mémoires*, 2 volumes. Ed. Frans Van Kalken. Brussels: Institut de Sociologie Solvay, 1958.

Ilegems, Danny, and Jan Willems. *De kroon ontbloot: Over de macht van Boudewijn*. Leuven: Kritak, 1991.

Israel, Jonathan Irvine. *The Dutch Republic: Its Rise, Greatness and Fall 1477-1806*. Oxford: Clarendon Press, 1995.

Jacques, Gérard. *In het hart van Afrika: De saga van de Lualaba*. Tielt: Lannoo, 1996.

Janssens, Gustaaf.
1. 'De Goffinets, archivarissen van de koninklijke familie en beheerders van het fortuin van koning Leopold II.' In Janssens and Stengers, below.
2. 'De reisdagboekaantekeningen van de hertog van Brabant: Een eersterangsbron voor een betere kennis van de ideeën van de toekomstige koning Leopold II.' In Janssens and Stengers, below.
3. 'De Goffinets, bijna honderd jaar lang discrete dienaars van de koninklijke familie.' In Janssens and Stengers, below.

Janssens, Gustaaf, and Jean Stengers, eds. *Nieuw licht op Leopold I & Leopold II: Het Archief Goffinet*. Brussels: Koning Boudewijn Stichting, 1997.

Janssens, Stef. *De namen uit de doofpot*. Berchem: EPO, 1998.

Josson, Maurits. *De Belgische omwenteling van 1830*, 3 volumes. Amsterdam/Tielt: Veen/Lannoo, 1930.

Juste, Théodore.
1. *Histoire du Congrès National de Belgique ou de la fondation de la Monarchie Belge,* 2 volumes. Brussels: Lacroix, Van Meenen et Co, 1861.
2. *Léopold Ier, Roi des Belges d'après des documents inédits,* 2 volumes. Brussels: Lacroix, Van Meenen et Co, 1868.
3. *Léopold Ier et Léopold II, rois des Belges, leur vie et leur règne.* Brussels: Weissenbruch-Muquardt, 1878.
Kalb, Madeleine G. *The Congo Cables: The Cold War in Africa from Eisenhower to Kennedy.* New York: MacMillan, 1982.
Kalisz, Serge, and Patrick Moriau. *Les cahiers d'un commissaire: Les coulisses de l'affaire Dutroux.* Brussels: Pire, 1998.
Kerckvoorde, Mia.
1. *Louise van Orléans: Het vergeten leven van Louise-Marie, eerste koningin van België 1812–1850.* Tielt: Lannoo, 1988.
2. *Charlotte: Van Laken tot Mexico: biografie van een keizerin (1840–1927).* Tielt: Lannoo, 1991.
3. *Marie-Henriette: Een vrouw in de schaduw van een reus, Leopold II.* Tielt: Lannoo, 1997.
Keyes, Roger. *Outrageous Fortune: The Tragedy of Leopold III of the Belgians, 1901–1941.* London: Secker & Warburg, 1984.
Kieft, David. *Belgium's Return to Neutrality: An Essay in the Frustrations of Small Power Diplomacy.* Oxford: Clarendon Press, 1972.
Kirschen, Gilbert. *Léopold avant Léopold Ier: La jeunesse romantique d'un Prince ambitieux.* Brussels: Jacques Antoine, 1988.
Knight, Ellis Cornelia. *The Autobiography of Miss Knight, Lady Companion to Princess Charlotte.* Ed. Roger Fulford. London: William Kimber, 1960.
Koninckx, Christian, and Patrick Lefèvre, eds. *Boudewijn: Een koning en zijn tijd.* Tielt: Gemeentekrediet/Lannoo, 1998.
Kossmann, E.H. *The Low Countries.* Oxford: Oxford University Press, 1978.
Kurgan-van Hentenryk, Ginette.
1. *Léopold II et les groupes financiers belges en Chine: La politique royale et ses prolongements 1895–1914.* Brussels: Académie Royale de Belgique, 1972.
2. *Gouverner la Générale de Belgique: Essai de biographie collective.* Brussels: De Boeck & Larcier, 1996.
3. 'Het persoonlijke vermogen van Leopold II.' In Janssens and Stengers, above.
Lademacher, Horst. *Die belgische Neutralität als Problem der europäischen Politik 1830–1914.* Bonn: Ludwig Röhrscheid Verlag, 1971.
Lallemand, Roger. 'La Belgique, pays d'incertitude.' In Pickels and Sojcher, below.
Lambrechts, Lut. *De twee levens van koningin Elisabeth.* Antwerp: Hadewych, 1990.
Lanzac de Laborie, Léon de. *La domination française en Belgique.* 2 volumes. Paris: E. Plon, Nourrit et Cie, 1895.
Las Cases, Comte Emmanuel de. *Le mémorial de Sainte-Hélène par le comte de las Cases,* 2 volumes. Ed. Gérard Walter. Paris: Gallimard, 1956–1957 (first published in 1823).
Launay, Jacques de.
1. *La Belgique à l'heure allemande 1940–1945: les années sombres.* Brussels: Paul Legrain/Marabout, 1986 (first published in 1977).
2. *Léopold Ier.* Brussels: J.M. Collet, 1982.
Leclef, Edmond, ed. *Le Cardinal van Roey et l'occupation allemande en Belgique: Actes et documents publiés par le chanoine Leclef.* Brussels: Goemaere, 1945.

Lefébure, René. 'La Donation Royale.' *Revue Générale Belge*, 1952: pp. 557–9.

Le Febve de Vivy, L. *Documents d'histoire précoloniale belge 1861–1865*. Brussels: Académie Royale des Sciences Coloniales, 1955.

Lekime, Fernand. *La mangeuse de cuivre: La saga de l'Union Minière du Haut-Katanga 1906–1966*. Brussels: Hatier, 1992.

Lemmens, P. 'Het Verbond V.O.S., H. De Man en Leopold III na de Belgische Capitulatie van 28.5.1940.' *Wetenschappelijke Tijdingen op het gebied van de Vlaamse Beweging*, 1993, pp. 176–82, 193–213.

Leopold I [King of the Belgians].
1. *Lettres de Léopold Ier: premier roi des Belges*. Ed. Carlo Bronne. Brussels: Charles Dessart, 1943.
2. *Les Lettres de Léopold Ier à sa sœur la princesse Sophie, à son beau-frère Emmanuel, comte de Mensdorff-Pouilly, et à son neveu Alphonse, comte de Mensdorff-Pouilly 1804–1864*. Eds. Jean Puraye and Hans-Otto Lang. Liège: Vaillant-Carmanne, 1973.

Leopold II [King of the Belgians].
1. *Léopold II: Pensées et réflexions*. Ed. Georges-Henri Dumont. Brussels: L'amitié par le livre, 1948.
2. *Le mariage de Maximilien et Charlotte: Journal du Duc de Brabant 1856–1857*. Ed. Victor Capron. Brussels: Victor Capron, 1986.
3. *Un voyage à Wildbach-Gastein en 1861: Journal du Duc de Brabant*. Ed. Victor Capron. Brussels: Victor Capron, 1987.

Leopold II [King of the Belgians], and Henri-Alexis Brialmont. *Complément de l'Oeuvre de 1830, établissements à créer dans les pays transatlantiques: Avenir du commerce et de l'industrie belges*. Brussels: Charles Muquardt, 1860.

Leopold III [King of the Belgians].
1. *De Opvoeding van een Prins: Gesprekken met Koning Leopold III*. Ed. Gilbert Kirschen. Kalmthout: Uilenspiegel, 1986 (first published in French as *L'éducation d'un prince: Entretiens avec le Roi Léopold III* in 1984).
2. *Kroongetuige: Over de grote gebeurtenissen tijdens mijn koningschap*. Tielt: Lannoo, 2001 (first published in French as *Pour l'Histoire: Sur quelques épisodes de mon règne* in 2001).
3. *Carnets de voyages*. Brussels: Racine, 2004.

Leroy, Pierre. *Journal de la Province Orientale, décembre 1958–mai 1960*. Mons: P. Leroy, 1965.

Lesage, Dieter. 'Federalisme en postkolonialisme: Over de natie als museum.' In Asselberghs and Lesage, above.

Les origines diplomatiques de la guerre de 1870, 29 volumes. Ed. Ministère des affaires étrangères. Paris: Flicker, 1910–1932.

Lichtervelde, Comte Louis de.
1. *Léopold of the Belgians*. New York: The Century Co, 1929 (first published in French as *Léopold II* in 1926).
2. *Léopold Ier et la formation de la Belgique contemporaine*. Brussels: Albert Dewit, 1929.

Liebaers, Herman. *Koning Boudewijn in spiegelbeeld: Getuigenis van een grootmaarschalk 1974–1981*. Leuven: Van Halewyck, 1998.

Lieven, Princess. *The Private Letters of Princess Lieven to Prince Metternich 1820–1826*. Ed. Peter Quennell. London: John Murray, 1937.

Lobkowicz, Prince Stéphane de. *Baudouin: Biographie*. Braine l'Alleud: J.M. Collet, 1994.

Lombaerde, Piet. *Leopold II: Koning-Bouwheer.* Ghent: Uitgeverij Pandora/Snoeck-Ducaju, 1995.

Louise [Princess of Belgium]. *Autour des trônes que j'ai vus tomber.* Brussels: Le Cri, 1997 (first published in 1921).

Louise [Queen of Belgium]. *La cour de Belgique et la cour de France de 1832 à 1850: Lettres intimes de Louise-Marie d'Orléans, première Reine des Belges au Roi Louis-Philippe et à la Reine Marie-Amélie.* Ed. Comte Hippolyte d'Ursel. Paris: Plon, 1933.

Luykx, Theo. *Politieke geschiedenis van België van 1789 tot heden.* Amsterdam-Brussels: Elsevier, 1973.

Luyten, Dirk. *Ideologie en praktijk van het corporatisme tijdens de Tweede Wereldoorlog.* Brussels: VUB Press, 1997.

Lyttelton, Oliver Viscount Chandos. *The Memoirs of Lord Chandos.* London: The Bodley Head, 1962.

Mabille, Xavier. *Histoire politique de la Belgique: Facteurs et acteurs de changement.* Brussels: CRISP, 2000.

Mahin, Lucien. *Qué walon po dmwin? Eradication et renaissance de la langue wallonne.* Gerpinnes: Quorum, 1999.

Marchal, Jules. *L'histoire du Congo 1910-1945,* 3 volumes. Borgloon: Paula Bellings, 1999-2001.

Marie-José [Queen of Italy]. *Albert et Elisabeth de Belgique, mes parents.* Paris: Plon, 1971.

Maskens, Alain. *Mono-Vlamingen en mono-Walen: Dwaalwegen en gevaren van mono-identitaire ideologieën.* Brussels: Ockegem, 2000.

Mattachich, Comte Geza. *Folle par raison d'état: La princesse Louise de Belgique.* Brussels: Le Cri, 1998 (first published in 1904).

Mertens, Pierre. *Koninklijke rust.* Bussum: Thoth, 1996 (first published in French as *Une paix royale* in 1995).

Mesnil, Christian. *La Question Royale.* Brussels: Vokaer, 1976.

Meuwissen, Eric. *Richesse Oblige: La belle époque des grandes fortunes.* Brussels: Racine, 1999.

Meyers, W., and F. Selleslagh. *De vijand te lijf: De Belgen in het verzet.* Kapellen: Helios, 1984.

Meynen, Alain. 'Economic and Social Policy since the 1950s.' In Witte, below.

Michaux, O. *Au Congo: Carnet de campagne.* Namur: Librairie Dupagne-Counert, 1913.

Michielsen, Stefaan, and Béatrice Delvaux. *Zes huwelijken en een begrafenis: Grote en kleine geheimen van de Belgische haute finance.* Tielt: Lannoo, 1999.

Miller, Jane K. *Belgian Foreign Policy between two wars 1919-1940.* New York: Bookman Associates, 1951.

Molitor, André. *La fonction royale en Belgique.* Brussels: CRISP, 1979.

Moloney, Joseph Augustus. *With Captain Stairs to Katanga.* London: Sampson Low, 1893.

Monteyne, André.
    1. *De Brusselaars: In een stad die anders is.* Tielt: Lannoo, 1981.
    2. *Karel Buls.* Brussels: AMVB, 1981.

Monthaye, Lt.-Col., and Alfred Germain. *Notre Dynastie.* Brussels: Rossel, 1910.

Morel, Edmund Dene.
  1. 'King Leopold's American Intrigues Exposed.' In Twain, below.
  2. *E.D. Morel's History of the Congo Reform Movement*. Eds. William Roger Louis and Jean Stengers. Oxford: Clarendon Press, 1968.

Mouchet, R., and A. Pearson. *The Practicle Hygiene of Native Compounds in Tropical Africa, being notes from the experience of the first eighteen years of European work in the Katanga*. London: Baillière, Tindall & Cox, 1923 (first published in French as *L'Hygiène pratique des camps de travailleurs noirs en Afrique tropicale* in 1922)

Mouchet, R., and R. Van Nitsen. *La main d'oeuvre indigène au Congo belge: Les problèmes qu'elle évoque*. Brussels: Impr. des Travaux Publics, 1940.

Mottoulle, Léopold. *Politique sociale de l'Union Minière du Haut-Katanga pour sa main-d'oeuvre indigène et ses résultats au cours de vingt années d'application*. Brussels: Libr. Falk fils, G. Van Campenhout, succ., 1946.

Moyersoen, Ludovic. *Prosper Poullet en de politiek van zijn tijd*. Bruges/Brussels: De Kinkhoren/Desclée de Brouwer, 1946.

Nefors, Patrick. *Industriële 'collaboratie' in België: Galopindoctrine, de emissiebank en de Belgische industrie in de Tweede Wereldoorlog*. Leuven: Van Halewyck, 2000.

Neuckermans, Luc, and Pol Van Den Driessche. *Albert: Koning na Boudewijn*. Leuven: Van Halewyck, 1995.

Nicholas, Allison. *Elisabeth: Queen of the Belgians, her Life and Times*. Bognor Regis: New Horizon, 1982.

Nicolas, Jean, and Frédéric Lavachery. *Dossier pédophilie: Le scandale de l'affaire Dutroux*. Paris: Flammarion, 2001.

Noterman, Jacques A.M. *De val van Albert I*. Leuven: Van Halewyck, 2004 (first published in French as *Le Roi tué: La première enquête approfondie sur la mort d'Albert 1er* in 2004).

Nothomb, Pierre. *Le roi Albert*. Brussels: Editions Rex, 1934.

Olson, Mancur.
  1. *The Logic of Collective Action: Public Goods and the Theory of Groups*. Cambridge, Mass.: Harvard University Press, 1965.
  2. *The Rise and Decline of Nations: Economic Growth, Stagflation and Social Rigidities*. New Haven, Conn.: Yale University Press, 1982.

Oncken, Hermann. *Die Rheinpolitik Kaiser Napoleons III von 1863 bis 1870*, 3 volumes. Stuttgart: F.A. Perthes, 1926.

Oukhow, Michel. 'Arbeidersbeweging en Vlaamse kwestie 1855–1875.' In Dhondt, above.

Paoli, Dominique.
  1. *Prinses Clementine: De strijd om het geluk*. Tielt: Lannoo, 1993 (first published in French as *Clémentine, princesse Napoléon* in 1992).
  2. *Henriette, duchesse de Vendôme*. Brussels: Racine, 2000.

Parc Locmaria, Thérèse du. 'Un témoignage inédit: L'exode des princes royaux en mai 1940.' *L'Eventail*, Oct. 1993: pp. 22–7.

Pauwels, Jos, ed. *De waanzin van Charlotte: Prinses van België, keizerin van Mexico*. Berchem: EPO, 2000.

Pauwels, Luc, and Pieter-Jan Verstraete. *Vlaamse macht: In herinnering aan Lode Claes (1913–1997)*. Wijnegem: Delta-Stichting, 1998.

Pauwels, Luc. 'Joris van Severen en Duitsland.' In Cailliau, above.

Peeters, Wim, and Jérôme Wilson. *L'industrie belge dans la Russie des Tsars*. Alleur-Liège: Editions Du Perron, 1999.

Pellender, Heinz. *Chronik der Stadt und der Veste Coburg der Herren und Herrscher über Coburg und das Coburger Land.* Coburg: Fiedler Verlag, 1983.

Peltzer, Marina. 'De prins van Saksen-Coburg en Rusland.' In Sabbe, below.

Petacco, Arrigo. *Regina: La vita e i segreti di Maria José.* Milan: Mondadori, 1997.

Petrie, Glen. *A Singular Iniquity: The Campaigns of Joséphine Butler.* New York: The Viking Press, 1971.

Picard, Leo. *Evolutie van de Vlaamse Beweging van 1795 tot 1950,* 3 volumes. Antwerp: Standaard Uitgeverij, s.a.

Pickels, Antoine, and Jacques Sojcher, eds. *Belgique toujours grande et belle.* Brussels: Editions Complexe, 1998.

Pinder, John, ed. *Foundations of Democracy in the European Union: From the Genesis of Parliamentary Democracy to the European Parliament.* Basingstoke: MacMillan Press, 1999.

Pirenne, Henri. *Histoire de Belgique,* 7 volumes. Brussels: H. Lamertin, 1900–1932.

Pirenne, Jacques. *Mémoires et notes politiques.* Verviers: André Gerard/Marabout, 1975.

Plowden, Alison. *Caroline & Charlotte: The Regent's Wife and Daughter 1795–1821.* London: Sidgwick & Jackson, 1989.

Polspoel, Guy, and Pol Van Den Driessche. *Koning en onderkoning: Over de invloed van het hof en de macht van Jacques van Ypersele de Strihou.* Leuven: Van Halewyck, 2001.

Posse, Otto, and Manfred Kobuch. *Die Wettiner: Genealogie des Gesamthauses Wettin.* Leipzig: Zentralantiquariat Leipzig, 1994.

Potts, D.M. and W.T.W. Potts. *Queen Victoria's Gene: Haemophilia and the Royal Family.* Stroud: Sutton, 1995.

Provoost, Guido. *Vlaanderen en het militair-politiek beleid in België tussen de twee wereldoorlogen: Het Frans-Belgisch militair akkoord van 1920,* 2 volumes. Leuven: Davidsfonds, 1976.

Putman, Luc. *In dienst van koning Boudewijn.* Merendree: Sintjoris, 1997.

Quaghebeur, Marc, and Nicole Savy, eds. *France-Belgique (1848–1914): Affinités-Ambiguïtés.* Brussels: Editions Labor, 1997.

Ranieri, Liane.
  1. *Les relations entre l'Etat Indépendant du Congo et l'Italie 1876–1908.* Brussels: Académie Royale des Sciences Coloniales, 1959.
  2. *Léopold II Urbaniste.* Brussels: Hayez, 1973.
  3. 'Stedenbouw: Een vroege passie van Leopold II.' In Janssens and Stengers, above.

Raskin, Evrard. *Prinses Lilian: De vrouw die Leopold III ten val bracht.* Antwerp: Houtekiet, 1998.

Rastoul de Mongeot, Alphonse. *Léopold Ier, Roi des Belges: Sa vie militaire et politique.* Brussels: Lacroix, 1846.

Raymond, G. de. *Léopold II à Paris: Souvenirs.* Bruges: Desclée de Brouwer, 1950.

Reid, Escott. *Time of Fear and Hope: The Making of the North Atlantic Treaty 1947–1949.* Toronto: McClelland and Stewart, 1977.

Reinach-Foussemagne, Comtesse H. de. *Charlotte de Belgique: Impératrice du Mexique.* Paris: Plon, Nourrit et Cie, 1925.

Rhodes James, Robert. *Albert, Prince Consort: A Biography.* London: Hamish Hamilton, 1983.

Richardson, Joanna. *My dearest Uncle: A Life of Leopold, First King of the Belgians.* London: Jonathan Cape Ltd, 1961.

Rimanque, Karel. *De grondwet, toegelicht, gewikt en gewogen.* Antwerp: Intersentia, 1999.

Roelofsen, C. G. 'The Right to National Self-Determination in the 18th and 19th-Century — An Emerging Principle of Public International Law?' In Sybesma-Knol and Van Bellingen, below.

Roeykens, P. Auguste. *Les débuts de l'oeuvre africaine de Léopold II (1875–1879).* Brussels: Académie Royale des Sciences Coloniales, 1955.

Rudolph, Joseph R. Jr. 'Belgium — Controlling Separatist Tendencies in a Multinational State.' In Williams, below.

Runciman, Steven. *The White Rajahs: A History of Sarawak from 1841 to 1946.* Cambridge: Cambridge University Press, 1960.

Ruys, Manu.
1. *Achter de maskerade: Over macht, schijnmacht en onmacht.* Kapellen: Pelckmans, 1996.
2. *Een levensverhaal.* Tielt: Lannoo, 1999.
3. *Waarom Lumumba moest sterven.* Antwerp: Pelckmans, 2000.

Sabbe, Et., ed. *Leopold I en zijn tijd.* Brussels: Algemeen Rijksarchief, 1965.

Saerens, Lieven. *Vreemdelingen in een wereldstad: Een geschiedenis van Antwerpen en zijn joodse bevolking 1880–1944.* Tielt: Lannoo, 2000.

Sanderson, George Neville. *England, Europe and the Upper Nile 1882–1899.* Edinburgh: Edinburgh University Press, 1965.

Sandner, Harald. *Das Haus Sachsen-Coburg und Gotha: Eine Dokumentation zum 175-Jährigen Jubiläum des Stammhauses in Wort und Bild (1826 bis 2001).* Coburg: Neue Presse, 2001.

Schepens, Luc.
1. 'Is er meer dan één koningskwestie in België?' *Ons Erfdeel,* 1973/2: pp. 37–48.
2. *Koning Albert, Charles de Broqueville en de Vlaamse Beweging tijdens de Eerste Wereldoorlog.* Tielt: Lannoo, 1983.

Schepens, Luc, and Emile Vandewoude. *Albert & Elisabeth 1914–1918: Albums van de Koningin, nota's van de Koning.* Brussels: Gemeentekrediet, 1984.

Scherer, André, and Jacques Grunewald, eds. *L'Allemagne et les problèmes de la paix pendant la première guerre mondiale,* 4 volumes. Paris: Publications de la Sorbonne, 1962–1978.

Schiel, Irmgard. *Stéphanie, princesse heritière dans l'ombre de Mayerling.* Gembloux: Duculot, 1980.

Schmidt, Royal J. *Versailles and the Rurh: The Seedbed of World War II.* The Hague: Martinus Nijhoff, 1968.

Schmitz, Yves. *Guillaume Ier et la Belgique.* Brussels: Goemaere, 1945.

Seberechts, Frank. *Ieder zijn zwarte: Verzet, collaboratie en repressie.* Leuven/Ghent: Davidsfonds/Perspectief, 1994.

Séguy, Philippe, and Antoine Michelland. *Fabiola: Koningin in het wit.* Antwerp: Hadewych, 1996 (first published in French as *Fabiola: La reine blanche* in 1995).

Senelle, Robert. 'The Current Constitutional Sytem.' In Boudart, Boudart and Bryssinck, above.

Serrou, Robert. *Baudouin: Le roi.* Paris: Perrin/Presses de la Renaissance, 2000.

Seton-Watson, Hugh. *Nations and States: An Enquiry into the Origins of Nations and the Politics of Nationalism.* London: Methuen, 1977.

Severus, Claudius [Severeyns, Lodewijck]. *Vlaanderens Weezang.* Antwerp: Drukk. Mercurius, 1916.

Sherry, Norman. *Conrad's Western World*. Cambridge: Cambridge University Press, 1971.

Simon, Alois, Mgr. *Léopold Iᵉʳ. Brussels: La Renaissance du livre, 1963.*

Simons, Ludo. *Van Duinkerke tot Königsberg: Geschiedenis van de Aldietsche Beweging.* Beveren-Antwerp: Orbis en Orion, 1980.

Slade, Ruth. *King Leopold's Congo: Aspects of the Development of Race Relations in the Congo Independent State.* Oxford: Oxford University Press, 1962.

Smits, Arnoldus. *1830 Scheuring in de Nederlanden,* 4 volumes. Kortrijk-Heule: UGA, 1983–1999.

Snoy et d'Oppuers, Jean-Charles. *Rebâtir l'Europe: Mémoires.* Brussels: Duculot, 1989.

Sörensen, Patsy. *De maskers af! Over socialisme, prostitutie en mensenhandel.* Antwerp: Hadewych, 1994.

Spaak, Paul-Henri. *Combats inachevés,* 2 volumes. Paris: Fayard, 1969.

Speer, Albert. *Erinnerungen.* Frankfurt am Main: Ullstein, 1969.

Spencer, Metta, ed. *Separatism — Democracy and Integration.* Lanham, MA: Rowman & Littlefield Publishers, 1998.

Stanley, Henry Morton. *Unpublished Letters.* Ed. Albert Maurice. London: W. & R. Chambers, 1955.

Steinberg, Maxime.
1. *L'Etoile et le fusil: La question juive, 1940–1942.* Brussels: Editions Vie Ouvrière, 1983.
2. *L'Etoile et le fusil: 1942, Les cent jours de la déportation des juifs de Belgique.* Brussels: Editions Vie Ouvrière, 1984.
3. *L'Etoile et le fusil: La traque des juifs, 1942–1944,* 2 volumes. Brussels: Editions Vie Ouvrière, 1986.

Stengers, Jean.
1. 'Sentiment national, sentiment orangiste et sentiment français à l'aube de notre indépendance.' *Revue belge de philologie et d'histoire,* XXIX, 1, 1951, pp. 61–92.
2. *Combien le Congo a-t-il coûté à la Belgique?* Brussels: Académie Royale des Sciences Coloniales, 1957.
3. *Belgique et Congo: L'élaboration de la Charte coloniale.* Brussels: La Renaissance du livre, 1963.
4. 'Léopold II et le patrimoine dynastique.' *Le Bulletin de la Classe des Lettres et des Sciences Morales et Politiques de l'Académie Royale de Belgique,* 5, VIII, 2/4 (1972): pp. 63–134.
5. 'Léopold Iᵉʳ et le catholicisme en Belgique: documents inédits de 1859.' In Braive and Lory, above.
6. *Léopold III et le gouvernement: Les deux politiques belges de 1940.* Gembloux: Duculot, 1980.
7. *Congo: Mythes et réalités: 100 ans d'histoire.* Paris/Louvain-la-Neuve: Duculot, 1989.
8. *L'Action du Roi en Belgique depuis 1831: Pouvoir et influence.* Louvain-la-Neuve: Duculot, 1992.
9. *De koningen der Belgen: Van Leopold I tot Albert II.* Leuven: Davidsfonds, 1997.
10. 'De uitbreiding van België: Tussen droom en werkelijkheid.' In Janssens and Stengers, above.
11. *Histoire du sentiment national en Belgique des origines à 1918,* 2 volumes. Brussels: Racine, 2000–2002.

Stenmans, A. *La reprise du Congo par la Belgique: Essai d'histoire parlementaire et diplomatique*. Brussels: Ed. Techniques et Scientifiques, 1949.

Stephanie [Princess of Belgium]. *Je devais être impératrice*. Brussels: Le Cri, 1997 (first published in German as *Ich sollte Kaiserin werden* in 1935).

Stinglhamber, Gustave, and Paul Dresse. *Léopold II au travail*. Brussels: Editions du Sablon, 1945.

Stockmar, Christian. *Memoirs of Baron Stockmar*. Ed. Ernest A. Stockmar. London: Longmans, Green and Co, 1872 (first published in German as *Denkwürdigkeiten aus den Papieren des Freiherrn Christian Friedrich von Stockmar* in 1872).

Stols, Eddy. 'Les Belges au Mato Grosso et en Amazonie ou la récidive de l'avonture congolaise (1895–1910).' In Dumoulin and Stols, above.

Strachey, Lytton. *Queen Victoria*. London: Penguin Books, 1971 (first published in 1921).

Suenens, Cardinal Leo-Jozef.
1. *Terugblik & Verwachting: Herinneringen van een kardinaal*. Tielt: Lannoo, 1992.
2. *Koning Boudewijn: Het getuigenis van een leven*. Ertvelde: FIAT, 1995.

Sybesma-Knol, Neri, and Jef Van Bellingen, eds. *Naar een nieuwe interpretatie van het Recht op Zelfbeschikking?* Brussels: VUB Press, 1995.

Talleyrand-Périgord, Charles-Maurice, Prince de Bénévent. *Mémoires du Prince de Talleyrand*, 5 volumes. Ed. Adolphe Fourier de Bacourt. Paris: De Bonnet, 1967 (first published in 1891).

Terlinden, Charles.
1. 'Papiers du lieutenant général De Lannoy, gouverneur des princes royaux (1846–1849).' *Bulletin de la Commission Royale d'Histoire*, 1938: pp. 279–353.
2. *Impérialisme et équilibre*. Brussels: Larcier, 1952.

Thielemans, Marie-Rose. 'De politieke ideeën van Leopold I.' In Sabbe, above.

Thomas, Daniel H. *The Guarantee of Belgian Independence and Neutrality in European Diplomacy 1830s–1930s*. Kingston: D.H. Thomas Publishing, 1983.

Tindemans, Leo. *De memoires: Gedreven door een overtuiging*. Tielt: Lannoo, 2002.

Todts, Herman. *Hoop en wanhoop der Vlaamsgezinden*, 6 volumes. Leuven: Davidsfonds, 1961–1988.

Toebosch, Emile. *Honderd jaar ongewone debatten in Kamer en Senaat*. Brussels: Belgische Kamer van Volksvertegenwoordigers, 2001.

Tordoir, Joseph. 'Vorsten en koninklijke families.' In Janssens and Stengers, above.

Twain, Mark. *King Leopold's Soliloquy: A Satire*. London: T. Fisher Unwin, 1907.

Vanacker, Daniël.
1. *Het Aktivistisch avontuur*. Ghent: Stichting Mens en Kultuur, 1991.
2. *De Frontbeweging: De Vlaamse strijd aan de Ijzer*. Koksijde: De Klaproos, 2000.

Van Audenhaeghe, Léon. *Très-Belle: Blanche Delacroix, Baronne de Vaughan: Le grand amour de Léopold II*. Brussels: Didier Hatier, 1987.

Van Caenegem, Raoul. 'Mediaeval Flanders and the Seeds of Modern Democracy.' In Pinder, above.

Van den Berghe, Jan.
1. *Het intieme dagboek van een Koningshuis: Roman van een dynastie*. Antwerp: Helios, 1980.
2. *De Habsburgs en de Coburgs: Liefde en tragiek van twee dynastieën*. Antwerp: Helios, 1984.
3. *Noblesse Oblige: Kroniek van de Belgische adel*. Groot-Bijgaarden: Globe, 1997.
4. *Kroniek van 100 jaar Europese koningshuizen*. Ghent: Globe, 1999.

Vandenbroeke, Chris. *Hoe rijk was arm Vlaanderen? Vlaanderen in de 18de eeuw: Een vergelijkend overzicht.* Bruges: Uitgeverij Marc Van de Wiele, 1995.

Van Den Driessche, Pol, ed. *De kroongetuigen: Achter de muren van het Koninklijk Paleis.* Ghent: Scoop, 1998.

Vandenpeereboom, Alphonse. *La fin d'un règne: Notes et Souvenirs 1862-1867.* Ed. Marcel Bots. Ghent: Liberaal Archief, 1994.

Van den Wijngaert, Mark. 'Politieke en sociaal-economische mijlpalen.' In Koninckx and Lefèvre, above.

Van den Wijngaert, Mark, Lieve Beullens and Dana Brants. *België en zijn koningen: Monarchie en macht.* Antwerp: Houtekiet, 2000.

Van den Wijngaert, Mark, Michel Dumoulin and Vincent Dujardin, eds. *Een koningsdrama: De biografie van Leopold III.* Antwerp: Manteau, 2001.

Vandeputte, Robert. *Een machteloos minister.* Antwerp: Standaard Uitgeverij, 1982.

Van Der Essen, Léon. *La Belgique dans la Royaume des Pays-Bas 1814-1830.* Brussels: La Lecture au Foyer, 1923.

Van der Smissen, Edouard, ed. *Léopold II et Beernaert d'après leur correspondance inédite de 1884 à 1894,* 2 volumes. Brussels: Goemaere, 1920.

Vandervelde, Emile.
1. *Les 10 dernières années du règne de Léopold II.* Ghent: Soc. Coop. Imp. Ouvrière, 1910.
2. *Souvenirs d'un militant socialiste.* Paris: Denoël, 1939.

Van De Woestijne, Karel. *Verzameld journalistiek werk, deel 9: NRC, maart 1916-september 1919.* Ed. Ada Deprez. Ghent: Cultureel Documentatiecentrum 't Pand, 1992.

Vandewoude, Emile.
1. 'Het Huis van koning Leopold I: Een historische schets.' In Sabbe, above.
2. 'L'échec de la tentative de colonisation belge aux Nouvelles Hébrides, 1861.' In *De Belgische expansie,* above.

Van Geen, F.M.L. *De Generaal van Geen.* The Hague: Blankwaart & Schoonhoven, 1910.

Van Goethem, Herman, and Jan Velaers. *Leopold III: De Koning, het Land, de Oorlog.* Tielt: Lannoo, 1994.

Vangroenweghe, Daniël.
1. *Leopold II: Kongo.* Bruges: Vangroenweghe, 1985.
2. *Rood rubber: Leopold II en zijn Kongo.* Zaventem: Elsevier Librico, 1985.

Van Haegendoorn, Maurits.
1. *Het geld van de Vlamingen.* Leuven: Davidsfonds, 1978.
2. *Geel & zwart van de driekleur.* Leuven: Davidsfonds, 1979.

Van Isacker, Karel.
1. *Het Daensisme: De teleurgang van een onafhankelijke, christelijke arbeidersbeweging in Vlaanderen 1893-1914.* Antwerp: De Nederlandsche Boekhandel, 1959.
2. *Mijn land in de kering 1830-1980,* 2 volumes. Antwerp: De Nederlandsche Boekhandel, 1978-1983.

Van Kalken, Frans. *Histoire du Royaume des Pay-Bas et de la Révolution Belge de 1830.* Brussels: Lebègue, 1910.

Van Nitsen, R. Brussels. *L'Hygiène des travailleurs noirs dans les camps industriels du Haut-Katanga.* Brussels: G. Van Campenhout, 1932.

Van Overstraeten, Raoul.
1. *Albert I & Léopold III: Vingt ans de politique militaire belge 1920-1940.* Bruges: Desclée de Brouwer, 1949.
2. *Sous le joug: Léopold III prisonnier.* Brussels: Didier Hatier, 1986.

Van Roy, Louis.
1. *Het taboe van de kollaboratie.* Kapellen: DNB-Pelckmans, 1987.
2. *Brieven aan een Kardinaal: Bijdrage tot de studie van de na-oorlogse periode.* Wielsbeke: Oranje-De Eenhoorn, 1994.
Vanthemsche, Guy. 'Kongo en het privé-fortuin van Leopold II.' In Janssens and Stengers, above.
Van Ypersele de Strihou, Anne.
1. 'Enkele aspecten van de persoonlijkheden van koning Leopold I, van koningin Louisa en hun kinderen, geschetst aan de hand van voorwerpen die hun vertrouwd waren.' In Sabbe, above.
2. *Astrid 1905-1935.* Brussels: Gemeentekrediet, 1985.
Van Ypersele, Laurence.
1. *Le Roi Albert: Histoire d'un mythe.* Ottignies: Editions Quorum, 1995.
2. 'Een natie neemt afscheid van haar koning.' In Koninckx and Lefèvre, above.
Van Zuylen, Baron Pierre. *L'échiquier congolais ou le secret du roi.* Brussels: Charles Dessart, 1959.
Vaughan, Baronne de.
1. *Quelques souvenirs de ma vie.* Ed. Paul Faure. Paris: Flammarion, 1936.
2. *Presque Reine: Mémoires de ma vie.* Brussels: Le Cri, 1998 (first published in 1944).
Vellut, Jean-Luc. 'Mining in the Belgian Congo.' In Birmingham and Martin, vol. II, above.
Verberne, L.G.J. *Geschiedenis van Nederland in de jaren 1813-1850,* 2 volumes. Utrecht/Antwerp: Het Spectrum, 1958 (first published in 1937).
Verhaert, Paul [Schrevers, René]. *Un Appèl aux Bruxellois: L'Avenir de la Belgique et le Mouvement Flamand: Le Rôle de Bruxelles.* Brussels: Van der Bergen, 1934.
Verhofstadt, Guy. *De Belgische ziekte: Diagnose en remedies.* Antwerp: Hadewyck, 1997.
Verhulst, Adriaan, and Luc Pareyn, eds. *Huldeboek Prof. Dr. Marcel Bots.* Ghent: Liberaal Archief, 1995.
Vermeersch, Arthur. *La Question Congolaise.* Brussels: Ch. Bulens, 1906.
Vermeir Piet. *Leopold I: Mens, vorst, diplomaat,* 2 volumes. Dendermonde: Vermeir, 1965-1967.
Verslag van de Commissie van Voorlichting op 14 Juli 1946 door Zijne Majesteit Koning Leopold III ingesteld. Brussels: Goemaere, 1947.
Verstraete, Pieter-Jan. *Stefaan Laureys: Het tragische lot van een Finland- en Oostfrontvrijwilliger.* Kortrijk: Verstraete, 1998.
Viaene, Vincent. 'De monarchie en de stelling van België in Europa onder Leopold I en Leopold II (1831-1909).' In Janssens and Stengers, above.
Victoria [Queen of Great Britain and Ireland].
1. *The Letters of Queen Victoria: A Selection from Her Majesty's Correspondence between the Years 1837-1861,* 3 volumes. Eds. Arthur Christopher Benson and Reginald Baliol Brett, 2nd Viscount Esher. London: John Murray, 1908.
2. *The Girlhood of Queen Victoria: A Selection from Her Majesty's Diaries 1832-1840,* 2 volumes. Ed. Viscount Esher. London: John Murray, 1912.
3. *The Letters of Queen Victoria, 2nd series,* 3 volumes. Ed. George Earle Buckle. London: John Murray, 1928.
4. *The Letters of Queen Victoria, 3rd series,* 3 volumes. Ed. George Earle Buckle. London: John Murray, 1932.
Vinks, Jos. *Borms.* Brecht: De Roerdomp, 1974.

Vlaemynck, Carlos H.
1. *Dossier Abbeville*. Leuven: Davidsfonds, 1977.
2. *Naar Engeland gedeporteerd*. Antwerp: De Nederlandsche Boekhandel, 1984.
Vos, Louis. 'Reconstructions of the Past in Belgium and Flanders.' In Coppieters and Huysseune, above.
Wangenheim, Rita von. *Baron Stockmar: Eine coburgisch-englische Geschichte*. Coburg: Hirsch Verlag, 1996.
Ward, Yvonne M. 'The Womanly Garb of Queen Victoria's Early Motherhood 1840–42.' *Women's History Review*, 8, 2 (1999): pp. 277–95.
Waysblatt, Adeline. 'Les Juifs en 1940.' In Gérard-Libois and Gotovitch 1, above.
Weber, Patrick. *Elisabeth de Belgique: L'autre Sissi*. Paris: Payot & Rivages, 1998.
Weintraub, Stanley. *Albert: Uncrowned King*. London: John Murray, 1997.
Weverbergh, Julien. *Leopold II van Saksen Coburgs allergrootste zaak*. Brussels: Manteau, 1971.
Wiedau, Kristin. *Eine adlige Kindheit in Coburg: Fürstenerziehung und Kunstunterweisung der Prinzen Ernst und Albert von Sachsen-Coburg und Gotha*. Coburg: Coburger Landesstiftung, 2000.
Wiener, Sam. *Les traités matrimoniaux des princes*. Brussels: Veuve Monnom, 1906.
Willemsen, A.W. *Het Vlaams-nationalisme: De geschiedenis van de jaren 1914–1940*. Utrecht: Ambo, 1969.
Willequet, Jacques.
1. 'Léopold Ier et le Portugal: Une mission de Van de Weyer en 1836.' *Revue belge de philologie et d'histoire*, XXVIII, 1, 1950, pp. 97–130.
2. *Le Congo belge et la Weltpolitik (1894–1914)*. Brussels: Presses Universitaires, 1962.
3. *Paul-Henri Spaak: Un homme, des combats*. Brussels: La Renaissance du Livre, 1975.
4. *Albert Ier, Roi des Belges: Un portrait politique et humain*. Brussels: Presses de Belgique, 1979.
Williams, Colin H., ed. *National Separatism*. Cardiff: University of Wales Press, 1982.
Wilmet, Louis.
1. *Albert: Roi des Belges*. Charleroi/Paris: Dupuis, 1937.
2. *Le Prince Baudouin: Frère aîné du Roi Albert*. Charleroi/Paris: Dupuis, s.d.
3. *Elisabeth, reine des Belges*. Bomal: Jean Petitpas, 1965.
Wils, Lode.
1. *Kanunnik Jan David*. Leuven: Davidsfonds, 1957.
2. *Flamenpolitik en aktivisme*. Leuven: Davidsfonds, 1974.
3. *De Messias van Vlaanderen: Frans Van Cauwelaert 1880–1910*. Antwerp: Hadewych, 1998.
4. *Frans van Cauwelaert: En de barst van België, 1910–1919*. Antwerp: Houtekiet, 2001.
Witte, Els, ed. *Political History of Belgium From 1830 onwards*. Brussels: VUB Press, 2000.
Ydewalle, Charles d'.
1. *Elisabeth de Belgique*. Paris: Flammarion, 1964.
2. *Reines*. Ostend: Erel, 1976.

Index

Abbeville massacre (1940), 202–3, 214
Aberdeen, George Hamilton-Gordon, Earl of (1784–1860), 25–6, 32–3, 39, 65
Abetz, Otto (1903–1958), 209
Abdullah bin Abdul Aziz al-Saud, Prince of Saudi Arabia, *later* Crown Prince (b. 1924), 312
ABN-Amro, 321–3
Abortion Act, Belgian, 292–3
Adair, Sir Robert (1763–1855), 49
Adelaide of Saxe-Meiningen, Duchess of Clarence, *later* Queen of Great Britain (1792–1849), 22
Akihito, Emperor of Japan (b. 1933), 302
Aktivism, Aktivists, 157–8, 161, 163–6, 179, 197, 215
Albert of Saxe-Coburg, Prince Consort of Great Britain (1819–1861), 1, 19–20, 22–3, 63–4, 71, 77, 126, 130
Albert I, Prince of Belgium, King of the Belgians (1875–1934):
birth, family background and youth, 129–31; character 130, 138–9, 144; education, 130–2, 134; and socialism, 131, 135, 139–40, 144–7, 159, 167, 177–8, 289; and Brück's Law, 131, 134; and the Flemings, 132, 135, 150, 157, 159, 161–2, 164–5, 169, 178, 180, 187; duties as Crown Prince, 134–5, 138; anti-Semitism, 135, 154, 180; dislike of 'Anglo-Saxons,' 135–6, 154, 181; marriage, 136–8, 140, 182; appearance, 138; and his wife Elisabeth, 138–9, 151, 181; and the Catholic Church, 140, 178–9; conspires against the government, 145–6, 168; and the Belgian politicians, 146–7, 159, 162–3, 169, 176–8, 180, 187; on Belgium and the Belgians,

147–8, 186; and his (legitimate) children, 147, 153, 181–2; in favour of neutralism, 149, 153, 183–4, 187; commanding the army in World War I, 150–2, 154, 161, 163; negotiations with the Germans, 154–6, 158–9, 163; and the Loppem Coup, 167–8; installs corporatist regime, 169, 171–2, 195; admires Mussolini, 172, 184; establishes press agency, 176; and Einstein, 180–1; promiscuity, 181; at Mosley's wedding, 182; financial worries, 182, 184; last years, death and funeral, 185–7, 189; on Leopold II, 131, 186; memory of, 191, 247
Albert II, Prince of Belgium, Prince of Liège, King of the Belgians (b. 1934):
birth, family background and youth, 184, 241; and his brother Baudouin, 249–50, 266, 305; and his uncle Charles, 252; on Lumumba, 259; marriage, 261, 308–9; and his father, 266; character, 305, 308–9; civil list, 306; motoring, 308, 321; and his wife Paola, 308–9, 311, 321; promiscuity, 311, 321; trade missions 311–3; involvement in ESH case, 312–4; implicated in sex abuse scandal, 315; interferes in bank merger case, 322–3; and the Dutroux case, 328–9, 331–2; resents public prosecutor, 333; wants to restore Belgium's standing, 334
Alen, André, Baron (b. 1950), 293
Alençon, Emilienne d' (1869–?), 101
Alexander, Prince of Orange (1818–1848), 63
Alexander, Duke of Württemberg (1771–1833), 5, 20
Alexander, Duke of Württemberg (1804–1881), 62

The 1975 Referendum on Europe
Volume 1: Reflections of the Participants

edited by Mark Baimbridge

250 pp., £17.95/$34.90, 1845400348 (pbk.)

Volume 2: Current Analysis and Lessons for the Future

ed. Mark Baimbridge *et al.*

250 pp., £17.95/$34.90, 1845400356 (pbk.)

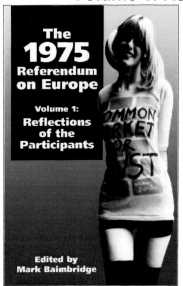

These books provide an analysis of the past, current and future relationship between the UK and the EU, treating the key overarching issues in the 1975 referendum and looking ahead to the prospect (eventually) of further referendums. Contributors to Volume 1 include David Owen, Tam Dalyell and Teddy Taylor. Mark Baimbridge is senior lecturer in economics at the University of Bradford with research interests focused on European integration.

Alarming Drum: Britain's European Dilemma

Peter Morgan

Alarming Drum is an analysis of the UK's past and present relationship with the European Union, together with a scrutiny of global strategic prospects for the next half century. The thesis is that European countries need trade, defence and security treaties, but the EU treaties actually in force are seriously misconceived. The author lived in Paris for eight years as Marketing Director for IBM Europe and, as DG of the IoD, was involved in the negotiations for the Maastricht Treaty, EMU and the Social Chapter.

'Peter Morgan shines a laser beam into the Euro-fog.' **Peter Jay**

'This book is a mine of facts and data which are likely to be used by everyone writing or speaking about the EU for a long time to come.'
John Mills, *Eurofacts*

'*Alarming Drum* is the product of intensive research and as such is a valuable resource for anyone who needs easy access to the facts.' **Matthew Attwood**, *European Journal*

'An authoritative history and critique . . . with a refreshing lack of hysteria.' *This England*

'A thorough and masterly job.' **Patrick Minford**

'A challenging and important analysis.' **Tim Congdon**

300 pp., £19.95 / $39.90, 1845400151 (cloth)

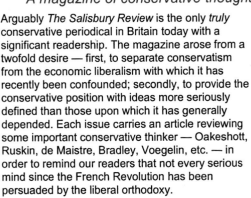